3/28/2010

To Kathryn;
I hope you enjoy the stories that captivated my life prior to defense of property rights! I admire so greatly all the effort you folks put forward to defend our liberty. Good luck & health!
Fred Kelly Grant

JUSTICE MY ASS!

FRED KELLY GRANT

Order this book online at www.trafford.com
or email orders@trafford.com

Most Trafford titles are also available at major online book retailers.

Note for Librarians: A cataloguing record for this book is available from Library
and Archives Canada at www.collectionscanada.ca/amicus/index-e.html

Printed in Victoria, BC, Canada.

ISBN: 978-1-4269-2180-3 (sc)

ISBN: 978-1-4269-2179-7 (dj)

Library of Congress Control Number: 2009940718

*Our mission is to efficiently provide the world's finest, most comprehensive book publishing
service, enabling every author to experience success. To find out how to publish your book, your
way, and have it available worldwide, visit us online at www.trafford.com*

Trafford rev. 11/13/2009

 www.trafford.com

North America & international
toll-free: 1 888 232 4444 (USA & Canada)
phone: 250 383 6864 ✦ fax: 812 355 4082

Acknowledgements

My wife, Lodice, would not be proud of all that is in this book, but she would be proud that I finally
Finished, what I started. She was my greatest fan, so in defense of me she would have found a positive
justification for its contents. I can still hear her voice at the end of one of my stories told to friends: "I
was SO PROUD!" NOT. Everything good that I have done, I owe to her encouragement; everything bad
I have done, she forgave. Nothing of merit that I accomplished would have been possible without her.

My family, particularly Jon and Staci, have encouraged me to finish and have given me critical help in writing, editing and finding a publisher—without their pushing and shoving, I never would have finished the book. I am thankful to Andy for reading the manuscript, ready to tell me if the effort should be scrapped.

My work would not be complete without Staci. I often take credit for the things she does and yet she is always willing to take on more. She works a thankless job with never a complaint. To her I am truly grateful.

I am also thankful to my long-time good friend, Cindy Bachman for taking on the editing and counseling on content clarity. Cindy edited the daylights out of a county plan we worked on together two decades ago; she is a stickler for detail, and has unlimited patience with the fact that I'm not.

Another long-time good friend, Ralph Nichols has edited for style, and I appreciate his effort and advice. Ralph is a free-lance writer in Seattle who has written for the Idaho Statesman, the Idaho Press Tribune, the Seattle Times, the High Line Times, and the Anchorage Times. Ralph and I have been through many wars together.

Countless rancher friends have urged me to write these stories down, and without their encouragement and "pushing" I probably would never gotten to it. I can't begin to name them all, but some went above and beyond in urging "write the book". My thanks to Mike and Linda Hanley who have demonstrated to me what it is to have passion for an idea, to Tim Lowry and his family for showing the meaning of sheer determination in pursuing what is "right", to Dick and Karen Bass who have pushed me for three decades, to Richard and Connie Brandau who were always willing to listen to "just one more story", to Dr. Chad Gibson whose high level of intellect never seemed to stand in the way of enjoying the stories of the street, to Dennis Stanford who has often reminded me that I need to take time from work to finish the book, to Brenda Richards who told me that I should write a book the first time she heard the "Mose" moonshine story, and Dick Freund and Gary Aman---both good law enforcement officers who love the drama and comedy of the courtroom.

Another close friend, Layne Bangerter, has gone out of his way to urge me on. Layne and I have fought through some difficult times together, and his loyalty and support have been priceless.

In Texas, Margaret and Dan Byfield have encouraged me for years and years. Then, a few months ago, Ralph Snyder, a giant of a Texan and my close friend, said to me in his deep Texas accent, "Finish that book." I took it seriously. When his boss, Marcia, smilingly nodded in agreement, I knew it was a Texas mandate.

I am naturally lazy. My South Carolina grandmother said to me many years ago, "Freddie, honey, you better work at something you can use your brain for." I wanted to finish the book which was on my "bucket list", right between "walk across the Golden Gate

Bridge" (which I did with my two sons and family friend David Johnson) and "spend an entire day in Chicago's O'Hare Airport waiting for United Airlines to find even one mechanically sound plane" (which I have now done with Jon and Staci). So, the book's time had come. But, without the urging and encouragement of my family and friends, I wouldn't have finished.

So, to all who encouraged me, I say "like it or not, you share the blame for what appears on these pages."

PREFACE

Normally, a writer would not start by explaining what the writing is NOT to be. But, as my old boss Charles E. Moylan, Jr., former States Attorney for Baltimore City would tell you, he could never count on my being normal or, doing anything the normal way. If Charley has gray hair today, I'm sure I caused most of it, even belatedly.

This is NOT an indictment of police officers, prosecutors, defense attorneys, judges, or court personnel and administrators. It is NOT a serious, social analysis of the "criminal justice PROCESS," which I choose to call the "criminal justice SYSTEM." It is NOT a weighing of our "process" against that in any other governmental or social setting in the world.

It is NONE of those things. It is NOT meant as an insult to anyone but me. It is simply a collection of experiences within the process which a retired Los Angeles detective and I shared with our drinking companions—a collection of the stories that show why dedicated people in the process must find humor, often dark and sick, in the tragedy that surrounds them each day.

Red Merritt, the retired detective and I thought that we were dedicated professionals. We believed that we did our best at our jobs, and that our "best" was not a search for "justice" but for success. His success was in arresting lawbreakers in a way that could lead to conviction. Mine, as a prosecutor, was working hard with the officers to get convictions on good cases. Then, as a defense attorney, it was working hard to get dismissals, acquittals, or at least verdicts for offenses less than what I had offered in plea bargains.

What kept us from going any crazier than we were, was quite frankly, the thrill of the challenge—the challenge to "win." I loved trial work, the effort to persuade a jury of twelve regular citizens, and to persuade a judge when the issue was law or sentencing. Sometimes I loved success too much—as you will see.

"Normally" that would end this Preface. But, in reading recent news accounts of the criminal process in Baltimore, I am overwhelmed by the fault finding and finger pointing that goes on between detectives and administrators, and the state's attorney's office. I am amazed at some of the news stories that chronicle botched investigations, and then, frankly, botched prosecutions. I cannot imagine a prosecutor in Charley Moylan's office putting an investigator on the stand who would have to admit "I don't know" or "I don't remember" in answer to questions about the crime scene. I cannot imagine a prosecutor in his office who would make the decisions about calling or not calling witnesses, which are evidenced in the news articles from the *Baltimore Sun*. It seems so needless to me in a city like Baltimore.

So, I abnormally go on at some length in this Preface to talk about the quality of people with whom I had the privilege of working. There obviously is an answer to the problems currently experienced in Baltimore the city needs to turn back the clock, to a day when quality prosecutors and quality detectives cooperated fully. Not that we didn't have problems, but those problems were never allowed to stand between us and success.

I worked in Baltimore with some of the finest people I have ever known. Charley Moylan had a brilliant legal mind, and he was a great trial lawyer. Long before I became a prosecutor, when I was still clerking for the Court of Appeals of Maryland, I watched him prosecute a stripper for the murder of a Philippine doctor she had picked up. She killed the doctor in a downtown hotel and set fire to his body in the bath tub. Charley tried a magnificent case, and I decided during that trial that if I could ever approach his level of ability, I would be a good trial lawyer.

As a State's Attorney, Charley was a sound leader. He was willing to give his lawyers their head, even though he often rued the days on which he did that with me. He worked hard with the politicians to keep our salaries up, and he always had our backs.

His chief deputy, George Helinski, was a prince of a man, very bright, very level headed and even keeled. He too was a very good trial lawyer. And I'm sure I caused George some grey hair too.

Howard Cardin, the chief of the trial division who succeeded Charley as State's Attorney when Charley was appointed to the intermediate Court of Appeals, was a good friend and one great trial lawyer. Howard was one of those "no nonsense," "no frills" prosecutors who knew exactly how much evidence to put on and stop. He understood the "bottom line" of prosecution better than anyone I ever saw in Baltimore or here in Idaho. Howard prosecuted a fish store operator who had raped and murdered a fifth grade student. For some it would have been a difficult case to put together—with lots of facts to be interlinked—but Howard did it with apparent ease.

Peter D. Ward, who later became a member of the Supreme Bench, was an excellent trial lawyer, and well-organized supervisor. Once, when two of Pete's murder cases got scheduled back to back, he found himself in a bind when he had not finished the first case and another court was ready to start the second. I took his outline of witnesses and evidence, and, with only about 20 minutes to read his notes, speak with the homicide officers and their witnesses, I tried that case to a jury. With that, I won the 2nd degree verdict that we sought. Pete's outline led me right through the testimony to the closing argument that he had outlined in his notes.

(Pete, from Birmingham, England, had a wonderful English accent that got stronger, it seemed, the longer he was in Baltimore. When I was in the United States Attorney's office, I met Pete, who was appointed to represent a federal defendant. One day my great friend Roger Duncan remarked that he didn't care for Pete and his "fake Roland Park accent." I said, "Rog, that's a real accent, Pete is from England." "Oh," said Roger, "Well I think he's a pretty good guy then." From that moment on, Roger had the greatest respect for Pete.)

Steve Harris, who would later become the first appointed Public Defender in Baltimore, an office limited at first to the Municipal

Courts, was another good friend and a very good trial lawyer. Steve was sensitive to victims' feelings and confidences, and worked hard to get successful results at trial.

Bobby Fertitta, who succeeded me as chief of the organized crime division when I went into private practice, was a special friend who went on to head the College of Prosecutors for the National District Attorney's Association. I learned a lot by watching Bobby's finesse and diplomacy in dealing with police officers, with difficult judges, and in persuading juries in difficult cases. Bobby married the absolute best assistant that I ever had, Diane, a true friend who helped me immensely through tough work loads in the prosecutor's office.

At one time or another, I had the privilege of not only working with, but supervising Pete, Bobby, and Michael Kaminkow, who was a very good trial lawyer as well, and who got better with each case he took on.

Two young prosecutors who came into the office and worked with me in organized crime cases were Bob Stewart and Joseph Kiel. Hard working, well organized, detail oriented, good trial lawyers they were. They were exceptional leaders of investigations conducted for special Grand Juries.

One last prosecutor, who has come to my mind many times over the years, is Anton Keating, who came into the office as a young lawyer not too long before I left. Anton was a hard worker, and much later I learned, what an excellent trial lawyer he was. Anton handled the post-conviction proceedings, where the judge found that I had badly over-reached as a prosecutor—the judge pointing out that I mislead the jury and used inappropriate pre-trial publicity—which resulted in a new trial for the murder defendant. A lesser lawyer than Anton would not have won that case, and his examination of me on the stand, showed meticulous preparation and skillful questioning.

As I began to read more about Baltimore in getting ready to put my experiences together, I saw that Anton ran for state's attorney several years ago. He ran at a time when, like today, the prosecutor's office was plagued with a horrible record in success rates in trying murder cases. He offered to solve those problems by returning to a close working relationship between the police and the prosecutors, with emphasis on training prosecutors in the law and trial tactics. He would have been a fine state's attorney. He is obviously well-organized, and he knows how to operate a successful office by having worked in one.

On the defense side, one of my very close friends was Milton B. Allen who, I always called "the Honorable" even before he became state's attorney and then a judge. Milton was as dedicated a defense attorney as I ever saw. He pursued successful results as much as any of us, but always honorably. I well remember meeting him in the hallway of the courthouse on the first morning that I came to work as a defense attorney. He saw me, smiled that big smile, pushed his glasses up on his forehead and said, "Hey there boy friend, now you're gonna find out what it's like to fight with nothing but a big stick."

One of the hardest times in my life in Baltimore was when George Helinski, Howard Cardin and the Honorable Milton all ran against each other in the first primary election after Charley was appointed to the bench. All were my friends, all were honorable, and would have made a good State's Attorney. I supported Howard because we were very close friends, and because I really thought he would be able to work more easily with the city administration for funding and support.

As both a prosecutor and defense attorney I had the privilege of practicing before some of the finest trial judges who could ever exist. Judges Anselm Sodaro, Charles Harris, Joseph Carter, J. Gilbert Prendergast, George Russell, Basil Thomas, Albert Sklar, Solomon Liss, Tom Kenney (who had been my boss when I was an assistant U.S. Attorney) and William O'Donnell (referred to as "Wild Bill O'Donnell" by most of us because of his active and often aggressive interference in a prosecutor's case); and in the counties J. DeWeese Carter in Caroline County and Stuart Hammill in Garrett County. Judge Meyer Cardin was special to me. He was so practical in approaching the regular, daily case loads, working through a docket with the fewest postponements possible for us as prosecutors, and with common sense results for us as defense attorneys. We could always count on a "square deal" during the trial from all these judges, even though at sentencing some of them were not the most desirable for the defense. They far surpassed present day judges with whom I have experience.

I can't imagine any of those judges putting up with the kind of activities that are chronicled in the news stories over the past four to eight years. I read that in one case, the judge said, from the bench, "pitiful" at the performance of a prosecutor. I can't imagine any of the judges who sat in the 1960s and early 70s putting up with the failures to disclose and other prosecution and police failures noted in the news stories about today's Baltimore. They wouldn't have stopped with "pitiful." They would have been in our faces and in Charley's and George's faces on a daily basis until something got straightened up.

I can just imagine what the training would have been like if we had been caught not disclosing evidence in accordance with the rules. We would have first been confronted by the bench, then by testing until we all knew discovery rules backward and forward. I remember once when a judge just mildly complained about a prosecutor who wasn't familiar enough with a Fourth Amendment application. Charley subjected the entire staff to a series of weekly meetings where we had to read and study the classic Fourth and Fourteenth Amendment case decisions and then be tested on the cases just as though we were in law school again. The *Baltimore Sun* got wind of the meetings and tests and ran a story about the State's Attorney taking his staff back to school. We were all subjected to jokes at our expense, but within a few weeks we all were up to date on the principles existent in the Fourth Amendment. To his credit, all of us were subjected to the testing even if we already had proficiency with the concepts of search and seizure.

One of the reasons that I find it so hard to believe that homicide cases have become such a problem in Baltimore is that the working relationship between Charley's office and the police investigative units was so good. Police officers like Captain Anton Glover of homicide, Steve Tabeling who was a sergeant in the Northern District during most of my days working with him, Leon Tomlin who was a sergeant in the small narcotics squad during most of my days working with him, and the officers they supervised, were superb officers. When I crossed the street from the federal prosecutor's office to the State's Attorney's office, I found to my surprise that there really were different degrees of murder cases from the standpoint of how the process treated them. Fights in bars, domestic fights, and street fights between "friends" were obviously treated differently from felony murders committed during robberies or for hire. And, every homicide case was assigned specially to an individual prosecutor from the time it came into the office. Charley and George both expected, and got, a close working relationship between each prosecutor and the homicide detectives under Glover. Our success rate was exceptional.

I see that there have been complaints that detectives and investigating officers don't call the prosecutors for advice before charging. That lack of relationship did not exist during Charley's time as State's Attorney and Glover's time as homicide captain. Often, a prosecutor was called by homicide to come to Central District to help analyze the evidence and the charge, and/or to help with developing the interrogation strategy for a suspect. When I read about today's problems stemming from fault finding and lack of cooperation, it is not the Baltimore that I knew. I would hate to try to calculate the number of hours spent by prosecutors working after hours with detectives from the districts as well as Central administration on search and arrest warrants.

Every person I have named worked hard and with dedication to perform his or her functions successfully, and worked with pride.

All of us shared the humor that might offend those who don't work in the midst of the people involved in the criminal process. Some of the humor, and many of the complications that caused us all concerns, are pointed out in this collection. And that's really all that the book is intended to do.

An Introduction

This collection of stories and opinions has been in the sausage grinder for four decades. The title makes it clear what I think of the criminal justice system in America: it is dysfunctional. That became crystal clear during the Baltimore riots that followed the assassination of Dr. Martin Luther King, Jr. On April 4, 1968, Dr. King was shot down as he stood on the balcony outside his room at the Lorraine Motel in Memphis, Tennessee. He had been resting prior to a scheduled speech that would have been emotional, moving and critical to the embattled, striking municipal workers in Memphis. When he awakened, he walked out on that balcony and was shot from ambush.

Two days later, the racial riots began in Baltimore.

The uniquely talented, world-revered civil rights leader was shot by a hiding, cowardly white unknown racist James Earl Ray. It goes without saying to most experienced law enforcement folks that Ray did not act alone. But, the "establishment" was willing to accept that conclusion to avoid a protracted investigation that could have resulted in bitterness and even more racial violence when the conspirators were named.

The same interest in avoiding inconvenience to government's orderly plodding led to the official acceptance of the theory that Lee Harvey Oswald acted alone in the assassination of President John Fitzgerald Kennedy. To me, perhaps the most disappointing thing about the conclusion of the Kennedy Commission was that Earl

Warren allowed the conclusion to be reached and published under his name.

Throughout the decades since Dr. King's murder, many activists and writers have focused on the unfairness of the killing, which took so much from so many. But there is really nothing that guarantees any of us "fairness." When I was receiving alcohol rehab treatment in the Mercy Care Unit (a 12 Step oriented counseling center) in Nampa, Idaho, in 1985, I whined one day about the unfairness of being afflicted with alcoholism. The clinical psychologist assisting the Care Unit, looked me squarely in the eye and said, "Fred, 'fair' is the carnival that comes through town in the summer time."

It is useless to consider the unfairness to all of Baltimore that resulted from the riots. The days of the riots proved to me that a major civil disobedience will bring the "system" to its knees. The rights of lawful citizens were forfeited, the rights of criminals were mauled, and the rights of victims of crimes were ignored. All that happened in spite of the best of intentions on the part of most police, prosecutors, defense attorneys, judges, administrators, and politicians.

But, even during ordinary days, the "system" is dysfunctional in the way that it re-victimizes the victims of crime over and over and over. Innocent victims of rapes, for example, are brutalized on the witness stand. The rape victim's sexual history, the way she was dressed at the time of the attack, whether she had been having a good time and even "flirting," whether she had been drinking—all are fair game to the defense on cross examination, while the defendant can refuse to testify. And even if the defendant does testify, he is spared many of the styles of character attack that the rules allow against the victim.

The victim's witness in a case often has to sit or stand with, or in the midst of, the family and friends of the defendant while waiting to testify. Many prosecutors don't make the effort to protect their own witnesses during the pre-trial wait. This is true in both crowded big city courthouses and small rural courthouses. I remember a murder case that went to trial in rural Canyon County, Idaho, in the early 1980s. Two brothers robbed a neighborhood grocery store just eight blocks from my house. They murdered the owner, a man who was loved throughout the city. One day as I wandered down the hall from my law clerk's office, I noticed witnesses for the state surrounded in the hall by members of the defendants' family. The witnesses looked very uncomfortable in the midst of a group making loud, rude comments about the unfairness to the defendants. Two of the state's witnesses were relatives of the victim. It wasn't any of my business, but I stepped up to the two and told them and the other witnesses for the prosecution to come with me. I took them down to the law library, and then went up the back hall and took a note into the prosecutor to tell him where his witnesses were. Neither the court nor the state had made any arrangement for protecting those witnesses prior to trial.

Many dedicated law enforcement people work daily in a "system" that moves criminals along a conveyer belt, which loops them through police stations, courtrooms, jails and back again. Some consider themselves to be "sanitation engineers" or garbage men just trying to keep the streets swept daily, only to repeat the job the next day.

Unfortunately, those dedicated professionals often find themselves working in the midst of people who are just doing a job for a paycheck, to get experience so they can move on to better jobs, or to make a living better than they could in private life. Combine that with the fact that these professionals are also surrounded by psychotics, sociopaths, sexual predators, pedophiles, rapists, murderers, sadists, masochists, robbers and thieves, racial hate-mongers, and just plain slime, and you can see why dedicated workers have to resort to humor in the darkest situations—just to preserve their sanity.

To say that the system was and is dysfunctional doesn't mean that I didn't enjoy my work. I loved the courtroom—the challenge, both when I was prosecutor and then as a defense attorney defending people that I had tried to put away for years. The excitement of presenting the facts to a jury, or the law to a judge, in a winning effort never dimmed or dulled. Finding the cutting edge strategy that works in a given case is like an aphrodisiac.

But the love of the courtroom wasn't enough. I drank too much, being a disavowed alcoholic. Life for my wife, Lodice, was lonely because work and drinking kept me away from home way too much. Finally, she persuaded me to return our family to Idaho where she and I went to school, and to return in time for our sons to go to school outside the Baltimore system. At first, the move cut down on my drinking, as a change in life-style always does for an alcoholic. But, I succumbed to the boredom of small town life and used that as an excuse to spend a lot of time in bars recounting the stories, repeating he comical situations found in an all too tragic system.

A retired Los Angeles detective, James T. "Red" Merritt, joined me in telling the stories, and joined me in believing that if we hadn't found comic relief in tragedy, we would have lost our minds completely. As we told and retold the stories, we decided that we should write a book.

But we convinced ourselves that we couldn't write a book until we settled on a title. This was the alcoholism finding a rationalization for not diving into the task of writing, which requires immense self discipline. The problem, of course, was that alcoholics don't have such discipline.

One night, as we discussed a failure in the Idaho parole system, we inadvertently stumbled onto the title. A three-time rapist serving a life sentence "without the possibility of parole" was, in fact, paroled, and three days later was arrested for murder and rape of a nurse in Seattle. To Red, I said, "That's justice." Red's reply was, "Justice, my ass." The title was born.

THE ROAD TO JUSTICE MY ASS

1

I wanted to be a preacher—an evangelist. I wanted to inspire congregations with moving sermons, ending with a choir roaring out "Precious Lord, Take My Hand and Lead Me On." I heard Governor Frank Clement of Tennessee give such a speech at the 1956 Democratic Convention, and saw all those conventioneers jump to their feet as the Great Organ sprang into the hymn. I wanted to bring a crowd to its feet like that. What a way to make your way to heaven.

Instead, I became a lawyer and no doubt diverted myself to Dante's Eighth Circle of hell. But if I hadn't gone into the field where "truth" is at best a variable, I wouldn't be able now to write this book.

What now could I write about preaching that hasn't been written better, by better authors and better people? In this book, I can write about strange experiences that better writers don't even know about. So, it's a good thing I suppose, that I became a lawyer.

2

How did it happen? How did I get off course so far? Ego—that inner element that is designed to keep one balanced, if you can control it.

I was always shy, with an inferiority complex. But, for some reason that didn't stand in the way of my participating "on stage." I loved dramatics, and then in the ninth grade, an English teacher named Byron Yoseloff introduced me to the wide world of competitive speech through debate. Once experiencing the rush of winning a debate, I was hooked on speech and performance.

Then, starting with a high school prank, I took performance up a notch and got the feel of persuading a "jury" to interpret facts the way you want, regardless of what the facts actually support.

My good friend Bill Mainwaring was a straight arrow kind of guy. His father was a prestigious newspaper publisher, far removed from the type of mentality that would condone prankster activities in school. In many ways Bill was like his dad, and he would become the editor and then publisher of the Salem, Oregon, newspaper. Bill unfortunately fell under the spell of my good friend Bob Campbell and I. One night on the way home from an upset victory over our arch rival in basketball, we came to a stop at a portable stop sign in the middle of the town of Meridian. We decided that it would be a good trophy for our night of victory. Bill was assigned to get the sign dislodged and loaded into the backseat of Bob's two-door, cut-down hot rod. Somehow, he managed to accomplish the task. Riding in back hunched up with the sign, Bill survived detection from several police cars we passed on the twelve-mile drive home.

We took the sign to Bob's parents farm equipment store and hid it among the equipment waiting to be repaired, then forgot about it. Not until years later was it discovered when the store was sold to be moved to a new location. By that time none of us knew anything about the sign. With his new-found spirit of rebellion, Bill initiated the prank that led me to a "mock trial" where I got a taste of jury performance—and liked it. Bill and I both had physics class "taught" by Webster "Doc" Caldwell, part-time teacher, full-time realtor, and part-time Justice of the Peace. Doc was an interesting piece of work, but hardly an inspirational teacher. He really did know his physics technicalities, but he couldn't help one decipher instructions, much less build a lever or explain a lever and pulley. But Doc was a fun guy to run a class hour.

There was a "Doc Clique" that gathered each day during the first period "home room" and the lunch-time hours. Doc gave a seminar on virtually everything in the world, whether he had any specific knowledge about the subjects or not.   I used his home room first period as the time I went to practice debate or speech; our agreement was that I wouldn't bother him about teaching me physics. I could use the hour to do my extra work, and he would provide me with the answers to study, along with the questions.   Doc presided over the Clique workshops with a gavel that was his pride and joy. It wasn't linked to any special occasion, just a gavel, but to him it was a symbol of authority.

We all joked about what would happen if the gavel disappeared; even joked with him about it and he threatened torture to anyone who took it.

Well, one day the gavel was gone. Doc wasn't quite sure when it disappeared. He worked as hard at pinpointing a suspect and suspect time as Captain Queeg did in measuring the strawberries in *The Caine Mutiny.*

He finally focused on a time right before the "Clique" arrived before school. Bill had opening period home room, so Doc decided that Bill was left alone with the gavel while Doc was in the office picking up bulletins for the day. So, he accused Bill of taking the gavel.

Obviously, Bill denied guilt. Doc, who always loved to hold forth on trial techniques that he had observed as Justice of the Peace, decided to hold a "mock trial" to determine guilt. He named two of his key Clique leaders to be prosecutors, and told me I had to defend Bill. It must have been by sheer instinct, but I didn't ask Bill whether he had taken the gavel—I just assumed that he had.

Never having studied anything about law or trials, other than in history classes, I needed help. My dad knew Earl Garrity, one of the most famous trial lawyers in Idaho. Garrity had been Owyhee County prosecuting attorney when my dad was Justice of the Peace and Coroner in the county. They had become steadfast friends. Dad liked to tell of the day he met Garrity on a road out in the county just after Garrity had lost re-election to his job. Dad was freighting supplies from Murphy to Silver City (which at the time was the County Seat even though it was hours and hours of travel from every populated area of Owyhee County; the County Seat designation still survived the Gold and Silver days of the late 1880s when Silver City was a metropolis of over 50,000).

Dad had just delivered the week's supplies to a moonshiner. Dad always left the supplies under a bridge on the creek, and picked up a jug of moonshine that was left hanging by rope from the bridge, just low enough to dangle in the cool water. As he moved on up the road, he ran into Garrity coming down by horseback. They stopped to talk, and Garrity was worried. He had not campaigned, thinking that he was a shoo-in for re-election. But, he had been defeated. He told my dad that he didn't know how he would survive without the salary. I think Dad said it was $35 a month. Dad assured him that he was a good enough trial lawyer that he could make a good living in Nampa, the nearest town to Owyhee County-and a railroad town with lots of litigation. Dad broke out the jug of illegal moonshine and the two sat and got pretty drunk. Dad had to camp out there by the creek until morning and then finished his trek into Silver City. Garrity decided to head on down and somehow he made it safely.

My dad suggested that I go talk to Garrity about trials and get some ideas as to how to defend Bill. He arranged it, and I spent over two hours with a guy who by then was a trial giant in the state. Garrity told me that the key for me would be to object to hearsay evidence. He said that since no one actually saw the theft of the gavel, almost everything that would be offered against Bill would be "hearsay" and inadmissible. He explained the hearsay rule to me, and then loaned me a handbook on evidence to study. I spent more time on that handbook than I did on class homework for the three weeks before the "trial" started.

The trial became a "big thing" in the school. The school newspaper carried a feature on all the participants, and announced when the trial would be held. It became clear that there was a big crowd interested in attending, so it was set in the evening, to be held in one of the largest rooms in the school.

We picked the jury from those who attended the trial, and fortunately Bill had a lot of friends. Most of the jurors were good friends with Bill and with me. Doc presided, using a hammer as his gavel to highlight the absence of the real thing. The two prosecutors started calling witnesses to try to show that each had "heard" when the gavel was taken, who had taken it, and how it had been hidden. Of course, all the witnesses would point their "facts" toward Bill. But I started objecting to the testimony on the basis of "hearsay" and the rule against admitting such evidence. A clearly surprised Doc ruled with me on every objection. As a result, most of the evidence damning to Bill was kept out. Still, the prosecutors did paint him into a pretty good circumstantial case, coming close to pinpointing him being alone in the room with the gavel.

I put Bill on the stand and he denied that he took the gavel, and claimed that he did not see it when he was in the room before school started. Then, following the rules in the evidence handbook that Garrity loaned me, I presented one character witness after another to say that they knew Bill to be a generally honest person.

I made my closing argument very factual and pointing out what "reasonable doubt" was as described in the evidence handbook. When I finished summarizing the lack of evidence, and the honest character of Bill, I built up to a very emotional ending where I called for the acquittal of "honest Bill Mainwaring." The crowd gave me a standing ovation, Doc had to quiet the room with his hammer, and I was hooked. When the jury returned a "not guilty" verdict, it was pleasing, but the real rush came when the crowd stood and applauded. Ego? Absolutely.

Doc's gavel showed up on his desk the next morning. I started reading everything about trials that I could get my hands on.

3

By the time I started college, I had fixed Clarence Darrow as my idol. My wife had never wanted me to be a preacher or radio announcer, and from the beginning of our dating promoted my becoming a lawyer. She gave me the book *Attorney for the Damned* for the first Christmas after we were married. It contained all the great speeches that Darrow had made to juries and to courts in his famous cases: the Loeb-Leopold case in which he argued for a life sentence instead of death for the kidnapping and murder of Bobby Franks, the son of a wealthy Chicago family; the Scopes trial where the teacher in Tennessee was charged with teaching Darwin's theory of evolution in violation of state law; the trial of the man hired by union organizers to murder a former governor of Idaho who was anti-union. Reporters who covered the argument in the Loeb-Leopold case said the judge shed tears at the conclusion of Darrow's argument. That was the standard that I would work toward.

The image of standing before a jury at the end of a criminal case is what kept me going through the arduous life at the University of Chicago law school. The movie *The Paper Chase,* and the subsequent television series by the same name was not an exaggeration. It was a brutal life.

At Chicago, Karl Nickerson Llewellyn, famous for his teachings and writings on commercial law and the fundamental principles of the law, inspired me to keep working toward a life as a litigator. He told us that those of us who didn't want to be trial lawyers ought to be in a business school. As I performed in the Moot Court program, he judged my team in our first-year argument. At the conclusion of the arguments, he called me aside and said, "You've got the instincts of the jackal, by God use them."

I did. And I was never disappointed in the courtroom drama— the strategic maneuvers, the effort to gain the edge on every witness, exhibit, objection, motion, and argument—the twists and turns that came in witness testimony and in opposing counsel's techniques and miscues. During my trial days, I never took time to worry about where I was situated in the quest for "justice." As a prosecutor, I focused on doing the job of getting a verdict consistent with the evidence. As a defense attorney, I never had a client who asked me to get him or her "justice." Clients wanted acquittals or minimum sentences which they could serve "standing on their heads."

4

I gave up my career as a trial lawyer in Baltimore, and returned to Nampa, where my wife, Lodice, and I had grown up. Lodice wanted our boys to go to school here, where she thought the values of life were taught better than in the city. So we came back to the place where our parents lived, where we had gone to school, and where she wanted to make our permanent home. I admit that I did so reluctantly, feeling that I would miss the excitement of the city and the trial courtroom. And, of course I was right—miss it I have.

The abandonment of my love for the courtroom, of a great talent I had for the courtroom, did not result from a loss of excitement or interest. I can't imagine how the thrill of walking into a courtroom, with a person's life or liberty on the line, can be matched by any other line of work in the world. I can't adequately express the excitement of confronting an able opposing counsel. I have tried to describe it and cannot. The feeling is electric, and at the end of the day, there is nothing left but exhaustion. Yet discussing the day's work with your associates revives the energy level and makes it difficult to simply settle down to family conversation and concerns. Often the stop for "one drink" to share the day's events led to many, many drinks and a lost night for the family. So I can understand my wife's desire to leave that lifestyle and come home to simpler life in Idaho.

When we decided to move, our friend Roger Duncan offered to drive a U-Haul truck with our furnishings. He had always wanted to see the west, and thought this would be his best chance to do that. After we arrived, and got the truck unloaded, he spent a few days being entertained by the "old west" stories of my dad.

Dad had freighted into Silver City, the historic center of the mining area high in the Owyhee Mountains in the southwest corner of Idaho at the ION (Idaho, Oregon and Nevada) triangle. He had owned and operated the only garage in Murphy, which by then, had become the County Seat of Owyhee County. Dad operated the state liquor store in the office of his garage, had a slot machine in the same office, and served as Justice of the Peace.

On the night before Roger returned to Baltimore, I took him up to the Holiday Inn near the Boise airport and stopped in to share a last drink with him. He said, "Pudge, you're gonna be nuts within a year." When I simply said, "Hope not," he said, "You're gonna miss the headlines about your big wins, the excitement of the courtrooms, and all else about the city." Roger was more right that night, than I think even he knew.

But Lodice had followed me in every step of my career, and now, when she so wanted to come home, I came with her. I was so burned out with the constant pressures of a criminal trial schedule, and my constant drinking, that I was not sure I wanted to practice law any more. But, I gave it a try.

5

I practiced for a year under a permit from the Idaho Supreme Court while I decided whether to take the bar and continue practicing. I worked with Bill Brauner, an old school friend who had always wanted us to practice law together. I liked Bill and his partners. But just before Christmas one of his clients wanted eviction papers prepared for two families living in his apartments. I got the papers ready and asked the client when in January he wanted them served. He said he wanted them served on Christmas Eve, and he meant it.

I was done. My love was in the trial courtroom with a criminal case, not this.

I went to work for my old friend Dale Haile, the sheriff of Canyon County, Idaho. He was as good a sheriff as ever served. But he, too, had a serious drinking problem. (Actually, that is a misnomer; no real drinker has a problem drinking. He has problems CAUSED by drinking, not a problem drinking.) As I worked in Dale's office, I heard about a Nampa cop who had worked in LA, and had been in Watts during the big riots there. The name was "Red" Merritt.

A narcotics task force had been set up in the sheriff's office, with officers from Canyon County and two cities(Nampa and Caldwell) working together. Dick Appleton headed the task force, an officer I would grow to have a lot of respect for. He was planning an arrest, and asked me to go along. I thought, "Why not?" We walked into the suspect's house; Appleton told the guy he was under arrest. The suspect turned and walked toward his mother who was coming into the room from the back of the house. He reached out his hands to his mother as if to take her hands and say goodbye. I saw him pass a clear pack with some white substance in it to her hands. She turned as though to walk toward the back of the house. I walked over to her and said, "Maam, I need you to hand me what is in your hands." She said, "I don't have anything," and I told her that I had just seen her son handing her a package of something white. She then turned it over, and later a lab test showed the pills to be unlawful narcotics.

When the defendant's attorney scheduled a motion to suppress, the prosecutor called me to testify as to how I saw the narcotics passed. Defense counsel didn't know my background; he only knew that I was an attorney licensed to practice in Maryland, so he challenged my expertise as to my observation of narcotics being handed off. The prosecutor had anticipated this, so deliberately did not put my experience into the direct testimony.

The defense attorney started off strong, asking me if I had ever participated in a drug arrest before. I answered "Yes." He asked whether I had any experience at all in observing occurrence of facts leading to establishment of "probable cause." ("Probable cause" is the standard by which a judge decides whether an arrest or search warrant should be issued. It means there is enough evidence that would cause a reasonable person to believe it is probable that a crime has been committed and that the defendant did it. The term does not require proof that the defendant committed the crime, only that it is reasonable to believe that a crime has been committed, and to establish a link between the crime and the defendant. As to a search warrant, the test is whether there is sufficient evidence to persuade a reasonable person that there is evidence of a crime on the premises to be searched.) Again, I answered simply "yes." That led him to ask me generally about my experience. I then explained my experience in Baltimore as prosecutor, Chief of the organized crime unit, and then a defense attorney. I said that in all, I had participated in hundreds of probable cause situations, and in arrests and searches. He was so surprised by the answer that he just sat for awhile staring first at his file and then at me, and then back at the file. Once his examination was ended, the judge ruled immediately that probable cause existed. So, the narcotics evidence was admitted and the defendant then changed his plea to "guilty."

Appleton was so pleased with the result that he spread the story of how the defense got "sandbagged". He was especially pleased because they had tried to get this defendant "dirty" or in actual possession of drugs for a long while, and to have him fall right into the trap was a blessing.

I didn't know that the story had spread all over the valley. One day not long after the hearing, I was sitting with a friend in the sheriff's office, engaged in one of the most predominant activities in any police station—drinking coffee. I noticed a tall lanky redhead walking three prisoners in custody, into the jail. He had the three handcuffed with the middle man's arms crossed in front of him with each wrist cuffed to the outside arm of the men on his right and left. So, with only two pair of handcuffs, the prisoners were rendered unable to move any arm to attack the officer. By being attached as they were, they could do nothing but shuffle along like three old men trying to keep their balance. (Until recently, I had never made that connection, but now I know what it is like to shuffle in order to keep your balance.)

I had seen the cross-over cuffing in Baltimore many times. I figured this must be the big city retiree. I walked over to him and asked, "Are you Merritt?" He looked at me and said, "Yeah, you must be Grant. Recognize the cuffs?"

We went that afternoon to a bar, had a beer, and started telling stories. Often the humor was classless, pure trash, but it was the humor that carried us through some bad, bad days on the job.

We told our stories with real gusto, but never got around to writing. We even settled on the title, "Justice My Ass" but, typical of alcoholics—we talked endlessly, without ever taking the time to focus on writing. Writing time would have interfered with drinking time.

Red liked to drink as much as I did, and most of our story telling occurred in bar settings. In 1985, after a very rocky period in my marriage, I went into a Care Unit for alcoholism. When I came out, I was sober and never have had a drink since. I still spent a lot of time with Red, he with his beer and me with my club soda. And we still talked about our stories, but never got around to writing.

I lost touch with Red a long time ago. He left Nampa, returned to security work in northern California, then went somewhere in Oregon, and I lost his trail.

6

Red and I agreed, based on our experiences, that there was no sound "system" involved with the criminal process, and that we always should refer to it as the "criminal justice process"—not system. We agreed that there was little search for justice in the process, that money had much to do with the results of the process, and that victims of crimes were the persons treated with the least respect and consideration in the process—by prosecutors, clerks of the court, judges and defense counsel.

We agreed that if "justice" was the result of any given case, it wasn't "justice" to all—because there is no way that both the defendant AND the victim could both get "JUSTICE." Only if the defendant has enough money to get the best lawyer, or, through sheer luck, gets the best possible attorney, either through the lottery of court appointment or through a public defender's office that has adequate counsel employed, can he get "justice." And normally, unless the victim is very wealthy, he or she has no influence on the process and its result, so will not get "justice". We also agreed that the public hardly ever gets "justice".

We both predicted long before the verdict that OJ Simpson

would be acquitted because he had Johnny Cochrane, who was not only very good but would be able to exploit a key investigator who was racist. As it turned out, Simpson won the verdict, but lost all his money in a civil case; the investigator gained a career as "writer" of true crime and "analyst" for the cable channels that have to rely on "talking heads" to fill 24 hours with an hour's worth of news.

During the OJ trial, the so-called experts on Court TV, like Nancy Grace who has been precisely described by Gerry Spence in his book, *Bloodthirsty Bitches and Pious Pimps of Power*, saw no doubt that OJ would be convicted. Grace continually talked about her experience as a "real trial lawyer," but apparently never noticed how Cochrane was goading Darden, and how Shapiro and Bailey were leading Marsha astray.

What a marvelous job of strategy the defense pulled off. Cochrane tantalized Darden about whether the gloves were even OJ's gloves. Red and I talked about how Cochrane was leading Darden into the trap, but didn't know whether anyone on the prosecution team was smart enough to avoid the trap. The answer was "no."

When Darden asked Simpson to try on the glove, it was all over. It was a dumb move for at least three reasons, which a well prepared prosecutor would or should have known: 1. The two gloves had been tested for blood and blood had been taken from the gloves for typing. The exposure of the gloves to the chemicals necessary to do that would naturally make them shrink. 2. It is very easy for anyone to make gloves not fit. All you have to do is spread your fingers as wide as possible, and the glove, which tends to pull the fingers together snugly, will not go on the hand. 3. OJ was on arthritis medicine. If he stopped taking it, as he had, his hands would swell. News stories had pointed out that OJ had stopped taking his medicine in jail.

So when Darden had OJ standing before the jury, fingers spread, not being able to squeeze the shrunken glove on his swollen hand, he had presented the defense with the line for acquittal: "If it doesn't fit, you MUST ACQUIT."

The taxpayers of Los Angeles County paid a dear price for an ineffective prosecution team. If the team of Marsha and Darden was the best they had, it was a bad office. But I suspect that the team was put together as a gender-race strategy: Marsha as a woman to go after the killer of a woman and Darden as an *Afro-American* lawyer to neutralize the white officer vs. *Afro-American* defendant racial theme. If that was the thinking behind selection of the trial team, it was a serious blunder. If this was truly the best the office had, the taxpayers of the County really were cheated.

Ask our justice question about the Simpson trial. Who was actually owed justice? I would say justice was owed to the victims, the defendant, AND the taxpayers of the County. Many people would not include the taxpayers. They would argue that justice is owed only to the defendant, and perhaps to the victims. But, to my mind, justice should not be looked at only from the individual's standpoint. The community is entitled to have a criminal justice system that serves the community with justice. Why? Well, for one thing, the community is paying a high price in taxes for that "system." When you total the expense for the police, the prosecutors, the courts, the jails, and, in many cases, the defense, you have probably 75 percent or more of a local government's budget. And, for another, unless community justice is achieved, there is a feeling of failure that doesn't deter wrong-doers. Justice for the community justifies the high expense for "protect and serve." Finally, the community is interested in justice to be sure that when and if members of the community are themselves summoned before the so-called "bar of justice", they will be afforded justice.

What would have been "just" in the Simpson case? One would think that it would have incorporated a competent investigation and an effective prosecution in the name of the "people of the County of Los Angeles." It would have incorporated retribution on behalf of the victims, that is to say, revenge for what befell them. It would have incorporated a constitutionally correct process—from investigation through arrest, through trial—for the defendant, and a correct result on the evidence resulting from the process.

In fact, justice was done only for the defendant. The taxpayers were cheated by the incompetent investigation plagued by participation by racists, and by an ineffective prosecution. There was no "revenge" or retribution for the victims; in fact, the victims were vilified. The defendant did get a constitutionally correct process, at least in the courts where it counted—including competent defense counsel for which he paid handsomely. The question of a correct result became moot when the correct court process led to a not guilty verdict. Justice? "Justice, My Ass."

This book was never intended either by Red or by me to be an analytical dissection of the "system," but rather a collection of stories of how the "system" failed or succeeded in spite of itself. It was never intended as an indictment of police, prosecutors, defense attorneys, and/or judges. Most of the individuals who toil in the criminal court process are decent, competent people. To emphasize MOST of them try their best to do their jobs in a competent manner. That's all they can do to make the system work. Each element of the system must work in each case in order for the community to get its moneys worth—police must do their work efficiently and effectively (avoiding constitutional violations and rejecting any temptation to be racially or gender or socially selective); prosecutors must work with the police in preparing adequately to present the evidence, follow all the rules, and persuade the jurors; and the judges must perform competently in order to see that costly mistrials and appellate reversals are avoided and that jurors are properly informed of the law.

Defense attorneys are a different cup of tea. When they perform competently, they push the system to its maximum stress level. When they are successful, only the defendant wins.

This book was designed just to tell the stories of how we found the "system" to succeed and fail, and some of the strange things and people we encountered along the way. To the surprise of most of my friends and family, I now have reached the writing stage.

So, Red, here we go....

TRIAL LAWYERS

7

A **good trial lawyer must** capture the courtroom from the first moment of the trial. The trial lawyer must actually be in charge, even while allowing the judge to think that they are in charge. Without the command of the room, the lawyer can't move the trial in the direction he or she needs it to move. Verdicts are not won by chance, by sheer luck, or by skilful presentation alone. They are won because of better, more complete mental and physical preparation.

I have never seen a good trial lawyer read an argument to a jury; I have never seen a good trial lawyer carry a note pad when approaching the jury box. He or she can't be looking constantly at an outline or notes, because he or she must have almost constant eye contact with the jurors. Jurors have to be able to "see," as well as feel, the sincerity of the lawyer giving the argument.

A good trial lawyer must have a personality that can convey intense feeling, the ability to use emotion when called for, and to rely only on reason when called for. A good trial lawyer must have, or at least understand, common sense. I have never seen a good trial lawyer who didn't understand common, plain, everyday people, as well as sophisticated elitists.

A jury can be made up of weird combinations of all kinds of people, all races, all nationalities, all income levels, all educational levels, all retention levels and all interest levels. The good lawyer must be able to relate to all of them, without over-emphasizing to any one of the groups. A good trial lawyer understands, even if he doesn't appreciate, all types of music, literature, movies, sports and entertainment. He or she is a person who can relate to all people and all activities.

During jury selection, good trial lawyer never asks questions of prospective jurors that would embarrass them, never asks convoluted questions that would confuse them, never uses big uncommon words that would confuse or embarrass them, never asks questions or acts in any way that would make them uncomfortable. When the *voir dire* (questions asked of prospective jurors before they are selected to serve on the jury) ends, the juror(s) should feel good about the lawyer or there will be trouble for the lawyer in the jury room. Many times I have seen opposing counsel get a look from a juror that would be a dead turn-off for me, only to see the lawyer leave that juror on the panel.

A good trial lawyer understands the psychology of communication, the psychology of living, the psychology of feeling. He or she has to understand the local community—the neighborhood from which the juror comes. He or she has to understand the kind of work that is done by any juror left on the panel. He or she has to be able to "read" jurors' faces, especially their eyes, in order to know whether the intended message is getting across. He or she has to be able to pay attention to the jurors' reactions as opposing counsel's examination of witnesses is going on, and as his or her own examination is going on.

For example, if it appears that jurors are getting put off by an attorney's examination of a witness, the good trial lawyer must factor that in when he or she begins examining the witness. If opposing counsel has really torn into a witness, and it appears to have annoyed one or more of the jurors, the good trial lawyer will take a gentle approach—keeping in mind that most times it is the nature and timing of the question and the line of questioning, that gets the intended message across, rather than the energy used in pushing at the witness.

If a witness has just answered in an unbelievable way, often the best impact can come with a lowering of the glasses down to the bridge of the nose, or lifting the glasses up off the face, and simply asking "really?" in a tone that says, "I am amazed that you would answer that way."

A good trial lawyer pays attention to what prospective jurors say during the *voir dire* questioning. I saw one of the most highly regarded lawyers in Idaho embarrass himself one day by not paying attention. The court had asked that any juror who had experienced litigation identify himself or herself. Several raised their hands. The lawyer then began asking specific questions, and asked one of the ladies for the details of her experience with litigation. She said that her two daughters had been involved in an auto accident, and she provided details as to how they were injured and subsequently went through civil litigation. She discussed her daughters' cases for a good fifteen minutes. Then the lawyer went back to his scripted *voir dire* questions, and asked her, "Do you have any children?" To which she responded, "Do you mean other than the two daughters that we've been discussing for the past half an hour?" Very embarrassing to the lawyer, as the courtroom full of prospective jurors laughed.

The good trial lawyer treats the judge with respect, but doesn't hesitate to make him the enemy. Often I have been told by jurors that they resented the way the judge ruled against me time after time. That differs with whether the lawyer is prosecuting or defending. The prosecutor, in my opinion, should rarely object, and never if the evidence isn't crucial. I tried not to come across as trying to keep anything out of evidence, being ready and willing to confront any punch the defense could throw. On the other hand, as a prosecutor I might offer evidence when I knew the judge would sustain the defense's objection. When I did that, I offered the question as I was approaching the bench, so that when the defense objected and the judge sustained the objection, I could turn back toward my table, facing the jury with a look of disbelief on my face. That's when I shrugged and took on the "Well, okay, that's not fair, but I'll just have to prove it another way" look.

As a defense attorney I tried to limit my objections to those things that were clearly inadmissible AND critical. If possible, it was good to get a string of sustained objections. And, somewhere in the middle of the string, I could throw in a "Now, judge, the prosecutor knows better than that. You've already told him that he isn't allowed to offer irrelevant evidence, so once again I object." Sometimes the prosecutor would object to my editorializing, and that gave me the chance to shrug and say, "Well, if you're going to keep trying to do something that's illegal, I have to tell you about it."

The court would strike my remark, but it didn't get stricken from the jurors' minds. By limiting my objections to crucial evidence, I got more attention from the court to the substance of my objections, and sometimes got some sustained that ought not to have been.

I have seen attorneys start objecting at the first sign of a leading question, but I never objected to "leading" until we got to the heart of the testimony. My experience was that when I held my objections until that point, the judge would be more likely to sustain, and it gave me a chance to say, "Objection, your honor, counsel is trying to testify for the witness by leading." That made it seem worse than just a leading question and made it seem that the witness was being spoon-fed.

One of the most comical objections I ever witnessed came in a complicated federal drug conspiracy case where I represented one of the defendants. The evidence in the case had been procured through wiretaps. Eight defendants were joined for trial, and all filed motions to suppress. Chief Judge Roszell Thompson presided. One of the defendants was represented by an older lawyer from Baltimore County who was long past his most active days. I was told that he had been a good, successful trial lawyer.

During the suppression hearings, he had several martinis at lunch. Then, in the afternoon sessions, he had a tendency to doze off. One afternoon, as he was nodding, the assistant U.S. Attorney took an unusually long time between questions, as he checked and re-checked his notes. All of a sudden, the lawyer popped his head up and said, "Objection your honor." Judge Thompson, who had gotten a little more upset as each hour of the complicated process passed, nearly broke his pencil as he slammed his hand down on the bench and exclaimed, "There is no question before the court, there can be, no objection. Counsel, please pay attention to the proceedings."

A minute or two went by, the assistant U.S. attorney asked a question and several of us objected at the same time. Judge Thompson said, very firmly, "The objection is sustained." Our aged companion looked up, raised his hand and said, "I told you so your, Honor."

A good trial lawyer also knows when and how to limit his or her cross examination so that he or she doesn't allow the witness to reiterate the testimony given on direct. I have seen counsel go through a series of questions that allows the witness to give the full details of the testimony all over again. Particularly, I have seen this with attorneys not experienced in trying criminal cases. It often appeared that some attorneys don't realize the difference between a civil and criminal case.

The trial lawyer must also know when to press a witness and when not to press. I recall a rape case that I was prosecuting, where the defendant's grandmother testified to establish an alibi. The defendant's room was on the second floor and the grandmother's room was on the first floor. The defendant could come down the steps and get out the front door without passing the grandmother's room, but she testified that she always heard him when he came down. She said that on the night in question, a year prior to trial, at 10 p.m. she knew he was in his room upstairs, so he couldn't have been at the rape site. The lady was obviously stressed over her grandson's plight, and I had two excellent eye witnesses. So, my cross examination was simply this, "Mrs._____, you love your grandson an awful lot don't you?" She got misty eyed and said, "More than anything." I said, "Thank you, maam, I have no other questions." What more could I have gained, and how much more I could have lost by discrediting her with details?

When I gave my opening statement, I always included some statements to the jury about what the judge would instruct on the law when the case was over. Then, in closing, I would remind them what the judge would instruct them on, and I alerted them to listen for it. It didn't matter whether the instruction I discussed was crucial or not. In most every trial, when the judge hit that spot in the instructions, at least one juror, usually more, looked at me and either smiled or nodded "yes." By saying something that I knew had to be in the standard instructions, my credibility was boosted when the judge actually did instruct in the way I predicted.

Many times, people asked me how I constructed my closing arguments. My answer was that I knew what my closing was going to be when the trial started. What I had to do during the trial was make sure the evidence got introduced to support what I intended to argue. As a result, when a trial ended abruptly for some reason, in the middle of an afternoon, I had the advantage over a lawyer who had to think about what and how he was going to argue. The only "pat" part of any of my arguments was the emphasis, as a defense attorney, on the fact that the jury had to prove itself by taking seriously the burden of proof. Nothing else was set in stone—each closing argument was put in terms determined by how I sized up the jurors.

8

The *voir dire* **of prospective** jurors is extremely important. A good trial lawyer knows those questions can be used to gain support, credibility, and an emphasis on that part of the case important to him or her. The questions really don't ever get a juror to admit bias. The juror who admits bias is really trying to get excused from service.

Most times, when opposing counsel went into great detail in questioning, I would simply say, "This juror is certainly acceptable, your honor." I did that even though I had every intention of challenging the juror at the end of the *voir dire*. It showed that I was satisfied with the quality and character of the jurors, and in the end, when I challenged one of these jurors and he or she was the only one who remembered that I had passed him or her with the "certainly acceptable" line.

Once, when I was defending a Philippine sailor on a murder charge, an extremely attractive young woman, seated as a prospective juror, was seated in the front row of the jury box. She had on a very mini mini-skirt. There was no "modesty panel" at the front of the box, just a brass rail that extended upward to about waist high. She certainly didn't seem embarrassed, even though it was obvious that the judge, clerk, prosecutor and I kept our eyes on her.

I don't remember why, but the young prosecutor challenged her. I was kind of disappointed because she would have been a pleasure to the eyes and I thought she had smiled faintly a couple of times when I made some remark to the court. The judge called counsel to the bench and really read the young kid the riot act. He said something to the effect that "You two get to try the case, so you'll have something to interest you. I have to sit here and be bored through the whole thing. At least with her there I had something to enjoy. Why the hell did you challenge her?" I knew he was just getting some comic relief for himself at the prosecutor's expense. But the kid said, in effect, "I'm sorry judge, I could withdraw my challenge." I said, "Well, judge, when he makes that withdrawal, then I will ask my client whether he has any objection."

So we went back to the trial table and the prosecutor said, "The state would like to withdraw its last objection, and have the juror seated." I said, "Your honor, one minute while I confer with my client." I then told him, through the interpreter, "This is a good juror, and we want her on here." Then I said, "Your Honor, this juror was always satisfactory to the defense, and we are sure as ever that she will try this case fairly." When she took her seat, she looked at me and smiled, not faintly this time.

The next morning when court convened, she was dressed in a very nice slack suit. The enjoyable sight was gone, but I felt that we had a very sympathetic juror.

A good trial lawyer has to be confident and show confidence to the jurors, but not be cocky. He or she has to be serious but not afraid to laugh or smile when something funny does happen. He or she has to show concern for the witnesses but not to the point of being condescending. The good trial lawyer makes eye contact with the jurors every time they enter and leave the room. When the jury is seated to begin the day, I always said "Good Morning," looking right at them, and all usually responded. The same when they came in after lunch, "Good Afternoon."

When I knew that an objection or motion of mine needed to be heard outside the presence of the jury, I always alerted the court and counsel ahead of time. When we reached a certain piece of evidence, and I needed an out-of-jury presence argument, I simply reminded the court that the matter we had previously discussed needed to be taken up. He would excuse the jury, and it didn't look like I was demanding all of a sudden that the jury be excluded from something. I always tried to time the incident near the time that the judge would have called a mid-morning or mid-afternoon recess, and that usually prompted the judge to say something to the effect that "this is a good time to take a recess anyhow." I tried never to make it appear that all of a sudden I was afraid of the jurors hearing something and asked for their removal.

As a prosecutor, it was much easier to put all these things into practice, because I got to set my order of witnesses. I also could time the testimony so that I could put on some dramatic evidence just before lunch recess or just before evening recess, when the other side didn't get a chance to cross examine until after the recess, after the drama had sunk in.

I knew what my burden was, and I knew that no matter what the law was, the only important thing was that the jurors believed that I had proved the defendant's guilt beyond a reasonable doubt. As a defense attorney, I knew that I had to convince the jury that the state's burden was heavier than just "reasonable" doubt, that I had to convince the jury to be looking at beyond "any" doubt.

One of the most elementary things for a good trial lawyer is never to show shock or undue concern when a big surprise hits. Because, in almost every case, there will be at least one surprise—some more critical than others.

9

One of the most shocking surprises that ever hit me came in a murder-conspiracy trial that had been removed from Baltimore City to Oakland, the county seat of Garrett County in the far western corner of Maryland, closer to Pittsburgh than to Baltimore.

A prisoner in the Baltimore City Jail escaped custody during a medical trip to the Baltimore City Hospital on the city's east side. He had gotten a message to his wife, telling her the time of his visit. She went to the Baltimore City Hospital armed with a handgun. When her husband was brought out of the hospital for return to the jail, she approached him along a loading ramp. As she reached him, she shoved the gun into his hands. He fired at the guard and escaped with her in her car.

A maintenance man was working on the ramp and observed her hand the gun to the prisoner. As he put it, he saw her hand him something that looked "like a piece of pipe."

The next night, a tip was called in to the homicide unit that the escapee was in a downtown lounge/restaurant. An off duty detective passing through the office took the call. He relayed the message to dispatch and headed for the lounge. As he drove up and started to enter the lounge, the escapee came out and shot and killed the officer. By this time other cars were arriving, and the escapee fled across the street into a parking lot. As officers surrounded him, he put the gun to his head and shot himself dead.

The case took on even more importance because of the detective's murder. With the killer dead, the focus turned to the wife who assisted the escape and furnished her husband with the murder weapon. I took the case to the Grand Jury, which returned charges of conspiracy, escape, and murder. The murder charge was based on her status as an accomplice.

We still were not sure how criminally involved the guard was. But, there was enough evidence for the Grand Jury to charge him with aiding an escape and conspiracy. Since the murder charge allowed an automatic change of venue, and because of the extreme impact of local publicity, defense counsel moved for the change. I asked the Court to send the case to Garrett County where Judge Stuart Hamill was presiding judge.

10

The town of Oakland was a small western Maryland town in the center of a tourist area around Deep Creek Lake. The courthouse was an old building, with an unusual courtroom in the format of an amphitheatre. The court, jury and trial counsel were on the main floor, with the audience seated in the balcony on three sides of the floor. This case was such a big newsworthy case, and would be such an attraction in a quiet little town, that the court decided to issue tickets to members of the public. A ticket entitled a holder to a certain number of hours. At the end of the time, if there were people waiting to get in, the ticketholder had to yield a seat.

Bob Stewart had assisted me with the case through the Grand Jury and went with me to assist at the trial. Lt. Tom Coppinger who headed the police squad assigned to the States' Attorney's office, went with us to help with witnesses. The police officers involved in the investigation of the escape and the murder, the ballistics expert, two citizens who witnessed the shooting of the detective at the lounge, and the maintenance man from the hospital were all taken to Oakland.

Counsel for the jail guard offered to have his client testify and identify the defendant if we would just drop the conspiracy charge, leaving a misfeasance charge to be faced. I turned down the offer, pointing out that I didn't need him, thus we didn't have to deal away the charge.

On the first day of trial, the jury selection and opening statements took up most of the day. We put on evidence that the prisoner was incarcerated legally at the City Jail, and the court recessed for the day.

On the second day, we put on the stand, the officers who set the stage for the escape, and then proved the shooting of the detective by the escapee. The day was finished out with the civilian witnesses to the murder of the officer.

On the third day, Bob was going to examine the ballistics expert to prove the same gun that fired the bullets found at the Baltimore City Hospital was used to murder the detective. That testimony would be followed by the maintenance man who would finally identify the defendant as the woman who passed the murder weapon to the escapee. That morning, I arrived with the maintenance man at the courthouse early so we could make him feel comfortable with the court surroundings.

I took him first into the balcony and let him look down on the main floor where the court, parties and the jury would be seated. I showed him from there where he would be sitting as the witness. We then went on to the main floor, he took his seat in the witness chair, and I asked him a series of questions to get him adjusted to his surroundings.

We finished up some loose ends as to the escape, the call to homicide, and the response to the murder scene, then called the ballistics expert. Bob took the expert through his testimony very skillfully, and the expert was not damaged at all on cross. We were sitting in good shape as the court broke for lunch.

11

During the lunch break, I went over the maintenance man's testimony with him one last time. With his testimony in the afternoon, we would seal the defendant's fate. He was a slight man who never had been involved in anything of importance in his whole life. But he didn't seem nervous as we approached testimony time.

I lead him through his testimony—he came to work, started to perform his maintenance and clean up chores, was working on the loading ramp when the guard and the prisoner in jail uniform came out of the hospital onto the ramp, and saw a woman approaching the prisoner. He testified that he saw the woman hand the prisoner what looked like "a piece of pipe." I showed him the gun, and asked him to compare the barrel of the pistol to what he saw that resembled a "piece of pipe." He said the barrel looked like what he saw the woman hand the prisoner.

Right after the woman handed the object to the prisoner the witness turned his attention away for a few seconds and heard gunshots. He jumped off the loading ramp into the parking lot and hit the ground. From that position, he saw the woman and the prisoner jump in a car which she drove away.

We had the full story —all that we needed now was identification of the defendant as the woman. I let a few seconds go by without any question. I flipped through a few pages of reports for effect, letting the drama build up for the jury. I turned to Bob and conferred for a few seconds, just building up the drama. Then, in an absolutely still court room, I asked him "to look around the courtroom and tell the ladies and gentlemen of the jury whether you see in the courtroom the woman who walked up to the prisoner and handed him what looked like a piece of pipe, just before gunshots were fired."

He began slowly looking around, and I saw that he was focusing on the balcony where the public was seated. At first I didn't worry because I had asked him to look around the courtroom, but as seconds passed I got a sinking feeling. He finally said, "No." I said, "I'm asking you to look around the courtroom very carefully again and tell me if you see the woman." The defense objected, but the court overruled the objection. The witness looked around the balcony again, and said, "No." Very quickly, I said, "No further questions, your honor." The defense said, "No cross," and I asked the court to recess for the day. The defense objected and asked for a bench conference.

Before going to the bench, I turned to Tom Coppinger and told him to keep the witness separated from everyone until we could find out who paid him off. I also told him to call the guard's attorney and ask him to be ready to talk to me as soon as I got back to the motel. Finally, I asked him to get transportation ready to bring the guard to Oakland that night. Tom asked me whether I had any idea where we would find the guard, and I said I didn't but we would as soon as I talked to his lawyer. I told Bob and Tom to act smoothly as though we had expected the witness to testify as he had.

Bob and Tom left with the witness to start making arrangements to try to resurrect our case. Fortunately, there wasn't any evidence that the jury knew we were in trouble.

At the bench, defense counsel asked the court to require me to dismiss the charges. I objected and said that the court had no basis for making such an order. I said my next witness will prove identification. Counsel asked what witness and I named the guard. That prompted a loud retort from the defense, saying that I couldn't call the guard because I hadn't disclosed his name as a witness. I disagreed pointing out that his name was on the indictment form itself as a witness. I also pointed out that defense had not filed for written discovery, but that I had let him review the entire file including the guard's statement. He objected again to my calling the guard as a witness and the court overruled the objection on the basis that I had identified him on the indictment form. Next, counsel objected on the ground, that he had been misled into not interviewing the guard. I committed to the court that I would make the witness available at eight the following morning for interview by the defense.

Judge Hamill then recessed the court and excused the jury, telling them to come the next day a little bit later, at 10:30 a.m., and be prepared to stay until a verdict was reached.

As the jurors filed out, I turned and saw Tom and Bob motioning to me. They told me that the witness wanted to tell me that he saw the woman now and that he had been mixed up and was looking in the wrong place. Tom said he didn't think the guy was really smart enough to have done anything deliberately. I told Tom I still wanted him to check the witness out, that it was just too pat.

When I walked out of the courtroom, the defendant and counsel were conferring, and counsel was not as chipper as he had been just half an hour earlier. We went into the clerk's office and I talked to the witness. He was now scared, and told me that he just hadn't looked in the right place. He said if we went back in he would know where to look this time. I explained that we had passed by that opportunity.

12

About an hour after returning to the motel, we were able to reach the guard's attorney. I told him I wanted to deal in order to seal up the verdict. He said he would let his client testify if I would drop the criminal charges—both the conspiracy and the misfeasance. I talked it over with Bob and Tom and the homicide detectives—we all decided it was worth it. The homicide detectives had satisfied themselves through their investigation that the guard really had taken no active role in the escape. They had concluded that he violated his duties by agreeing that the prisoner could meet and talk with his wife, but they also knew that administratively he was not going to be working at the jail.

I called the attorney back and we made the plea agreement. Then the task was to find the guard. His attorney had been trying to reach him from the time he got my first message. We made arrangements for him to call homicide as soon as he reached the guard so that someone could pick him up and get him to Oakland. It was easily a four-hour drive, with the last hour and a half being through the mountains.

We went to dinner, hoping for the best. Arriving back at the motel we had a message that a detective was on the way with the guard. He arrived about 2 a.m., and we finished our interview and preparation at 4 a.m. I remember that when the detective arrived with the guard, the homicide lieutenant who was with me on the case told the detective he had to turn around and head back to Baltimore right away. That nearly caused the exhausted detective to have cardiac arrest. After a good laugh, the detective went to bed while we worked on through the night.

We arrived at the courthouse at 8 a.m. and, after a conference with the court and counsel, at which I revealed that I would be dismissing the charges against the guard, we turned him over to the defense. At 10:30 a.m., the interview over, court reconvened and the defendant pleaded guilty under a deal in which I recommended, and the court agreed to, a ten-year sentence.

The plea was taken and Judge Hamill ordered a presentence report. I dismissed the charges against the guard, and the court called the jury in and discharged them. I am positive that no juror even had a hint at the surprise that hit us the previous day. I have never been kicked by a mule, but I have a feeling that it couldn't be much worse than the pain that had hit me with that single word "no."

Neither Bob and Tom, nor the officers, nor I let on that we were hit hard. And that's how it has to be.

The officers were satisfied with the outcome, but two months later we were enraged when the judge imposed the 10-year sentence but suspended it and placed the defendant on 10 years probation. So her time spent behind bars was just over a year. Just another example of the strange twists that a case makes as it meanders through the "process".

13

A final point that has always seemed important to me in assessing the duties of a trial lawyer is he or she must be imaginative in devising a strategy for allowing the jury to view the facts from the standpoint of the witnesses, the victim and/or the defendant. Often it is necessary that counsel create the mechanism for the jurors to actually "see" and "feel" the events that form the base of the charge.

Back to when I was defending the Philippine sailor, I was faced with the problem of being able to convey to the jury the hopelessness of a paranoid individual in the midst of people whose language he neither spoke nor understood. The sailor was charged with murder in the stabbing death of an unarmed man in a west side bar. He was on shore leave, spoke and understood no English, and somehow had gotten to a dive frequented by some pretty tough guys.

The story that I got from witnesses who worked at the bar painted such strange actions by the defendant, prior to and after the stabbing, that I felt I needed a mental evaluation. The result was that the defendant suffered from paranoia, which of course was enhanced by his inability to understand what was being said around him. His mental state was not of such level as to avoid trial, but it certainly mitigated his culpability in my mind. After conferring with officials at the embassy, I offered a plea of guilty to manslaughter. The prosecutor turned it down, wanting second degree. The Embassy officials were against such a plea and the sailor was following instructions from them.

So we went to trial. On cross of the state's witnesses I was able to show the anxiety that began to build in the defendant the longer he stayed in the bar. One witness even acknowledged, after being led pretty unmercifully by me, that he seemed to get more and more afraid the longer he stayed. He started talking loudly to himself, and finally in almost a frenzy, he stabbed the guy sitting next to him at the bar.

I called the psychiatrist who testified about his finding of paranoia, and he explained how paranoia works to build toward an unnatural and unreasonable fear that people are endangering the paranoid. He explained that the fear would come on sooner and harsher if the paranoid did not speak or understand the language being spoken around him.

I felt that the story was in the record, but the psychiatrist was not the most lively of witnesses, and I had no idea how much of the theory had sunk in. So, I asked for a recess until the next morning so I could get some things set up. After court, I met with the embassy officials, the defendant, and the interpreter and explained what I wanted to do. I wanted to have the defendant waive his right to have his answers translated into English, at least for a period of five to ten minutes. We worked it through to all of their satisfaction, and I was sure that the defendant understood. But I didn't know whether I could get it past the court.

Overnight I decided not to push the envelope too far, and decided to try to waive translation on only four questions relating to the defendant's feelings right before the stabbing. Frankly, I didn't research the issue because I didn't have time, and even if I had, I'm not sure I wanted to know what the law might be.

As I explained what our strategy was, the state objected and the court was less than enthused. I pointed out that it was the only effective way that the defense had to make it clear to the jury the state of the facts as they appeared to the defendant at the time of the stabbing. I argued that we were entitled to get that evidence before the jury. I also argued that since a defendant could in fact waive his right to jury trial, his right to keep silent (leading to an actual confession of guilt), and even his right to trial itself by pleading guilty, he should be able to waive the right to have some of his answers translated. The court's position was that the jury had the right to hear the answers, and I simply submitted that what we would be offering the jury was the same evidence that faced the defendant. The judge took a recess, but could find no quick law. Finally, he agreed that he would let the defendant waive the right to have four answers translated as they were given, provided that the same four questions and answers would then be repeated for the jury.

That was the best I was going to get so I went with it. The judge instructed the jury as to what was going to happen, and the defendant took the stand. When we got to the last few minutes prior to the stabbing, I made the formal waiver and my next four questions were translated to the defendant but his answers were not translated. The courtroom seemed very still during the process and, without looking at the jury I hoped they were feeling a lot of discomfort. After the four answers had been given and not translated, the court reporter read back the questions and the interpreter translated the answers.

During closing argument, I stressed the quiet discomfort in the court room during the time when none of us knew what the defendant was saying. I tried to tie that to a feeling of what the defendant had been going through in the bar prior to the stabbing.

I had no idea how effective the strategy was, and still don't know to this day. The jury was out for four hours, and then reported that they were deadlocked. The judge declared a mistrial and refused to ask the jury what the vote was when they decided they could reach no verdict. But the clerk asked the foreperson (who was the attractive young lady in the mini-skirt that the state had earlier challenged and then reinstated) in the hall and reported back to us that it was eight for manslaughter, two for second degree, and two for not guilty. I conferred with the embassy officials, and then pleaded the defendant to manslaughter.

During the time pending sentence, the embassy worked some kind of deal with the State Department. The defendant was sentenced to 10 years, but through some governmental manipulations was released to the embassy for transport out of the United States and back to the Philippines. I had the distinct feeling that the defendant was more afraid of what he was going to face in his home islands than what he would face in prison. But the verdict returned was the same as what I had offered prior to trial, so I felt that my job was well done.

14

The good trial lawyer is always able to adjust strategy at a moment's notice if and when surprise hits. And surprise will hit, sometimes in a series of cases one after the other, and then again only at long intervals. But whenever, he or she must be ready.

Pete Ward, as I have said, was one of the best organized and prepared lawyers I ever saw. He had the most effective means for preparing for those ever-troublesome child sexual molestation cases. Knowing that children have trouble getting through necessary testimony as to parts of the body, and having experienced problems resulting from that troublesome aspect of their testimony, Pete devised a sketch of the human body. It was not anything but a penciled sketch of the outline of the body, and the proper names of the parts of the body relevant to a molestation case were written in on the form.

Pete had his witnesses' parents or guardians bring child witnesses in early on trial day so he could go over the drawing with them, getting them comfortable with using the correct names of the parts of the body involved in the case. A big problem was getting them comfortable with using the word "penis," but use of the drawing and just explaining the testimony, worked beautifully for him.

One day, Pete was leading off with Judge J. Gilbert Prendergast, a retired navy captain who ran a tight ship in the courtroom. Pete was on my trial team at the time. Charley Moylan had set up teams of trial assistants, a supervisor and three assistants who worked together in a courtroom for a month, then moved on to another courtroom. He had devised this plan to cure the problem of postponements and mix-ups caused when a prosecutor assigned to a court had a case that carried over to a second and/or third day, thus messing up the assignments he had in a different court on that second and third day.

My team had been assigned to Judge Prendergast as our first assignment. The Judge was insistent that his court be ready to start at 10 a.m., not 10:01 a.m. but 10 a.m. And that meant not just ready to say to him "we're ready," but that when he walked on the bench at 10 a.m. we had the case ready to start.

So we picked one case for each day and the assistant to which it was assigned had to have it ready—had to spend time before trial day making sure the witnesses were ready and would be there early. Then, while that case got underway, we could round up our witnesses on the regular docket schedule and get the other trials set. One person had the "lead case" assignment for each day, and one had the "second case" assignment, then each had to gather together witnesses in the other cases on the docket to get a case ready when the two lead cases were finished.

But when Pete had a molestation case, it was our automatic "lead case" because of his habit of having the witnesses in early. We did so well with the good judge that Charley extended our stay for a second month, so we got to know Judge Prendergast very well. It wasn't all bad. He was a fine judge, a real gentleman, who didn't interfere in your case, so long as you were prepared. And we were.

On this particular day, I had the second case and, fortunately, had time the day before to get it ready. My witnesses were ready and in the courtroom, and Pete went ahead with the lead. He was grumbling under his breath, in that delightful Birmingham accent, "Dammit, she didn't get her in early enough." The mother had not gotten the girl in early enough to suit Pete. I asked him if he needed me to take mine first. He said, "No. I think it will be all right." The witness had time to go over the drawing with him, but apparently she had a problem in simply saying "penis."

Pete did his usual fine job of getting the details of the crime into evidence. For a formal Englishman, he had such a way with child witnesses, and particularly little girl witnesses. He was amazing in how he could bring them through difficult cases with comfort. But when it came time for her to identify the "penis," trouble arrived like an early summer evening thunderstorm. He directed her attention to the drawing, and asked her to look at it and tell the judge what part of the body the defendant put in her "vagina." She looked at the drawing, put her finger at the crotch and started to say "penis" and then just lowered her head and let out a big sigh and then a big sob.

"Damn," said Pete aside to me, and went up to the witness stand to comfort the little girl. He calmed her down, and then made a go of it again, got to the same spot and instead of saying "penis" this time she just broke down in a series of big sobs. "Damn, damn," said Pete. "I wish she had gotten her in earlier." He went to give the little girl his handkerchief and calm her and Judge Prendergast took a five minute recess.

The little girl got calmed down again. Pete said he didn't know whether she was going to get the word out or not, and maybe he had better try to have her just mark and initial the spot of the body and circle the word. I asked whether the little girl had a brother, older or younger, and Pete immediately hit on an idea. When court resumed, he asked her whether she had a little brother. She said yes, and then he started his success: "Does your brother have a part of his body that is the same part as that part of the defendant's body he put in your vagina?" Answer was "Yes." So Pete asked whether the family had a name that they called that part of her brother's body. "Yes," she said kind of smiling now. Pete was headed into the final stretch now, feeling very happy with himself: "Now dear, using the name that your family uses for the part on your brother's body, what is the part of the defendant's body that he placed in your vagina?" She hardly hesitated at all in getting out the name: "His chicken neck."

Judge Prendergast sat up straight in his chair, and said, "His WHAT?" Without a second's hesitation, Pete was on his feet, fairly shouting out, "His chicken neck, your honor, his BLOODY chicken neck!"

The crowd was afraid to laugh out loud in the judge's courtroom, but many had to get up to leave so that they could laugh outside. We lost most of the police officers to the hallway. Pete had done what he had to do—alter the game plan and WIN.

15

Bobby Fertitta, like Pete, could make that split-second answer or switch that victory requires. My first experience with Bobby came on my first day in the State's Attorney's office. I had just moved across the street from the U.S. Attorney's office where any case, misdemeanor or felony, had a file complete with FBI reports that documented every witness and his or her testimony, all the evidence, any problems to be encountered and other specific trial details. FBI agents always scheduled your witnesses to see you and be interviewed the day before the trial.

On my first day, George Helinski escorted me to Judge O'Donnell's courtroom where Fertitta had the docket. George's final remarks to me were, "Welcome to this side of the street where the happenings happen."

As I took my seat next to Fertitta at the trial table, he was beginning the second day of a jury trial. He handed me a file with two sheets of paper in it—an indictment and a one-page transcript of the Grand Jury where our assistant simply summarized for the GJ what the witnesses would prove if there. He asked me to get it ready for trial. That meant that I had to go through the courtroom quietly while he started his case, find the witnesses, interview them in the hall, and be ready to try a FELONY ARSON case. To my amazement, the witnesses were there, the officer was there, and I felt we had a case ready to go.

So I returned to the table just as a witness was explaining to the defense counsel that he couldn't remember how close to the curb the victim's foot was. Fertitta had just offered into evidence a series of photos taken at the crime scene, but evidently they didn't include a shot of the curb that would answer the question. O'Donnell (who earned the nickname "wild Bill O'Donnell" because he had been State's Attorney before Charley and thought he knew more about prosecuting than we did or could ever know, and because he aggressively interfered with the prosecutor's case) got that little sardonic grin on his face and tossed Bobby an insulting snide remark about being able to have that answer if the prosecutor had only introduced a photo of that curb space. I think he believed the office had been ineffective in not making sure that all necessary photos were in evidence. Bobby was on his feet right away. "Your honor, I do have that photo and didn't introduce it for a VERY good reason. Would you like for me to state that reason for the court and jury?" O'Donnell lost the grin; he didn't want to risk mistrial, so he simply said, "No, there is no need."

The defense counsel didn't want to ask any more about the curb space, for fear, I guess, that Bobby would offer that photo, and he had to wonder at this point what he had missed in this photo. He went on with his examination of the witness, and when I couldn't stand it any longer, I wrote Bobby a note and passed it over to him. It said, "What was the reason?" He read the note, leaned over to me, kind of grinned and said, "I forgot to offer it." Remarkable. Bobby turned a forgotten thought into an answer that had to stir the jury's imagination, and took care of the judge's interruptions for the rest of the trial.

Bobby (I guess he should be Robert since he became the very dignified Dean of the College of Prosecutors for the National District Attorneys Association) had a real talent for the finesse, diplomatic way of moving through things that Pete and I would just bulldog through. Bobby was a very talented lawyer, always ready to make the swift decision and change of plans.

16

Red and I often talked about how trial lawyers accomplished more with juries by what they didn't say. An example was the introduction of murder scene photos. For the most part, prosecutors introduce such photos just for the shock value to the jury, in an effort to prejudice the jurors. Red knew several attorneys who did as I often did in avoiding the appellate risk of offering the photos in evidence. Instead, we would put the photos face down on the trial table where the jury could see they were the backs of photos. In one case, I picked up the photos, showed them to my second chair, shook my head, and put them face down. Throughout the trial, every once in a while I would notice the jurors looking at the face-down photos. I was sure I got more value through the mystery of them than I would have by offering them.

Red told of two lawyers who would face the jurors, holding the photos up with the backs to the jurors, stare at the photos and shake their heads almost in disbelief. They then would lay down the photos and never go back to them during the entire trial.

Red also loved to tell the story of remarkably talented Johnny Cochrane and how he pulled off a strategic gem before the Scarlet

Lady in the LA courts. She was judge with a fashion statement—she wore a Scarlet robe. Cochrane was a young lawyer who was representing a guy caught with enough drugs to justify a long sentence. The officers wanted to pin him good because he had refused to become an informant for them. The Scarlet Lady was a prosecutor's judge who knew the rules of evidence and used them against the defense at critical times.

Cochrane objected to all the evidence at the beginning of the case, and after discussion the Scarlet Lady overruled his objection. On the first question to the first agent witness, Cochrane objected; overruled. Then he moved that his objection be continuing on every question and answer during the trial. Scarlet Lady said it can't be done that way. Cochrane showed her and the D.A how it could be done under the rules. So she ruled with him. Then Johnny sat back and asked no questions, made no other statements, and participated in no other way through the case. As a result, the D.A. got sloppy with no Johnny to worry about. The D.A. rested, and hadn't formally offered the drugs into evidence. With no objection having been stated and argued, he had just overlooked the technicality of offering it. Johnny put on a witness who said that the defendant was with him about an hour before the arrest. That's all he said. On cross, the D.A. made it clear that the defendant could have been with him as he said, and still have been at the scene of the arrest. Johnny had no redirect and he rested.

Then Cochrane moved to dismiss the case because no evidence of illegal drugs was in the record. The D.A. then said it was simply an oversight that could be cured on rebuttal. Cochrane objected to rebuttal unless it had to do only with where the defendant was an hour before the arrest. He pointed out that the state rested without introducing the drugs, then even participated in the defense, so had full opportunity during both case in chief and in the defense to offer the evidence and did not. The Scarlet Lady was trapped by the rules and had to dismiss. As Cochrane and his client walked away from the trial table, the Scarlet Lady called to Cochrane and said to him, "You were lucky today, not good, but lucky." Johnny smiled that smile and said, "Thank you maam." She then hurled back at him, "This is a warning, next time you won't dance through here!" Cochrane at that broke into a soft shoe dance routine and danced down the aisle and out of the courtroom. Red said the Scarlet Lady fumed, and took it out on every other lawyer present in court that day—and on all defendants.

17

Not all surprises and challenges come to lawyers trying criminal cases. One of my biggest surprises came in a civil case in which I played little or no part. In several misdemeanor criminal cases I represented a guy who operated on the Block. I didn't know much about his "operations" other than he sent to me people charged with misdemeanor drug charges, pornographic possession cases, traffic citations, and some burglary and receiving stolen property cases. His "girlfriend" who lived with him was a gorgeous dancer in one of the non-strip dancing bars. These bars featured younger women who danced in high heels, skimpy bra and skimpier shorts on the bar along which customers sat and drank. Music was by juke box, and even though it would run automatically and free, the girls solicited change for the "box" from the customers.

These bars were simply the precursors to bars of today where customers stock up with dollar bills and then reach up and slip them inside the bikini bottom of the dancer. Baltimore's city law enforcement standards did not permit that kind of conduct at the bar. Tips were just left on the bar and the dancers picked them up when they finished.

Few of the dancers really put their heart into the dancing. Often, you would notice a dancer staring out an open door to the sidewalk beyond, and all of a sudden wave to someone on the sidewalk and start a shouting conversation with the person while entertaining the guy with the dough at the bar.

When a dance was over, the dancer then circulated the bar to see who would like to have her sit down for a closer look. All he had to do was buy a heavily overpriced glass of ginger ale or soda water masquerading as champagne. In the lower level bar's, or those owned by people with less "protection," the contact was limited to buying drinks, although for a magnum the guy could sit in a booth up close to the girl.

Neither the Block nor the bar owners had yet advanced to the current practice of selling no alcohol and featuring completely naked dancers on the bars right in front of the soda drinking customers. The threat of the liquor control board was far greater to the Block owners than the threat of the police. Loss of the liquor license would cripple the bar.

In the bars with a little better tie-in to police protection, the dancers were older, although well preserved. When they finished a dance, they aggressively pursued drinks, using hands on the guy's body to convince him that it was in his best interest to buy the lady a drink. If he bought a magnum, he got to go to a booth, where for a cash deposit he could buy sex in many forms—right there under the table.

One of the latter bars had a pretty good looking older woman who stood in the door, as though she was just bored and looking out on the street to see who was coming by. If someone slowed or seemed to look with interest, she lifted her dress up to the waist and was naked underneath. She was tireless, working days and nights. The first time the detectives and prosecutors walked down for lunch to disrupt things a bit, she wasn't familiar with our group. When the first prosecutor passed her door, up went the dress, and then quickly down when she recognized a detective right behind the prosecutor. We kidded the detective as to how she knew who he was in order to cover up so quickly.

Well, again I digress. It's easy to do when remembering the

Block and it is colorful, with shady and seedy, atmosphere. My client's girlfriend came to me to file a workman's compensation claim. As I said, she was an absolutely gorgeous, tall blonde woman in her twenties with not a fault that I could tell. Had I ever seen her dance I would have been better able to tell, but I knew from her boyfriend that she was the top tip receiver at the bar. She was the one everyone came to see and eagerly bought her drinks at the bar just to have her sit with them for a few minutes. He reported that she did not do the sex act routine.

She said she hurt her back stepping on to the bar in stiletto heels. She was able to go on with the dance, but that strained her back even worse. Her lower back was in pain enough that she missed two nights of work, heard about workman's comp and came to see about it. I asked how long she had been out of work, she said just the two nights, that she had gone back the third night and been dancing since. But, she said, "it hurt" when she climbed on the bar and when she stepped off.

I told her that she might get a small claim, but it would be small. I knew the adjusters would know the kind of dancing that was done in the Block, and would know that someone with a real bad lower back couldn't be doing it. She wanted to go ahead with it. I arranged an appointment with a chiropractor to whom claimants with minimal claims always went first, and received fairly high reports of damage. We got a very good report from our choice. I told my client not to get her hopes up because the commission would now send her to a doctor who would not be nearly so generous. In a few days we got the name of the examining doctor for the commission. I checked around and found that he was very, very conservative—as in "cheap."

She went to the doctor, and called me that evening and said that she had one more evaluation to go through. Her appointment was two weeks out, and I forgot about the case. Several weeks later, I got a copy of his report to the commission and was shocked. He raised damages well over what our own doctor had. This doctor even predicted continuing pain into the future, too speculative to fix now, but which could be determined within six weeks.

I called the client and asked her what happened. She said she didn't know. On the first visit she just undressed and was sitting there naked when the doctor came into the room. She told him she couldn't find any gowns or towels, and he said this would be better because his examination could be more precise. She said he told her that he wouldn't be able to make his report until he had given her massages to test the depth of the tissue injuries. So he set her for twice-weekly massages for six weeks, at the expense of the state. She got a very handsome settlement from workman's comp, and got to continue her massages at the doctor's own expense, I imagine. She continued to dance throughout the treatments.

18

I think maybe all trial lawyers dream of having at least one Perry Mason moment—where the client is innocent and the innocence is proven at the very last second. My closest came with a court appointment to represent a guy charged with bank robbery. I looked at the police file, then went in and talked to the detective and lieutenant in the robbery division of Captain Anton Glover. They told me how sure the witness was, and that this was a guy with a history of armed robbery. When I went to visit the defendant in the City Jail, I was pretty sure I had a losing case. As was my habit, I did not ask him what he had done. I asked what he told the police. He told me that he told them he didn't do the robbery and couldn't have because he had an alibi. They asked him what the alibi was, and he asked for an attorney.

His alibi was that he was in the City Jail on another robbery charge when this bank was robbed. I checked with the records office and found that he was telling truth. I got a certified copy of the record, went back to the office and prepared an affidavit to present to the court and get a dismissal. Suddenly it hit me— I had to let this case go to preliminary hearing so I could prove my client was innocent.

I asked for a preliminary hearing and it was scheduled before Judge Brocollino, a little Italian good guy who stayed close to his Little Italy roots, if you know what I mean. But, if your case didn't go against one of his "folks," he was a good, objective judge.

The prosecutor put on the bank teller, who was an extremely good looking, well dressed, young lady. Prosecutor, clerk and bailiff were all taking steps to make her feel comfortable as she took her place in the witness chair. She testified very clearly and directly as to the robbery, and how the gunman put a "big gun" right in her face and demanded money. I had looked at her description of the robber in the police report, which was given to me that morning. It sure fit my client.

She testified as to how she picked out the robber from a photo lineup that the police brought to the bank to show her. Then she identified the defendant as the gunman. On cross, I asked her when she gave the police the description of the gunman. It turned out she did that after picking the defendant from the photo lineup. I asked whether she knew why the police did not have a physical line-up. She said the police told her they couldn't find the defendant.

Then I started taking her through her reasons for remembering the defendant and being so certain of her identification. One by one, I took her through the features she emphasized, and Judge "B" looked at me like I was crazy. Finally, I got to the question of what feature of the defendant made her remember him so certainly. She thought about it for a minute and then said, "His eyes." I asked, "What about his eyes make you remember them so well?" She went through several answers, winding up with the "intensity" of his eyes. I finally got her to say that she would never forget those eyes. She also said she remembered the stature of his shoulders as he held the gun aimed at her. I had the defendant stand up, and she said, "Yes" his stature reminded her again of the certainty of her identification.

Judge "B" was just openly staring at me in disbelief. Finally, I said, no other questions, the state had no redirect and closed its case. I then asked to call a witness. That was unusual at a preliminary hearing, which defense counsel regularly used only to hear what kind of witness the civilian made. But I was entitled to call a witness, so I called the records keeper at the City Jail. I asked her to identify herself, and then had her produce a certified copy of the records showing that the defendant was in jail on the date of the bank robbery, had been there for five days prior, and was still there. She testified that he was there on a robbery charge. I offered into evidence the certified record which contained the photo and fingerprints of my client.

When the witness was finished, I moved to dismiss and the prosecutor had no objection. Judge "B" dismissed the case, and then said to me, "Why didn't you just tell us that, and save everybody's time?" I said, "What, and ruin my only Perry Mason moment so far and maybe forever, having an innocent client and proving it in a hearing in court?" I added, "Besides, I won two cases today. I won this one, and when they find the right guy for the bank job, it's going to be hard to convict when the defense counsel has the transcript of the eyewitness from this hearing." He laughed and, shaking his head left the courtroom.

As the lieutenant of robbery passed by me he said, "Lousy scumbag," I turned and said, "Thanks, that's the nicest thing you've called me lately." He laughed and waved as he went out.

Out in the hall, the teller thanked me for preventing her from making a big mistake. She wanted my card in case she ever needed a lawyer, and said the lieutenant had just told her that I was "the best." I gave her my card but unfortunately she never needed a lawyer I guess.

That was my Perry Mason moment. By the way, the defendant wanted me to move to replace his court-appointed attorney on his other robbery charges. I told him the court wouldn't let me do that. With what I knew of his other charges, there would be no Perry Mason moments.

PROSECUTORS

19

The prosecutor's presentation on trial day begins when he or she leaves the car at the parking lot. This is true whether the city is big or small, urban or rural. The person getting out of the next car may well be one of the pools of prospective jurors that had been called in for that day's trials. The prosecutor will not know it, and the other person probably will not know the prosecutor.

When the jury pool comes into the courtroom for the selection of the trial jury, the prosecutor will not recognize that juror from the parking lot, but the juror will recognize the prosecutor. So everything the prosecutor did in getting out of the car, on the way into the courthouse and to his office may, and probably will, have been observed—and remembered. The difficulty for the prosecutor is that the juror is not going to say, "I have no trust in you because I saw you do 'X' this morning."

If the prosecutor has not acted professionally, he or she may end up with a juror who already has no confidence. And to be successful, the prosecutor must have the confidence of the jurors, who must believe the prosecutor is not going to steer them into an incorrect verdict.

From the time the jury pool arrives for the trial jury selection, the prosecutor must continue to act very professionally. This doesn't mean he or she can't be jovial with the other people in the courtroom, but it does mean he or she can't be seen as being overly friendly with the defense counsel, and certainly not with the defendant. I always ignored the defendant as though they were not in the courtroom—I didn't want to appear hostile, yet I didn't want even the slightest hint that I considered the defendant to be a human being, with human feelings.

The jurors became the center of my attention when they arrived. I watched all of them coming through the door, smiling when one of them smiled, making sure they all saw that I made eye contact with them. During the general *voir dire* questions by the judge, I turned my back to the judge and watched the jurors as they listened to the questions, and then as each person offered any information in answer to the questions. If one of the jurors stated a reason why it was really critical, economically or family wise to avoid jury duty, I made sure I was first to suggest to the Court that juror be excused. I wanted it to appear to all the jurors that I cared about them as human beings, and I didn't really want someone on the jury who was going to be concentrating on something other than my case.

When the individual jurors began to be called into the box for final *voir dire* by the attorneys, I carefully reviewed the specific biographical information provided by the jury commissioner. I always tried to avoid asking a question that was already answered in the profiles.

I remember a time when a very good trial lawyer just had a mental lapse during *voir dire*, and it was embarrassing to him. The juror had already told the court he had three brothers who were law enforcement officers. The lawyer had apparently missed the comment about the officers being brothers, and just remembered that the juror knew law enforcement officers. So, on individual *voir dire*, he asked the juror something to the effect, "Would you tend to believe the officers that you know, simply because they are police officers?" The juror said, "No, I would believe them more because they are my brothers." The laughter was embarrassing, and the lawyer's challenge of the juror became far more noticeable than it needed to be.

A prosecutor can get himself in trouble by pursuing questions too far with individual jurors. These folks for the most part are not real happy that they have been summoned for jury duty. They aren't making a lot of money for their service, and their lives are being complicated and maybe even compromised by having to serve. So they don't like to be grilled. I always simply challenged a juror if I had any doubt that would have caused me to ask a lot of questions. For example, if I had the slightest hint that a juror might have an axe to grind with law enforcement, I certainly didn't pursue the matter. I might get an answer that I didn't like, and when I got it, the entire pool of jurors had heard it. I remember one case in particular in which the prosecutor probed and probed as to why the juror didn't want to sit in a case where police officers were witnesses. Finally, the juror said that she had proof that police officers had lied in a case involving a friend. Oops.

When I accepted a juror, I never just said, "The state has no challenge" or the "state accepts the juror." I always said something to the effect that, "The state is satisfied that this juror will be fair to the state and the defendant." Each time I said it, I hoped that every juror in the box heard I had faith in them.

Most important to me, as a prosecutor, was the juror's body language. I paid attention to each juror as questions were asked and answers given. When defense counsel was questioning, I was watching the other jurors already in the box, watching their facial and body reactions to each question. Body language, work information provided on the written bio profile, and just plain "gut instinct" played the largest role in my selections; my questions were very limited.

20

The result was that I can't ever remember it taking more than an hour to pick a jury in one of my cases—except once, on a removed case to the eastern shore of Maryland, when the judge had to send out for more jurors.

The defendant in a capital murder case had the absolute right to change trial venue away from Baltimore City. As a usual matter, the judge asked the state where it would like the case transferred. A lot of my associates just picked Baltimore County because it was closer and more convenient. I normally picked either far western Maryland or the Eastern Shore of Maryland because of the quality of the judges.

Judge DeWeese Carter, sitting in Denton, the County Seat of Caroline County, was one of the very best trial judges—he prepared for the case, he did thorough research, he was fair and objective so appeal reversals would be rare, and he didn't overly interfere in the attorney's presentation.

This particular murder case that I had transferred to Judge Carter's court involved an attorney who used all 20 of his challenges pretty quickly, and we ran out of the pool jurors with only nine seated in the jury box. The judge sent the sheriff out to round up jurors and bring them in. Under the law, if the available pool ran out, the judge could have the sheriff bring in other qualified jurors. So the sheriff went out and started rounding people up off the street and sending them to the courtroom.

We all sat in the courtroom and waited as the extra jurors came in, some of them pretty irritated at having their daily errands interrupted with a jury call. One mother came in with three little children, obviously not prepared to bring them into a courtroom. I quickly exercised one of my challenges by telling the judge that I was concerned about her and her children being brought in without adequate time for arranging a sitter. She appeared very grateful, and I hoped that the message got home to the other jurors that I really cared about their welfare.

One of the jurors who came in had been stopped in his truck at a traffic light when the sheriff directed him in. He was a butcher, making a delivery, and had on his very bloody apron. He became our twelfth juror, and was allowed to go home and change clothes before beginning the trial. That also gave him time to get his brother to run his deliveries and his shop during the trial. It was a whole different world down there. In the City, these people would be moaning and groaning. Here, in rural Eastern Shore country, they just accepted their fate and did their duty.

I always had my opening and closing arguments all prepared in my mind before I started picking the jury. I had the evidence presentation clearly in my mind as to how I wanted it to proceed. So my efforts at picking the jury were directed toward getting a jury that I thought would best fit my case. Again, my decision was based on me being comfortable with my observations of their body actions, and keeping in mind the type of job they held, or school they had attended or were attending. Once the jury was picked I usually had a pretty good feeling about how the case would come out.

21

One very important jury trial caused me some real doubt. I took a chance, a big chance, and was a little worried as the case began. It was the first trial jury that I picked after the pool selection process was altered in Baltimore, so that far more Afro-Americans and minorities were included in the jury pool.

I think the most important legal change that occurred while I was in the State's Attorney's office was this change in jury pool selection. Previously, jury pools were made up mostly of whites, often older and retired whites, many of whom volunteered to be on jury panels. I know that's hard to believe in this day and age, but it is fact. Seldom was a Black juror spotted in a jury pool. If there was a Black juror, it would have been a professional man, or a man with a managerial-type job.

Black defendants were not eager for trial by jury because the jury pools included no low income, working class Black citizens. The jury pools did not include young Blacks who had experienced life on the streets and grown suspicious of police and other government officials. So jury trials were a rarity to us when the defendant was Black.

When the law required expansion of selection criteria to include elements of data that brought into the pool a more representative number of working class Blacks and other minority people, the tendency to waive jury trials changed. While court (judge) trials were still predominant, far more jury trials were held. I know that as a defense attorney I tried far more jury trials of Black defendants than I would have under the prior selection process.

I had been out of the trial courtroom for several weeks when the jury selection data base changed. I was working in two special Grand Juries, which had been impaneled to investigate major narcotics deliveries and conspiracies, professional burglaries, murders for hire, and gambling and corruption.

During this time, several murder cases had been tried before the "new" juries, and none of them had resulted in "unqualified verdict." In Maryland, the possible verdicts in a first degree murder case were not guilty, guilty without capital punishment, and guilty. Under the "qualified" verdict limited by the "without capital punishment" clause, the judge could give only a life sentence. Under an "unqualified" guilty verdict, the judge could give life or death.

It appeared that with the "new" juries, there was a hesitance by the jurors to deliver "guilty" verdicts. Charley and George assigned a cab driver murder case to me, with instructions to get an unqualified guilty verdict.

From a practical standpoint, it might not have seemed very important that juries under the new selection system were not allowing imposition of the death penalty. Since 1955 there had not been an execution in Maryland. The constitutionality debate had even resulted in a general understanding that the governor was not going to allow anyone to be executed.

But the threat of an unqualified verdict, the threat that death might be imposed, and the possibility that authorities might begin allowing executions were still important bargaining chips in getting a plea in a murder case. Without that threat, there was no incentive to plead to first or second degree murder. The maximum penalty for second degree murder was life, so there was no real incentive for the defendant to plead to a life sentence when that would be the worst that could come from a jury verdict

As a prosecutor from another county had said, "We know they won't be executed, but they don't know it, and they won't take a chance on it when it's their lives on the line." Getting the unqualified verdict was an important part of the prosecutors' weapons in Maryland.

Opinions varied as to why the "new" juries were not returning straight "guilty" verdicts. I think the predominant theory was that the "new" juries included more young, somewhat militant Blacks—citizens who had a completely different view of the police and criminal investigations than the prior predominately white juries, jurors who didn't have the same faith in the white-dominated judiciary to be fair to people of all races.

22

The case assigned to me involved the murder of a Black cab driver during a robbery that netted the killer thirteen dollars. A Black defendant was charged with the crime, all the witnesses for the state were Black, and the defense attorney was Black. I planned to end up with an all-Black jury. I didn't want to risk a polarization that might result if the jury included a small group of whites among a majority of Blacks, or a small group of Blacks among a majority of whites. I planned to try this case, to and for, the Black community.

I wanted the defense attorney to think that I was deliberately trying to get a white group of jurors, so I wasted four of my ten challenges. He started using his twenty challenges to get rid of whites. I kept an eye on the racial balance of the rest of the pool, and wasted one more challenge, which led to his using several more of his twenty to get rid of the rest of the whites in the pool. With his challenges gone, I was able to use my few remaining to get a jury of young to middle age working people, a group that included shift workers, city employees, stay-at-home mothers and teachers.

I wanted them focused on the victim of this crime, a hard working man who supported his family with the earnings from cab driving, which he did as a second job. He worked all day at his primary job, then "rented" another cabbie's vehicle and worked a few hours every night. The police found the dead cab driver slumped over in the seat of the cab, which was sitting in the street on Wakefield Avenue in Baltimore. He was shot three times in the back of the head for the thirteen dollars he had in his pocket.

The police had received a "tip" and had picked up the defendant, Cornelius Thomas Strong, for questioning. The witnesses that I had were the defendant's cousin, Doug Johnson, another cousin, JoAnn Johnson, and a lady at whose house the defendant played cards on the night of the murder. According to a witness, Strong was playing cards on the night of October 20, 1968, and had lost all his money, and then lost money he borrowed from other players. About 9 p.m. he got mad, pulled out a handgun and left, saying, "I'll pay you your money. I got to go pick up some." He returned to the game between 10 and 10:30 p.m. with the thirteen dollars.

Doug Johnson testified that Strong came to his house and asked that he drive the defendant up on Wakefield Avenue. Johnson did as asked, and then the defendant stopped a Sun cab. They got in, and after a short ride, Johnson said that Strong pulled out a "long, black .22 caliber, put it in back of the cab driver's head and said, " Stop right here.'" Johnson said the cabbie looked back and said, "Take my money, but please don't kill me." Johnson testified that he was scared and jumped out of the cab and started running up through a wooded area. He heard three shots and then Strong was right behind him. He testified that Strong said he shot the driver because he needed the money. The two got back to where Johnson's car had been parked and drove to JoAnn Johnson's house, another cousin. JoAnn Johnson testified that on the night she heard about the murder on Wakefield Avenue, she heard Doug Johnson and Strong talking about a killing. She testified that the following Sunday, Strong came to her house and was talking about the cab driver that got shot, and told her that he did it. A final witness testified that sometime later Strong asked if she remembered the cab driver getting killed up by some park, and he told her that he did it.

From the beginning of the trial, I focused on the victim—in opening statement, and in testimony about him and his work. I felt good about the evidence, but the problem would be the verdict. I knew what I had known from the start of the trial: the form of the verdict would depend on the strength of the closing argument. I focused again on the victim, his life, his work, his family, his death for only thirteen dollars, that he was unarmed, that he pleaded with the defendant not to kill him, that there was absolutely no reason for the murder because the victim was not resisting, and that he was murdered by the defendant who showed him no mercy what-so-ever. I reiterated several times that the defendant had shown no mercy to the victim.

I told the jury in the courtroom that day, that they set the rules for Baltimore City. They were superior to the city council, to the mayor, the governor of Maryland, to the police department, to the judge himself. I told them they had the power that day to decide the rules for their community and their city. I told them that an unqualified verdict was necessary to send the word to other potential murderers of cab drivers, of bus drivers, of sales clerks, of everyone who worked with the public, especially at night they were not safe in Baltimore City.

I told them that an unqualified verdict would mean the defendant would be given the message that the full impact of the law was facing him for his callous murder. I told them also that an unqualified verdict would permit the judge the widest possible discretion on a first degree murder case, allowing him to be unrestricted in doing his duty under the Maryland Constitution. I went through the division of authority between the jury and the judge, and that the sentencing power was within the judge's jurisdiction, but the only way his hands wouldn't be tied was if they returned an unqualified verdict.

And I told them that the judge, with an unrestricted verdict, would be given the opportunity to look at the defendant from the bench and determine whether to give the defendant mercy—mercy the defendant had denied to the victim. Several times during my comparison of the two forms of verdicts, and of the differing jurisdictional jobs of the judge and jury, I repeated the testimony of the defendant's cousin, "The cab driver looked back and said, 'Take the money, but please don't kill me!'"

I remember building up to the final point, at which time I

picked up the handgun and said, "What it took God 42 years to develop into the man that the victim was, the defendant destroyed this quickly." I pointed the gun at the ceiling and pulled the trigger three times. In that quiet courtroom, with marble walls, the "click-click-click" was at a minimum, dramatic. After that demonstration, I repeated again the cab driver's last words, "Take the money, but please don't kill me!" and I pulled the trigger three times more, "click-click-click," and sat down.

I don't remember how long the jury deliberated, but it wasn't exceptionally long—maybe three hours. The verdict was an "unqualified guilty."

I honestly do not remember whether the verdict stemmed the tide of unqualified verdicts, but it did prove that the "new" working class Black jurors who were being selected were serious citizens who would pay attention to the safety of their city.

Strong was sentenced after I had left the state's attorney's office. Judge Carter imposed the death penalty.

23

A prosecutor often needs luck, even help from unknown sources. I was assigned a first degree murder case on which I couldn't take a plea of anything less than the main charge. No plea bargains even to second degree. In Maryland, the maximum punishment for second degree was life-in-prison. For first degree, it was life or death. In a jury trial, the verdict had to be "guilty" for the judge to be able to impose the death penalty. In a court trial, the judge had to make the initial decision when he found guilt.

For all practical purposes, a plea of guilty to second degree was a fine plea bargain for the state—avoid the mistakes and the witness foibles that can occur during a trial; secure the life sentence; save the family of the victim from having to relive the tragedy through the trial; and save the time of the court, the prosecutor's office and the police.

On occasion there were those cases in which the State's Attorney, an elected official, simply couldn't make the plea bargain. Charley assigned this one-such case to me. The owner of a popular sports bar, lounge and restaurant was shot down during an armed robbery. He was sitting at the bar when the robbers came in. Witnesses said he gave no resistance, nothing to provoke the robbers, but one of them shot him.

The victim, a very popular Irishman, was popular not only because of his place of business but also because he was a very charitable man, known to give willingly to community causes and to police funds and drives. The murder made headlines, and pressure was on the police to make the case.

One of the robbers, given up by an informant, identified the others, and identified the gunman. All the defendants were arrested, a solid lineup was held, and the witnesses not only picked them out but identified the gunman.

When Charley told me I had the case, he also told me, "No second degree pleas, we have to get a first degree verdict. Then it's up to the judge. But we have to hand him a first degree verdict."

The defense attorney was a good attorney, but one who faced facts. When she had reviewed what I had in my file, she talked with her client and then told me he would plead to second degree murder. I had to turn the deal down, and told her that I wouldn't be able to change my mind.

We got ready for trial. On the morning of the trial, I met with defense counsel in the judge's chambers and once more offered her the chance to plead to the charge, to avoid my putting on victim testimony, witness after witness. She said no, but offered second degree. I told her and the judge, again, that I couldn't do it. And I emphasized again how good my case was.

When it was clear that there was no deal, the judge had his secretary call for the juror panel. In a case like this, where the defense had twenty challenges and the state ten, the jury commissioner sent a full courtroom of jurors. As I went out to the table, the defense attorney was huddled with her client. She walked over to me and said, "He wants to plead, if he can avoid the death penalty."

We walked back to chambers and I said that I could take the first degree plea and make no recommendation as to the sentence, thus leaving the penalty completely to the judge. I had already talked this situation over with Charley, although I didn't think it would happen. He told me the sentence was in the hands of the judge; we wouldn't object to any decision he made. So the judge agreed that he would not give death, but would impose life.

As we waited for the jurors to leave the room, I asked counsel what happened. She said she didn't know. When she walked out to the trial table, he said he wanted to plead to first degree, if the judge wouldn't sentence him to death. The plea was entered, and we all went on about our business of the day. The press had their story, the family witnesses were relieved, and the police were satisfied.

That afternoon, about the time courts were cleaning up for the day, and just before the bus would have arrived to pick up the defendants to go back to City Jail, the guard who was in charge of the defendant came into my office. (There was a lockup of several cells in the basement of the courthouse, and an elevator served all the main courtrooms in the central core of the building. Defendants were brought up the elevator into the hallway behind the courtrooms and brought from there into courtroom. When a defendant was brought in for trial, the guard had to stay with him throughout the trial, no matter how long it lasted. A bus brought the defendants in for trial, in the morning. They returned them to City Jail after court was over for the day. When a trial was held outside those rooms in the core of the building, the guard had to bring the defendant up and through the main hallway into the courtroom. This trial was to be in one of the outside courtrooms, so the guard had walked with the defendant a long way between the courthouse lockup and the courtroom.) He opened the conversation that afternoon with, "We did a good job today." I said, "Yeah," and he asked, "Did I do good?" I asked him what he meant.

The guard said he was talking to the defendant that morning and asked him why he wasn't pleading. The defendant told him he didn't want to face the death penalty, and his lawyer thought there was a good chance of getting second degree. The guard said when the jurors came into the court-room, he leaned over to the defendant and said, "Hey man, do you see anybody in that courtroom who's your color? Grant will have a field day with a jury from that crowd. When Grant turns it on in final argument, you won't have a chance." They talked for a few minutes, and the defendant asked him if he thought it was too late to try to make a deal about the death penalty.

The guard said he told the defendant, "I don't know, but if it was me, I'd sure as hell try, and not let Grant get hold of them in his final argument." When the defense counsel came into the courtroom, he told her he wanted to plead.

So was saved a trial. Thanks to the system? No—thanks to a guard who didn't want to spend four days sitting in a courtroom where he couldn't make the rounds of the building and collect all the gossip as he went.

24

Apart from luck, sometimes a prosecutor has to use an on-the-border strategy to put and embellishment on the trial presentation—or at least thinks he does.

For several weeks, a band of bank robbers called the "Panty Hose Gang" had been successfully robbing banks throughout Baltimore City. No clues were left behind. No word was forthcoming from informants. Police and the FBI were stymied. The robbers all wore panty hose over their heads, stretching their faces to indistinguishable shapes. They were heavily armed, with sawed off shotguns and automatic weapons.

One afternoon, as I was finishing a court trial day, Charley's secretary told me he needed to see me in his office. He told me the police had a man in custody who had been arrested by the FBI in a Baltimore County bank robbery. They had him identified from a finger print—one lone print that was found outside the bank. (Early in my law life I had helped an associate in a big law firm with a federal bank robbery case, where his client was linked to the robbery by a finger print on a coffee cup abandoned in a gutter outside the bank. Witnesses had observed men sitting in the car drinking coffee for a good length of time prior to the robbery; the FBI does a good job of finding finger prints.)

Charley told me the guy said he had information about the Panty Hose Gang, but wouldn't talk to anyone but the prosecutor who was going to try the case. The guy told the police he didn't want to talk to anybody but the man who was going to try the case, the man who was going to stand there and tell the judge what had brought about the arrests and convictions. Charley told me he was assigning me the case, and I had a free hand with making a deal with the guy in custody.

In the Central District homicide-robbery division, I met Charles Clifford Cofield. He was a good looking, young, very articulate guy. Captain Tony Glover introduced me to him, and Charles began to question me. He wanted to know whether I would be the one to try the cases—actually try them, not just supervise. I told him I was not the State's Attorney, just a trial lawyer and Charley had assigned the case to me so I would be the one who would try the case. He wanted to know whether I would be the one to ask the sentencing judge to be extremely lenient with him if he testified against the other members of the gang. I told him I would be.

Cofield told me that he couldn't go to jail, either before or after testifying. He had a wife and young child, and he would be killed if he went to jail. He said that if he went to jail pending trial, the gang would threaten to, and would, kill his wife and child to keep him from testifying. He said if they did kill his family, then they would kill him too. He told me these gang members were steely cold and would kill in an instant. I asked him if he was the same as they were. He said, "Yes, if it was one of them giving me up, I would kill to prevent it. And so would they." He also said that if he did testify, and went to jail, he would be killed—that there was no kind of protective custody in prison where he would be safe. He said, "I would find a way to kill anyone who gave me up, and so will they."

I told him that I would have to hear what he had to say before I could make any kind of deal that big. He said that wouldn't work. He wanted the deal before he gave me any information. Captain Glover told him I could be trusted and said, "If Grant tells you he will make a deal if your information is good, he will do it." The answer was still, "No."

I went in the other room to talk to Glover and his officers who had been talking to Cofield before I got there. They said they were convinced he was the "real thing," that he was one of the gang and probably could deliver the whole crew. They told me the Bureau thought they had a good case against Cofield, so he had every reason to talk if he wanted to avoid jail.

Based on their feelings, and a gut feeling of my own, I then made the deal with Cofield. I told him if he gave me the names and addresses, and enough information to get convictions, and then would testify against the gang members, I would recommend to the Court that he get probation and not go to prison. I told him that I couldn't guarantee that he wouldn't go to prison, but I would make as strong an argument for probation as I could make. I also told Cofield that he would have to be charged with the robberies, so that I had something to hold over his head. I also told him that I would find some way to keep him with his family prior to the trials.

Cofield had formed some kind of bond with Captain Glover, Sterling Fletcher and George Christian. He looked at them and asked, "Can I trust him?" They all said he could, and Cofield made the deal.

Cofield started talking at about 5:30 p.m. and we didn't finish taking his statement until after 11 p.m. As soon as we got about half-an-hour into the interview, I called for Charley and couldn't reach him. But I talked to George Helinski, told him what was going on and asked him to send Bob Stewart down to help me with statements and details. Bob showed up quickly, and we went back to taking a long, detailed statement.

About 9 p.m. I called Judge Joseph Carter at his home and told him what we were doing. I asked if we could come to his house with affidavits and warrants when we got them ready. He said, "Come anytime, just call ahead if it's real late and I'll be ready when you get here."

Cofield gave us names, places, amounts of money, apartments that had been rented within a block of the banks so the robbers could just retreat there and wait for the hubbub to die down, addresses of the robbers, and information about weapons storage between jobs. Bob started putting together affidavits as the interview continued. In the affidavits, we named Cofield as the member of the gang providing the information, and we wrote a second affidavit for him to sign. We attached his affidavit to our overall affidavit detailing the arrest and the information he was providing. I wanted his affidavit not only as support for the warrants, but also as a sworn statement to use against him if he changed his mind anywhere along the line.

As we were completing affidavits, and Cofield was finally having a sandwich and some coffee, Captain Glover was gathering detectives to take part in the search parties. He was also alerting the district station house commanders that we would be asking for uniform support for some searches later in the night, or early morning. Of course he told no one what we were working on and just said that we had some drug-related searches to be made.

Glover and his men wanted to execute the warrants just before dawn, before the gang members had a chance to get up and hit the streets for the morning. They wanted to hit simultaneously and hopefully get all members at the same time. They feared that anyone we didn't get on the first sweep would take off and be hard to find. I favored this approach, because I didn't want to have to worry about any of the actual gang members being free to try to harm Cofield, or his family.

As the captain was breaking down assignments for the raiding parties, one of the detectives took Bob Stewart and me to Judge Carter's home. In the wee hours of the morning, the judge reviewed the affidavit, and signed warrants for day or night service on the houses and hangouts identified in the affidavit and on the face of the warrants.

The search parties were ready when we returned to homicide-robbery, and each was assigned a warrant and briefed on the whole operation. The head of each search team was told to radio the appropriate district for uniform support once they were en route and to have the uniforms meet them some six to eight blocks away from the site of the search. Once there, the teams would brief the uniforms and all would then move to the site. All warrants were to be executed at the same time throughout the city. It was the first time I had actually sat through a "watch synchronization" exercise.

Bob and I went with the party that accompanied Captain Glover.

It was summer time, and the night had been Baltimore hot. But, as always, at first light it got chilly. The chilliness was always worse when you were standing with a police raiding party and heard the officers chug the shells into the shot gun chambers. Just at dawn, officers struck at over a dozen different sites throughout the city. All the members of the gang were arrested, and guns, bank money bags and panty hose were seized at the various locations.

25

Once the raids were completed and we could review the evidence, we started preparing for the morning's Grand Jury. I wanted to take Cofield to the Grand Jury to get him sworn-in, to appraise his performance as a witness, and to get presentments and indictments in order to avoid the necessity of a series of preliminary hearings. I wanted to get Cofield's pre-trial duties finished quickly so t we could get him into protective custody.

As Bob was getting presentments ready, and drafting indictments, I was meeting with Charley and George to discuss how we could keep Cofield and his family safe. I knew that with the arrests that had been made, the word was already out about him, and extra security had to be used. Even as we talked, the press had realized something special was getting ready for the Grand Jury, and word circulated among the reporters that several early morning arrests had been made. The rumor was that the Panty Hose gang had been caught.

We came to agreement that the ideal security would be to place Cofield and his family somewhere way outside the city in a rented house or apartment. That would avoid the hundreds or thousands of overtime hours that would be necessary for around-the-clock police protection.

Charley said he would make calls to city hall and arrange for us to meet with Mayor D'Alesandro after my Grand Jury presentation was completed. We would have to get City approval for funding such a project because the State's Attorney's budget didn't have such funds available. We recognized the danger that Cofield would take off, leaving us holding the bag, but we weighed that danger against the reality that he would probably not run. He had too much at stake. If he ran, he would ultimately be found, face life-in-prison on five robbery charges, and then he would be killed in prison. The "hit" would be put on him for turning on his cohorts even if he didn't actually testify against them.

I took the cases into the Grand Jury, briefed the jurors on what had happened during the night, and then brought in Cofield to testify. Normally, we didn't bring a witness of this caliber before the jury. We would just summarize the testimony, present his statement and let the Grand Jury act. But, as I said, I wanted to get Cofield's testimony under oath, and I wanted to see how good a witness he made.

He made an excellent witness appearance, listening carefully to questions and answering in a deliberate, articulate, to-the-point manner. The jurors were mesmerized by the appearance and testimony of such a dangerous robber. I felt like we had a good case. Now he needed to be protected.

Charley and I went to see the Mayor. Charley had briefed him, and he had the members of the Board of Estimates present. This was the body that would have to approve the money for any safe-keeping project. Charley made an introduction as to how we came to meet with Cofield, and then I detailed the story, including the danger to Cofield if he were committed to jail. I pointed out that keeping him in a different jail wouldn't work because someone could still get to his wife and child.

The mayor, Tommy D'Alesandro, whose father "Big Tommy" had been the Richard J. Daley of Baltimore, remarked that this had all the characteristics of the "old dime detective stories" with "real life" added to it.

I laid out our idea for renting a house in western Maryland, several hours from Baltimore, and the need for secrecy as to where the house was. Even the city finance people couldn't know where the house was. Every problem known to any public finance department was present in the case. But, the Panty Hose gang had been such a plague to the city, that everyone was somewhat excited about cleaning them up. The mayor supported us and assured the money would be made available. He arranged for an advance that day so we could get Cofield on the road as soon as possible.

Captain Glover picked two detectives who would be the only people to know where Cofield and his family were. I went with the detectives to talk to Mrs. Cofield and explain the whole story to her. Meanwhile, Cofield was being guarded in an office well within the confines of our offices in the courthouse. Mrs. Cofield gathered together some clothes for Charles and the child, and two detectives transported her and the child to the old Southern Hotel just a block from the courthouse. They would stay there until a house was rented by the two detectives, who were solely responsible for picking the town and house. By the time the news broke that night on television about the arrests, charges, and searches, the Cofields were in protective custody.

After working all night, I went home to get cleaned up and changed, had an early dinner, and went back to debrief Cofield as to what we found in each of the searches. Before I left the police station that night, I was told that a house and town had been selected and the first month's rent paid. The next day, the Cofields' property was loaded on a U-Haul truck, and off they took for their safe-house, riding in one of the detective's private vehicles while the other detective drove the truck.

As we worked toward the trials, if I had questions, I gave them to the detectives and they brought back answers. Once, when I felt that I had to talk to Cofield about some corroboration evidence, the detectives picked him up and brought him to meet me at a state police barracks west of Baltimore.

In Maryland, a conviction could not rest on the testimony of an accomplice without corroboration, which had to be in the form of evidence not related in any way to the accomplice's testimony. For example, finding a gun in the house of one of the gang members was a good find, but the gun had to be identified by someone other than the accomplice. Corroboration could take place in many ways: an independent witness could have seen one of the gang members near the bank on the date of a robbery, a witness could identify a weapon as belonging to one of the gang members, a witness could testify as to some statement that a gang member had made, a bank money bag found stuffed behind a furnace in one of the houses could serve as corroboration.

26

The gang's *modas operandi* **was,** they would case a bank, make the decision to rob it and set the date for the robbery. They would find and rent an apartment or room within a block of the bank and several hours prior to a robbery. They would go singly and in pairs to the apartment and just hang out. When it was time for the robbery, the gang would leave the apartment, again singly and in pairs, head for the bank, and put on the pantyhose masks just before entering. When the robbery ended, they left the bank, took off the masks by the time they reached the corner. Then singly and in pairs took different routes back to the apartment where they holed up while the police were swarming the bank. The gang would divide up the money and, many hours later, after dark left again singly and in pairs, and walked to where they had left their cars.

The first case we scheduled for trial was that of William Oliver Gardner. It was a robbery in which Cofield did not participate because he was in jail at the time. We picked that case because I felt that the corroboration was strong from outside witnesses. But the corroboration was in the form of circumstantial evidence, and

Cofield's testimony would put all the circumstances together. The jury would have to believe him without doubt.

To say that I was nervous would be the understatement of the century. A lot was at stake. By the time the trial was scheduled in October, 1968, several thousand dollars of city money had been spent in house rental and supplies for the Cofield family. Charley, of course, reminded me how important it was that we won the cases—not only from the standpoint of successfully prosecuting the gang, but also from the standpoint of justifying the expenditures and the mayor's administrative trust in us.

Hundreds of hours had been spent in preparing for the cases. Charley's word to the Mayor and finance officials was on the line, as he had assured them we had good cases. Glover's pride and reputation were on the line because he had committed so many hours of his homicide squad to a series of robbery cases. And, even though the FBI agents had been happy to have us trying the cases in state court, the FBI management would have loved nothing better than to be able to say, "We could have done it better."

The case was set before Judge Basil Thomas. He was a good judge who understood the rules of procedure and evidence. His courtroom was well run. His court clerk, Jerry Flanagan, was one of the best, if not the best in the courthouse. His court reporter Barbara Zentz was the best. We couldn't have picked a better courtroom cast and setting.

The robbery in the Gardner case occurred at the Union Trust bank on North Avenue. It took pace just after 9:30 a.m. while Cofield was in jail on another charge.

The investigating detectives had turned up a witness, Jerry Glass, who was a businessman with a somewhat shady past—a fraud conviction and a discharge from the police department under a cloud. Glass had seen Tommy Lucas, one of the leaders of the gang, outside the Union Trust Bank just before it was robbed. Glass told us that he was afraid for his safety if he testified. He said that he had already received threatening telephone calls warning him not to tell the police anything. The police agreed they would provide regular drive-by service at his home. On that basis he agreed to testify.

So when called to the stand, Glass testified that at just after 9 a.m. on the day of the robbery, he was on his way into the bank when he saw Lucas standing with another man in front of the bank. Glass had previously known Lucas and talked to him for a few minutes. He heard Lucas refer to the other man as Gardner. Glass then entered the bank and the two men stayed outside. Glass testified that he went into the bank and met with the manager for a few minutes, and that when he left the bank, Lucas and the other man were still standing in front. When Glass started to get into his car, he saw the two men enter the bank.

Glass identified the photo of Lucas as the man he knew and saw outside the bank with the man Lucas referred to as Gardner. I then asked Glass to identify the man who had been with Lucas outside the bank just prior to the robbery. Glass looked around the courtroom, asked a man in the audience to stand so he could get a better look at him. Then said he could not identify anyone in the courtroom as the man known as Gardner. I asked him whether he had identified the man from photos prior to trial and Glass said he must have been mistaken.

I asked for an immediate recess, and asked that the judge order sequestration of the witness. Judge Thomas granted the requests over objection by the defense. I turned to Lieutenant Tom Coppinger and asked that he take Glass to my office immediately and hold him there until I got there. I asked him to call Glass's lawyer and ask him to come to my office as soon as possible because his client was probably going to be charged. I also asked Tom to talk to Steve Harris, an assistant State's Attorney who knew Glass previously, brief Steve on what happened, and ask him to talk to Glass.

The jail guard handcuffed Gardner and removed him from the courtroom. Meanwhile, Bob and I talked to the other witnesses who had been kept outside the courtroom in a witness room. We explained that the case had extended into another day, and they needed to be back the next day even though we might not have to call them back to the stand.

Then Bob and I discussed Glass and whether he might have been paid off. We decided that I was going into my office and advise Glass's attorney that he would be charged with obstruction of justice and perjury. One way or the other he stood every chance of conviction:

either he gave a false statement to the police in obstruction of justice, or he lied on the witness stand. With a prior record of fraud, he had a good chance of serving time. We knew Glass would understand the trouble he was in, being a former police officer discharged under a cloud.

When we got to our offices which were then on the fourth floor of the courthouse, I made sure that Glass could hear me making plans for presenting charges of obstruction and perjury to the Grand Jury the next morning. I said it loud enough that he could hear my plans and know that I was extremely upset— as in angry. Diane, my assistant, and the best legal assistant I ever had or saw, told me that Glass's lawyer was on the way, and Steve had been talking to Glass.

So, after I stormed around a bit, making sure that Glass knew my intentions, I talked to Steve. He told me Glass said he was threatened prior to coming to the courthouse and the caller threatened his daughter, knew what she had on that day, and where she went to school. The caller also knew the Glass babysitter and knew which police cruiser had been around the Glass home that morning.

Steve said Glass wanted to talk to me, and he was scared I was going to charge him. Steve and I decided to let Glass cool his heels until his lawyer got there. So, Steve went back to Glass and told him I refused to talk to him, that Steve had tried to reason with me, but I was too angry to even consider giving Glass any break. Steve told Glass he had better wait until his lawyer got there.

When Glass's lawyer arrived, Steve briefed him on what had happened, and we let the lawyer meet with Glass for as long as he wanted. About half-an-hour later, the lawyer came in and said his client would like to meet with me. I agreed, and asked Steve and Bob Stewart to join us.

Glass told us the story—he received a call that morning before leaving for court that warned him not to testify. The caller described the clothes his daughter had on that morning, when she went to school, knew which school she went to, what time she got dropped off, and knew the name and address of the babysitter who cared for the daughter after school. He also identified the police cruiser which had been around his home that morning. Glass said the caller told him the police couldn't live with him and his family forever.

Glass reluctantly agreed that he would go into court the next day and tell the jury why he had lied, and he would identify Gardner.

We discussed whether to charge Glass and keep him in custody, or whether to put him in protective custody. He pleaded with us not to charge him and lock him up. His lawyer said he would vouch for him showing up for trial the next morning. So, I agreed that he could go home, and return to court the next morning. He did ask for extra police coverage that night, and Captain Glover arranged for it. In fact, we had police drive him home, leaving his car downtown, and arranged for the police to return him to court. It was agreed that his daughter would say home from school the next day and that police would be at his home with his family.

Bob, Steve and I did some research as to rehabilitation of a witness who wanted to change their testimony. We found case decisions allowing the witness to explain to the fact finder why he was changing his testimony, and found the rule of procedure allowing for such rehabilitation in Maryland.

The next morning, we re-called Jerry Glass to the stand, outside the presence of the jury. I explained to the court that Mr. Glass wished to testify, change his testimony and would explain why he did not tell the truth during his prior testimony. The defense attorney objected and argued that any explanation as to threats would be unduly prejudicial to the jury. I cited the case decisions and provided copies to both counsel and the Court. Judge Thomas took a recess and retired to his chambers to review the cases. He also asked defense counsel to present him with any authority which opposed rehabilitation. Defense counsel retired to the law library on the sixth floor of the courthouse. Glass was taken, with his attorney, to a witness room where he would be segregated from the other witnesses waiting there. We retired to our offices.

Detectives, Steve Harris, Bob Stewart and every other assistant on the floor gathered, drank coffee, told nervous jokes, and became more and more nervous as time went by. It was during times like these that classless jokes about some of the misery we saw every day seemed to ease us through. We particularly joked about what Charley would do to me if the cases all went down on the "lie" of Jerry Glass. One suggestion was that he would offer me up as an indentured servant to the city to make up for the city funds expended. That was one of the gentler suggestions as to what he would do. Twice during this time of waiting, Charley's secretary Annette called to see whether there was any word. George Helinski checked in with us, but Charley stayed clear.

After awhile, Glass's attorney joined us for a few minutes and wanted to know if he couldn't be sworn in an assistant state's attorney so that he could get paid for his time. I told him that if we won, I would take it up with Charley who would be in a better mood than he would be if we suggested it right then. It was all in jest, and helped us get through some very difficult time. I told them all that Charley had wished me good luck the night before the trial started, and then said he didn't want to increase the pressure—but to remember that I had to win. Charley had a habit of nodding his head affirmatively several times after he made a special point to you, and as he said, "You have to win." His face and head were emphasizing the words.

Finally, after about two hours, Judge Thomas's secretary who was a very close friend of mine, called to say that he was ready. I tried to find out from her what he had decided. She just laughed and asked, "Wouldn't you like to know?" I said, "Hell yes, I want to know!" She asked, "How much is it worth to you to know?" I said, "How about dinner?" She laughed and said if that's all I had to offer, I could just wait until I got to court.

When we walked into the courtroom, I looked to Jerry Flanagan and Barbara Zentz for clues as to the judge's decision—nothing but straight faces. Judge Thomas came in, took the bench and said after considering the authorities, and doing some checking himself, and receiving nothing from the defense, he was prepared to allow the witness to rehabilitate himself by telling the jury about the threats to him and his family. Judge Thomas said that he would instruct the jury that, none of that testimony could be considered as evidence of guilt of the defendant, or even as evidence that the defendant was involved in the threatening telephone calls in any way. He said that he would instruct the jury they were to apply the evidence only in determining the credibility of the witness.

Judge Thomas then asked the bailiff to advise the jury that we would resume after lunch, and he recessed for lunch. What a collective sigh of relief came from prosecutors and detectives. I went back by Charley's office to tell him the result, and Annette said he knew and had gone to a luncheon meeting. George just sat in his office, nodding and smiling, saying, "Lucky, lucky."

Bob and I spent the lunch hour getting our thoughts back into sync. When court resumed, when the jury was in the box, I then recalled Jerry Glass. I asked him whether he wanted to change the testimony he had given the previous day. He said, "Yes" and I asked him again if he could identify the man outside the bank with Tommy Lucas who Lucas had called Gardener. Over defense objection, Glass was allowed to point to the defendant and identify him as Gardener. I then asked Glass to explain to the jury why he had lied the day before. Again, over defense objections, Glass was allowed to tell the jury about the threatening call, and give details about the call.

On cross examination, defense counsel really attacked Glass's credibility. He asked him why he had not come forward to tell the police about his experience as soon as he heard about the robbery. Glass said he was afraid and he knew enough about Lucas to be afraid to get involved. Counsel then asked why he, at first told the police he knew nothing about the robbery. Glass again relied on his fear, and on threats that he had gotten, warning him not to get involved. Counsel then wanted to know why he changed his mind and cooperated. Glass said that he cooperated only after the police agreed to keep his home and family under regular watch.

When Glass finished his testimony, we had Gardner placed with Tommy Lucas outside the bank just before the robbery, and—entering the bank immediately prior to the robbery.

27

The bank manager testified that Glass did come in to meet with him just after 9:00 a.m. on the day of the robbery. He said Glass left about 9:30. Right after Glass left, he heard a scuffling sound, turned and saw a customer on the floor. Two men wearing panty hose masks and carrying guns were yelling a robbery was taking place.

The customer, who had been knocked to the floor of the bank when the robbers entered, testified that she picked the photo of Tommy Lucas from mug shots, not from his face which was distorted by the panty hose, but from the stature of his head. She identified the photo of Lucas she had picked out prior to trial.

A piece of wood had been found in the bank, and I introduced the wood into evidence. The wood was accepted subject to my linking it to the defendant, through other evidence.

When we completed the presentation of all these circumstantial facts, we were ready to call Charles Clifford Cofield. With all the circumstances in place, Cofield had to be believed by the jury. It was always worrisome when you had to rest a case on an accomplice's testimony. The defense could attack the accomplice all day on his making a deal to save himself, and on his being willing to lie in order to save himself. In this case, they also knew that we had been paying to keep Cofield and his family safe, so they could attack him on being willing to lie to have his life paid for.

I worried about two things first, I worried that in fact the gang's friends would try to kill Cofield, even in the courthouse, and second, I figured that we had to come up with something to make it apparent to the jury that, not only was he a dangerous robber, but Cofield was in danger from other dangerous robbers because of his testifying.

As I was painting the breakfast room in our house, I called Bob and told him I was going to stop and talk to Cofield one last time in the morning. I asked that Bob call the Central District police and arrange for a dozen or so shotgun armed guards to be at the courthouse. I explained that as Cofield came into the courtroom I wanted the shotgun guards to precede him and stand guard as he testified. Cofield would be protected, but also the jury would see he was in fact, endangering himself by testifying. Bob agreed then asked me whether I was painting. He and my fellow workers knew I hated painting, and how my mind worked when I had to paint.

When I got to the courthouse, Diane said the Central District Captain had been calling every ten minutes and needed desperately to talk to me. She called him for me and he pleaded with me, not to ask him to bring in a bunch of shotgun wielding uniform police officers. He was afraid that people would panic and it would create a terrible furor. I thought about if for a minute, and told him I would settle for a dozen detectives with their gold badges showing from their lapels. In just a few minutes, Captain Glover called me and wanted to know where I wanted the detectives, and when.

When court commenced, and the jury was settled in, I rose and announced, "The State calls Charles Clifford Cofield." A detective stood at the door in the back of the courtroom. I turned and looked at him, he nodded and opened the door and said down the hall, "Charles Clifford Cofield." We heard a door open, and heard many sets of footsteps coming down the hall. In came the detectives, all with gold badges showing, and they marched right up to the witness chair, forming a line. In came Cofield, followed by three other detectives. He was dressed in a suit, walking with his head up looking right at me he nodded, just before he took the witness chair. The detectives stayed in place. I asked Charles to state his name, and

I sat down at the trial table. Bob leaned over and said, "The jury is really paying attention."

Cofield was articulate, answering directly in that settled voice I had come to know pretty well. He showed an almost steely deliberateness. He testified that on April 22nd, Lucas, Gardner and he cased the bank on North Avenue, and on that day he saw a sawed off shotgun in Gardner's care Trunk. He testified that they went back to the bank on the 26th and then made the decision to rob in on May 10th. The plan was to be the same, find a place near to the bank where the three of them could get to quickly right after the robbery to wait out the investigation chaos.

He testified that the only reason he wasn't with Lucas and Gardner on the day of the robbery, May 10th, is that he was in jail in Baltimore County on a robbery charge. He testified that when he got out on bail, he met with Lucas and Gardner on May 25th and again saw the sawed off shotgun, but this time it was missing a piece of wood that was missing from Gardner's sawed off shotgun when he saw it two weeks after the robbery.

Cofield then identified Gardner as the person with whom he and Lucas planned the robbery. He identified Lucas' photograph, and I turned him over for cross examination.

The cross examination Cofield handled beautifully, saying of course he was testifying in order to stay out of jail. But, he managed to slip in, if he wasn't telling the truth, we wouldn't have found other evidence of guilt. He said he offered to testify because he feared for his family, and he would do anything to protect his family. I don't know what possessed the defense counsel, but he challenged Cofield on whether he would do "anything" to protect his family. He asked a question in the nature of, "If you thought I was a danger to your family would you kill me?" Without batting an eye, Cofield looked him right in the eye and said, "In a second."

The jury was out about two hours and came in with a guilty verdict. It was a big relief, not only to me, but to everyone who had put faith in the witness. As I heard the verdict and looked around to see Captain Glover, I saw Charley opening the door to leave the courtroom. He had slipped in to listen to the verdict from the back of the courtroom.

Now, I don't know how important the strategy of the "protective detectives" was perhaps the verdict would have been the same. But, I wasn't willing to risk it. I wanted the jury to realize what danger Cofield was putting himself in when he testified. They had to realize that he was in fact a major crook, endangering himself to help convict other major crooks. Our strategy of trying Gardner first, a case in which Cofield did not even participate worked.

The case that worried me most from a corroboration standpoint was that against Tommy Lucas. But, several weeks after the Gardner case, Lucas pleaded guilty and was sentenced to forty years.

At one point prior to the Lucas pleas, we were looking for a person we thought might have corroborating evidence. The detectives had been unable to find him. No one wanted to tell them where he was. No one on the street really wanted to be identified as cooperating in any way in this case.

One afternoon, Captain Glover and I decided we should make an effort to stir up the regular hang-outs of our reluctant potential witness. That night, he had all his homicide and robbery detectives on duty. They armed themselves with shotguns, put on their bullet proof vests, and we set out in three teams for three different bars. Bob Stewart and I joined a team that went to a bar on Greenmount Avenue. We went in, and the armed detectives covered the front and back entrances inside the bar. One of the detectives unplugged the juke box, and in the quiet that followed, we said we were looking for the witness. And, it would be to his advantage if he turned himself in and asked to talk to me. That was the message delivered at all three bars.

At 4:30 a.m. I got a call from the Central District saying that the guy was there, looking for me and wouldn't talk to anyone else. The sergeant tried to tell him to go down to the courthouse after 9:00 a.m. but the guy said he wasn't leaving and he would wait right there. I got dressed and headed down to Central. Captain Glover and Fletcher met me there and we questioned the guy for about two hours. He was not a witness to the robbery, but he did give us some information that allowed us to gather one slight piece of corroboration against Lucas. That piece of corroboration convinced Milton Allen, counsel for Lucas, that there was sufficient corroboration to permit a conviction on Cofield's testimony.

28

When the trials had all successfully ended, Cofield appeared before Judge Charles D. Harris, who was that year presiding as the Chief of the criminal bench. Cofield had entered his guilty pleas to five counts of armed robbery before the Gardner trial, but sentencing had been postponed.

I advised Judge Harris of the complete cooperation given to us by Cofield, how he had been completely honest with us and had stayed steadfast through the trials. I told the judge of how we had protected Cofield prior to trial at the expense of the city, and told him that I truly believed that Cofield's life would be in danger if put in prison. I told the judge that I had promised Cofield that we would protect him and his family prior to sentencing, and that I would recommend probation at the time of sentencing. I pointed out how the others in the "panty hose gang" had now been convicted or plead guilty, and all were serving prison sentences, thanks to Cofield's information and testimony.

Judge Harris imposed five sentences of twenty years, made them consecutive, suspended the sentences and placed Cofield on one hundred years of unsupervised probation, with permission to leave the state. The judge wished him good luck and told him that the citizens of Baltimore City were indebted to him.

After court adjourned, I shook hands with Charles, thanked him, wished him good luck and told him to let me know if there was ever anything I could do for him. The same two detectives who had kept him and his family secretly located, took him out the back way from the courtroom, and I never have laid eyes on him, heard from him or about him to this very day.

29

A prosecutor must always be careful not to overstep the legal or ethical bounds, careful not to overzealously risk reversal on appeal.

I prosecuted a rape trial in which there was nothing to tie the defendant to the crime other than the identification by the victim. She did not know the defendant, and had never seen him before. He did not live near her, did not work near her, and we had no evidence as to why he was even in the area.

The victim was much older than the nineteen year old defendant. She worked as a nurse and was on her way home from the bus stop, when she was attacked by a knife wielding young man. He forced her into a large construction pipe and raped her at knife point.

She called the police when she got home, just three blocks from where she was attacked. After reporting the attack, she went by taxi to the hospital as directed by the police. The examination showed there was tearing that would corroborate rape, rather than consensual sex. The officers who responded to the hospital took her description of the attacker and asked her to come to the station the next afternoon to talk to detectives.

When she arrived at the station house, she saw the defendant, who was being brought in on a warrant for probation violation. She immediately identified the defendant to the desk sergeant. He had the defendant held at the desk for detectives. The victim was taken back into the detectives' office where she was questioned about her identification. She never varied or wavered in her identification of the defendant.

This pre-trial confrontation at the station house came during a time when challenges to pre-trial identification processes were running rampant. The Wade case had been decided, which insisted that pre-trial identification lineups had to meet a standard of objectivity, and they had to allow for attendance of counsel at such line-ups.

When we got to trial, I had no intention of using the pre-trial identification because it was a one-on-one confrontation where there had been no opportunity of assuring unbiased observation or presence of counsel. I put the victim on the stand. Her testimony was very clear and certain.

But, clearly, she had little time to observe the defendant's face during the knife wielding attack. It came at night, after dark, with little or no street light illumination. On cross examination, the defense counsel made some real mileage I thought by showing there was nothing such as prior relationship or prior exposure to corroborate her "in court" identification. Counsel kept returning to the short amount of time the victim had for observation. Counsel asked whether she wasn't influenced in her identification by the fact the defendant was the only one on trial, the only one charged with the crime, the only one in the courtroom who was in custody for the crime.

I felt that she withstood the cross as well as could be expected, but I was concerned. I felt that I should now use the "in station" identification to show that the victim had identified the defendant other than in the court room. I went to talk with George Helinski about my strategy. We talked about my feeling of confidence with the jury, and with the identification as it stood. I told him I wasn't comfortable with her "in court" identification. We discussed the risk of using the pre-trial, one-on-one "in station" exposure at the station house. The "in station" identification came, just one day after the event, when it was still very fresh in her mind. The "in court" identification came six months after the rape.

I felt it was worth the risk of appellate reversal to get the corroboration of the "in station" identification. George said he could see no flaw in that position, and we discussed the fact that a prosecutor cannot run scared of an appeal. He must do what he thinks best for the case at trial.

On redirect examination the next day, I asked her to recount her identification of the defendant at the station house. She went through the details of how she was at the station to report to the detectives, when all of a sudden there was the defendant, the man who attacked her. She testified that she identified him at the station house because she knew it was the attacker, not because anyone pointed him out to her.

I asked her whether her "in court" identification was based on her memory of the attacker, and not influenced by either the prior "in station" confrontation or by seeing him "in custody" in the trial room. She assured the jury she remembered him from the attack, and she remembered him from the attack when she identified him at the station house the day after the attack.

I asked her whether her "in court" identification was because she had previously identified him in the station house or because she remembered him from the attack. Her answer repeatedly was she remembered him from the time of the attack.

The jury convicted the young man of rape.   On appeal, the conviction was affirmed, but one member of the court dissented on the grounds the "in court" identification was not sufficiently shown to have been, based upon independent and objective memory. The court found no reason to reverse, because of the pre-trial "in station" identification.   I took the chance, thinking I was right in doing so, to protect and support the victim's "in court" identification.

30

In another case, a post conviction court found that I overreached. It cost a reversal of a first degree murder conviction and the death penalty. Walter "Kidd" Henderson, a well known prominent figure on Pennsylvania Avenue in west Baltimore, and rumored to be a kingpin of the drug trade, was shot and killed in his bar. The same day as the murder, Irving Wilson turned himself in to the Western District police station. Wilson said he had killed Henderson in self defense.

When the police arrived at the bar, they found Henderson dead on the floor. He was not armed. Wilson was charged with first degree murder. As soon as the police realized that Henderson was the victim, Captain Glover contacted me because of the drug connections of the victim.

For several months, we had been accumulating information about Henderson from informants, hoping to get sufficient information for a search and arrest warrant. But, Henderson protected himself from contact with people outside his small group of trusted lieutenants.

We secured warrants for his house, his club, and another two houses, which were listed on the property records of the City as his personally owned properties. We were obviously looking for evidence of narcotics violations, believing that Wilson had killed Henderson to take over his organization and drug trade. Wilson was a known lieutenant of Henderson's.

The swarming raid teams, which swooped in on Henderson's property so quickly after the murder, caught the attention of Mamie Oliver, reporter for the newspaper *Afro American* who covered narcotics cases. Ms. Oliver interviewed me whenever she could, after any big drug raid in a Black area of the City.

After the organized crime division was created by Charley, and I was put in charge, we queried as to why we never had cases in narcotics court against any big dealer. Mostly our cases were against some of the lowest and most vulnerable drug users. We began to ask officers why we never got to the dealers. We heard many reasons drug arrests were allowed only by the central narcotics detective group made up of ten or twelve officers. We also heard that the big dealers had bought influence with certain command officers in narcotics and in the central police administration.

My narcotics group, composed of three other assistants and I, decided that we would authorize officers to arrest all users and addicts discovered at drug sites when warrants were executed. We then talked with those users, or had the police talk to them, and promised immunity or no charges at all, if they would give us information about their dealer, and his dealer. As we gathered information from all the users arrested, we began to put together cumulative and continuing affidavits listing everything we could learn about the "big wahzoo" who dealt to the users.

We prepared many, many warrants for the officers, not only in narcotics but in the detective units in each district. Bob Stewart and I started participating in the raids, so we could identify users we especially wanted as informants. Joe Kiel began participating in the raids with us. One of us went with the raiding teams, usually consisting of 4 officers.

The slogan "Grant and 4" was created on the streets, especially in the Western District. With that kind of publicity, Ms. Oliver interviewed me often, trying to get me to identify the big drug dealers we were after. Of course, I would not and did not identify them.

But, after Henderson was murdered and his houses and places of business raided "before the corpse was cold," according to "*The Afro*", Blacks began to demonstrate their anger against the officers and the prosecutors. Ms. Oliver wanted to know why the warrants were served. I decided to tell her, rather than hide the reason. So, in a fairly long interview, I answered her questions. I said I believed that "Kidd" Henderson was executed by people, who wanted to take over his drug trade and gambling enterprise. I justified the eagerness of the police to enter the premises on the fact that they had never been able to gain inside information about "Kidd's" protracted activities or his organization. I said they were searching for evidence that would show whether a conspiracy was involved with the intent of taking over his street operations.

Ms. Oliver asked me why I thought "Kidd" was murdered. I said that I thought it was an execution by some "one or more" who wanted to take over his organization. Gradually as I talked, she seemed less and less militantly anti police for having desecrated the dead man's houses and belongings.

"*The Afro*" ran a big front page story with photos and lots of quotes attributed to me. Of course, what I was telling her I really believed at the time. I had no doubt at that time, Wilson either wanted control, or was the shooter for someone who did want that control.

Defense counsel moved for a "change of venue", based on too much publicity having been generated to allow the defendant to receive a fair and impartial jury trial.

While the defendant had the right to remove the case without stating any cause, the fact is an aggressive defense attorney would have tried this case right in the courts of Baltimore City. Here, virtually all Black jurors "would have known" that Henderson was a criminal, and the shooting might have been the only reasonable method for curbing this giant size criminal. This case would have presented the Black jurors with the opportunity to go easy on someone, who was trying to remove or cure the drug problem from and on the City streets.

Nevertheless, counsel in one of the more bizarre moves I saw while in the criminal practice, asked for a change of venue. I asked that the case be removed to Caroline County, to be tried by Judge DeWeese Carter.

31

During the trial of the case, the defense counsel called ME to the stand to testify for the defense. I objected to my being called, but since I had an assistant sitting second seat at the trial table, Judge Carter ruled that I could testify. I couldn't then, and certainly can't now, understand why in the world he would want me on the stand. He knew from Ms. Oliver's article, I considered this case to be an execution, gang style.

Nearly half a day of trial time was wasted by my testimony. At one point, he asked me for my opinion, as to why Henderson was killed. I hesitated, and remember even looking at Judge Carter before I answered. I should have either refused to answer, or said that I didn't have an opinion since that was a question for the jury to decide. But, I didn't. I answered truthfully—I thought it was, and treated it as, an assassination. What would have been acceptable for me to argue, to the jury on the facts, was not acceptable for me to testify to, as a witness. Granted, it was foolish, and I think inappropriate and inexcusable, for the defense to call me as a witness. Granted, I think the court was wrong in allowing me to testify, when I was lead prosecutor. But, I shouldn't have testified as I did. I should not have answered that question.

The jury convicted the defendant of murder in the first degree and Judge Carter imposed the death penalty.

Years later, after I had left practice in Baltimore, and in fact had left Baltimore, a "post conviction challenge" to the conviction was handled by Anton Keating for the Public Defender's office. He questioned me as to why I submitted the facts of the case to a newspaper, which fully reported them prior to trial. I explained what I was trying to do with Ms. Oliver was to prevent hostile reaction to the police searches. Keating questioned me about the "American Bar Standards" as to pre-trial publicity. I had to admit, that at the time of the trial, I had not even read those standards. As I recall, I think I had to admit that what I revealed to the press did violate those "Standards". I know now the "Standards" were violated, and the proof in the post conviction challenge was the "Standards" had been violated—even though I really was not aware of them.

Keating also questioned me very skillfully as to the testimony I gave when called by the defense as a witness. The court condemned me quite unmercifully in an eighty some page opinion, which set aside the conviction and sentence. The court decided I recklessly mislead and influenced the jury.

The verdict and sentence were set aside. Wilson was taken off death row and appeared in court to plead guilty to a manslaughter charge. He was sentenced to ten years, and given credit for time served (which was about eight years).

I went over the line, according to the post conviction court. Do I agree? I suppose I do. I know what happened was set up by a defense attorney who was not capable of trying such a murder trial. I know that it was virtually insane for him to call me to the stand, to ask a question about an opinion which he knew I held, about this being an assassination.

I also think, had I been defending myself in this case, the result would not have been as clear. But, at that point, I was far from caring about defending my actions. I also think that a lesser lawyer than Keating might not have won the case.

But, that's the way this "game" is played. Some you win, some you lose even, when you win. Would I today, do what I did in that case? No, I would have handled it quite differently, and I believe had I pressed the issue, I could have convinced Judge Carter not to allow me to testify. Would the pre-trial publicity have been enough for the reversal? Maybe—maybe not. At any rate, I did go over the line.

32

Just as I said as to trial lawyers, the prosecutor has to be ready to deal with surprises, even as to mistaken identification. I prosecuted a rape case where the defendant was charged with twenty six rapes. His attorney told me that the defendant denied that he committed rape—because none of the women used such physical resistance that he was forced to use his weapon.

His rapes had occurred over a period of months. His victims were school teachers, professional women, clerks, all chosen at random and often on a whim. In one case, the defendant was walking through a hallway when he saw the victim ironing in her apartment. She had left the door open, in the access controlled building to help cool the apartment. He walked in, pulled a knife and raped her.

The defendant was a salesman who picked his victims at bus stops, in stores, at church, and then followed them to their homes. All of his victims were strikingly pretty. The case was a court trial, and I decided to try ten of the twenty six rape charges—where I thought the victims would tell their stories in the simplest fashion.

The detective who worked up the cases was very helpful in pretrial preparation, bringing in the victims for interviews and making sure they were early on trial day. In the months that went by between the rapes and the trial, he kept in touch with the victims so they knew what was happening at each stage of the case.

The first victim to take the stand was a school teacher. She did a phenomenal job of testifying to the lead-up of the rape, the rape itself, and her explanation of why she didn't try to physically and forcibly resist in the face of the defendant's knife. After she had laid out the facts of the case in clear, detailed, yet concise fashion, I then asked her to look around the courtroom and tell me whether she saw the man who had committed the offense against her.

The defendant was sitting to her right, at the end of the trial table, dressed in a suit, with a legal tablet in front of him. His attorney sat next to him. She said she did see the man in the courtroom. I asked her to point him out to the court. She pointed directly toward me and said, "That man sitting on the front row right behind you." She was pointing out Detective Penny, who had worked with her so many hours getting ready for the trial. A lady who hadn't shown even one ounce of nervousness during her testimony, had nervously fixed on a face she knew, and she identified the investigating officer.

I tried to rehabilitate her by showing her a set of photos from which she had picked the defendant right after the rape, but the court wasn't having any of that. So, I excused her. There was no cross, and she was escorted to a witness waiting room. As she was leaving the room, I turned to Detective Penny and laughingly told him that he better have a good alibi because she was a "damned impressive witness." He just shook his head in utter disbelief.

The rest of the morning went well, and by lunch, we had four cases proven. During the lunch break, the witnesses who had testified were brought into the courtroom so I could tell them where we were in the case. As the first witness came in, she passed detective Penny. When she walked up to me, she wanted to know why the defendant was walking around without guards.

I had to tell her that she had picked the wrong man, that she had picked the investigating officer. She just shook her head and her eyes began to tear up. I put my arms around her and told her we were all right, we would convict him on all the other charges.

But, believe me I had detective Penny change seats right after her testimony, and move to the back of the courtroom.

The court convicted the defendant in the other nine rape cases, and then imposed nine consecutive life sentences. After the sentencing, the defense attorney told me the defendant had charted out his "sexual encounters". The defendant had to help the attorney keep track of the cases. We knew of twenty six; the defendant had identified forty eight rape cases.

DEFENSE ATTORNEYS

33

It is an old wives tale that only a fool acts as his own attorney. It is not totally true. Sometimes I have seen defendants who were, or could have been, better off, or at least as well off, without the lawyer's fee.

Mose was an old Black man, a confirmed moonshiner who made whiskey in old abandoned tobacco barns in southern Maryland. He was arrested and charged by, Alcohol, Tobacco and Firearms agents who set up in surveillance and waited for smoke to drift up from one of the abandoned tobacco barns. They had been on surveillance for 2 weeks, three of them, and finally scored with old Mose.

The big government in the sky puts no emphasis on serious crimes such as transporting of illegal automatic weapons into and out of our urban areas. Nor does the big government in the sky put any emphasis on the interstate running of alcohol but best concentrates particularly on cigarettes transported from sales tax states to non sales tax states. The lost state revenues don't begin to compare in importance to the political heat and reduction of lobbying "gifts" which would come from anti-guns and anti-tobacco interests.

Well, back to Mose, victim of a two week, three agent surveillance. In a grove of trees within site of an abandoned tobacco barn, located deep within private property where crops once grew.

Mose's case was taken to the Grand Jury by Roger Duncan who handled all the moonshine cases. He took a gallon mason jar of 'shine into the Grand Jury and let them pass it around and smell it, as he explained how it was made. Moses' shine was good quality, looked (through coloring) and smelled like scotch.

To digress for a bit—there was a rumor that circulated among some of the assistants and FBI agents that the 'shine played a role during the Orioles/Dodgers World Series in the fall of 1966. It was the first World Series the Orioles had been in for an awful long time, the first after they got Frank Robinson from Cincinnati in the best acquisition by a Baltimore franchise since the Colts made a less than twenty five cent telephone call to Johnny Unitas, who was playing sandlot ball in Pittsburgh. Rumors had it that some of the Assistants, wheeled around from the evidence room (with complicit FBI agents), a stolen color TV set, opened a gallon mason jar of 'shine, opened three bottles of coke, and enjoyed that great opening day victory by the Orioles—on a home run by Paul Blair, an underrated little centerfielder.

What always annoyed those who were involved in the rumor, was not knowing the identification of the rat among the secretaries who told the head office. Fortunately, Mr. Kenney, the US Attorney, was at the game and there was no evidence left the next day. I thought I knew who the rat was.

My secretary was so loyal to the office and its budget that she would seek me out in the bathroom, if someone in D.C called and it would mean a long distance fee for us to call back. Usually when she knocked on the door of the "Men's" room across the hall, I would just ask her what she wanted and would tell her I would call back. She always reminded me that it would cost us long distance to call back. I always said, "It's costing D.C's office more in long distance while you chase me down at the urinal, than it will cost us to call back. The money comes from all our taxes." She would respond, "But, that's out of their budget." I would remain silent until she went away—but, when I was in a stall, I didn't answer her.

One day, Paul Kramer, who shared the suite of offices we were in, walked in and called out "Fred". I answered and he came to the door of the stall and told me she was very anxious to reach me to give me a message from D.C. He said she was trying to give the convoluted message through him. Paul said he would just come in and tell me that she had a message. I said, "Paul, have her come in." He laughed and said, "Good deal." I thought I was making a point—she could wait for my bathroom break. But nooooooooo! The next thing I heard was her voice right outside the stall, calling, "Mr. Grant" as she tapped on the stall door. She then proceeded to give me a five minute convoluted message I could do nothing about, sitting on the toilet. I said, "Okay I'll call him when I get through." That satisfied her and I heard her wash her hands and leave the Men's Room.

I returned the call, and it was nothing critical. In fact, the caller had intended to just put it in an internal memo when he didn't get me. I told him that my secretary delivered the message to the stall door. He laughed and made me promise to never tell his secretary about that technique. Later that day, my secretary thanked me for letting her deliver the message in person. She said it would be a lot easier now she knew she could just enter. I started going to the locked bathroom clear around the building, on the FBI side. They let me use their key.

I was sure she was the snitch, and nobody had a better nominee.

Well, anyway back to Mose. Roger scheduled Mose's Grand Jury appearance so his case would go to Judge R. Dorsey Watkins for arraignment, plea and sentencing. Watkins was the most lenient on 'shiners. Roger was not a fanatic against the old 'shiners who made their product the old fashioned slow way, in the grand traditions of the South. Bath-tub gin made in the city was a different matter. That stuff would blind or outright kill you. So, Roger treated those cases as serious matters.

Mose appeared before Judge Watkins on a day when I had the arraignments. We handled arraignments a lot differently in the federal court than in the state court. We had the files on each case.

We were prepared to answer questions, make recommendations as to seizure and destruction of product, the matter of bail, and then ultimately, on sentencing.

Mose told the judge that he didn't have a lawyer yet and had no money to get one. I confirmed for the judge that Mose was unemployed and received no social security or benefits. Judge Watkins questioned why, and he directed me, as officer of the court, to conduct an inquiry as to why Mose was not getting social security or any other age benefits. As I will tell later, Judge Watkins often made the assistant U.S. Attorney work for "the people" instead of the government.

Mose was in jail, put there by the Magistrate, on initial appearance when he had no money for an attorney. Judge Watkins had started discussing appointment of counsel, when Mose interrupted, very politely, to ask permission to, "buy" his "own lawyer". Mose said, "Yo honuh, Ah don wan you to haf to buy my lawyuh. Ah wants to buy him mahself."

Judge Watkins debated with Mose for awhile, obviously tickled and impressed by Mose's intelligence. Finally, he said, "Mose you have no money, you have no job. If I let you out, you will just go back to making moonshine to "buy" your lawyer. You can't even pay for a bail bond to get out, to make more moonshine."

Mose said, "Yo honuh, suh, if you let me out on my recognition [he meant "recognizance" even though he had the basic element correct---it is a release trusting to the individual's recognition of his duty to appear in court.] Ah'll git the money and "buy mah lawyer", An I won't make no mo 'shine."

Finally, to the bottom line, Judge Watkins asked, "Mose, if you aren't going to make more moonshine where will you get the money for a lawyer?" Mose, with incredible honesty said, "Yo honuh, suh, I will jes sell the 'shine I dun made and hid and they didn fin."

Judge Watkins tipped his head in almost disbelief, broke into a mischievous grin and said "Mr. Grant?" I said, "The government has no objection your Honor." He said, "Neither does his Honor. Good luck with sales Mose."

Sometime later Roger told me Mose got one of the best trial lawyers down in southern Maryland. Judge Watkins put Mose on probation, with no fine or restitution of costs. Judge Watkins usually did not give probation in moonshine cases. He gave short, but definite, city jail sentences. But, Mose won probation, and my money was on Mose's absolute honesty when representing his self, that made the difference.

34

During my time in the US Attorney's office, we were in the midst of the Vietnam War. It was the time when Cassius Clay became Muhammad Ali and declared his ministerial status, because of his objection to the draft and the war. John Steadman wrote a damning sports column about Cassius Clay betraying his heritage as an American. He blasted him unmercifully for degrading the great contributions made by the "Brown Bomber," the greatest of Heavyweight Champions, Joe Louis, who volunteered to serve during the Second World War. Switching sports, Steadman condemned Clay by comparing him to the great Ted Williams, the "Splendid Splinter," perhaps the greatest pure hitter in the history of ball. Williams, left fielder for the Boston Red Sox, served even as late as the Korean War, at a time he was in the apex of his career.

Many never forgave Ali, not only because he didn't want to fight in the military, but because he abandoned his "given Baptist" name and took on a "militant" name. I didn't respect him for many years, but not because of his taking on the change of name. I never resented Lew Alcindor for changing his name to Kareem Abdul Jabar. I resented Ali because I had to handle so many cases where true conscientious objectors had to be sent away from home to work in the worst of situations. I had young husbands and fathers sent away for four years to clean latrines in mental hospitals, to handle the worst assignments in hospitals, and to risk death on the battle front as medic assistants. Ali lived in the lap of luxury, and didn't minister to anyone. "Fly like a butterfly, sting like a bee", was not exactly a homily.

As I grew older, I put some of those thoughts behind me. I appreciated Ali for his talent and for his courage in handling a crippling disease with dignity. But, I have to say I probably would have appreciated him more, if he had done his time in a hospital or as a medic assistant.

In those days, any Black who took a Muslim name was immediately considered anti-American, a person who turned their back on all that America had done for them. For a long time, Ali did not sit well with the American public, even the fight fans. I can remember rooting for his opponents for some time. I thought it was cowardly for Ali to hide behind what I considered to be a phony claim to ministerial status, behind a Black Muslim sham membership.

Conscientious objectors who refused to be drafted into the military service, but didn't claim a clearly false ministerial claim under a Muslim or some other label, were charged by the F.B.I. with draft evasion. The statutory penalty for the charge was five years. The standard in the District Court in Maryland was a four year sentence, to be served not in the penitentiary, but in health services for the United States. Usually, these young men were sent to Veteran's hospitals or mental hospitals to serve as an orderly or aides, and sometimes to serve as military corpsmen.

Roger Duncan had a case in which a Black Muslim was charged, and the case was scheduled before Judge Harrison Winter— the most disciplined and the most severe of the federal judges. When a defendant was sentenced by Judge Winter, the attorney was best served if he started by arguing mitigation from the maximum sentence downward.

The judge was from very wealthy background, and lived in the highly exclusive Roland Park neighborhood of the City. His white hair, blue eyes, stern chin and face, gave him quite an Arian look. But, while he was strict, he was a fair and objective judge. He did however insist on the decorum traditional to the courts from English days. I enjoyed trying cases before him because he applied the rules objectively, with no favoritism to government or defendant.

But Judge Winter was not the judge to take a draft evader before, for sentencing. Any defense attorney could arrange a convenient arraignment schedule with the federal prosecutor, and—any competent one would have arranged with Roger for a different judge.

The attorney for this defendant did not, and he appeared with his client for the purpose of pleading guilty and being sentenced. Prior to the beginning of court, he told Roger that he would save his presentation of mitigation for the pre-sentence investigator who would prepare the pre-sentence report. Roger warned him that Judge Winter had been known to sentence without benefit of such a report, but the warning fell on deaf ears.

When the Judge entered the courtroom, and everybody stood, the defendant, who was still wearing his skull cap, remained seated. Judge Winter almost got to his chair, when he spotted the defendant sitting beside the standing defense counsel. As he stood there looking, Judge Winter asked the defendant to stand and remove his headgear. The defendant said, "No Sir." Judge Winter looked at counsel, and said, "Counsel?" Instead of having reasoned with his client before coming into court, or even at that moment, the attorney just responded that his religion didn't permit him to rise to honor a court of man or to bare his head as an honor to a court of man.

Judge Winter directed the Marshall to stand the defendant up, to remove his skull cap, and to gather all the assistance he needed to do the job. Fortunately for us all, when the bulky Marshall arrived at the back of the chair, the defendant did get up and take off his skull cap. Judge Winter than took his chair, and we all buckled our seat belts for a wild ride.

Roger called the case formally, the defense attorney entered a guilty plea, and Winter then questioned the defendant to be sure that he knew his rights and was waiving them voluntarily. I noticed that he spent much more time on the advice than normal and leaned over to Roger and whispered, "He's sending him to the Pen."

When satisfied that the defendant knew and understood his rights, Winter accepted the plea and asked if the defendant was ready for sentencing. Defense counsel said "we'll make a statement to the pre-sentence investigator judge." Winter replied "there will be no need for a pre-sentence investigation. The crime is clear, the defendant's plea is clear. His prior record has no relevance to his refusal to serve his nation at a time of war. So, I will pronounce sentence." He then imposed a 5 year, maximum sentence in "the custody of the attorney general of the united states."

We were stunned. This, of course meant 5 years in prison. No medic team, no hospital service, just service to the other inmates in a federal prison.

As to the form of the sentence; when sentencing a defendant to prison, the judge sentenced him to the custody of the Attorney General, because the Justice Department, Bureau of Prisons, decided where the defendant would be incarcerated: at low risk "camp", a medium security prison or a maximum security prison such as at Lewisburgh.

As Roger and the attorney were leaving the courtroom, the attorney said "well, it could have been worse." Roger, stunned, looked at him and asked "how could it have been any worse, he got the maximum." The attorney said "he could have sent him to prison." Roger asked "what?" and the attorney said, "he sentenced him to the custody of the attorney general, he could have sent him to prison." I kid you not!

The attorney was quite taken aback to hear that all that meant was that the defendant would serve 5 years in some federal prison. He said he had better hurry down to the Marshal's lock up and confer with his client about withdrawing the plea.

We laughed and said "fat chance" of withdrawing the plea before Winter, and wondered what the attorney thought when he heard that sentence. We wondered if he thought that his client would be dining with Robert, Ethel and the kids in Arlington that night, maybe attending classes at Georgetown, accompanying the Kennedys to the Cape, maybe helping earn his way by chauffeuring the Kennedys, or better yet chauffeuring Ted Kennedy so that he could avoid drunk driving incidents.

The attorney didn't get to meet with his client as soon as he got to the lock-up. He showed up soon at Roger's office seeking advice as to how to help his client. It seems that he hadn't even advised his client to come to court "clean". When he was booked in by the Marshal's office to be taken to the city jail to be held for transportation marijuana was found in his wallet. So, right then he was being booked on federal possession of controlled substances. The attorney didn't see how they could charge his client with extra crimes when they were booking him in for prison. Roger tried to explain to him that one had nothing to do with the other.

We wondered, later, whether the attorney would let the drug charges be scheduled before Judge Winter too. This is a time when the defendant could have done no worse by representing himself. Maybe no better, but certainly no worse, and it would have been cheaper.

I have to divert from "ineffective counsel" for just a minute because of the thought of the attorney not thinking his client could be charged for additional violations on the basis of evidence taken while he was in custody.

Sargeant Tabeling's detective unit from the Northern District was being plagued by a series of robberies of convenience stores, ice cream shops, sandwich shops, and other "fast and grab" shops—all robberies being committed by the same pistol packing person who carried the gun in a brown paper bag, and all committed between 12 noon and 2pm.

They had victims go through scores of mug shot books, to no avail. Then, they focused on recently arrested and convicted small time, petty robbers. They came up with a series of photos, whether the accused were in prison or not. The victims, to a one, picked a guy who was in prison. This was, of course, before I sprung a defendant because he was in jail when he was accused of a bank robbery.

We talked about it and I said that since so many of the victims picked the same guy, lets first check and make sure he was still in prison. The next day Tabeling's man called me and told me the suspect was still in jail, but had been moved to a half-way house within four blocks of every robbery site.

The half way house was a site where the defendants were taken before being released on parole, and where they could spend the night after working at a paying job outside the house each day.

We got a warrant for his arrest, based on the identifications plus the freedom of the suspect to use the streets in the area to get to his job. The detectives arrived at the half-way house about 4:30pm and were told that the defendant was "away at work at his job". So, they waited for him. About five o'clock here came, the suspect strolling down the street. They approached him and told him of the warrant and showed it to him. He said, "You can't arrest and search me, I have already been arrested and now am in prison." It was reported to me that the regular undercover guy called "animal" said "watch us sport." In the brown paper bag that the defendant was carrying was a hand gun which fit the description of the gun used in all the robberies, and six rolls of quarters as well as 75 one dollar bills. When the officers checked with the desk sergeant, they learned of a robbery within the past two hours just four blocks away. Sure enough, six rolls of quarters and 75 one dollar bills had been taken. Another crook's myth destroyed: You can be arrested while being in jail.

35

One of the worst cases of inadequate counsel I ever saw occurred right here in Canyon County, Idaho long after I left Baltimore. I was serving as law clerk to Judges Ed Lodge and Jim Doolittle in Canyon County, and one of my jobs was to review cases that were in for Motion Day. (One judge a week spent one day hearing criminal arraignments and motions to dismiss, to suppress, to require discovery in civil case motions.)

I reviewed a burglary and receiving stolen property case, and looked at the motion to suppress filed by the attorney. The motion to suppress challenged all the evidence that tied the defendant to the crime, on the grounds of unlawful search and seizure. I looked at the Preliminary Hearing Transcript, and the defense brief and affidavits and told Judge Doolittle the defense had a good case.

I worked on the law for half a day and it became clear that it was a slam dunk motion to suppress, and without the evidence there was no case against the defendant. So, it would be a case where the state would have to dismiss.

The attorney was appointed by the court. The attorney was a very good researcher but not really good in the courtroom. And, the attorney's personality was not one of a good, aggressive lawyer. Quite frankly, he did not look the part of a trial lawyer. But, the research was good, the motion was well done and the conclusion of suppression and dismissal was clear.

Three days before Motion Day the defense filed a request for postponement and a notice of withdrawal of counsel and entry of appearance by a new lawyer. The defendant or someone in his family or among his friends had raised enough money to hire an attorney. Obviously not understanding how solid his defense was, the defendant had put up good money for an attorney that I knew wouldn't understand how good the defense was.

Apparently, the defendant and family were not impressed by the appearance of the appointed attorney. So, the new counsel was sought. I told the Judge that the Motion would never be heard, that the new attorney would end up pleading the guy guilty without ever knowing that the motion was sound. This lawyer was a real ladies' man, at least in his own mind he talked a good show, but didn't have real legal talent. And, he was lazy.

He was so lazy that he looked at this case as a real good chance for probation because of the defendant's young age and lack of criminal record. It wouldn't make any difference to the lawyer that a plea would give the defendant a felony record that would follow him forever. The appointed attorney had seen that problem and found a way to get a not guilty verdict.

Sure enough, just before Motion Day we got a notice that the motion was being withdrawn and a change of plea would be entered. Judge Doolittle said he was going to have to be very careful in questioning the defendant thoroughly as his understanding of all he was giving up. We talked about it, and he said he was going to go specifically into the motion and his knowledge and understanding of what he was giving up.

The day of the hearing, the attorney came back into the hallway behind the courtroom, sought me out and said "what do you think my chances are for probation?" I said I didn't know, but asked him about his view of the motion. His response was "I didn't pay much attention, knew that no legal technicality was going to get us probation."

In court, the Judge put the defendant through the most rigorous questioning that I ever saw in a courtroom before accepting the guilty plea. He specifically referred to the Motion to Suppress, and asked the defendant whether he understood that if the motion were granted the state would have no evidence against him. He explained to him that the state had not even responded to the motion, and that could mean that there was no real defense against the motion. To all, the defendant said he understood and wanted to give up the right to have the Motion decided. Then, the judge did something that he didn't usually do. He turned to counsel and asked "are you satisfied that this plea is in the best interests of your client?" When the attorney said yes, the judge asked "have you reviewed the motion to suppress, and reviewed it with your client and given him your advice as to the likelihood of success of that motion?" The answer was yes, and, satisfied that he had done all he could do as a judge, Judge Doolittle accepted the plea and ordered a pre sentence investigation on his own.

The pre-sentence report showed no criminal record, but showed a recent propensity for hanging out with the wrong crowd, and for some drinking. The attorney made no plea other than submitting on the basis of the report. It didn't matter because when Judge Doolittle first read the report he said he was going to have to give probation, because he knew in his brain and heart that he would have granted the Motion to Suppress and ordered a dismissal. So, probation was the best he could do in the face of incompetent counsel.

The judge entered probation with some restrictive rules about drinking and drug usage. As we left the courtroom, the family and/or friends had gathered around the lawyer just beaming and congratulating him. They thought he had pulled off a miracle; no doubt he had told them how hard it would be to get probation in this case.

His client obtained a criminal felony record that day. And, it will follow him forever. The attorney? He became a district judge through election by the voters. Then later left the bench after having it disclosed and confirmed that he had molested a minor girl in his own home prior to becoming a judge. Rumors persisted about his conduct in the courthouse itself, but I was gone from the courthouse by that time and have no idea. I wouldn't doubt that the rumors were true, but I'm not sure enough to repeat them here.

36

As a defense attorney, I never had a client who asked me to do justice or to get justice for him or her. I always am amused when I hear people call defense attorneys "shysters" and worse, blaming them for the return of criminals to the streets to commit again. But, those folks are the same as those who will go to the most noted criminal attorney when any member of their family is charged with a crime.

The job of a defense attorney is not to acquire justice, or even strive for justice. It is his or her job to make sure that his or her client is not taken advantage of by the "system", that the state is forced to meet the burden of proof that has been placed on it.

The so-called "presumption of innocence" is no defense for any person charged with a crime. From the time a person is detained by the police, the "system" does not presume him or her innocent. The presumption is to the contrary. If the detainee does not get counsel as soon as possible, the "system" will continue to gather evidence, direct or circumstantial or manufactured while he or she remains unable to take care of the business of self protection.

Often I found it useful to remind a jury at the end of a criminal trial that the jurors had not really accepted the "presumption of innocence" at the beginning of the trial. I then called on them to rectify that error by seriously and rigidly requiring the state to meet its burden. The argument was something like this: "When we started this trial, you told the judge and I that you accepted the presumption of innocence, that my client in your minds was presumed innocent and that you would continue to presume his innocence until the state had satisfied you that he or she was guilty beyond a reasonable doubt. But, you and I know that you didn't tell the truth about that presumption. How could you presume that my client innocent? He or she is the only person in the courtroom who has been charged with this crime. You were told that he or she had been indicted by the Grand Jury, which meant that a group of citizens like you had said that he or she committed the crime. You knew that he or she was the only one in custody for the crime. You knew that he or she was the only one the prosecutor was seeking to convict. And, from television and radio and newspapers, you knew that there had been any number of times that he or she would have been released before trial if innocent. It is only reasonable that you would have presumed the opposite of innocence, that you would have presumed guilt. And, it is only reasonable that you would tell the judge and I that you did accept the presumption of innocence because that is what the system expected you to say. But, now is the time of reckoning. You can now make it up to the defendant, to the judge and to me by forgetting about whatever you said at the beginning of the trial. Now is the time for you to concentrate on the constitutional requirement that the state prove my client guilty beyond a reasonable doubt. Now is the time for you to make up for not accepting the presumption of innocence. Now is the time for you to hold the state's feet to the fire and require that the evidence satisfy you beyond a reasonable doubt. If you're not satisfied, then you must find that the state has not done its constitutional duty. If you do that, then you will have satisfactorily performed the most important duty any citizen has—that of passing judgment on a person charged with a crime. Then, you can forget about any statements about the presumption of innocence. Then, you can rest tonight with the knowledge that you did what was right."

Often, after a verdict was in, a juror or jurors told me that this is the part of the argument which got to them. This was always linked to the emphasis that I put on the fact that they didn't have to answer to anyone but themselves when they went into the jury room.

37

It was this argument that lead to one of the best "victories" in my career, a hung jury. Not long after leaving the prosecutor's office, a man charged with possession of drugs with the intent to distribute came to me to represent him. His "street name" was Pearl Street Reds. I knew of him because his name had been mentioned in warrant after warrant during my time in the organized crime division.

The state's evidence was that the police executed a search warrant on a house in which they found the defendant lying naked in a bed, asleep. Right next to the bed was a locked portable two drawer file cabinet. The key to the cabinet was in the defendant's pants pocket. Inside the cabinet was enough heroin to satisfy the "intent to distribute" statute. There were also papers in the cabinet in the defendant's name.

He was willing to plead guilty to a two possession charge, and take a maximum of five years imprisonment, and I made that offer to the state. The two prosecutors, both young and very good, had worked under me in the organized crime division. They refused the deal, holding out for a 20 year sentence. That was not acceptable to the defendant or to me. So, we went to trial.

In the jury selection, I focused early on some members of the panel brought into the courtroom who I thought might not be favorable to police testimony. Based on age, on job, and on appearance, I had picked out some folks that I hoped to get on the jury. At the time, the appearance of the "Afro" hair cut was considered somewhat militant, so I chanced that the hair cuts on several prospective jurors were favorable to me.

When the state had used its challenges, I had four left, and that worked to my favor. I used those four to go through 8 jurors and ended up with four of the people I had focused on. When the jury was empanelled and sworn by Judge J.Gilbert Prendergast, he excused the jury while we finished preparing to begin the trial. When they were in the jury room, he asked counsel, "Well gentlemen, shall I declare a mistrial now or do you want to go through the trial first?" The lead prosecutor asked what the court meant and he said something to the effect "Mr.Grant has picked his jury, and at the very best the state will get a hung jury. So, do you want the court to declare it, now?" They said that they were satisfied with the jury, and he smiled and said "Don't say I didn't warn you."

Judge Prendergast was one of the best trial judges I ever saw. A retired Navy captain, he maintained strict discipline in the courtroom, squarely and fairly applied the rules of evidence, and applied the rules and the law as he saw it, not as required for victory by the state. He did not assist the state in securing convictions, nor did he assist the defense. Some judges bend over backward in favor of the defense in order to avoid the threat of reversal on appeal. This judge didn't worry about that. He called the rules as he saw them, and if the appellate court didn't agree, so be it.

The state made its opening statement and I told the court that I would reserve my opening until the end of the state's case. Ordinarily I reserved my opening until after the state's case, that way I knew exactly how the testimony had come in, and what I had to counter.

There were six officers involved in the search. The smart thing would have been for the state to call only one of the officers. All the evidence could be admitted through one witness, and that would have limited my cross examination. But, fearing that I would argue that by not calling all the witnesses they were trying to hide something, they called all six. (In a case tried the prior week, I had made that argument, which proved effective with the jurors who acquitted my client.)

In all my years of practice, I never saw six police officers, or six civilian witnesses, who would tell the same story of an incident without contradictions. It is just human nature that each witness observes a set of facts in a different way.

I stressed each and every contradiction on cross examination of the witnesses. Not one of the contradictions, in and of itself, was of importance. What was important was the overall perception that there was real question as to whether the officers were expecting to find my defendant in the house. One contradiction after another lead me to an argument in closing that the officers went to this house looking for a completely different drug suspect. Now, what legal difference did that make? Of course, none, but, it gave my four jurors a reason to not like what the police had done in the case.

Opening statements were limited to discussion of the evidence to be presented, and were not to be used for argument. So, when the state completed its case, I intended to focus on the reasonable doubt standard of proof. I hoped that in doing that, I could draw an objection from the prosecutors. I wanted to try to use that objection to make it appear to the jury that the state was interested only in conviction, not justice.

I advised the jury that the defendant would rely on the facts shown in evidence to show that the state had not met the constitutional standard of conviction only when the facts showed guilt beyond a reasonable doubt. Sure enough, both prosecutors objected, which allowed me to turn to the court and ask "your honor, is the state objecting to the constitution and to the rights of the defense under the constitution?" Judge Prendergast said, in sustaining the objection, "come now Mr. Grant, you know better." I said something to the effect, "I'm sorry your honor, I will keep in mind the state's objection to the defense reliance on the constitution." My point was made. I knew that the whole exchange was not lost on the last four of the jurors I had selected.

The fact that I made an opening, made the prosecutors believe that I intended to call the defendant to the stand. That would have opened him to cross examination as to his criminal record. Such record was useable only for purposes of challenging the credibility of the defendant. So, they almost gleefully began sorting through the criminal record cards for my client. They would have crucified him with the many prior convictions on his record.

When I finished my opening, to which they had objected, I went back to the trial table and then turned and said, "Your honor, the defense rests." Both prosecutors jumped to their feet objecting. The judge excused the jury, and then asked the basis of the objection. They said that the defendant had to testify because I made an opening statement. Of course, they had no basis for that objection. But, they argued that I should not have been allowed to make an opening if I didn't intend to call witnesses. The judge simply answered, "Gentlemen, Mr. Grant has just demonstrated how the defense can get the opening final argument, and then get a second final argument after you finish."

In my closing, I emphasized every contradiction in the police testimony, and paid little attention to the evidence linking my client to the heroin. I made it a "police contradiction" versus "reasonable doubt" test. I used the argument I outlined above about the jury not really believing in the presumption of innocence at the beginning of the trial.

After three hours, the jury reported that it was a hung jury. The judge sent them back to consider awhile longer in order to avoid the expense of a trial with no verdict. After two and a half more hours, they reported still being hung. So, the judge declared a mistrial. Ordinarily, he did not ask what the vote was, but this time he did. It turned out that my four jurors had convinced four others, so the vote stood at eight to four, for ACQUITTAL. I couldn't believe that myself.

Jurors weren't often anxious to talk to the parties, but they opened up to the bailiffs who became their caretakers during the course of the trial, and during deliberations---taking care of their needs, drinks, food, phone calls and all the daily needs. After this trial, one of the jurors who voted for acquittal said that my young Black woman with the Afro hair do, sat down near the door of the jury room, said she was voting not guilty and was going to read her book until the jury either acquitted or decided it couldn't decide. Apparently, she said to the others, in effect, the following "I wouldn't believe one of those officers if he told me my name, the prosecutor showed how they couldn't even get their stories straight. Don't bother me with questions or votes. My vote is not guilty, I won't answer questions and I won't discuss the case any further." With that she turned to her book and read. She was the juror that Judge Prendergast referred to when he asked the prosecutors if they wanted a mistrial quickly at the beginning of the trial.

Right away, the prosecutors said that rather than re-try the case, they would accept the five year sentence offer. Without even talking to my client, I said "No, you guys put all your witnesses on, now their testimony can be transcribed, and you lost eight jurors. You can't improve on the testimony, so no deal." Then, I talked to my client and asked him if he would plead for a two year sentence and he jumped at the chance. So, I offered the two years, the prosecutors accepted, the judge took the plea and we walked out to await preparation of a presentence report. My client said, "I can do two standing on my head." Justice?

38

Moylan reiterated early in my career that as a prosecutor or defense attorney your job was to make the jury believe that you were helping them make the toughest decision that any one of them would ever make. Llewellyn said that your job was to help them interpret the facts that had been presented in evidence, to make them feel that as they left the jury box and entered the jury room for deliberations that you had taken the hand of the twelve juror out of the box and were walking into the jury room to help them analyze the evidence. I always tried to do just that, to argue the testimony as though the meaning was clear and undeniable. I tried to reason them to my view of the testimony through analysis (even though emotional) rather than browbeating.

From the time the entire panel of jurors entered the courtroom, before the twelve were selected, I took every precaution to appear to be interested only in finding the truth, or as close to the truth as we could get. As a prosecutor, I always included in my opening statement that it was our job, the jurors and mine, to come as close to the truth as humanly possible. Emphasis on that aspect of truth began to prepare them for the end of the trial when it was necessary to the state that they not hold us to absolute truth, to not hold us to "beyond all doubt."

So much for the treatment of the constitutional aspects of trial and burden of proof. It was my job as defense attorney to use every legal means to force the state to do its job. Strategy was critical. He who planned for and executed the best, most creative strategy won.

39

I always asked for a jury trial at arraignment. Most times I would waive that right when we got to the trial, or the settled plea bargain. But, at the time of arraignment, no one knew in which court, and before which judge, the case would be scheduled for trial. So, having asked for a jury trial, I was always protected if we got to a judge who made a court trial impossible.

That practice often paid off when the prosecutor had such a long docket that he couldn't try a jury trial against me and still move the majority of his cases. So, many times I got the delay I wanted, without having to ask for a postponement. When the state had to postpone because it couldn't try a jury trial, it went against the state on the record, not against the defense.

One of the first paying defendants that came into my office after I left the prosecutor's office was an alleged professional burglar. He had never been charged with or suspected of burglary of a residence, only commercial establishments and most often warehouses.

I was interviewing him about the case against him, and he asked "You don't remember me do you?" I said, I didn't," and he told me that I once had prosecuted him on a stolen car charge. He gave me the details and I remembered the case. He said "I got convicted and did time for it, but I didn't steal the car, I don't steal cars." I asked him why he came to me if I got a conviction when he was innocent. He said "well, I figured if you could convict me when I didn't do it, you might be able to get me off if I did do it."

The guy was charged with a commercial burglary of a chemical warehouse. The police stopped his car, and during the stop, searched the trunk and found several multi-gallon jugs of chemicals taken during the burglary. He was arrested and charged with the burglary.

They had no search warrant, and I felt they had no probable cause for the search without a warrant. It was a "fishing expedition" search the officers were not looking for him for any offense, and would not be able to show any emergency reasons for having to search the car. If they had reason to arrest him, they could have secured the car until a warrant was issued. So, I felt that I could get the evidence suppressed.

But, he was also charged with a robbery in an unrelated case. While he was free on bail on the burglary charge, he got into a confrontation with a taxi driver. The defendant was driving along down a street near his home, when a taxi driver cut him off in traffic. The defendant nearly hit the taxi, and in swerving to avoid collision almost hit two other cars. He set out in pursuit of the cab.

About two blocks up the street, the taxi stopped at a red light, and the defendant got out of his car and walked up to the taxi to confront the driver. Pretty heated words led to my client reaching in the window and grabbing the cabbie by the shirt. Before he actually hit him or took even worse action he got control of himself and let the cabbie loose.

My client drove on home. The cabbie turned him in and accused him of robbing him of cash that was in the front pocket of his shirt. The pocket was ripped when the cabbie reported to the district police station. The cabbie had the license plate number and had also followed the defendant to see where he went. So, the police had no trouble locating him at his home, and arresting him. When he was released on bail he came to me for representation on both charges.

He already had counsel on the burglary charge, but when he got charged with the robbery he decided to come to me. He told me he was innocent of the robbery, said the cabbie's shirt was not ripped by him, and he didn't take any money from him. As he explained it, he would never commit a robbery. His prison record was as a burglar (with the one car theft which he related to a burglary type charge), and he explained that burglars were given a certain type of deference in the prison population. He said that robbers were not treated with that same deference, and no professional burglar ever wanted to go to prison with a robbery conviction.

Well, I took on the cases, knowing that I had a real problem. He was charged with a burglary which he probably had committed, but I thought I could win that one through a motion to suppress. He was charged with a robbery which I thought he had not committed, but which I thought I could not win. I was faced with an eye witness identification and accusation of robbery. There were no other witnesses, the cabbie had the license number and had no criminal record. So, it was going to be the word of a non-criminal, working guy against a defendant with a prison record. Not much chance that either a judge in a court trial or a jury would believe the defendant even if I could put him on the stand.

So, I delayed the trial as long as I could. Two years later, it was scheduled before a hard sentencing, but fair judge. I was out of postponement material. I walked in the morning, waited my turn to talk to the young prosecutor who was surrounded by other attorneys talking pleas. Finally, he got to me and I said "You know I have a jury trial". He flared up and said "Oh no, you can't pull that at the last minute without notice." I said "Son, I always ask for jury trial at arraignment. That has been on the record for two years." He said that his docket didn't show it. The clerk of the court spoke up and said "Fred always asks for a jury trial, and the arraignment shows that he did in this case."

The poor kid was trapped. He had a long docket and if he started my jury trial, he would have to move about ten other cases. He said, "Well, you'll just have to come back this afternoon." I said, "Fine" and winked at the clerk and walked out.

What the young prosecutor did not know about his judge is that he hated to start any jury trial in the afternoon. The judge usually enjoyed a couple of drinks at lunch when he wasn't involved in a jury or serious court trial. And, after that, he didn't like to start a jury trial. That was a fact that was valuable to know.

When I went back at a little after one p.m., the prosecutor said I would have to come back about three p.m. because he had not completed through his guilty pleas yet. I just nodded and walked out. I spent the next two hours just visiting with clerks and secretaries in the other judges' chambers up and down the hall. Then, I visited with the assignment clerk in the state's attorney's office and gave her some cases to set for trial. It helped to know her, and it was to my advantage that I would bring cases to her for setting. I asked for particular judges and she would set them there because that scheduling would avoid my getting a postponement, thus helping keep her cases moving along.

Finally, at three p.m., I went back to court and the prosecutor was ready. He called my case and said "This is a jury trial, judge". The judge looked up and said "What? Why are you calling a jury trial to start in the afternoon? Why didn't you call this case this morning?" The prosecutor had to admit that he wasn't prepared to handle his docket around a jury trial and he didn't know that I wanted a jury. The judge said "He always asks for a jury trial" and really was not happy with the prosecutor and showed it. He looked at me and asked "Fred, does this have to be a jury trial?" I asked to approach the bench and he waved us up.

I said, "Judge, you know me, I would try this case before you, but my client is scared to death of you and your stiff sentences. So, he figures I've got a better chance with a jury."

He asked, "What kind of case is it?" I said, "Well judge, it's a real problem case for me. He's charged with a burglary which I can win on a motion to suppress. But he's charged with a robbery which I can't win, but he didn't do it." He asked me how I knew he didn't do the robbery and I told him the full story about deference to burglars, sparing no detail. I also told him that the cabbie had no criminal record, even though he wasn't well thought of at the cab company because of strange things happening to his fares. And, I couldn't beat him with my client even if I put him on the stand, not with his burglary convictions.

He then asked me how I would win on the motion to suppress and I explained the case to him. He said, "Yeah, I would rule with you on that. So, why can't we work out the case?" I said, "Judge, I could plead him guilty to the burglary and not file the motion, but I can't plead him guilty to the robbery because it will be on his record and he will be labeled a robber if he goes to prison, now or ever again." He asked me what kind of a sentence I was looking for and I said, "He doesn't want to go to prison. He is professional enough to know I can win the burglary and he doesn't want to go to prison for something he didn't do. Besides, if he goes into prison with a robbery case, even if it gets dropped, he'll be tagged as a robber, and that ruins his prison status. The judge just blurted out "This seems like a probation case to me" and turned to the prosecutor. The young guy who was really nervous because the judge had not spoken nicely to him, said "Whatever you say judge." The judge leaned back and said "Okay, let's get it settled." I said, "Judge I've got to clear this with my client, I haven't discussed this with him". He said, "Well, talk to him and do your best."

I walked back to where my client and his wife were sitting in the front row of the courtroom. I kneeled down in front of him and said "Now, don't you dare smile. You look very serious and do not smile while I'm talking to you." I then explained what I had worked out and what the judge had agreed to. He started to smile and I warned him again "Don't you dare smile. You look straight at me, then turn and look at your wife, say a few words about dinner tonight, and then look back at me and nod your head up and down." He did just what I told him, and I walked back up to the bench. "Good work, Fred" said the judge. We entered the plea to the burglary, the state dropped the robbery charge, the defendant was put on probation and we walked out.

During the two years that I had delayed the trial, the defendant had sent many friends and acquaintances to me, and that continued at an even increased level. He was much better than a signboard or yellow page ad, or even by today's standards an internet ad, he was a walking success story.

40

One of the defense attorney's most important weapons is knowledge and information about court personnel. He or she should know the judges and their idiosyncrasies, know clerks who can be invaluable, know the bailiffs, know the police officers and know the prosecutors and their propensities and capabilities. Another important weapon that goes hand in glove with knowledge is being considerate of and being on good terms with as many of these actors in the criminal field as possible. It pays to have them like you. That doesn't happen by chance. It comes from being considerate of their jobs and schedules, from never embarrassing them in court or in front of the judge, from not finding fault with them, and from not misleading them.

I often had cases scheduled in six or more courts on a given day. As I entered one courtroom, the clerk would remind me that I had a case in another courtroom. My secretary could leave messages with the clerks and stay in contact with me through the day.

41

I mentioned earlier how the "good citizens" of the world look down on criminal lawyers, call them shysters and think that it is terrible that this rogue band of lawyers do their damndest to get people off in criminal cases. But, let one of them get a charge, and they want the best of the "shysters".

One Sunday night I got a call from an assistant state's attorney whose dad was a member of a Blue Chip New York City law firm. He needed the best criminal lawyer in Baltimore to handle a case quickly and successfully. The assistant told him about me and said he would talk to me about the case. I heard that it had to be moved and concluded within a week at the most. I told him I would take it, talked to the client that Sunday night and then the next day in my office.

He was from the mid-west, and had been promoted to an ultra high level in a litigation oriented division of a federal agency. He would be within the top three persons in the division. He had been at a training session in DC for a week before being sworn in and assuming his duties the next week.

All week, he had heard stories about "The Block" in Baltimore.

The Block is a stretch of Baltimore Street in downtown Baltimore running from Gay Street where the Central District Police Building stood to the corner of Baltimore and Calvert, a block from the Courthouse. It was home to pornography stores, strip clubs, bars where anything from sex to murder could be purchased, bookie joints, gypsy fortune telling stands, famous Pollock Johnnie's sausage and chili dog store and a charcoal broiled hamburger joint with a score of public telephone booths in the back for bookies.

The Block also was home to the Gayety Burlesque House which still booked in some big name strippers. The Gayety was famous for the fact that the set-up strippers were totally naked before the first song of their set was finished. It sometimes took the star a couple of songs to complete nakedness.

So, the client, who had worked hard to get the training in within a week's time, had planned to relax a little on the Friday night after training ended. He drove his rental car over to Baltimore and went to the Block.

My client was a man of distinctive taste, and the Block was a good bit below what he expected and what he would have enjoyed. He, like so many people, pictured the Block and its inhabitants as portrayed in "Call Me Madame" or "Gypsy" which Ethel Merman and top stars played the "ladies of the night" and their friends. They thought of the Block as portrayed by Damien Runyan in his famous writings of New York and its racing, gambling, pornography subculture.

The difference is the Block was real—real as it wasn't possible to portray in words or in music. The people there were real, with flaws and faults. They were dangerous because they lived in a dangerous world. Larceny was in their hearts and minds. Not a one of the strippers or bar girls that would handle a customer sexually under a table for a drink (of expensive "champagne" which was really cheap ginger ale) plus tip really had a yen for the guy as she claimed. When a customer walked in, the girls saw dollar signs, and the managers watched how well the girls performed in getting those signs changed into dollars changing hands.

Baltimore home-boy's, didn't drink beer from a glass on the Block. They didn't order whiskey that had to come from a watered down bottle and be poured into and drunk from a glass. They drank beer right from the bottle—for cleanliness reasons.

So, my client went into one bar, ordered a beer, drank part of it and was hit on by a dancer who immediately fondled his crotch and asked for a drink and some fun. She told him, she had been waiting for a class guy like him all night, and she would give him far more than he paid for.

He really hadn't gone to the Block for active participation, but for a drink and to observe. So, he left and went to the Gayety. The show had already started, and a naked dancer was turning cartwheels on the stage. He was the only person in the audience save for ten or so oriental guys in suits and using binoculars which they were busy keeping in focus as the dancer moved through her cartwheels and then somersaults. They were in the front row, about 10 feet from the dancer, so it was a struggle for them to keep their binoculars in focus. He didn't like the atmosphere or the sticky floors, so he left.

Deciding to try one more spot, he went into a bar at the invitation of a barker claiming that the classiest ladies on the Block were performing inside. He sat at the bar, ordered a beer, and watched one dancer who quickly got down to a very brief "g string", looked at herself in the side mirrors examining her hair and makeup, seemed to be completely bored, slapped herself on her buttocks a few times, and moved her feet back and forth in a box fox trot step. He drank half his beer, was hit on by another dancer, and left.

He had consumed not quite one full beer and had seen enough of the Block. On the way out of Baltimore, he came to a rather confusing portion of the highway leading into the Baltimore-Washington Parkway. A police car had stopped another car, and was not fully off the roadway. Confused by the changing lanes, the client hit the back fender of the police car. It was only a slight scraping, but it was a scraping, and the client stopped.

The officer came to his car and was very apologetic. He said that it was his fault, he hadn't pulled completely off the highway as he should have, said that he had his attention on the driver and his passenger and on getting radio information on them, and just overlooked where his car was parked. He told my client that he hated to hold him up even though there wasn't any damage, but that since it was a police car, he had to report it to a sergeant of traffic patrol.

The officer went to his car, called for a sergeant, and returned to my client's car and said that a sergeant would be there in just few minutes, they had been lucky to have one near. At that time my client, honest to the core, said "I really I didn't have more than one beer." That sparked the officer's interest and he asked my client if he had been drinking before the accident. The answer was yes, but not more than one beer. Well, the officer had heard that one thousand and nineteen times, so he said he would have to report that to the sergeant, that he couldn't test him because he was involved in the accident. The sergeant would have to make the decision. He even told the client that he didn't appear to be under the influence.

When the sergeant arrived, my client told him the full story of his trip to the Block, and the fact that he didn't finish either of the two beers. Obviously, the sergeant had heard the "One or two beers" story even more than the patrol officer, and since a city car was involved, he decided to give my client a breath test.

Some people can drink a lot and still pass that test. I once took the test as "a test" after drinking all day on a holiday where I had fixed dinner with my wife for 20 people, drinking all the way through preparations. One of the twenty was in a job where breath tests had to be taken accurately. So, he gave me one and I passed. My mother had had less than one drink and she failed.

My client failed. Now, I believed his story about the beers. He was a fastidious man and I can just see how he would recoil at the seedy insides of the spots on the Block. Nevertheless, the test was it and he was charged with driving under the influence of alcohol. His appearance was set for Tuesday in Traffic Court. His job was to start on Thursday.

42

I told him that I would waive a jury, take a court trial presented on a statement of facts, and then ask for a verdict of inattentive driving. The verdict really fit the case facts much better than driving under the influence. We had researched the personnel and law enforcement standards relating to his new job—doing it surreptitiously though New York. We knew that an inattentive would not hurt him, but a driving under the influence, pending or pleaded, would kill the job.

I had followed the same process in scores of cases, far worse than this. In each of them I asked for and got an inattentive verdict where, as here, the client had no driving under the influence records, no criminal records and was caught by just drinking one or two too many. On Tuesday morning, the judge was John Hargrove, one of only three Black judges on the entire Municipal court. He was a practical man, had been a prosecutor and defense attorney, and had a good sense of which cases should and could be dealt and which should and could not.

Within the previous three or four months, the *Baltimore Sun* had run a series of investigative articles which focused on assertions that the Municipal Court judges took payoffs and bribes to fix traffic tickets and worse. The central focus had been on the traffic judges, where "fixing a ticket" was not looked at fiercely by most of the public. Just about every person in the City would have had a ticket "fixed" if possible—everyone but my wife, Lodice, who would have felt a moral obligation to pay her fine.

The Municipal judges were all a little nervous, expecting that any day there might be indictments, federal or state. I knew that my old friends Bob Stewart and Joe Kiel were working on the case, but had no idea what they had or didn't have. I know that Hargrove had not been one of the judges that I had heard mentioned as even being a suspect. I also knew that there were a lot of nervous folks on the streets—folks who worked for "figures" generally believed to be Jewish and Italian bosses who controlled public jobs, public contracts, gambling, and corruption of all types.

I explained that the judges were nervous, but there should be no problem with this case, and we were doing it in open court, straight forward and direct. But, I also explained that if something went wrong, I would take an immediate appeal and walk it up to the Supreme Bench in the courthouse just a couple of blocks away. I explained that this is the only way we could speed the process, because if I prayed a jury trial to take it "downtown" to the Supreme Bench, the paper process would delay the outcome for days. We had only two days.

We walked into the crowded courtroom a few minutes before 9 a.m. when traffic court opened. Often, the judges would call first the cases where the defendants were represented by counsel because the lawyers usually had cases scheduled for trial at 10 a.m. in the main courthouse. Hargrove and I had always gotten along very well, and I had always found him to be reasonable and bottom line common sense. He called my case first and said, "Got a big case downtown counselor?" I said I did at about 10:30 a.m. and we were off to a congenial start. I waived the jury, agreed to trial by the court, statement of, and the officer told what happened. He stated that he had no idea that the defendant had been drinking, and in answer to my question said that he did not believe that the beers had anything to do with the accident. He said that it was his fault that the police car was parked in the right of way. I only asked him two other questions: 1. Was the defendant cooperative? (he answered "yes" and then pointed out that he wouldn't have known to even ask for a breath test except for the defendant's volunteering the information about having beer) and 2. Was he opposed to a verdict of inattentive driving? (his answer, was to the effect of "absolutely not.")

I put in the history of the defendant, how the Block visit came about, the importance of the job the defendant was going to take, and the importance of a verdict of inattentive driving to that job. Then I rested and asked for a verdict of inattentive driving.

I was stunned when Hargrove launched into a sermon about how the judges were under scrutiny by the press, and how he was not going to take part in back-door deals for reducing driving under the influence to a inattentive driving. I took advantage of a pause while he took a breath from his rant, and pointed out that there was nothing "back-door" about this case. We had brought the facts into the open in open court, allowed the officer to put in all the facts, determined that the officer had no interest in this being higher than inattentive driving, and then openly asked for the type of verdict which fit the facts.

Hargrove once again asked, "What would the *Sun* papers say if I went along with the request?" I replied, "Your honor, I'm sorry, I didn't realize that this case was being tried in the *Baltimore Sun* editorial board room, by the *Sun* editors. I thought we were in a court of law, presided over by a judge who decided on facts not on a whim as to what might please the newspapers." He jumped around in his chair and said, "Guilty of driving under the influence, now I guess that takes care of the new job, doesn't it?"

I asked the clerk to fill out the verdict and hand me the slip so I could file an immediate appeal. Hargrove, who had already started the next case, interrupted counsel who was talking and said to me, "Appeal won't save the guy's job you won't get it heard in time." I couldn't believe him, but I hurled right back at him, "We'll see about that."

I waited while the court clerk filled out the papers, I had the defendant pay the fine, got the receipt for the fine, and took certified copies of the citation, the docket entries, the verdict, the payment of the fine, and left for the main courthouse.

In the court, I sought out an assistant who wasn't in court, explained the case to him, showed him the papers, and told him about the job the man was taking, and the attitude and demonstration of Judge Hargrove that morning. He took the case and we went to the courtroom that his team was working in that day. Judge J. Harold Grady was the judge. Grady was a former states attorney and Mayor of Baltimore. He was a common sense, fair and objective judge except where one of his "old political friends" was involved in the case.

Most defendants waived juries and took court trials with Judge Grady because he was so practical and fair. We went into court, sat down and waited until the case being tried was concluded. The assistant went to the bench and talked briefly to Judge Grady who then beckoned me up. He asked something like, "The traffic judges running a little scared are they?" I laughed and said, "I guess so." He agreed to hear the case.

While the next case was being heard, we added the case to the docket, got the papers filed and to the clerk of the courtroom, and waited. Our case was called next. I waived the right to jury trial on appeal, asked for a trial de novo (a defendant had the right to a new trial at the appeal level, by taking that approach we could put the evidence on in open court so that there was a full factual record rather than just an appeal on paper work), and agreed to call the defendant and have him testify under oath. The prosecutor agreed, and we proceeded. The defendant told his story, how he got to the Block, had about one beer, hit the police car, volunteered that he had been drinking, failed the test and went on trial that morning. The officer felt so bad about how the case had went, that he followed us along through the appeal process. I called him as a defense witness and had him tell how he didn't believe the accident was the defendant's fault and how he thought a verdict of inattentive driving was appropriate. He testified that he had verified that the defendant had no record, criminal or traffic—never even a parking ticket. We rested, and Judge Grady entered a verdict of inattentive driving, stating that the verdict more correctly fit the facts than a driving under the influence. He pointed out that the breath test created a presumption, but that with the officer's testimony we had overcome that presumption. He imposed the same fine imposed by Hargrove and ordered that the defendant pay the costs for the appeal. The defendant thanked the judge and Judge Grady wished him good luck in his new job, said that it was important to have good men in jobs that important, and told him to stay away from the Block. The defendant promised never to go there again.

We both thanked the officer and the assistant. I told the officer if there was every anything I could do for him or any family member or friend to let me know. I said goodbye to the client and wished him luck. He thanked me and told me if I ever needed a favor to let him know.

I had a lot to do that day, and should have gotten to it. But, I just couldn't without doing one thing very important to me. I asked to get a certified copy of the disposition on the appeal, waited for it and then walked back up to the traffic court. At 11:30a.m., less than three hours from the time of the trial in traffic court, I walked in and stood at the back of the courtroom. Hargrove noticed me, and let me stand there through several trials. Finally, just before the lunch break, he said something to the effect "Well, Mr. Grant, back again, want to have me reconsider, well I'm not going to." That was my opening, and I said, "No, your honor, I'm just waiting until the clerk has time to enter the paper work. The appeal has been heard, and Judge Grady has entered a verdict of inattentive driving, the defendant is on his way to his job, and I haven't spotted a *Baltimore Sun* editor anywhere along the way. The members of the Supreme Bench don't try cases looking over their shoulders at the *Sun* papers." He just looked shocked. I walked over and handed the papers to the clerk, who muttered, "good job" under his breath.

I never tried another case before Judge Hargrove. I had lost all respect for him that day, and I successfully moved to disqualify him every time a case was set before him. One day in the Central District, he stopped me in the hall and asked me if we were ever going to talk over our problem, I told him no because I had no problem to be discussed.

43

As luck would have it, a few weeks later Peter Angelos called me and asked if I would help him out with a case in the Grand Jury. I met with him about a client who had been summoned to the Special Baltimore City Grand Jury. Angelos thought my experience with Grand Juries might be helpful to him and his client. I agreed to take on the case which, of all things, involved the investigation into alleged corruption at the traffic court. His client was due in the Grand Jury the next day.

I met the witness that afternoon and he looked just awful. He had no color but grey in his face. He was short of breath, grey all over and so nervous his hands were shaking. He told me that the prosecutors, Stewart and Kiel, had talked to him and told him that they had proof that he was the "bag man" who delivered "gifts" to Municipal Court judges in cases that had been "fixed". He denied knowing anything about it, and they issued him a summons to the Grand Jury.

I did not ask him anything about the facts. I told him that the facts discussion would have to be between him and the Grand Jury when he got there, but that I would try my best to prevent his appearance for awhile at least. His daughter was with him, and I told her to get him some help with getting some sleep that night. I asked her about his health. She told me that he had been a heavy smoker for years, but had really been ill since this "whole mess" came up. She told me that the people being named by the prosecutors were dear and long time friends of his, and the stress on him had been terrible. Once again I told her to get him some help from a doctor so that he could sleep that night because I was going to need him to be able to stand strong the next day.

I met the client in my office at 9:00 a.m. His appearance was scheduled for 10:00 a.m. He still looked grey, frail and bad. He was still shaking. I really did worry about him having a heart attack. At the time I didn't know much about heart attacks except the general warning signs that everyone talked about. But, he demonstrated all of them: he had chest pains, he was grey in color, he had shortness of breath, he was shaking, he had indigestion in addition to pains, and he had pains in his arms.

I had worked most of the night on some pleadings, and Dana my assistant had them typed and ready by 9:30 a.m. I walked across the street with my client. I deposited him in the back row of Court room three in the Courthouse and told him not to move. I went to Howard Cardin's office. I had alerted him that morning that I had a special pleading to file with him. Howard was the interim state's attorney who had been appointed by the Supreme Bench after Charley Moylan had been named to the Special Court of Appeals by Governor Mandel.

44

The pleading was a petition to the Equity Court of Baltimore for delay of appearance before the Grand Jury while the Medical Department of the Court examined my client to determine if he was physically and mentally able to appear before the Grand Jury as ordered. Having served it on Howard, I picked up my client and took him and the pleading to Judge Perrot in his chambers. My client sat in the secretary's office while I was discussing the pleading and the affidavits supporting it, Judge Perrot's secretary came in and said that Bob Stewart and an officer had just taken the client into custody and removed him from her office. The Judge was furious. He signed the stay order, and the order for examination, and asked me to deliver the papers to Judge Sklar who was presiding in Criminal Court 1 which oversaw the Grand Jury.

As I entered the criminal court room, Stewart and Kiel were standing before the judge with my client. Judge Sklar said, "Well, you're a little late counsel." I said, "Well, judge I'm not late. I served on the State's Attorney of Baltimore this morning a petition for a stay order by the Equity Court in order to have this man examined by the medical department of this Court. While I was with Judge

Perrot, my client was removed from the equity court and brought to this court. I have the signed stay order and order for examination for personal delivery to your honor, along with Judge Perrot's invitation to you and the prosecutors to formally appear in the Equity Court to show a cause why you are not in contempt unless you honor the stay order."

Sklar looked at the papers and with a beet red face turned on the prosecutors. He demanded to know whether they took the man from the Equity Court while this petition was pending. They said they had no knowledge of the petition. I told the court that he would note that it was served on Mr. Cardin that morning at about 9:30 a.m. I said that when I was in the office, service on the state's attorney was sufficient to put the office on notice. I said I wasn't aware that things had changed so that individual assistants were superior to the State's Attorney. I couldn't help myself. As long as I had them on the defensive, I poured it on.

I asked Judge Sklar whether he intended to obey the order of the Equity Court, or whether I should go back to Judge Perrot and advise him that his order was being disobeyed. I pointed out that Judge Perrot was waiting, and was holding up other cases so that he could act immediately with contempt proceedings if necessary. Judge Sklar said to advise Judge Perrot that his orders would be honored to the letter. He then ordered the state's attorney's office and its police squad to release my client immediately to my custody. I told the court that I would take my client to the medical department (which by the way, as an interesting but unrelated fact, had been advised by Dr. Manfred Guttmacher until his death; he testified for the defense in the Jack Ruby trial for the murder of Lee Harvey Oswald who murdered John Fitzgerald Kennedy) for examination.

I delivered my client, and the staff began an examination. It was late afternoon when we got the report that my client's heart was in good enough condition to support him through testimony, and that there was nothing physically or mentally that would prevent him from testifying. The doctor did note an obvious high level of stress.

Equity court proceedings had long since ended for the day and Judge Perrot had left the courthouse. So, we scheduled the report and consideration of the stay order for the next morning. Once again I cautioned the witness's daughter to see that he got some sleep. I cautioned him about talking to anyone, not a prosecutor, not a friend, not a stranger—no one. I warned his daughter to protect him from others for the night, warning that newspaper reporters who had followed the proceedings that day might try to get to him through some subterfuge. I told her that no matter the caller or visitor said, he or she was to deny access to her father and to call me at once.

45

The next morning, I met my client in my office and we went across the street to the Equity Court where Judge Perrot took up the case at 9:30 a.m. The report was put into evidence. I had reviewed it very carefully and could find nothing in it to help us delay appearance any further. So, I submitted the report but asked that the judge take into account the reference to the high stress level. The prosecutors contended that the report cleared the way for Judge Perrot to rescind his stay order, and he agreed. However, he did warn them about the report's reference to a high stress level, and told them to carefully monitor his physical condition during the time he was before the Grand Jury.

So, with the stay order rescinded, we returned to Judge Sklar's courtroom where I filed three other written motions that I had conjured up during the night. Each one was argued and denied by the Court. Today, I can't even remember what the motions were. I know that after the written motions were denied, I started making oral motions, each one being argued and denied. As one motion was being argued by the prosecutors, I was coming up with another. We started in the criminal court at about 10 a.m. and I was still making oral motions at noon. I can't remember now, but I think the number went to something like twenty- eight motions. I can't remember the motions, but I remember the time because I had tickets for the opening day game of the Baltimore Orioles. I had bought tickets for several friends, who were waiting for me at my office. They were going to wait until 12:30p.m, and leave without me. Earlier that morning I told them I would be at the office by 10:30 a.m. I didn't honestly see how I could delay any longer than that. At 11:00 a.m. I sent word for them to leave when they were ready and I would join them later.

My client had come in that morning looking much better. There was color to his face and his daughter said he rested well. As we proceeded through the motions, it seemed to me that he gained in strength. At least he looked better and there was more color to his face. Finally, I said to Judge Sklar that I was out of motions, and it was time for me to advise my client that he had to appear before the Grand Jury and answer the state's questions honestly. The judge asked me if I was sure I had no more motions, and said he was beginning to enjoy the mental exercises. I said that I had no more.

At that point, my client said that he would like to ask me a question, and the court allowed it. He asked, "If they charge me with perjury will you represent me?" I said, "Wait a minute, Judge, I want the record clear that I am advising my client to testify truthfully to the Grand Jury, that it is his duty to testify truthfully." Judge Sklar asked my client if he understood my advice and he said he did, but he said, he still had the same question, whether I would represent him if he was charged with perjury. I said, "Judge I want the record clear..." and he interrupted me with a grin on his face. He said the record was clear, the witness understood that I was advising him to tell the truth, but he said your client is asking whether you will represent him if he is charged with perjury. The judge was clearly enjoying my discomfort with being connected in any way with an idea of committing perjury before the Grand Jury.

I said one last time for the record, directing my statement right to my client, that I did represent him, my advice to him was to tell the truth to the Grand Jury, that it was his duty to tell the truth, and that I was his attorney and would represent him on any charges. I asked the Court to put the witness on record that he understood that I was telling him that he MUST tell the truth in the Grand Jury. The Judge made the record very clearly, and the witness was turned over to Stewart for appearance before the Grand Jury.

I shook hands with my client, wished him good luck and said that I would see him the next day. His daughter thanked me for helping her dad and said that he looked and felt so much better— he had felt so alone during this whole stressful process.

I left and raced home to pick up son Andy who was about two at the time. He was going to his first Oriole game. When I got home, Dana had called and I almost didn't call her back. I thought something had gone wrong and I was going to miss the game with friends and Andy. She said that Bob Stewart had just called and congratulated me. It appeared that the witness testified that he had no knowledge of any gift deliveries, or any case "fixings", that he had no knowledge or information about anything they asked him. It turned out that he was their only hope for indictments, and without his testimony they had no place to go. The Grand Jury was dismissed without any charges being returned in the traffic court inquiry.

Andy and I joined my friends at the old Memorial Stadium for his first Oriole game. To this day he still has a foul ball hit into the stands by Merv Rettenmund of the Orioles, caught on the fly by my friend Jerry Flanagan who gave it to Andy. The Orioles won, and all in all it had been a good day, a very good day.

For the rest of my days in Baltimore, I had trouble losing cases before several members of the Municipal Court. For the last few weeks prior to our moving from Baltimore, I worked for Steve Harris who had been appointed the first public defender in Baltimore. It allowed me to stay in court without taking on private cases where often speedy trial was not what either the client or I wanted. Working for Steve meant that I didn't have to leave a case unfinished when we moved. That first public defender appointment provided service only to the Municipal Court for misdemeanor cases. So, I was in Municipal Court every day of the week, and before most of the judges had an exceptionally successful record.

46

During the brief time that I practiced in Idaho after relocating, I got another chance to help defend a homicide case. That trial furnishes evidence of how sheer luck sometimes aids the defense as much as skill or favorable facts.

But, the lawyer won't be helped if he isn't prepared on the facts when luck wanders along. My year spent in Bill Brauner's law office allowed me to work with Jim Doolittle before he became a District Judge. Jim was appointed to represent a defendant charged with murder stemming from a stabbing in the Tico Tico, a Hispanic bar infamous for trouble requiring police response. It was Jim's first murder trial, and he prevailed on Judge Edward Lodge to appoint me to assist him in the case.

The bar was crowded on the night of the fatal stabbing, but every witness was "in the bathroom" at the time of the fight. I went down to the bar to look at the crime scene. I wanted particularly to see this bathroom. The men's room was just big enough for one urinal and one stall and a cramped sink. Any more than two men in the room at one time and no one could even move. But, there must have been twenty who said they were in there when the stabbing happened. The women's bathroom had one stool and a small sink. It would have accommodated no more than two at a time; ten claimed to have been there.

The defendant told us that he was afraid and acted in self defense. But, of course we had no witnesses, because everyone was "in the bathroom." The stabbing took place behind the bar, in front of a big cooler where the beer was stored. The area behind the bar was not unlike that area in most bars. It was a large, wide area where several people could easily stand at a time. The bartender claimed he didn't see the fight because he had his back turned while mixing a drink. I didn't bother to question him since it was a beer only operation at the time.

I then went to the police station to see the photos and other discovery materials. I looked at all the photos shown me by the Sergeant. I made notes about each one, and one in particular was of interest because it showed a broken beer bottle on the floor behind the bar in the area near where the stabbing took place. I remember that I thought that the picture might come in handy for arguing that the broken beer bottle was left from a fight which the defendant ended with a knife. If we could show a fight, it would be a ground to argue to the jury that the case was manslaughter rather than murder.

I also saw the victim's tee-shirt, with several large holes in it showing the places where material was taken out by the lab to study the blood for typing. I just took notes about it and the holes.

There wasn't much in the way of help in the discovery, but I did mention the broken beer bottle to Jim to keep in mind to argue that a fight did occur. We knew we couldn't put the defendant on the stand, but he had made a statement to the police that he and the victim had fought. The photo might be acceptable to the jury to corroborate his story.

We went to the prosecutor and tried to plead the defendant guilty to manslaughter. I was amazed when he wouldn't accept the plea. This would never have even been scheduled for trial in Baltimore. The prosecutor who got the case would have called the defense, offered to accept manslaughter and the case would have been over.

But the prosecutor said that the "public" would not accept a plea bargain. I asked him who in the public had opposed a guilty plea to manslaughter in a stabbing death at the Tico Tico. He just bristled and said he couldn't reveal that. I looked at Jim, and asked whether that was even possible. The prosecutor wouldn't even discuss it further, and he seemed incensed when I told him this would be a slam dunk manslaughter case in Baltimore. He said something to the effect that human life was more valuable here than in Baltimore. I said, I doubted that, but just thought that maybe the excitement of a murder trial was too much to let him let go of it. That didn't go over very well.

Several other lawyers then told me that the prosecutor was paranoid, that he always thought that everyone was plotting against him—police, defense attorneys, the public, elected officials, the bar association and everyone.

47

We got to the trial. The prosecutor called the Sergeant to the stand and he presented his testimony, and got the tee shirt introduced into evidence. On cross examination, I wanted to show the jury that all the holes in the shirt were not from knife wounds, only one was. I started out by simply asking the Sergeant if the shirt was in the same condition now as it was when it was taken off the victim the night of the killing. He said, "Yes" it was. I didn't want to trap him. I asked him to hold the shirt up in front of him and look at it carefully. He did, and as he looked, you could see his eyes and face through all the holes that were cut in the shirt by the lab people long after the shirt came off the victim. I then asked, "Now, is the shirt in the exact same condition today as it was when it came off the victim the night of the death." He looked through the many holes and said, "Yes sir."

I said, "Your honor, I'm not trying to trap the witness, the defense would be glad to stipulate with the state that the holes in the shirt were made by the lab people removing material for the testing of blood." Up jumped the prosecutor and said, "The state doesn't need the help of the defense in presenting its case. We don't need a stipulation." So, Judge Lodge said, "All right Mr. Grant, keep trying."

I thought that the Sergeant having heard my offered stipulation would now know the answer. I asked again, "Sergeant, now would you hold up the shirt and look at it very carefully and tell me how it is changed from the way it looked when it came off the victim the night of the death." He looked at it and surprisingly said, "It hasn't changed."

I tried again, by asking him whether the shirt had been sent to the lab for blood analysis. He said yes it had. I asked him whether material usually got destroyed when lab people checked it for blood typing. Up jumped the prosecutor and said that he resented the fact that I was suggesting that the state had destroyed evidence. I looked up and Judge Lodge had his file up in front of his face, hiding from the jury the fact that he was about to break up laughing.

Since the prosecuting attorney had not objected, I just went on with the questions, asking the Sergeant now whether it appeared to him that the lab had taken pieces of material out of the shirt to test for blood. The prosecutor objected that I was suggesting destruction of evidence, but I could see that the Sergeant finally got the point. The judge overruled the objection, and without any further question, the Sergeant now said that the lab had taken some of the material out and left holes in the shirt.

The prosecutor was just fuming, still having missed the point, thinking that I was claiming that the lab destroyed evidence. As the sergeant left the stand, Jim leaned over to me and said, "This is the dumbest testimony I have ever heard!" I just said wait until you hear the next one.

When the Lieutenant got on the stand, the prosecutor introduced the photos through him. I kept track of the photos as they were offered, and the number was one less than I had seen at the police station. From my notes, I could tell that the broken beer bottle photo was missing. I couldn't believe the good fortune. Now, maybe I could make it appear that the state deliberately left it out. I doubted that because I didn't think the prosecutor or the lieutenant was smart enough to have connected the broken beer bottle with the concept of a fight. But, you never know.

I went through on cross examination, how I had come to the police station and looked at the photos. I clarified that I looked at each of the photos which the police had identified by number on a police report. I said, in preface to a question that the notes I took at the police station showed one photo more than the ones he introduced. I asked him to look at the police report and tell me whether all the photos had just been introduced in evidence. He looked at the police report and said, "No" there was one photo that had not been offered in evidence. I asked him to tell me what the missing photo showed. Up jumped the prosecutor and again ranted his resentment at my impugning his integrity by claiming that he had withheld evidence. I said, "Your Honor, I am just asking the witness about the photos and he has said that there is one missing."

The objection was overruled and the Lieutenant looked at each photo and found it on his notes on the report. Finally, he said that he could identify which photo was not introduced. It was a photo taken behind the bar. I asked whether that photo showed a broken beer bottle right near where the stabbing took place. He said, "Yes it did." I asked why he had that photo taken. He said, "Well, the defendant said there had been a fight, and a broken beer bottle might have shown there was." I couldn't believe our good fortune. Again, the prosecutor jumped up, and with a beet red face just raged about my accusing him of withholding evidence. He threw a folder across the trial table at me, and said, "See if you can find a photo there". I just took the folder, opened it, took out a manila envelope, and lo and behold there was the photo of the broken beer bottle. I showed it to the Lieutenant and asked him whether that was the missing photo. He grinned, obviously happy that he hadn't lost the photo, and said," Yes it was."

I offered the photo taken from the prosecutor's file as defense exhibit one. The prosecutor jumped up and said it was not a defense exhibit, the police had taken the photo and it was a state exhibit. I didn't have to say anything, the judge said no, the state hadn't offered it, the defense offered it and it would be defense exhibit one.

The prosecutor had become so unnerved that he never got focused again on the case. Jim made a great closing argument, bringing to the fore the police belief that the broken beer bottle might have corroborated the defendant's story of a fight, and actually relied on police expertise in arguing credibility of the fight theory.

The jury was out about two hours and came back with a manslaughter verdict, the same result that we had offered weeks before. The prosecutor never got over that case. Even after he was defeated and replaced as prosecutor, and entered private practice, he remembered that case. When I later became Judge Lodge's and Judge Doolittle's law clerk, he mentioned one day that he hoped that I didn't take it out on him on his case that was before Judge Doolittle. I asked him what he meant, and he said that now that the trio from the Tico Tico trial was together, he might not get a break in court. (By the "trio he meant Judge Lodge, Judge Dolittle and I. That was six years later. This was the same prosecutor who tried to hide from Red Merrit in the Larson case that I talk about elsewhere.

So, luck was with us, but being prepared made it possible for us to take advantage of the break.

The sergeant and the lieutenant continued their partnership. They drove an unmarked police car, but it was easily spotted even by new crooks on the street. It was the only car in Idaho—in fact, the only car in America, I think—that had a long antenna bent from the back of the car where it was installed, looped over the top of the car, and attached at the very top of the windshield with some kind of binding material. They explained that this made the car more unnoticeable that it would have been with the antenna standing up straight from the point of attachment. I think they were the only two people in the world who would have thought so.

Red Merritt and his Nampa police buddies called them "Tweedle Dum and Tweedle Dee." I thought the moniker was used only behind their backs. But one day in the courthouse, as the couple was making it through the hallway, another Nampa detective passed them and said, "How's it going Tweedles?" They responded, "Fine" almost in unison.

When I was preparing to examine them in the murder case, Red told me a story about them. There had been a burglary of a barn on a small farm that was inside the Caldwell city limits. A couple of well—filled bright blue tool boxes were stolen along with some heavier electric tools.

A couple of weeks after the burglary, a Nampa patrol officer spotted two men standing by the open trunk of a car parked on the street. One was showing the other some tools that he was taking out of two bright blue tool boxes in the trunk. The second man counted out some cash, handed it to the first man, and took the tools that had been picked out. The first man then showed the second an electric drill, money changed hands again, and the second man walked away with the tools.

Remembering the bulletin about the burglary and the bright—blue boxes, the Nampa patrolman called the detectives. Red and his partner responded and got the officer's report. They parked their unmarked car up the block so they could keep the trunk in sight, and called the Caldwell police to send over their detectives. Red and his partner wanted to wait until the man in control of the tools came back, and then one of them try to make a buy of tools so they could get probable cause.

When the dynamic duo of Tweedle Dum and Tweedle Dee arrived, they said they would take over and Red and his partner could leave. The Tweedles then parked their car with the looped over antenna, bearing Caldwell Police license plates, DIRECTLY BEHIND THE CAR IN WHICH THE BRIGHT BLUE TOOL BOXES WERE LOCATED. They intended to put the car under surveillance from five feet away and observe the operator's actions when he returned to the car.

Red and his partner left laughing. As darkness came, the Tweedles were still sitting, and the man never showed up again. After they realized he might not be coming back, they remembered to check the car's registration and found that it been stolen. The burglary was never solved as far as Red knew.

JUDGES

48

Judges are normally held in fairly high esteem by members of the public. At least they used to be, they were when I finished law school, and, for the most part, they were during my active trial work in Baltimore.

Over the last few years, the news has captured for the public the stories of judges who disgrace the public trust, individual and groups of judges who wear "wrinkled robes" (the name given to an FBI investigation of corruption among New Orleans area judges). News reports have focused on activist judges who write their own laws, judges who are just stupid, judges who have no empathy at all for victims of crimes, judges that are caught in corruption stings, to the point that people are more generally recognizing that judges are just human beings—some are good and reliable and honest and have integrity, some are just the opposite.

It is important to realize that judges are APPOINTED, not ANNOINTED by a supreme being. They are exceptional only in that they were appointed by the highest power in the state to serve as judges or elected by the people to serve as judges. They are mere lawyers who have been elevated to the bench, carrying with them all the strengths and weaknesses that they had before appointment or election.

Just as with all lawyers, a lawyer who finished last in his or her class at law school is still called a lawyer. A lawyer who finished last in his or her class in law school who became a judge is still just a lawyer with extraordinary power.

We had examples of both in Baltimore City and Maryland, and since returning to Idaho I have found that the same is true here. As a matter of fact, I haven't seen a single district in Idaho that across the board has judges as competent and capable as the across the board members of the Bench during the 60s in Baltimore City.

In Maryland, the equivalent of "district judges" in many states, i.e., the judges who serve main level of trial jurisdiction both criminal and civil were called Circuit judges. The body of such main trial level judges in each county was the Circuit Court of the County.

Baltimore City is not part of a county. Baltimore County is independent of Baltimore City and adjoins the City on the northwest, north and northeast boundaries. The body of Circuit judges in Baltimore City was called the Supreme Bench of Baltimore. That body included civil and criminal judges, those presiding in civil courts as the Circuit Court of Baltimore City, and those presiding in criminal courts as the Criminal Court of Baltimore City.

In Baltimore City, the lower level of trial jurisdiction, i.e., misdemeanors and less in the criminal area, and minor civil cases, was known as the Municipal Court of Baltimore City. (Today this level of jurisdiction is the District Court of Baltimore City) The Municipal judges served the role of magistrates in the counties of Maryland. A distinct part of the Municipal Court was the Traffic Court of Baltimore City.

The Municipal judges who handled criminal cases held court in the district police stations throughout the city: the central (the central and downtown of Baltimore), the southern, the southeastern and southwestern, the eastern, northeastern, the northern, the northwestern, and the western. Each district station house had a courtroom, judge's chambers and a lock up which served to hold detained prisoners until they appeared in the municipal court. On felony charges, the defendants were held for an initial appearance before the Municipal judge who set bail. The defendant was either released on bail, or was committed to the City Jail to await further proceedings.

Misdemeanors could be tried by the Municipal judges, but if the defendant requested a jury trial, the case was transferred to what we called "up town", for trial by the Supreme Bench.

Members of the Supreme Bench rotated from criminal to civil courts on a regular, annual basis. Those judges assigned to criminal court, heard nothing but criminal cases Monday through Friday of each week of their year. It had to be a real grind, and pretty depressing, to sit through the constantly turning revolving door of criminal cases, day after day. But, some judges preferred it to civil assignments, and asked for and got longer assignments.

As I say in detail elsewhere in this collection, when I first went to the state's attorney's office, assistants were assigned to a court for one or two days at most, and then moved on to other criminal courts. As a result there was little, if any, consistency in handling postponements and cases that were scheduled and re-scheduled without connection to any particular assistant. Charley Moylan changed the system to address those problems of inconsistency which benefited only the defendants. He set up trial teams of four assistants who were assigned to a court room for a month's time, and then moved on to another court room for a month. This meant that for a month at a time, my team was assigned to the judge who presided in that court room. The system made for a much more effective case management process.

If a jury trial started on a Monday and carried over to Tuesday, the other team members could handle the rest of the docket assignments before and after the jury trial, and could move the other cases to any other criminal court which had spare time. Cases moved along at a far more efficient pace.

49

My team had to take its turn before a judge who was one of the most ineffective judges I have ever seen. During the month that we were there, several cases assigned to me by Charley had to be scheduled for trial. But, I couldn't in good conscience schedule them before this judge. So, while my team held the fort with the regularly scheduled cases, I was trying cases set before other criminal judges. Many of the cases drew press attention because of the major nature of the felonies charged. They were cases especially important to the office and to the city.

The cases were not set in the court to which my team was assigned, because in my opinion the judge did not have a good grasp of the rules of evidence, or if so, didn't show it. The judge did not have the ability, or willingness, to quickly apply the rules during the course of a trial. And, the judge seemed to me to be intimidated by defense attorneys who waved the "appeal" flag—resulting in rulings for the defense contrary to the rules themselves. So, the prosecution shouldered an additional and undue burden in that court. The State has the burden of proof and rightly so. But, once the rules of law and evidence are set, they should be evenly and fairly applied, and in my opinion this judge did not do that. Many of the cases I was trying were sensitive enough from the standpoint of meeting the burden that I didn't need an undue burden to meet.

While my team was in this judge's court, I helped administer the docket assignments and make sure absences were covered, but each day I was tied up in my trials in another court. It meant that basically, three members of my team served the judge, and they did it well and effectively.

But, the judge went to Charley and complained about the fact that I wasn't trying headline cases in that court.

Charley called me in and told me that I had to find a way to try a case or cases in the judge's courtroom. The judge had complained to him that if a person paid attention to the *News American* and *Sun* papers he or she wouldn't know that this judge was even on the bench.

Since most of these cases had been assigned to me by Charley, I asked him which ones he wanted me to subject to the judge. He didn't want me to change the scheduling of the major cases, but he told me that I had to pick something of importance from the regularly scheduled cases, something that involved a top name defense attorney, and try it in the judge's court.

I talked with Pete Ward, Mike Kaminkow and Zeke Orlinksky on my team, and we found a case involving a fairly significant drug case defended by one of the best criminal defense attorneys. The dealer had been arrested after he accidentally stumbled into a surveillance of a common street dealer. The dealer's name was "known" on the Avenue, and his arrest had been featured in both newspapers.

Defense counsel had filed a motion to suppress evidence, and the result of the motion would determine the outcome of the case. If the suppression motion was denied and the evidence admitted, the guilt was clear. If the motion was granted and the evidence held inadmissible, the case would be dismissed. Neither way was there going to be a jury trial.

The courthouse reporters inquired as to why I had taken on this particular case on the motion, and I just told them that I wanted to take my turn in the judge's court. I don't think either reporter believed me but they had nothing to support any other theory, so they covered the case just as a part of the regular assignment.

The officers had a common street seller of heroin under surveillance, watching him make a series of sales, then tracking the purchasers and arresting them when they were out of sight of the seller. All of a sudden, into the picture came this defendant to make a delivery to the seller under surveillance . Very stupid of him to make a street delivery, and very unusual and out of character for him.

Normally the seller under surveillance would have gone to a much more secluded and protected site to get delivery from this defendant. We later learned, from other informants, that this defendant did not trust the seller under surveillance, and decided to come on him by surprise to see what quantity of drugs and money he had in his possession.

Our officers got to watch the defendant accept money from the street seller and count it out on the street. The defendant took the money for his delivery and appeared to be about to hand a package to the seller when our officers decided to move in on him. When he spotted the officers, he took off fast.

One officer took off after him while the others secured the seller, hoping there would be enough evidence there to charge the defendant. As the officer chased, the defendant reached a street corner and, as he turned the corner, he reached his arm out toward a trash basket. The officer could not see him actually drop anything in the basket, but did see him reach out toward the basket. A second officer had pursued in the radio cruiser, and spun the car around in front of the defendant and blocked his path. This second officer saw the defendant as he rounded the corner, and saw him drop an object of some kind in the basket.

The defendant was now trapped and arrested. He had nothing unlawful on him, just a large amount of money. The officers had not had probable cause to arrest the defendant when they moved in on him and started the chase. They had not observed him commit a crime. Taking money from the street seller could have been as innocent as payment of a loan. Had the officers waited just a few seconds longer, they might have developed probable cause by seeing delivery of a wrapped package to a known drug seller. But, they didn't, and we were not relying on existence of probable cause at the point at which the officers began the chase.

The defendants running when the plain clothes officers moved in was not evidence of crime. It once had been, but the courts had changed he rule because in the City there was as much innocence connected with running when plain clothes officers moved in on a person as there was guilt. Street safety or lack there- of had made it an innocent act to try to get away from some stranger moving in on you.

We did not rely on there being any evidence of a crime as of the time the pursuing officer saw him reach his hand out toward the trash basket, or the time the second officer saw him drop a package into the basket.

Instead, we were relying on the evidentiary doctrine of "abandonment." Under that doctrine, any evidence abandoned or thrown away by a defendant is admissible against him at trial. I argued that the rule applied here where the defendant threw a package into a city trash depository into which the public threw garbage to be picked up by city garbage personnel. It was not a private garbage can to which the defendant only had lawful access. So, any evidence that he abandoned into a city garbage can would be admissible against him if we could prove that he is the one who threw the evidence into the garbage.

After the defendant was stopped, the officers searched the garbage basket and found the wrapped package that contained a white substance that proved to be heroin. The burden I had to meet was to make an unbroken track of observation that made it clear that the defendant threw the package into the garbage can.

My main witness that day testified as to the first part of the scene, culminating in his chasing the defendant when he ran. The officer testified that he did see the defendant reach his right hand out to the garbage basket as he rounded the corner. The officer continued his pursuit, and when he rounded the corner he found the second officer had detained the defendant. The officer identified the defendant as the man he chased, and the man that was detained by the second officer.

The second officer then testified that the man, who came

running around the corner toward him, dropped a package into the trash basket. He identified the defendant as the man who dropped the package into the trash basket, and identified a wrapped package taken from the basket as the package he saw the defendant drop into the basket.

I had testimony that tracked the defendant through the process of reaching out toward the trash basket, and dropping into the basket the package of drugs that was taken from the trash basket. All the judge had to do was apply the rule.

But, counsel on cross examination did his best to confuse the judge, or, as I suspected at the time, to simply give him something on which he could rely to rule for the defense. He focused on the brief period of time, during which the officer lost sight of the defendant. His questioning got so heated that I objected to counsel "badgering" or "harassing" the witness. The judge overruled the objection, making the statements that under the law there could never be a "badgering" of a police officer because the officer was a public official who voluntarily exposed himself to heated cross examination, by taking the stand. I don't know how long I sat and stared at him, in utter amazement at such a ludicrous statement. But, I let it go and moved along. I had accomplished what I was after, a brief break so the officer could compose himself.

On re-direct examination, I decided that I would sum up the case in one question and answer, so that the judge wouldn't have to sort through separate questions and answers. I asked the question based on a summary of every relevant fact that the officer had sworn to in his testimony. The question ran like this, "You have testified, under oath, have you not, that when you moved in on the defendant and the defendant took off running, you followed him, never losing sight of him, until he started turning the corner, and as he started to turn you saw him reach his arm out toward the garbage can, you continued to run, when you turned the corner you saw that the second officer had detained the same man you had been chasing, the second officer then told you he saw the defendant drop a wrapped package into the garbage basket as he rounded the corner, and then you retrieved the wrapped package from the garbage basket, the second officer told you it was the package he saw the defendant drop into the garbage basket, that there was no other package that looked like that in the garbage basket, you marked the package and took it as evidence to the lab for analysis, and have offered in evidence the analysis that shows the package contained heroin?" The officer replied, "Yes sir." Defense counsel objected to the question and moved the answer stricken, on the ground that I was testifying and putting words in the officer's mouth.

The judge agreed, saying that I was putting words in the officer's mouth. I replied to the effect of saying, "With all due respect, I was only summarizing in a court trial the testimony he has given and asking him to confirm that such was his testimony. Every fact in my question, he testified to on direct." The judge replied, "I don't think so" and looked at counsel and smiled.

I think the smile made me madder than the remark. I replied with something to the effect of, "Well the Court is dead wrong, and I request that the court reporter read back the officer's testimony." That removed the smile and the judge almost snapped, "I don't like your tone Mr. Grant" I jumped right on that remark, "Well, judge, tone or no tone, I have the right to have the court reporter read back the testimony." Defense counsel took advantage of the opportunity to drive a wedge between the judge and the facts, and also raise the specter of appeal. His statement was to the effect, "Your honor, it would be a waste of the court's time, and would place this case in danger of needing appellate review to allow this answer to stand and subject us all to a repeat of the testimony." I could see the threat of appeal having its effect, so I said, "Well, judge, if the court reporter's record shows that you and counsel are correct, there will be no appeal, because the reporter will prove you two are right. Then, you will correctly sustain objection, and strike the answer, leaving me to go through a half hour of redirect.

That did it. The judge ordered that the court reporter find and read back the officer's testimony. I could have avoided the whole thing and simply restated my question in a series of questions, but I really had just gotten stubborn when the judge remarked that counsel was right and gave the knowing smile. I shouldn't have pursued the demand that the testimony be repeated, but I had gotten bull headed over the clear failure of the court to listen to and remember the testimony. I remember when one of my wife's nephews had gotten into trouble for refusing to do something his mother asked him to do. He was sent to his room to think things over. After awhile, his mother went in and asked him if he had changed his mind. His reply was, "Nope, I'm stubborn now." He was five, so I guess I was reacting like a five year old.

Suddenly, I realized that we had a substitute court reporter. The regular reporter assigned to that court room was one of the very best. That's one reason why I insisted on the "read back". But, as we sat and waited for the reporter to find the testimony, I realized that the substitute was a reporter who didn't work often in the courts, but mostly in the calmer arena of civil depositions. She was not nearly as quick and sharp as Frank the regular reporter. She sifted through the spiral of note paper from the machine that contained the reporter's machine's code marks—no words—just code marks. She sifted back and read, and then sifted forward and then backward again. As I waited, I considered all the things that could go wrong—she wouldn't be able to find it, or she wouldn't be able to read the code marks as the officer actually testified.

Literally minutes went by, and during each long minute the Judge and defense counsel carried on this little joking dialogue about their time being taken up by a "red herring". The more they carried on, the more determined I got to hold firm on the question as I asked it.

Finally, she found the spot and began to read. I felt like hugging her, she read the officer's testimony and it included each and every element of my question. When she finished, the judge looked to defense counsel and said something to the effect that, "Well, I guess he has us, counsel. I will have to allow the question and answer to stand as asked and answered." I jumped up and said, "Your honor, I want the reporter to assure me that she got this latest exchange. I know she was getting her material put back together after her long search for the testimony, so I want to be sure that she got your statement to defense counsel. Did you Madame Reporter?" She nodded her head that she did. I said, "Could I get you to answer orally for the record?" She said, "Yes, I did get the statement verbatim." The judge asked something like, "What is that all about?"

"Well judge, I just want to be sure that the record shows that this court has taken the side of the defense in a case in which the court should be objective. I admit that I was shocked to hear you say that you guess that I 'had' you and defense counsel." I said that the remark meant to me that the court had teamed up with the defense in competition with the state. I said that I thought the Court of Appeals would find that interesting in case the judge ruled against me and I had to file an appeal.

The judge was pretty upset with my sounding off, and said, "Mr. Grant you don't know how close you are to holding this court in contempt." He didn't realize that he had turned his words around. He obviously had meant to say that he was close to holding me in contempt, not that I was close to holding him in contempt.

The devil made me say, "Your honor, I do know how close I am to that state of mind. In fact, I already am there." Fortunately, he didn't realize that I had just told him that I had contempt for him.

The moment passed, the judge reluctantly denied the motion to suppress and with the evidence in, the plea was changed to guilty.

By the time I got to Charley's office to claim credit for trying a case in that courtroom he had already heard about the exchange. He just looked at me, nodding his head, and said not to take any thing else into that court. He asked me in that way he had of telling me how difficult I made his life, "Do you know that if he holds you in contempt, he will also hold me in contempt?" It was a rhetorical question, I thought, so I waved good night and left.

50

The next time I was in the judge's court was on the final day of our
month's assignment. I had no special cases scheduled. I took the
whole assignment that day. It was a day of drug possessions, that
is possessions of paraphernalia, and the key paraphernalia was the
spoon that the user used to heat the heroin powder into a liquid
for injection. The spoon recovered by the police was usually burned
almost black on the bottom of the spoon. It was possession of that
spoon that constituted the crime. On guilty pleas, I didn't go through
the use of a spoon. I just reported that the officer seized the spoon
as paraphernalia.

I handled ten or twelve of the spoon cases that day, and several
of the defendants had long records, no jobs and no income. So,
they were given prison time which would probably be served in the
House of Correction, a prison that offered medium to high security.
So, these defendants were headed for heavy duty prison time because
of having a spoon in their possession.

I suddenly thought of a story that Red Merritt had told me
about a Los Angeles judge who was called the "Scarlet Lady" because
she wore a Scarlet robe. She handled a lot of non-jury drug cases

in which defendants were sent to prison for possession of common paraphernalia like spoons.

One day after Red had finished testifying she called to him and asked him to come into chambers. She told Red that she didn't approve of all that he did as a police officer, and that she suspected him of baiting and harassing defendants. But, she said, she thought she could trust him to keep her question in confidence. She asked him to tell her the significance of the spoon that was offered in evidence in the paraphernalia cases.

Red was stunned to find that this judge had sent defendant after defendant to prison on the basis of possession of spoons, without even knowing how the spoons were used, and thus how they fit the meaning of paraphernalia.

Red said he was so taken aback, that he simply explained how the spoon was used, and therefore constituted paraphernalia. She said, "Well, then I have been right in all these spoon cases." She laughed and thanked him for the explanation.

I couldn't help but wonder if the judge in front of me knew how the spoons were used, and why they were paraphernalia. I wouldn't have bet on it.

I had gotten used to the efficiency and wisdom of the federal judges in Baltimore during my time in the U.S. Attorney's office. I was surprised to see how this state judge fell short of the mark.

51

The federal bench consisted of four very different personalities, but all were sound judges. Chief Judge Roszell Thompson was a sharp, intellectual judge who did exercise common sense. Judge Edward Northrup was a former Maryland legislator who was very practical, not very creative, but understood the nuances of criminal law and procedure. Judge Harrison Winter was an intellectual judge who understood the rules and law, and applied them fairly, never yielding in any way to a threat or fear of appellate review of his actions (Once he reached a sentencing stage, he believed that if the Congress set a maximum sentence, that was his starting point and the burden was on the defense to convince him to reduce the maximum term).

Finally there was Judge R. Dorsey Watkins who was very wise but had little common sense in application of the law—he had little patience for rules that laid out the burden of proof for the government and would in a heart beat require the prosecutor to find any evidence that might benefit the defense.

One of my assignments in the U.S. Attorney's office was to represent the Farmer's Home Administration in any civil cases involving the agency. A contracting-engineering firm filed a lawsuit claiming that the Director had "black listed" the firm, resulting in the refusal of any financial institution to deal with them on FHA loan or mortgage cases.

At the time, the FHA main office was located in Maryland, as was the main office of Social Security. So, the lawsuit was filed in Maryland, was assigned to me to answer, and was assigned to Judge Watkins for hearings and trial. After doing just a brief bit of research, it was clear to me that the agency could not be held liable on the claim filed. The decision of the director fell within the parameters of discretion assigned to him by the statutes. In the government's answer I pointed out that the director did not black list the plaintiff but even if he did, the agency could not be held liable.

On the basis of the cases, I moved to dismiss the complaint. Even without hearing, the judge refused to rule on the motion, stating that he would take it under advisement and after trial would rule on it. He reasoned that the trial would not be lengthy, and he would like to hear the facts before deciding the motion.

The trial was scheduled. The testimony went as I expected. The two partners in the firm testified that the Director had grown angry over a dispute with them as to payment programs and threatened that they would never qualify for an FHA project again. They claimed that the list of companies he sent out as recognized and qualified did not include their name.

The director, of course, denied that he had threatened them, and said that the list he sent out was not intended to be an all inclusive list. He said that leaving the plaintiff company off the list was not intended as a black listing. He denied any intention of black listing, and said that the list was only a partial list. He pointed out that the list made the statement that it was not an all inclusive list.

At the conclusion of the case, counsel and I presented oral argument, and I pointed out that the cases were universally consistent that the agency could not be held liable on the facts and law applicable to the case. Plaintiff's counsel had no citation of authority in support of the case, and admitted it. Their argument was based on considerations of fairness, not on law.

Judge Watkins instructed us to file written briefs. In his concluding his remarks, he looked me directly in the eyes and said,

"Mr. Grant, you are an officer of the Court, and as a representative of the Department of Justice you serve the interests of all the people and of this court. I expect you to look for any case, any case at all, that in any way supports the plaintiff's theory of the case." Of course I don't remember his exact words, but that was the gist of it, he was instructing me to do the opposing parties' research for them. He urged me to be as diligent in looking for law in favor of the plaintiff as I would in looking for law in favor of my client, the government. He gave a short homily on how the government represents all the people, including plaintiff.

I knew what all this was about. He didn't believe the director any more than I did. His instincts told him that the director had indeed black listed the plaintiff and knew there was no way of proving it. He felt that the plaintiff had been treated unfairly as did I. He wanted to find a way around ruling for the government, and he thought I would do a better job of research than plaintiff's attorney who hadn't shown himself to be any whirlwind at his job.

I went to the U.S. Attorney, told him what the judge had ordered, and asked how in the world I was to be expected to present legal authorities in opposition to the government's position. I was concerned it put me into a conflict of interest with my own client, the U.S. Government. He agreed it put us in a terribly awkward, if not unethical, bind.

He asked me whether I thought there was any law favoring the plaintiff. I told him I didn't think so, I hadn't found anything so far. We both thought maybe we would be spared a problem if I couldn't find anything opposing our position. In order to get some cover for us, he wrote to the Attorney General for an opinion as to what course we should take.

I set out to find what I could. My brief in favor of the government was done quickly, with at least three Supreme Court cases leading the authorities. Then I went to work, looking for any kookish decision out there in the vast wonderland of the law in which a district judge decided to ignore the Supreme Court.

After several days of work, I found a very, very old case from some district in Iowa or the Dakota's which granted relief in a case somewhat similar to ours. It was distinguishable in a ton of ways, but the result was what Judge Watkins was looking for. I read and re-read the decision, talked it over with my friends Roger Duncan and Ron Osborne and then reviewed it with the boss. We all decided that I had to cite it and just try my best to distinguish it.

We had not yet received a written response from the Attorney General, by telephone the boss had been told to go ahead and follow the judge's directions. Neither the AG's personnel nor I thought I would find even one case, Watkins could use. But I had, and we checked one more time to be sure that D.C. would not come down hard on us. I made it clear I feared that Judge Watkins would use this case to decide against the government.

I disclosed the case decision, pointing out I was doing so under specific directions from the Court. I set forth the case honestly, and then spent several pages stating reasons why the case was distinguishable from our facts, and should not be applied. I pointed out that the decision was in direct conflict with the more recent Supreme Court decision. I reasoned that had the more recent Supreme Court decisions been in existence, the district judge in the case would probably have decided differently. I pointed out this decision was just a quirk midst the scores of decisions ruling for the government.

The boss also wrote a cover letter with the brief, pointing out, he had checked with the Attorney General and had been cleared to present a case contrary to the best interests of our client, the government.

Of course, I was right. Judge Watkins issued a decision which set forth the facts at length, making it clear the government's position was unfair, did harm to the plaintiffs business interests, and was not in the best interests of the members of the public who had projects with FHA. His statement of facts made it pretty clear that he didn't like or trust the director. He set forth the tons of law in favor of the government, recognizing the great weight of the law favored the government. He set forth the one decision, using my statement of the case almost word for word. He did not mention all the distinguishing factors, and relied on the case to find against the government. He directed that I prepare an order that the Director place the plaintiffs name on the list, issue a written statement to all recipients of the list he had overlooked the plaintiffs company and he was now including it as a qualified project company. He also awarded the plaintiffs their attorney's fees and costs.

It was the big joke in the office that I was the only living assistant U.S. Attorney to lose this kind of case. Some joke, but it made for loud laughter as my friends told of my quandary during drinks after work with other lawyers. My hope, of course, was that Judge Watkins would not submit the decision for publication, that Chief Judge Thompson would not approve its publication and the Administrative Office of the Courts would not approve its publication.

It wasn't to be. A few months after the decision was filed, it appeared in the Federal Supplement, with a special notice in Law Week for all of the, nation to see. There it was. Fred Kelly Grant was the only living AUSA to lose such a case. I can't tell you how many letters we got from USA offices around the country asking how and why the result was reached by Judge Watkins.

The day I was in the district court for the last day as an AUSA, Judge Watkins was presiding. When the docket was completed, he commended me on my work with the office, and stated I had done myself and the office proud by my diligence in seeing justice was done. I knew what prompted his remarks. I wished he could publish the remarks in the Federal Supplement to take the edge off the jokes that persisted about my "success" in the case.

But, Judge Watkins did not make his decision from a lack of intelligence, a biased position, or ill-will. He was seeking to do justice as he saw it.

52

None of the federal judges ever set out to thwart the judicial process from a position of bias, or because of a lack of understanding of the law.

On the other hand a judge appointed to the Supreme Bench of Baltimore just barely before I went to work for the State's Attorney, was one of the worst possible judges to preside in a criminal case. He was a very intelligent man, but was not fond of litigation. He did not function well as a trial judge. I wondered why anyone who didn't enjoy trial work would want to become, or even let himself become, a trial judge. I think the answer must be the prestige of the position which became more important than performance of the job. Thus, perhaps, the reason some judges seem to think they are "anointed", not appointed.

This judge was sitting in criminal court when a murder case assigned to me came up for trial. It was not a sensational case. It was a case in which five young *Afro American* men (late teens) were charged with kicking an old man to death. They robbed him of his money after he cashed his welfare check. He resisted. They beat and kicked him to death. As in most cases like that, there were no witnesses to speak of. It was amazing how empty the streets quickly became when a street crime like this occurred.

There was one witness. He was a friend of the victim. He watched his friend die from a place of hiding in an alley. He was an alcoholic. After he told the police who killed his friend, and they were locked up and held without bail, he went on to a real, long-lasting binge. He was rightfully afraid for his life. He knew the defendants by name and face. They lived in the very neighborhood of the murder. The identification process was not one which contained any issue as to misidentification from a line up or photo process. Friends and family of the defendants lived in the neighborhood and they threatened the witness on a steady and continuing basis. He hid and he drank.

I prepared Tom Coppinger, the police lieutenant assigned to the State's Attorney's office for the fact that he would probably have to find the witness on the day before the trial and find some way to keep him sober and safe. In ordinary street murders and robberies like this one, the danger to the witness became critical when the trial was about to start. That's when the friends and family would put the pressure of violence on the witness as he or she was getting ready to testify.

The five defendants had a terrible criminal record, each having convictions for robbery and assault. One prior murder case against three of them had been dropped because of the failure of the witnesses to appear to testify. In the prior case, the eye witness simply disappeared. The police officers on the case and our own officers in the State's Attorney's office really were interested in keeping them off the streets.

Unfortunately, I spent the month prior to trial recuperating from a late in life tonsillectomy performed in the Johns Hopkins hospital. The complications kept me in the hospital for three days and then the doctor directed me to take a month off work. I was not in the office to prepare the file for trial. The trial was scheduled for the first day I was back. My throat by that time was still sore enough that talking for any matter of time was difficult at best. The week before the trial date, another assistant moved to postpone the trial on the grounds it was set for my first day back and I hadn't had sufficient time during the month prior to trial to prepare. The attorneys for the five had no objection, because in a case like this one, the longer it took to get to trial the better the chance the witness would not show up, and the better the chance, the officers and prosecutor's office would lose interest.

Nevertheless, the judge denied the motion. He said, someone else could prepare the case and try it. He ruled the community had a right to have the case tried quickly, whether or not the defendants waived their right to speedy trial. The associate argued the case had been specially assigned to me and I was the one who had interviewed the eye witness, and the community would be better served by the postponement until the prosecutor who knew the case was prepared to try it.

The judge would not budge. This incident occurred prior to Charley's initiation of trial teams. There wasn't anyone else with enough slack time to get ready for the case, particularly since virtually the whole preparation would have to be at the last minute with the sobering up of the main witness.

On my first day back, still pretty weak, I had to try a five defendant murder case. I called Tom the day before the trial and he said he would start looking for the eye witness that day. Late that night, Tom had him in tow and put him at a friend's house in a different neighborhood for the night.

When I arrived on the morning of trial, Tom told me the bad news. Our witness had started drinking, got scared, and told his friend he was going to hide out until the trial was over. He left and the friend didn't know where he had gone.

I moved to postpone the trial and put on the record the fact the witness had been served with a subpoena personally by Coppinger. He had placed the witness with a friend to try to assure his attendance at the trial, and the state had acted with diligence in trying to produce the witness. Now, the defense attorneys objected, sensing the witness might not show up ever. The judge denied the motion to postpone and actually said we should have arrested the witness and held him in jail until the trial was over. I asked him if he really thought it would have been a good idea to arrest and hold the witness in detention with the defendants. His remark was to the effect "It is a big city jail" and he could have been held in a different "wing" where he would have had no contact with the defendants. What ignorance.

I asked Tom to take as many of our officers as necessary and go find the witness, while I started the trial. The defense counsel waived jury trials, and asked to be tried by the court. They knew waiving the jury decreased the time I had to find the witness before getting to the testimony stage of the trial. Moving through the stages of a jury process, I would likely have had until the next day before I had to present the one eye witness. I did have five other cases scheduled on that day's docket to move and get rid of, so that ate up some time. By 11 a.m. I was out of delays, and so started to present my case. Still no word from our officers as to whether they had found the witness. I knew that meant that he was still in hiding.

I put on the officers who responded to the call and had them testify as to the condition of the body when they arrived, the discovery of a board had been used by one defendant, and the fact the witness identified the defendants who were then arrested. Of course, the witness statement to the officers was hearsay and was not admissible for the truth of what he said. It was admitted only to show the basis for the arrest of the defendants.

I offered the statement only to delay, and I counted on all the defense attorneys to object to the statement. But, smelling the blood, they didn't even object, knowing the statement could not be used to prove guilt.

I managed to get past the lunch hour and up to about two in the afternoon before I ran out of "fill." Just before I finished with one of the medics, Tom came into the courtroom. I asked for a brief recess to confer with our officer and the judge denied even that motion. I then asked for one minute to confer with the officer. The judge asked if it had to do with the eye witness, as though he had the right to ask anything about the subject of my conference with an officer. I said I was trying to determine the status of the witness and he denied me even one minute. He said I would have to ask my officer on the record what the status of the witness was. I refused and said it was not the court's business or, the defense counsel's business to know the status of our case before I made determination in conference with our officer.

We were headed for a direct confrontation as to the state's right to confer with its own officers. When fortunately the judge had to take his own recess to take a telephone call he had been waiting for. Imagine this scenario: the state was denied even a one minute recess to confer with its officer about the status of its witness, but the judge could take a recess to take a telephone call.

Tom gave me the bad and good news. The good news is they found the witness and he was in the courthouse; the bad news is he was so drunk he hardly knew his own name. I quickly went to Tom's office to see how bad the witness was. He was in very, very bad shape. Slurring his words, he wasn't able to put a simple sentence together. Leaving them to try pouring coffee down the witness, I went back to court.

53

I was honest with the court and counsel. I told them the witness was in the building and had been put into custody by our officers for failure to honor his subpoena. I told them he was in no condition to testify because he was drunk but we were doing what we could to sober him up quickly. I told the court and counsel what he would testify to, and provided them with copies of what the police had reported as to how he knew the defendants and as to how he watched them beat and kick the victim.

I requested a postponement only until the following morning, with assurance we would maintain custody of the witness over night so, he would be sober enough to testify. I also offered to make him available to defense counsel the next morning before he testified so they could better prepare cross examination. The judge denied the request without even hearing from the defense. I made out a case for the recess based on current Maryland Court of Appeals case decisions and pointed out, under those decisions the trial court should grant the postponement unless the defense could PROVE prejudice or harm to their case. I pointed out the delay in calling the witness would not prejudice their case. It would be the same result to them as if I had another witness to put on, delaying the witness appearance until the next day. In fact, I pointed out any possibility of prejudice had been removed by my disclosing the details of his testimony.

We only had about an hour and a half of the court day left at that point. Again, without hearing from the defense to require them to articulate the particular prejudice that the delay would cause as required by the Maryland Courts, the judge denied the request.

I called the second medic, and the judge asked me to prefer the witness's expected testimony. Then, without any objection from the defense, he ruled the testimony would be cumulative and inadmissible. I pointed out the defense had posed no objections and in any event, objection would be premature when made prior to the witness taking the stand. At this point, I was prepared to take up all the time I could in oral argument.

I argued that to decide the evidence was inadmissible without objection by the defense showed a bias against the state which was grounds for the judge to disqualify himself. He denied the motion to disqualify himself, and ruled the testimony of the medic would be cumulative and not admissible with or without objection by the defense. That decision was clearly in violation of Maryland law; in fact it even presumed the court could deny the defendants the chance to cross examine the witness.

I then requested a one hour recess and with assurance to the court I could finish the state's case by the end of the court day even with the hour recess. Of course, the motion was denied.

I called the witness. Tom went to get him. When he came into the courtroom, he had to be helped to the front and to the witness stand. I asked he be sworn, but the clerk couldn't even get him to take the oath. I told the judge he could see I had truthfully represented the witness's condition and again asked for a recess. The judge denied the request and asked me whether the state rested. I knew by this time the judge was going to dismiss the case, so I refused to rest. I told him since he had taken control of the case. He would have to enter an order that the state had concluded its case because I refused to do so. He then just entered a verdict of not guilty, not a dismissal, but a verdict of not guilty.

By this time I didn't really care what he did to me, so I put a strong statement on the record as to what the witness would say as to how the defendants kicked and beat an old man to death after robbing him of his only means of support. The newspaper reporters were now in the room, having been alerted by the court room observers as to what was going on.

The judge said he had to protect the community's right to speedy trials and I responded that I doubted the community would prefer ramming through this case at the expense of reaching a just result as to the guilt of the defendants who engaged in such vicious conduct. I made sure I included the full details of the murder and the records of the defendants.

The papers did run the story including the fact the judge denied even a one hour recess so the state could hopefully sober up the witness. The judge complained to Charley, my presentation made him look bad in the press.

Well, the defendants did come back. Two of them evaded further court action though because they were killed themselves in a street brawl. The other three were charged with robbery and assault, when they robbed and beat another welfare recipient.

Whose fault was it that justice was denied in this case? Mine. I should have been more alert during my convalescence and had someone in the office either take on the case, or put in for a postponement very early when I knew I was going in the hospital. I should never have let that case get scheduled before someone I knew was a novice at criminal law and process.

The major problem with the "system" is its effectiveness is dependent on quality performance from every human participant in every stage of the cases. Human failure, like mine in this case, throws the system out of whack so justice is the last thing that is served—especially justice for the victim and for the people of the community.

54

My second experience with the good judge came during a summer session when he was sitting during a vacation week. I had assignment for his regular docket and didn't see any problem cases in advance. The first case on the docket assignment was not ready for trial because defense counsel was not present. All the state's witnesses were present and ready. The judge twice during the day moved the case down so that the defense attorney could accommodate his clients in civil courts. I couldn't help but wonder at the comparison between this and his denial of a one hour delay to sober up a prosecution witness in the murder trial.

Finally defense counsel's civil court commitments being satisfied, we got to this assault case. The defendant, a cab driver, was charged with using a tire iron to strike an irate passenger. The testimony was the passenger argued about the fare and the poor driving of the cabbie; so the cabbie took out a tire iron and tried to club the passenger. The cabbie testified in his own defense and one of the issues of the case was the actual time of day the events occurred. The cabbie claimed not to have been aware of the time and claimed he never wore a watch. It seemed strange to me because I have never ridden with a cabbie before then or until this very day and who didn't have a watch or clock in the cab so he knew the time of day.

During my lengthy cross examination, I crossed him up on several parts of his testimony and finally trapped him into admitting he was in a hurry because he had to get to some event at his grandchild's school. I asked a question to the effect, "If you didn't have a watch and didn't know what time it was, how did you know you had to hurry?" I felt good, knew I had him. He just sat there like the proverbial deer in the headlights.

But, the Judge interrupted, recessed the case and said something to the effect, "This seems to me to be a matter we should be able to work out by just mediating, not subjecting these parties to the rigors of litigation." I objected the case had been tried on the defendant's not guilty plea and if he had wanted to "deal" it should have been before he got trapped on the stand. I did turn to the defense counsel and asked, if he was changing his client's plea?

The Judge interrupted and said, he was not talking about the defendant's plea, but about working this case out in the interests of the public. As I had in the prior murder case, I questioned whether the general public would have an interest in "working out" such a case in which a taxi driver took a tire iron to a passenger.

He ignored my point and actually began to negotiate the result of the case with defense counsel. I just sat and watched like a third big toe. When the deal was struck, the Judge said to me something like, "Well, don't you think justice has been served?" I remember my answer very well, "Justice never walked into this courtroom today." And I walked out.

55

A third time I was plagued by the good judge. I was prosecuting a defendant charged with assault, assault with the intent to kill and assault by threatening with an explosive device. No, it wasn't a terrorist case. It was a case of a guy who was overly amorous and went too far trying to get a young lady into bed.

The victim was a seductively pretty woman of about twenty six, as I remember. She was single and lived alone in an downtown apartment, in the section of Baltimore. One night she went with a friend to a country music bar in Dundalk, a community in east Baltimore which is definitely blue collar. It sits in the portion of Baltimore which most presents the picture you would have of a steel workers community.

She and the friend often went to this particular bar when they wanted to drink, dance and be seduced. She told in pre-trial interviews that she rarely "struck out" when she went there. And, she admitted she was there enough, that most of the regular guys knew she could be available "if they played their cards right."

Her friend cashed in her chips early that night, and went home with a regular. She stayed behind, having a good time "just playing the field and enjoying free drinks." But, the defendant had a different idea as to what would be a fun way to spend the rest of the night. He pursued her and got upset when she didn't show any interest in him.

She told me "he was all right" but she knew his girlfriend and knew her to be pretty "mean spirited." She said on several prior nights she had seen the girlfriend "get right in the face" of some woman the defendant showed any interest in. My witness didn't want any kind of trouble that would ruin her fun in a favorite hangout.

The defendant started to confront every other guy who bought the witness a drink or asked her to dance. His threats to the other guys in the bar started to dry up her supply of free drinks. Guys who didn't want trouble started avoiding her. So, she decided to dance just once with the defendant, thinking maybe then he would leave her alone. It was the wrong choice.

She said he was more interested in groping than dancing and she broke away from him, leaving him standing on the dance floor. He cursed her and stormed out of the bar. She decided to head for home before real trouble started.

She drove home, apparently not noticing the defendant had taken a cab and was following her. When she got home, she parked her car on the street, walked up the stairs to her second floor apartment, unlocked the door and went in. She pushed the door closed but didn't check to make sure it locked because she had to hurry to use the bathroom.

She heard loud knocking on the door and shouts from the defendant to let him in or she would be sorry. He was shouting she couldn't get away with teasing him and then leaving him "hanging." She heard the door open and remembered she had failed to check it. She said she was afraid to go out and confront the defendant because he sounded very mad. So, she went through the door from the bathroom to her bedroom and hid behind the clothes hanging in her closet.

She could hear him storming around and shouting she would either come out or he would find her and rape her. Then, she said that he said he had a firebomb and he was going to set it off, if she didn't come out. She claimed he repeated that threat two or three times as he walked through the apartment, stopping one time, right beside the closet door.

For some reason, he decided to leave and she heard him go out and close the door. Afraid whether or not he had really left, she said she stayed in the closet for almost an hour. Finally, she risked coming out, found him gone and called the police. From her description, they were able to learn his identity from the bar owner and arrested him.

She was really quite stunning. As a usual thing, when a prosecutor was interviewing a witness this good looking, his office became as popular as the Lincoln Memorial to tourists in D.C. A steady parade of prosecutors passed and anyone who could think of any reason to stop in for a "business chat" did so. This woman really sparked a parade.

Her story sounded a little strange when I first read the police reports. It was the first time that I had ever run across a case where a defendant threatened to use a bomb. The defense attorney had offered a plea to simple assault, with probation and I was inclined to take it. The threat with an explosive charge carried a much more serious sentence, but I just had my doubts about a bomb threat being realistic. I talked to the prosecutor who took her into the Grand Jury to get the indictment, he told me she made a convincing witness and I really owed it to myself to interview her.

Before I did that, I talked to the lead officer and he told me a neighbor confirmed the shouting and noise coming from "some man" in her apartment and the cabby confirmed taking the defendant there and waiting for him. The officer said the cabby said the defendant was in a "mean" mood. I interviewed her and decided she was telling the truth about the bomb.

I told defense counsel I would agree to an assault plea, but would oppose probation and request a sentence of at least two years. I explained to him I had corroborating evidence.

In those days, the rules of discovery, which now plague every level of trial work with exchanges of mountains of paper, had not yet been invoked. Discovery was provided for by the Rules but rarely used. It was so limited in nature, the defense hardly ever received anything of use through formal discovery proceedings. Defense did better by just working with the prosecutor and avoiding the nuisance of paper motions.

I told the defense everything I had including the cab driver. He called me back the next day and said his client said no. He told me the defendant couldn't plead at all now because he was trying to convince his girlfriend that he was completely innocent and had never pursued the witness. He said his client was more afraid of his girlfriend than he was a sentence.

56

We went to trial. I had hoped for a jury trial because I just didn't like trying court trials before this judge. But, the defense waived the jury.

I decided I wanted to create a credibility factor for the witness before she told her bomb story. I called the bartender first, who told about how the defendant pursued the witness in the bar and stormed out mad when she left him on the dance floor. I then called the cabby, and then the neighbor. The scene was set for the witness to tell her story, with corroborating testimony already in.

She did a good job on direct and held up well on cross examination. I had explained to her, the defense would attack her from a morals standpoint and she had to be honest about her going to the bar seeking fun which included sex for that night. She openly answered the defense questions and didn't attempt to dodge the issue.

On re-direct, I went back over the bomb threat and as she was answering questions, all of a sudden there is a loud voice from the audience yelling, "You lying bitch whore." I looked around and a woman was standing up in the second or third row, shaking her fist at the witness and continuing to shout curses. The defendant got up and hurried to her and he and a woman next to her finally got her to sit down. By that time the bailiff was there too and she just sat crying.

What does the judge do? Instead of just recessing until the room could get quiet again, and then going on with the trial, he says to the bailiff, "In five minutes bring that woman into my chambers." He then told counsel to come to his chambers and went off the bench.

When we got in chambers, he asked if anyone knew who the woman was. The defense attorney said it was the defendant's girl friend. I asked why the judge was going to talk to her, because she wasn't listed as a witness for either party. He said he thought she might be able to present a different light on the witness's story. I just looked at the defense attorney in disbelief.

I laughed and said something to the effect of, "No really, your honor, why are you going to talk with her." He said he had question about the bomb part of the story and wanted to hear what the lady in the courtroom knew about it. I was just beside myself. I told him there was nothing she could offer that wouldn't be hearsay because she was not present in the apartment and even if she did have admissible evidence it was up to the defense to call her in open court. I said it was improper for the court to hear her in the privacy of chambers. He asked defense counsel if he would call her to the stand and he said, "No". The judge said he had no choice then but to talk to the woman in chambers. Both defense counsel and I objected. Counsel didn't know what the woman would say and didn't want to be bound by what she might say.

The judge said the court had an obligation "to justice" to hear everything about a case. In came the yelling, disruptive woman. I felt sorry for her. She was still crying and obviously distraught. The judge forbade counsel from objecting during his questioning of the woman. We made a continuing objection and settled in for the show.

The judge asked her about her relationship with the defendant and she explained she was his live-in girlfriend. He asked her if she believed the defendant was innocent and to my surprise she said, "No". She then explained that he chased women every time she wasn't with him. The judge asked why she interrupted by shouting at the witness? She said, "I don't want him to go to jail. No body makes love to me like he does. He is just too good at oral sex to lose." It was all the defense counsel, the court reporter, bailiff and I could do to just not drop out laughing.

But, it wasn't funny to the judge. He excused her and then said to us, "This case doesn't belong in criminal court." He said because there were so many personal feelings involved, he was going to dismiss the case but would expect the defendant to make a promise to leave the witness alone.

I knew enough about this judge by this time to know there was no use in trying to explain the law. Of course defense counsel jumped at the chance. I told the judge I would request on the record that he explain why he was doing, what he was doing. He wanted to know why I made the request and I said something to the effect, "Because no body will believe me when I tell them this and I want it on the record."

We went out into court, the judge asked the defendant if he had anything to say and he promised to leave the witness alone by reading a statement that his attorney had written out for him. He carefully avoided admitting the crime, just in case I could get the case re-opened by some other judge.

The judge then dismissed the case and I requested that he put his reasons on the record. He said the only reason he needed to state was it was "in the interest of justice" and adjourned the court.

It was left to me to explain to a wildly mad witness and police officer why the case was dismissed. They were outraged as they should have been. I told them both it wouldn't do any good to appeal because once the trial began jeopardy had attached and under Maryland law we couldn't re-try him. I said the best advice I had was to report the judge to the Chief Judge of the Supreme Bench and the Court of Appeals. I don't know whether they did, I never heard about it if they did. But, you can believe I heard about it from my associates for the rest of my career.

Very likely it is the only time in history when a trial was decided by a witness talking to the judge in chambers, admitting that she thought the defendant was guilty, but pleading for him because she didn't want to lose his sex. Think that is a safe statement? I know the reason for dismissal was not one I ever learned about in law school. "In the interest of justice?" Please! Justice My Ass!

57

Most all the judges on the Supreme Bench were very good judges. In my years back here in Idaho, I have seen several good judges: Edward Lodge, Jim Doolittle, James Dunlap, Dennis Goff, all in Canyon County and several in Ada County who could have matched up with Baltimore judges. But for the most part, the quality of the bench here is not at a level equal to the Baltimore judges in the 60s.

Some of even the best judges did provide some comic moments in spite of their ability on the bench.

One of the very best judges from the standpoint of practicality, common sense, moving the dockets along without silly and undue delays, considering the plight of the victim in the case, considering the interests of the community in dispensing justice, and the rights of the defendant himself or herself, served in the criminal courts for several different year assignments during my time in Baltimore.

But, even he could make mistakes. In a court trial of a burglary charge he made a classic, comical error.

I put on the state's witnesses who proved the defendant was

arrested running from a liquor store with five sealed bottles of liquor in his arms. Officers had responded to an alarm, found the back door broken in and the defendant running up the alley with the liquor. The officers testified the defendant told them he was walking past the store when some man asked him to hold the liquor for him. They testified he ran when he heard the police arriving because he was afraid they would suspect him of the burglary.

When I completed the state's case, I said, "The state rests, your honor" and the judge said, "Ok, stand up Mr. Brown (not really the defendant's name, I can't remember it). Now, Mr. Brown the court finds you guilty. Do you have anything to say before I impose sentence?"

The defendant looked at his attorney and the young man finally said, "Uh, judge could we put on a defense before you get to sentencing?" The Judge looked surprised, and then said, "Oh, of course. Now Mr. Brown I don't want you to think that from anything I've said that I have any preconceived notion of your guilt. I have not made up my mind as to your guilt."

Brown took the stand, testified in a completely unbelievable fashion and I didn't even bother to cross examine. When the defendant rested, the Judge said, "Now, Mr. Brown, Are you ready for the verdict and sentence?" The defendant said yes, and the Judge found him guilty and ordered a pre-sentence report and rescheduled the case for sentencing.

Between cases, the Judge called me to the bench and with a twinkle in his eye, said, "No matter what the report says, I think this one better be a non-supervised probation, don't you." I agreed.

58

In Baltimore County there was a judge who mostly showed up only on pay day to pick up his check. Lawyers referred to him as the "phantom". And when he did show up, the lawyers and clients who got stuck with him and wished he hadn't.

A friend of mine told me of a divorce settlement he tried before the "phantom." When I first started practicing in Maryland, there was still a pretty strict defining line between cases heard in "equity" and those heard in "law". Those terms go back to our English legal heritage. "Equity" courts were those that had historically been the courts of the Church, courts dealing with cases on moral family and domestic issues. "Law" courts were those that were historically the courts of the Crown, courts dealing with criminal acts and torts, i.e., civil wrong doings such as intentional harm or accidental harm or contract disputes.

In Maryland, the courts still sat as equity courts in divorce, child custody, and injunction cases. This divorce settlement was heard in "equity." The case was heard by the "phantom" and weeks went by without a decision. Finally, the parties got a notice that he was ready to make a decision. In court, he announced that it had been a very hard case for him to decide. But, then he realized that he was sitting as a court of "equity," and that meant that he could apply just plain old common sense fairness. The week before, he presented the facts to the cleaning lady who was cleaning his office. She told him it seemed fair to her that the wife win. He analyzed the case as the cleaning lady had, decided she had a good view based on fairness rather than strict law, so he made her decision his.

This began a trend with him. Every time he sat "in equity," you could count on him conferring with the cleaning crews, the secretaries throughout the building, visitors to the courthouse, people in supermarket lines, fans at a ball game. As my friend said, it would have been an improvement on his decisions, if only the attorneys had been able to present their cases to the decision makers in the grocery lines and after hours in the courthouse. But, they were prisoners to his version of the facts as he gave them to his "helpers in equity."

His decision making and his absence from the courthouse seemed unique to me until I ran into Judge Gilbert Norris in the third judicial district in Idaho. He was a master at being a "phantom," not by disappearing but by finding ways to disqualify himself from hearing cases.

My good friend, the late Cy Rood, of Emmett, had one of the classic stories. Cy was involved in a civil damages action. It was a trial by jury and Cy had brought in medical experts from out of state for the beginning of the trial. Everybody was ready to go, when the Judge called counsel into chambers on the first morning. He announced that he would have to disqualify himself. Of course, Cy was outraged. He had just spent a lot of money to get his experts into town for the trial and he made that case to the Judge. But Norris said he had no choice. He told Cy that the pre-trial brief he filed cited an Idaho Supreme Court decision that Norris had participated in deciding. Often, the Court designated a district judge to sit with four members of the Court on cases to help move the case load along. Norris had sat with the Court on the case Cy relied on in his brief.

Now, that participation made no difference in the trial of Cy's case. The case was cited for a point of law, not facts. Norris was going to have to make no findings of fact because the case was a jury trial. Norris' explanation for why he couldn't hear the case just plain made no sense. A very angry Cy asked, "Does that mean, judge, that you are going to disqualify yourself every time you know what the law is?" But, the judge was unrelenting, he packed up his briefcase and he and his court reporter left the courthouse. A panel of forty prospective jurors out of town witnesses the parties to the trial all were left in his dust as he beat a hasty retreat back to Weiser, where his home chambers were located.

One day Norris disqualified himself because one of the parties was a member of a Kiwanis Club. Norris was a Kiwanian, but not in the same club, or even the same town. He did not know the man, and the Kiwanis Club was not one that Norris ever visited. He said that it wouldn't be fair for him to sit in a case where one of the parties was a fellow Kiwanian. Judge Doolittle suggested that he ought to get a list of all the Elks Club members in Idaho and start disqualifying himself whenever an Elk was involved.

He had presided over a jury trial on a product liability case involving a crop loss by a farmer who used chemicals that he had alleged were defective. The trial had gone on for ten days and was finally in the hands of the jury. It was a Friday morning when he jury began to deliberate. After lunch, when the jurors were in their third hour of deliberation in a ten day trial, I passed the judge and his reporter in the hallway and heard them talking about a snow storm coming. There were a few flakes in the air, and the judge and reporter had to make the forty five mile drive home when the case ended. Within a half hour, the judge had decided to declare a mistrial because he didn't want to get stranded in a snow storm. Over both lawyer's objections, he declared a mistrial, and ten days of court, jury and parties' time went down the drain. It never did snow that afternoon or evening.

The judge also drew a very controversial case involving a charge against a naturopath for practicing medicine without a license. The issue was going to revolve around interpretation of a convoluted portion of the "controlled drug" statute. The Attorney General's office was handling the case because there were several similar cases throughout the state. It was time efficient to have one lawyer present them all. The morning of the arraignment, my friend Dick Harris, the County prosecutor, came in the library just to visit. I bet him a lunch that Norris would disqualify himself. He said he would take the bet because on the evening before the judge had given counsel some written questions to help with his research. I went into court for the arraignment. When the case was called, Judge Norris began to discuss the complicated nature of the statute and the amount of time it would take for him to get "up to speed" on the statute. He then said it would be better for him to disqualify himself so that one of the other judges closer to the law library in Boise could handle the research.

As he started his justification speech, Dick looked back at me with the look that said he knew he owed me a lunch. The judge disqualified himself because he faced a contested question of law which would require some independent research and he was an hour's drive further from the state law library than the other judges. From that day on, he disqualified himself in cases in which there was a contested interpretation of a statute.

Dick Harris is a very close friend to me and to my family. He is a very skilful trial lawyer and as a prosecutor he knew just how much evidence to put in to meet the state's burden. Like my good friend Howard Cardin in Baltimore, Dick never "over-tried" his case as prosecutor. He put on just enough to satisfy the burden and had a good read on how much that "just enough" was. He is an Idaho lawyer who could have and would have held his own on the Baltimore scene.

Dick has a priceless story about the "Phantom" judge Norris and his willingness to put justice aside in order to avoid actually trying a case. His story about the "Phantom" is told so well that I have included his own words as to what he calls, "Justice Delayed is Justice Denied."

"An example of the well worn cliché that the wheels of justice grind exceedingly fine is the following story. As a deputy prosecuting attorney I prosecuted a defendant by the name of David Dalrymple. Initially Dalrymple was charged with stealing a checkbook out of his neighbor's pickup truck and forging some checks. The case against Dalrymple was fairly straight forward. The documents examiner opinion was the handwriting on the checks was that of Dalrymple. Dalrymple was identified by the clerks of the convenient stores where he passed the checks. He was not authorized to have possession of the check book or there was no consent to pass the checks. He was found guilty of forgery. Although this was Dalrymple's first felony crime as an adult he had an extensive juvenile record and was possibly looking at prison time. He was not incarcerated while awaiting sentencing.

Dalrymple was apparently angry that his neighbor would have the audacity to pursue the forgery charge against him. After all, the neighbor was out no loss. When the bank learned of the forgery they reversed the charges against the neighbor's bank account. But the neighbor testified against Dalrymple at the trial. Not only did the neighbor testify about the checkbook being stolen out of the pickup truck parked in the back of their house, he was permitted to testify about vandalism and other problems Dalrymple had committed against him over the years.

Dalrymple decided to retaliate against the neighbor. Sometime in early morning hours Dalrymple cut the lock on the neighbor's gate where he kept his pickup truck parked. The pickup truck was unlocked and the key was in the ignition. Dalrymple started the pickup and drove away.

The pickup truck had a large overhead camper attached. Dalrymple drove the pickup out of town to a point about seven miles in the country. He unlatched the ties that kept the camper attached to the pickup, attached a rope to the camper, and attached the other end of the rope to a power pole adjacent to the road. He then drove away pulling the camper off the pickup, dumping it along the side of the road. He then set the camper on fire completely destroying the camper.

Later in the day he took the camper to Lake Lowell, a large irrigation reservoir. The reservoir is located about eight miles southwest of the city and about six miles from the point he dumped the camper off the pickup. On the east side of the reservoir there is a park and an open sandy beach. He drove the pickup into the park, on to the beach and then drove the pickup into the lake. The pickup went into the lake far enough that the only part of the truck visible from land was the very top of the cab. There were a half dozen people at the park and walking on the beach when Dalrymple drove the vehicle into the lake. Three of those people knew Dalrymple from school. One of them asked Dalrymple why he drove the pickup into the lake. Dalrymple stated he did not like the guy that owned the pickup. The pickup was an almost new three-quarter ton Chevrolet. The damage to the camper and the pickup truck exceeded $30,000.00. The victim's insurance paid only about two thirds of the loss.

Dalrymple was charged with felony crimes of grand theft, malicious injury to property and arson. It was at that point that the justice system applied by the "phantom" judge Norris screwed up the case. Dalrymple, or more accurately his mother, hired Jim Doolittle, a competent local attorney, to provide his representation. After a preliminary hearing, his case was set over to the district court for trial. Judge Gilbert C. Norris was assigned to be the trial judge. Judge Norris was notorious for doing everything in slow motion. Although he was a trial judge he had an aversion to actually conducting a trial. All of his pre-trial maneuverings were designed to do everything possible to avoid trial. His sentences were designed to be so lenient as to openly invite defendants to plead guilty in order to avoid responsibility for the crimes committed. If the defendant did not plead, the judge would find the slightest excuse to postpone and continue any case that had the appearance of requiring a trial. He was known to order mistrials on the flimsiest of excuses. Cy Rood, a prosecutor in a neighboring county but within Judge Norris' jurisdiction provides a classic example. Cy stated that he took a defendant to trial charged with cattle theft. Cattle theft in that ranching community was a most serious crime. On the second day of trial of what was scheduled to take five days. Cy called a witness to the stand who had personal knowledge of the theft. Cy explained when he called the witness, Judge Norris seemed somewhat startled by the witness and kept a close watch over the testimony while Cy conducted his direct examination. At the conclusion of the testimony, Judge Norris announced that he must declare a mistrial. As the reason for the mistrial he stated that he was personally acquainted with the witness and knew that the witness was not credible. He therefore in good conscious declared that he could not let the testimony of the witness stand and the only solution for him to take was to declare a mistrial. The jury, who determined the matter of credibility of the witnesses, was dismissed, Judge Norris disqualified himself from hearing the case and the case was assigned to another judge. Cy attempted to find out what the witness had done that triggered such a response from the Judge. What Cy learned was this. Judge Norris had been part of a hunting party a year or two earlier in which a group from another camp spent the evening with them after a day's hunt, sitting around a campfire, drinking whiskey, and telling stories. The witness was one of the guys in the other hunting party that was a part of the festivities. After drinking enough whiskey he apparently was a good "story" teller and entertained the group with some tall tales. Some of those stories apparently stretched the truth a little. But Norris recognized the guy from that night in the woods, remembered those tales he told around the campfire and determined that he just was not a credible witness. Hence he could not allow the trial to proceed with the knowledge he possessed. Cy was totally dumbfounded by the Judge's actions because it was up to the jury, not the judge, to determine whether it believed the witness. But that was simply part of Judge Norris' particular eccentricity.

Judge Norris duly scheduled the Dalrymple case for trial. On the day of trial Judge Norris' court reporter had a cold and was not feeling well. Judge Norris only trusted his own reporter and would not permit a substitute reporter to record the trial proceedings. It was common knowledge that Francis Wander, the Judge's personal reporter at times would change the court record to cover some of Judge Norris' mistakes. Judge Norris was well aware of that fact and was reluctant to have another report the proceedings before him. The first date for Dalrymple's trial was vacated and reset. Because of the court procedure in place at the time and once a case is assigned to a particular judge that judge handled the case to its ultimate conclusion. The second Dalrymple trial was set out for about four months.

About two weeks before the second trial, Jim Doolittle called me and said he was having some difficulty with his client or more accurately Dalrymple's mother. The mother could not and would not believe that her son would commit such a crime as he was charged with. Doolittle informed me that he had gone over the evidence with her a number of times and could not convince her that factually the case was a slam dunk for conviction. Dalrymple wanted to fire him rather than take his advice to work out a plea bargain with the prosecution. Doolittle filed a motion to withdraw from the case citing irreconcilable differences between he and his client as how to best proceed with the case. That was music to Judge Norris' ears. He granted Doolittle's motion to withdraw and allowed Dalrymple to find a substitute attorney. Norris allowed Dalrymple a month to find another attorney and set the matter for an arraignment to appear with his new attorney.

Dalrymple hired Richard B. Eismann, an experienced attorney who knew Judge Norris and his proclivities very well. The matter was set for the third trial date in accord with Eismann's calendar about five months from the date of that arraignment. When that trial date approached Eismann moved for a continuance citing a conflict with another trial he had. Even though that trial was a civil trial which did not have priority over a criminal trial, Judge Norris granted a continuance. Dalrymple waived as a condition of the continuance both his statutory and constitutional right to a speedy trial. A fourth trial date was set again about five months out. When the time approached for that trial Judge Norris claimed illness and the trial was again vacated and continued. The matter was continued for the fifth time. At the next trial date, Eismann was scheduled for minor surgery and the trial was continued again.

Finally after a delay of over two and a half years the matter finally went to trial. At the commencement of the trial, Eismann made the standard motion to exclude witnesses from the trial so that the witnesses could not hear the testimony of the other witness. He also moved the court for an order that the witnesses not discuss their testimony with other witnesses during recesses and on breaks and particularly ordered the witnesses to not discuss the questions Eismann asked the witnesses on cross examination. That request was well beyond the requirements of the rule but Norris allowed it any way and entered the requested order.

We picked the jury, gave our opening statements and started

with witnesses. I called one of the kids at the lake and completed his testimony. I called another one of the kids and completed my direct examination. A recess was taken before Eismann started his cross-examination. When we reconvened after the recess, Eismann announced that he had a motion to be made outside the presence of the jury. The jury was excused after perhaps two minutes in the courtroom. Eismann then moved for a mistrial on the grounds that the witnesses were observed talking with each other in the hallway outside the courtroom during the recess. In support of his motion Eismann called Dalrymple's mother as a witness. She testified that the witnesses, particularly the one that had completed his testimony and been subject to Eismann's cross examination was discussing with the other witnesses the questions that Eismann had indeed asked him on cross examination and repeated the questions she said the witness told the others. Norris ignored the fact she had been in the courtroom during the cross examination and could not possibly have known the questions asked. After Dalrymple's mother testified, Eismann renewed his request for a mistrial. I knew I had an uphill battle to prevent a mistrial knowing Norris' proclivities. I called the three boys as witnesses and asked them what they had been talking about. Each replied that they had been talking about girls, school, cars, what they had done last Saturday night. They specifically denied talking about anything to do with the trial. They denied anything had been said about Eismann's cross examination questions. They each testified they scrupulously abided by the judge's admonition to them at the start of the trial. I called one of the boy's parents who had been present and another person who was just a spectator of the trial but who was familiar with what occurred during the recess. With that information provided to Norris it was up to him to make a ruling on the motion. He declared a mistrial even though he could not make a finding that the kids or the state's witnesses had violated his order. He brought back in the jury and dismissed them. But Norris was not through. After the jury was gone he declared that since he had now heard part of the evidence in this case that he could not sit as an impartial judge on any further proceedings in the case and disqualified him-self from hearing any further matters relative to this case and the defendant Dalrymple.

Another month went by before a new judge was assigned to the case. The New Judge was Robert B. Dunlap. Dunlap was elderly, approaching senility, crusty, gruff, and without what is commonly referred to as judicial temperament. But he was a judge who could make a decision and was the antithesis of Norris. The case was again set for trial. Dunlap ordered that any pretrial motions be made and heard at least twenty days before the new trial date.

Eismann waited until the last possible day in compliance with the order set by the judge to make a motion to dismiss the case. The motion was based on the grounds that Dalrymple, considering all the delays and the proceedings as whole, was denied his statutory and constitutional rights to a speedy trial and therefore could not receive a fair trial. Eismann requested the matter be dismissed. The motion was made notwithstanding that the record revealed on two different occasions Dalrymple expressly waived those rights in open court.

But Dunlap was overly angry at the dithering and dathering which occurred while the case was assigned to Norris. He pointed out all of the unnecessary delays including the blatant stupidity of the last mistrial and the Norris disqualification without any substantial judicial cause. As the result of the delays caused by the judicial system there was an inherent unfairness to require Dalrymple to continue with this proceeding. After a delay of over three years it was time to bring this matter to an end. Dunlap granted Eismann's motion to dismiss the case. So there it was, Dalrymple was "guilty as hell, free as a bird."

Justice, Not on your ass. The title of the book is appropriate.

ADMINISTRATIVE JUSTICE

59

There is a part of the process that we called "administrative justice." As we used the term we weren't talking about administrative procedure and issues decided by administrative agencies. Although there is a well -defined process in the administrative agency field, better followed than in the judicial process where often judges forget they were "appointed," not "anointed"- and maybe justice is achieved more often (but doubtful at best) in agencies than in courts- we were not talking about that well -defined process. Rather, we meant that many times people involved in the criminal process had to act "outside the box" to get at least a "fair" result. Many times, "justice" was achieved by these actions, which were not authorized, condoned, or even contemplated by the regular, normal judicial process.

We often took actions which aren't prescribed by law, rule, case decision, or even personnel manual. Prosecutors and defense attorneys may work out deals (not talking here about the normal plea bargaining) that settle, or avoid, or move along formal charges and cases. In most places the prosecutor enjoys great latitude in approaching the duties of his or her job. The term "prosecutorial discretion" is often used to describe the authority of the prosecutor to disregard a charge, dismiss a charge after it is filed, refuse to take a case to the grand jury, refuse to present a charge for the grand jury to return once the facts are heard there, or take or not take any other action falling within his criminal authority.

Sometimes, a prosecutor will use what is known as "prosecutor probation." That refers to a prosecutor agreeing not to file a charge if the potential defendant agrees to be on "unsupervised probation" for a certain period of time. The agreement is signed by the prosecutor, the potential defendant and his attorney if he has one. The only condition of the probation is that the potential defendant does not violate the law during the time period stated in the agreement.

"Prosecutor probation" is often used as a matter of policy, even when the procedure is not authorized or provided for by law. How can it be? It is because of "prosecutorial discretion." Since no court, no city council, no county government can REQUIRE the prosecutor to take a specific action, he can exercise his discretion as he wishes.

In Idaho, there is a judicial result known as a "withheld judgment," which means the court agrees to impose a penalty without a formal guilty plea. If the defendant goes through the next year without committing an offense of any kind, even the withheld judgment itself can be stricken from his or her record. With a "withheld judgment," the defendant can then claim, legitimately, that he or she has no criminal conviction.

60

The first case in which I sought prosecutor probation, as a defense counsel, arose in one of the rural counties of Maryland. A ranking police officer was charged with trespass and assault upon a farm owner. The officer was deer hunting on the property, thinking it was not private property. First, anyone who expects that deer hunting in Maryland is really "hunting" is mistaken. The "hunters" carry their guns and beer or beverage of choice out to a tree in which there is a platform up high enough that unsuspecting deer on the ground can be seen from quite a distance. They sit there imbibing and enjoying themselves, with bait for the deer around the base of the tree trunk, waiting for the deer to come at feeding time. When the deer come within firing range, the" hunters" shoot them like they were fish in a bucket.

Any resemblance between that style of "hunting" and what my dad used to go through in the high desert and mountains of Idaho is purely a figment of somebody's imagination. (First, to explain a term that causes non-westerners concern: "high desert." During the last few years my work in the high desert country of the West has been referred to in publications, leading people to ask me what a "high" desert is. It is a desert "high" in altitude, not at sea level or below as in Death Valley or the Mojave. The "high" deserts in Idaho and Nevada exist at altitudes of 3,500 to 4,000 feet. They don't sport cactus and other typical sea level desert plants. Rather, on the "high" deserts you will see sagebrush, junipers, greasewood and other forms of low- growing brush.)

My dad and his friends had to trek into the back country of that "high desert" to the mountains that rise up suddenly, and camp because it might take days to get their animal. The camp consisted of a canvas tent and if you were lucky, a folding canvas cot. If not lucky, a sleeping bag on the ground. Food was not carried in but prepared. They cooked meals over a campfire, usually in very cold weather. No one walked out of camp and climbed onto a wooden platform to lie in wait for the kill. Dad had to walk or go on horseback, for miles to actually locate the game. Usually the kill was made well back into the higher country and had to be carried out either by the hunter or on a pack animal if the hunt was by horseback. This hunting takes strength and effort, and the hunting occurs in the cold, rain, sleet and snow, often early at first light.

I remember one hunting trip, the last I made with my dad. We had walked for what seemed to me to be a thousand miles up a hill, down into the valley, up and through the valley, up the other side and over the peak then back down into the valley, up and over the hill to the camp. And, when I say "hill," I mean an Idaho- size "hill," not an East Coast -size hill. No animals sighted. As we sat around the campfire, dad having a cold beer, mom still finishing supper, we heard a shrill sound like a baby crying. From the other side of the creek, along which we camped, another shrill sound. Dad said, "That's cougar, there's deer somewhere." We got up and walked to the edge of the clearing and, in the dusk, across the valley, halfway up that high ridge, you could barely see a string of animals moving single file. Dad said, "There's the deer we were looking for all day." They were headed down the valley to some place where they no doubt watered and as they moved, two cougars had them spotted and were stalking. That was our last night in camp, so dad missed his deer that year. Later that month, one of my dad's good friends, dressed in bright red hunting jacket and a red cap, was shot by a hunter who was drunk. The friend died the next morning, and we never hunted again.

That's what I called hunting. I had to laugh when the officer told me how he had hunted. At any rate, he came to me to represent him. Funny, because he was one of the many who referred to every good defense attorney as a shyster and told me repeatedly that he didn't know how I could live with myself after I left the prosecutor's office and took up defense work. Yet, when he faced charges that would cost him his police job, he came directly to the "shyster" to represent him.

The first hearing before a magistrate in the county was scheduled at 7:30 p.m. It was because the judge had a "day job." He didn't make enough salary as a judge that he could give up the "day job," so he held court at night. I called the clerk of the court the day before and got the name and phone number of the complaining farm owner. I called him and arranged to meet with him early, before court, to discuss the case. He told me by telephone that it wouldn't do any good, told me that my client was such a jackass that he wanted to see him go to jail and lose his job. But he did agree to meet with me and let me buy him a burger and fries.

The officer and I drove to the town and I told him to get lost until half an hour before the hearing because I didn't want him anywhere near the farmer. The officer had told me that the farmer came driving up to the tree, jumped out of his truck, shook his fist at the officer and demanded he come down and fight. The client told me he tried to reason with the farmer, that he didn't even know he was the land owner, he didn't know who this was yelling at him to come down and fight.

The farmer had told me a different story on the phone. He said he found a car parked right in the middle of the path on which he was driving his tractor back to the barn, and had to maneuver the tractor over a rickety platform walkway across a drain ditch. He said he got his pickup and drove back to the parked car and yelled and honked the horn repeatedly. He said his property was posted "no trespassing" within fifty feet of where the car was parked and that the car would have had to drive right past the orange sign.

He said that when no one answered, he drove down into the

woods and could see a guy sitting up in the farmer's own personal tree platform (so that told me that the farmer was the same kind of "sportsman" as my client-one who laid in wait for the kill.) He said when he pulled up under the tree, he got out and my client started yelling at him and cursing him for "scaring the deer away." He said when he tried to tell my client that he was on private property, my client pointed his rifle at him and said, "I ought to shoot your ass for messing up my hunt." The farmer said he was afraid, but he did tell my client that he was on private property, and my client swore at him again and told him it wasn't private property, that he was a police officer from Baltimore and he would "arrest my ass" if I didn't quit interrupting his hunt.

The farmer said he left, went to his house and called the sheriff. A constable (often the small towns had a "kind of" police officer called a constable. This job was mostly a paper server and traffic controller) answered the call and accompanied him back to the tree. The constable had come from the field, meaning a farm field, so he didn't have on a uniform but had on farm overalls. When the farmer told the constable that the guy in the tree house pointed a rifle at him, the constable pinned a badge on the front of his overalls.

When they got to the tree, the man on the platform started swearing again and yelled at the constable, "Where the hell did you get that dime store badge?" The constable asked him to come down, and finally my client came down out of the tree house, pulled out a wallet, opened it and said, "Now, clown, that is a real badge, that's a Baltimore police badge, so get out of here and let me hunt." The farmer said my client then grabbed the front of his bib overalls, pulled him up close to his face and threatened to "stick his rifle up my butt." At that point, the farmer said he and the constable left and went to the house and called the state police number.

I really didn't believe the farmer's story. I doubted that my client went nearly as far as the farmer said. I had never seen a side of my client that would be consistent with the actions described by the farmer. But we were in the farmer's ball park. It was my big city client's word against local land owner. I hoped when I talked to the farmer in person, he might tell a less volatile story, one closer to my client's version of the whole situation being a mix-up on property lines.

As we ate our burger and fries and drank a beer, I didn't ask about the case. I asked about the town and the hunting and joked about the difference in hunting. When we finished and were having a second beer, I asked about any experiences he had with other trespassers. He told me that my client was the rudest hunter he ever came across. He said that usually a trespassing hunter would be real nice about the trespass and sometimes the farmer would let the hunter say on the platform.

We had gotten on fine and I thought I was on pretty good ground to start asking for a break for my client. I asked him what he really wanted to see happen in the case and he said, "I want to see your client boil in his own juices." That was pretty clear so I changed the subject back to the nature of the hunting experience itself. I told him the story about my dad and my last hunting trip. Our talk was now more relaxed. I then learned that he and the prosecutor were cousins. The prosecuting attorney was married to the judge's daughter and the three of them hunted together quite often. I had to shift into high gear.

I told him my client was a very good and brave policeman. I told him about his work and about a couple of tough cases that my client had cracked. I said, that in my days as a prosecutor I never saw an officer I could count on more to do a good job.

He softened up a little bit and said that he didn't really care whether my client went to jail, as long as he was convicted and put under the condition of never coming on his property again. I explained that a conviction, or plea to any form of charge, would cost my client his job, and asked if he would be willing to agree that the prosecutor drop the charge if my client promised never to come back to his property. He said, "No, he should have thought about his job before he threatened me."

He was getting riled up again, so I changed the subject again and told him my client was a good husband and father, just a plain good man. I told him that he had come in the country to relax from the heavy tension under which he worked. I said, "He just relaxed and was enjoying himself" when the farmer came up and interrupted him. I said he thought he was on a different platform with the owner's permission and he was probably embarrassed when he found he was in the wrong place and was trespassing. I said he just reacted badly when he realized he had made a mistake.

The farmer wanted to know whether he always acted so badly when he made a mistake. The guy was working me through the paces. I told him that was part of the problem—he worked under terrible pressure because of the need to handle every case without mistakes.

Finally, he agreed that it wouldn't do any good to lose a good police officer. He agreed to ask the prosecutor to just drop the charges if my client apologized to him in person, promised to never come on his property again and contributed to the rod and gun club fund for their annual festival.

I thanked him and told him we would meet him in the conference room up the hall from the courtroom. I went back, found my client and explained the deal to him. As soon as I mentioned apology, he got red in the face and said he would not apologize because it was all a mistake. He didn't think he had done anything wrong by just going on the wrong property. I said, "Okay, well write me a check for my $1,000 fee and we'll go on into court." He looked kind of shocked and asked why I wanted the fee right then. I said, "I want my money before you lose your job and can't pay me."

He really was shocked, and said, "You're not going in to try to get me off?" I said, "Look, you're a big city dweller who trespassed on a local's land." I knew I would have had a better chance to get Jack Ruby off than I would have had in getting him off.

All he could say was that I had told him I would only charge him two hundred and fifty dollars. I said that was before I had to buy the farmer a burger, fries and two beers. That eased him a bit, he laughed and we went to see the farmer. The prosecutor "withdrew" the citation as having been improvidently issued and agreed that if my client got into no trouble for the next twelve months, the citation would not be reinstated. It is what we call prosecutor probation. You won't find it in any law book.

I never told my client about the contribution to the rod and gun fund, I figured since the apology set him off so much, the contribution might have killed the deal. So I contributed to the fund. I don't like to lose.

Half a year later, the farmer called for an appointment and wanted me to represent his daughter in a juvenile case in the county. She had been charged with shoplifting along with a group of her friends who were smarting off in a store after school. He said the store owner was being a "stubborn old mule" and thought maybe I could talk him into dropping the charges. I guess he thought if I could talk his stubborn self into dropping a charge, I could do the same with the storekeeper. He was right, I did.

61

The first time I heard the term administrative justice applied was in a child abuse case. Now this was "child abuse" in a big city in the 60s. This was well before the game players in the process-legislators, counselors, psychologists, prosecutors and judges-really understood the extent of the physical mental and emotional harm that can be and is done to little ones. I make this disclaimer with the kindest of thoughts, hoping that all others were as naïve as I was at the time. We were dealing with brutal abuse, use of hair straightening irons to burn the child over all parts of the body, throwing the child down the stairs, using a razor to cut the child to teach the child not to cry or do something annoying, throwing the child against the wall and sticking the child's hand in a pot of boiling water on the stove and holding it there-yet the statutory maximum sentence for conviction was one lousy year.

Even where there was evidence of near -death, abuse rarely if ever was the defendant charged with assault with intent to murder. Under the circumstances of these cases, it was virtually impossible to prove intent beyond a reasonable doubt. And the defense would challenge application of the assault with intent statute because of the legislative intent shown by the specific child abuse statute that child victims were to be covered by the lesser sentence. As to both factors, the deciding power was the judge, not a jury.

The intent problem was posed when the intent of a defendant had to be proved through purely circumstantial evidence. You had proof of the injury, and even how the injury occurred physically. But normally there is no one present at the time of the injury to say how angry the perpetrator was, whether he made statements as to his intent, how he approached the child and all other elements that normally a prosecutor would introduce to prove intent. In some cases, in Maryland, intent could be inferred from use of a deadly weapon. For example, if a guy shot a child with a pistol or rifle or shotgun, the presumption from use of the weapon was that he intended to kill the child. It was easy to get to the intent when a deadly weapon was used. But most of the child abuse cases didn't involve the use of deadly weapons. They didn't involve the use of weapons of any kind. And it was harder to prove intent to a judge hardened by seeing brutality in the criminal courts over and over and over again than it would be to a jury seeing such violence perhaps for the first time. The judges, of course, were entangled with the niceties and technicalities of precedents and the desire not to be reversed on appeal.

In Maryland, or at least in Baltimore, most child abuse cases, in fact most criminal cases were tried by a judge and not a jury. Why? When I first joined the State's Attorney's office, jury trials were rare. Jury panels were not selected from the population at large, as now. Many members were volunteers, and most others were people retired or who held jobs or had businesses where they would be excused for jury duty. The volunteers we referred to as "civic pixies," often rich women who had nothing to do and wanted to "contribute," so they chose juror duty instead of hospital duty to give them something to add to the next luncheon conversation. They simply submitted their names to the jury commissioner or any member of the Supreme Bench, and they were on the central panel from which specific juries for trials would be picked. Since *Afro Americans* were rarely in a job where their bosses would let them off for jury duty, and rarely in business for themselves, which could operate in their absence, they were rarely called to jury duty. Even the home owner listings eliminated most *Afro Americans*.

Jurors were predominately older white men and women who had little empathy for the "cultural ways" of *Afro Americans*, no patience with those who continued to live in the ghettos, no understanding of the difficulty Afro Americans had in getting competitive jobs, a belief that most Afro Americans thrived happily on a life of welfare, and a general belief that young *Afro American*, men had a propensity to go around armed and ready to steal or rob. This observation comes not from any scientific collection of moods or opinions. It comes from talking to jurors, to neighbors and the people of Baltimore in churches, supermarkets and ball games. Respect for *Afro Americans*, in general, was reserved primarily for athletes or those who had achieved a professional standing as a lawyer, minister, or elected official.

As a result, few if any lawyers for *Afro Americans* ever asked for a jury trial in those early days of my time in the office. They preferred to be tried by a judge who might be more lenient because of his or her hardening from sitting in the criminal court for a year at a time. First, they would rely on technicalities that might be ignored by a white jury; they would compare the case to far worst cases they had heard and tried (something the white jury couldn't do) and the comparison would result in an acquittal or conviction of a lesser offense. Sometimes the judge just liked the attorney or owed them a favor.

The "circumstances" of the cases made it unlikely there would be jury trials included facts that the usual case involved, a mother on welfare who had a child or children by a different man or men than the boyfriend with whom she was living. The jurors would have been prejudiced from the outset for several reasons. They would have believed the worst of the defendant and would have given no credibility to his or her testimony or anyone else who might be involved in the family situation. They would have been incensed at the thought that their public tax dollars were being used to care for the children, while the mother and boyfriend went without jobs and fathers paid no child support. A defense attorney worth his salt did not take a jury trial.

The fact that these cases were tried by the more technically trained judges brought circumstances into play that frustrated me to the point of exasperation: (1) most of the time the defendant was a non-parent, usually the live in "boy friend" of the mother, who had been left in charge of the child while the mother was shopping, working, or checking in with unemployment or welfare (2) Most times the only witnesses were the offending boyfriend and the child, most often too young to be a testifying witness, (3) even though we could call the mother to the witness chair, we couldn't enforce the truth, and too often she wouldn't tell the truth (apparently preferring to keep the welfare grafting boy friend hanging around and supporting him over the safety and health of her child) (4) the state didn't have the opportunity to present obvious common street inferences to a jury, but instead had to rely on the technically oriented mind of a judge who stayed above the emotion of the case and (5) the maximum sentence of one year made it possible for a defendant who had hired a defense attorney never to serve a day in jail pending appeal. (If he had the money, most often through the mother, to hire an attorney, he could afford an appeal bond, and could stay on the street during the appeal.) In those rare cases where the state could present evidence from which the judge could make the inference that the boyfriend was the one who injured the child, the appeal was often successful because the evidence was so sparse. Often, the judge had to make too much of a leap from the evidence to the inference, and the appellate court reversed.

62

In one of the cases I tried, the defendant had been once convicted of child abuse and served three months of a year sentence, then convicted a second time and was free on appeal bond when he committed abuse again on the SAME CHILD. The little four year old girl was bruised from head to toe. Her mouth had been cut on both sides, by blows with a fist or some other hard object. One eye was swollen shut. Both her arms were in slings and an ankle in a cast. The doctors found over eighty five healed fractures from past beatings and she had eight compound fractures and a skull fracture this time. When she regained consciousness in the hospital, she had complete memory loss. It made me sick to think of even taking the case into court when all I could seek in penalty was one damn, insufficient year.

So I didn't. I "stetted" the case. That was a technique that was a variation on prosecution probation. The case was put on a "stet" docket, which meant it was inactive, and probably never would be reopened unless the defendant got into criminal trouble again. I announced to the court that I was stetting the case "in the interests of justice." My intent was not evident at the time. The defense attorney assured his client at the trial table that I just didn't want to lose.

I took the case to Jack, our Grand Jury prosecutor, and asked him to take it to the Grand Jury on an assault with intent to murder theory. He agreed and took the case to the Grand Jurors requesting that in this case they charge assault with intent to murder because of the repeated patterns of abuse. He presented the defendant's record, the medical history of the little girl, and the testimony of the police officer who examined the scene in the mother's house. In neither of the prior two cases had the mother testified truthfully, creating an alibi for the boyfriend, which we knew was false because of prior inconsistent statements that she had made. But you can't prove the truth of an event by simply showing prior inconsistent statements. You can only attack credibility of the witness that way. We could attack her credibility as to his alibi but it didn't help us prove the basic fact of what happened. It didn't help us to attack the mother's credibility when the only witnesses were the child and the abuser. And there was no way I could put that four year old girl on the stand to confront her disapproving mother and the guy who brutalized her. But Jack used the prior inconsistent statements before the Grand Jury to show the difficulty of proof when the mother and boyfriend stuck together.

The Grand Jury returned a presentment of assault with intent to murder, we filed the Indictment and then the case was rescheduled for trial.

In Grand Jury parlance, the prosecutor appears for the state and outlines the facts and then calls one or more witnesses to prove, "probable cause to believe that a crime was committed and that the defendant committed it." If the Jurors agree, they vote to present a charge to the presiding judge of the criminal bench, who turns presentments over to the prosecutor to issue Indictments. The document in which the Grand Jury's charge is specified is called the Grand Jury Presentment.

The prosecutor then has his staff type up an indictment or formal charge based on the Grand Jury Presentment. The presentment will normally contain only the charge the Grand Jury believes was committed, in this case assault with intent to murder. The Indictment, under Maryland law, had to include the charge, also every lesser penalty charge that would be included as a part of the charged crime. For example, a charge of murder in the presentation would lead to an Indictment charging murder, attempted murder, assault with intent to murder and assault. The law requiring the inclusion of all lesser included offenses often favored the defense because if counsel could raise any doubt at all, the trial jurors might compromise and find the defendant guilty only of one of the lesser included offenses.

The inclusion of all offenses often led to "compromise" verdicts when the jurors couldn't unanimously agree to guilt of the main charge. There is an adage in criminal trial parlance that "the jury wants to know who committed the crime, and doesn't want the one who committed it to get away with it." A wise old attorney told me that the first week I was in trial work in the United States Attorney's office. He told me it wasn't enough for most jurors just to believe that the state hadn't proved a case beyond a reasonable doubt. They had to know in their own minds, or at least have a rational explanation for, who actually did commit the crime before they would find "not guilty."

Over the years, I found that to be most often true. There were some major exceptions, but most often it has proven to be true. That's one of the reasons for Johnny Cochrane (one of the greatest) to get into evidence the possibilities of OJ's wife Nicole being involved in drugs and victimized by drug dealers. He thought the jury had to have some evidence of source of guilt if they were to acquit OJ.

63

In Ray Lewis's trial (Lewis, is line backer for the Baltimore Ravens, perhaps the greatest linebacker ever to play the game—and that's something for an old timer who saw Butkus, Taylor, Nitzke, and other greats from Green Bay, Baltimore, Detroit, Chicago, the Los Angeles Rams and Miami Dolphins play) the defense loaded the record with evidence of all the other people on the scene who could have committed the act with which Lewis was charged and reasons why the witnesses would lie about Lewis being the guilty one.

But inclusion of the lesser offenses could also benefit the state. If, during the trial, one element of the main charge wasn't clearly proved, the state could win on a lesser included and at least get the defendant some penitentiary time. Plus, the state could "deal" a case better with the defense by agreeing to take a plea to a lesser offense in order to get a conviction. Known as the infamous "plea bargain," the deal many times favored the defendant who wanted to avoid a major sentence.

The public does not like "plea bargains" and I don't blame them. The public thinks that too often an overworked prosecutor, a lazy prosecutor, or an inept prosecutor just gives away the farm with plea bargains to avoid having to go to trial. Police don't like plea bargains because when they have made a case, they want to see the defendant do the time for the crime he committed. In truth, without plea bargains, the incomprehensibly slow judicial process would screech to a stop similar to a metropolitan freeway at rush hour. If all prosecutors insisted on trying all cases, the strain on judges, clerks, bailiffs, jurors, prosecutors and public defenders would be so intense that the process would grind to a halt, or the public would be faced with monumental new taxes to provide for more of everything, including courtrooms paid for by the taxpayers. As it is now, when a citizen goes into a courtroom to watch a trial, he or she if a taxpayer, is paying for the building, the room, the utilities, the judge, the law clerk, the bailiff, the jurors, the prosecutor, and the defense attorney if the latter is public defender, as is most often the case. He is also paying witness fees for all witnesses who testify, and the salaries of all police officers, probation officers and jail officers who are involved with the case. Sometimes, if you are a tax paying citizen, you should go to your county offices and ask to see the budget for the district court in your county. You will be amazed at the amount, and at the percentage, it is of the total budget. Then imagine if you increased all those folks by six or ten, and all the courtrooms and buildings to facilitate all the new people. Yet, even with such increases, the process would still be slow.

Plea bargains can work the other way too. If every defense attorney asked for a jury trial in every case, the attorneys could bring a process to its knees in weeks, perhaps days. We are fortunate in this country that defense attorneys will not do that. They won't act together like that because it is not financially feasible for them. A good defense attorney gets paid well for moving his client through the process with the least penalty possible. That means he has to "play ball" with the others in the process, judges, prosecutors and schedule setters, so he can get favorable settings before favorable judges and not aggravate the prosecutors to the point at which the chief or lead prosecutors take on his cases. And, again, it is not financially feasible. Good defense attorneys don't make the majority of their income on trials. They make far more profit on plea bargains where they bargain away charges to the interest of their clients. And, keep in mind while Johnny Cochrane and the "dream team" were making hundreds of thousands in the Simpson trial, they were not handling hundreds of cases where they could make real good money for six minutes in court.

64

And back to the child abuse case. The indictment charged assault
with intent to murder and abuse of a child.   To gain a conviction
of the major charge, I faced the necessity of convincing the court
there was intent on the part of the defendant to murder the little
girl. The judge would have to infer the intent from the "totality of
the circumstances."

The four- year- old victim could not credibly testify because of
her memory loss resulting from her fall down the stairs, or blows
struck before she fell. The defendant, the live-in boyfriend, did not
have to testify. We could force the mother to take the stand, but she
would lie for the defendant. She had told officers that she arrived
home with groceries, and the defendant came out to help her in
with them. As they were on the front steps, she said, they heard
screams come from the little girl. They raced in and found her at
the bottom of stairs. The mother had told police the little girl was
clumsy and had a long history of falling and getting hurt. Since this
was before statutes authorizing and obligating medical personnel to
notify police and a doctor when seeing injuries that are inconsistent
with accidental explanations, hospital records would not have help

me because they would have described injuries but no conclusions as to causation.

I did have a doctor in this case who would testify. The doctor, who was part of the medical department of the Supreme Bench, had examined the x-rays and hospital records in the case and was prepared to testify as an expert that a fall down the stairs could not result in the severity of the head injury in this case, and to testify that the number and placement of injuries was consistent with abuse by an adult.

This was before the time when courts could admit opinion evidence that abuse had occurred, and when such testimony was sufficient to convict. So my evidence from the scene would be that the child fell while the two immoral adults were outside the house. The medical records would corroborate the mother's story that the child had repeatedly been treated for injuries "caused by accident (per) the child's mother." I knew that I couldn't use the defendant's story as contradictory as it was. A judge could easily make a finding that the defendant was not truthful and that still didn't give me the proof the defendant, rather than the mother, hurt the child.

The defense attorney was high priced and I knew he wasn't hired on the money that came to this unholy crowd through the mother's welfare. The defendant was valuable to someone with money and any income from that source did not show up in regular, lawful employment. I would get nowhere trying to show where he worked and who paid him. The money man had made sure of in providing expensive trial counsel to see he didn't get convicted.

I had scheduled the case before the most severe punisher on the bench and the attorney didn't want to take a chance on the legal technicalities winning for him. Neither did he want to count on the fact that the judge would refrain from leaping the evidence gap and inferring guilt from the witnesses' testimony. He offered to drop his double jeopardy argument and plead to the simple abuse of a child, with jail time of thirty days and probation. I told him the double jeopardy argument had no solid base, because I had stetted the prior charge the defendant never faced a jury or judge as trier of the facts and therefore was not in jeopardy. He knew that.

I then took a real chance and turned down the offer. I did tell him that I would agree to only two years in jail, if he would drop his appeal in the prior case and plead guilty in that case and the current case. I didn't want to do even that, but I knew the legal risk of trying the major charge, winning and having the decision successfully defended by the AG in the Maryland Court of Appeals (which is the Supreme Court of Maryland). The court was not famous for favoring inferences of guilt from circumstantial evidence. On the other hand, I understood also the risk that the judge himself would not be willing to take the chance of making the necessary inferences. Oh, for a jury in this case. But the defendant refused. Whatever he did for the lawyer's moneyman, he had street smarts.

We tried the case. Judge Carter, who was known as the "hanging judge," but was an objective trier of facts, first denied the defendant's motion to dismiss on the double jeopardy grounds. The defendant claimed that since I stetted the first charge, it was double jeopardy to bring back a higher charge. I knew the doctrine of double jeopardy didn't apply because the defendant is not put at jeopardy until a jury is sworn or a case begins under a court with jury waived. After all the testimony, Judge Carter found the defendant guilty of the main charge. Once I put the doctor on the stand, the defendant made the mistake of taking the stand, thinking he had to free himself from the cloud the doctor left in the air. Once the defendant was there, I could cross examine him on the prior cases of abusing this very child. Judge Carter relied on the prior cases to take this case outside the limitations of simple abuse. Whether that reliance, as substantive evidence, would hold up on appeal was questionable at best. The Maryland court had many times said that evidence of prior offenses served only to diminish the credibility of the witness but had never held in a case like this that admissions of prior offenses could serve as substantive evidence of a pattern. He then sentenced the defendant to the maximum twelve years in prison.

Within three days, the defendant's attorney filed an appeal and requested an appeal bond. The normal way for getting an appeal bond set was to take simply the appeal notice to the trial judge with the clerk's stamp on it showing that it had been filed. The trial judge then put an amount of bond on the notice and the defendant posted it and awaited the appeal on the street. Judge Carter denied the request and scheduled a hearing. At the hearing, I produced evidence of the prior convictions and evidence as to the facts in those cases. Judge Carter, calling the defendant a menace to this child and seeing nothing in the record that would persuade him that the mother would take any action to protect her child from this abuser, denied the bond.

It tickled the hell out of me, looking at the face of that attorney who had told his client that I was stetting the case because I was afraid to lose. No, I just didn't like to lose, not then, not today. It was hard to see who was most startled, the defendant or his attorney. I would have given most anything to see the look on the money man's face when he got the news and then had to worry about his guy starting to spill the beans to try to get out of jail free. It would have to be with someone else. I wouldn't have made a deal with that guy for all the money and successful cases in the world.

The next day, I had been assigned to the same courtroom and before beginning my assignment the judge called me back into chambers. He looked at me, smiled and said, "Well, he will get me reversed, but in the meantime he will be subjected to some administrative justice." It seemed to me to be the best concept I had heard in a long time. It wasn't something that I would have approved of upon graduation from the University of Chicago but after a few years watching the system not work, I thought it was a good concept. If I were to teach law now, I certainly would include a portion on administrative justice.

One element of the justice that the judge had imposed was the attitude the defendant would encounter in prison. Mostly unknown at the time to the general public, was the fact that inmates did not like child abusers and let the abusers know about it. By the time the Court of Appeals heard this defendant's case and reversed the conviction, he would have suffered even more than his four- year-old victim had suffered. And he would have known exactly why he was being abused by inmates, while in her innocence she would have had no idea as to why she was brutalized. The average time then for processing appeals was probably eighteen to twenty four months, so he had some serious time during which to regret his actions. As a bonus, the "money man" had to worry about his caving in and testifying as to what he did for a living.

65

I continued to handle these abuse cases when they showed up on regular dockets. The system in our office was that each attorney was assigned to handle the cases on the regular docket for that courtroom. The prosecutor didn't often see the cases until a couple of days before trial. Normally, the prosecutor looked over the files quickly and determined whether he had to talk to witnesses before the morning of trial.

If advance talk was required, it was usually necessary to talk to the officer on the case and try to get him to contact the witness. In most cases, there was no telephone number for the witness and often the address was wrong. So, no subpoena would have been served although sometimes the return of the sheriff showed delivery of the subpoena even when there was no house or building at the address where it was supposedly served. So contact with the officer was critical. Most often that contact had to come from home at night because of the officer's shift assignments and the prosecutor's office duties.

When a regular docket showed a child abuse case, you prepared it in the same, regular manner in spite of the difficult evidentiary problems existed. No advance notice was given to the prosecutor that a child abuse case was coming his way.

One night, as I was going through files for court the next day before Judge Anselm Sodaro, I saw that one of them was a very bad abuse case. Judge Sodaro was one of my favorites. He was Italian, soft spoken, but had been States' Attorney and a very good one. He was a quiet, solemn appearing judge who had a great sense of humor and sense of justice. A very short man in height, he barely saw over the huge marble benches that graced the Supreme Bench courtrooms.

He was serving his tour of duty as presiding judge of the criminal division. Sitting in the largest courtroom, he was in charge of assignments and could re-direct cases to other judges in the criminal division who finished their regular case assignments. The Supreme Bench judges were assigned for a year's time to either criminal, civil, or equity.

Regularly, the lead prosecutor of the two assigned to a courtroom met with the judge the day before and reviewed the docket as to whether there were obvious jury trials, motions for suppression, or any unique issues that the judge would want to be ready to handle. I didn't even discuss the abuse case because there were no procedural problems with it.

The case involved a child who was thrown down the stairs into a basement, after being burned in several spots on the body with a very hot object, probably a hair straightener. The straightener is a cast iron double-pole device is heated until almost red hot before use. I couldn't imagine how painful it must have been for a two-year-old to be burned with a red hot straightener in seven places on the body, including on both buttocks. The burns were so severe that the skin was gone and the wounds were bleeding. How can one imagine what kind of adult beast it would take to abuse a child like that and then cast him down the stairs as if throwing away an old worn out towel. The cries from that child must have been horrible and must have been heard throughout the neighborhood. But no one came forward to tell about it. No body called the police. Nobody discovered the little unconscious guy until his mother got home from work and found him sprawled on the basement floor.

I started my case by putting on the testimony of the police officer who was first on the scene. Arriving in front of even the medical ambulance (pronounced in Baltimorean language as ambeeelance). He found the victim lying in the middle of a pool of blood at the foot of the stairs that led from the kitchen to the basement. The child had fresh burn marks on his back and buttocks, which appeared to be made by a straightening iron. The marks were still bleeding. The child was unconscious. The mother said she had just arrived from work and saw the boy and called the police. She had not been into the basement, and made a special point of emphasizing that. In fact, according to the officer, she was more concerned about the facts of the case than she was about the condition of her child. Two hours into the investigation, she still had not asked how the child was doing.

The "at home boyfriend" told the officer at the scene that the baby must have moved the chair blocking the stairs. He told the officer he had no idea how the baby got the burn marks. The officer could find no straightener in the house and the mother told him that she did not hurt the baby, and that neither she nor the boyfriend used a hair straighter. Since the boyfriend did not testify in his own behalf, I could not cross examine him as to the truth of the story told to the police.

I called the doctor, with whom I had discussed the case the night before, and he testified that the head injuries as well as the other fractures of the arms and legs could not have resulted from a simple fall down the stairs. He also testified that the wounds from the hot iron were no more than two-to three hours old when he saw the child in the emergency room. The defense attorney called the mother, who testified that the boyfriend was with her when they discovered the child, that he had never lost his temper with the child, that he took care of the child every day while she worked and that she had left the child's father and took up with the boyfriend because the father was too rough with the child.

On cross, I took a real chance and asked whether the boyfriend had ever abused her, which she denied. I took another chance and asked the mother why the medical records at the same hospital that treated her child showed that she had shown up for emergency treatment and I struck pay dirt. It turned out that the guy had beaten her on several occasions that had required medical attention and that once he had grabbed her and tried to strangle her with the cord of a straightener. I quickly asked, "I thought you testified that you didn't own a hair straightener." She double talked a bit, and finally said that after he attacked her with the cord she threw the iron away. After he had straightened up she bought another one, which she could not find after the child was hurt. The defense made a mistake in calling her to the stand. But, while showing the defendant to be the brutal ass I thought he was, it didn't help with the base evidence from which the judge would have to take the inference of guilt.

The defense rested at the end of the mother's testimony. Judge Sodaro asked if I had rebuttal and I had to just shrug and say, "No your honor, that, unfortunately, is all the state can offer." His comment should have tipped me off as to what he planned to do. He said, "I understand, Mr. Grant. I've been there myself where there was nothing more I could do."

He then asked the defendant to stand, found him guilty, and set no appeal bail. He asked the clerk to note on the disposition sheet that "Judge Sodaro recommends no bail be set for this defendant." By placing this notation on the disposition sheet, Judge Sodaro was saying to the other judges, "This is a bad case and bail set will cripple my plan to get the defendant back on track."

That was the last case on the docket for the day. After the courtroom cleared I walked back into the court's chambers. When I walked into the secretary's office, the door to the judge's office was closed. I asked if he was in conference, and she said, "No. He said if you came in to have you go on in.

So I knocked and walked in. He was standing behind his desk, still in his robe, and a glass in his hand. He looked at me and said, "Fred, you know I will get reversed on that decision, but it will take them a year to get to the case, and by that time he will have served the year, so I don't regret what I have done."

I said, "Well, judge, it seems to me that you just did some administrative justice." He asked whether they taught that at Chicago. I said, "Oh no, judge, they insist on regular justice. I only heard about administrative justice the last time I was in Judge Carter's court." This time he laughed out loud and said, "Oh my God, do you mean I just applied the Joe Carter rule of law?" I said, "Yeah, but I think it's worth teaching at Chicago." He said, "Well, let's just hope that you and I don't have to apply it so often that I resemble the Star Chamber more than the Circuit of Baltimore."

I went to my boss's office that afternoon, and asked Charlie to relieve me of having to try child abuse cases. I told him, "I look at those kids and I think of my Andrew, and I look at these damn mothers who are willing to sacrifice their kids for some trashy or worse boyfriends and I cannot be objective. It bothers me too much, and I'm afraid that I will go to any ends to get convictions." Even though Charley didn't yet have kids, he told me that he never handled abuse cases either, unless it was homicide so he could go for "big time penalties." He said he couldn't really focus on them when there was no strategy that could be used to get around the blind laws that protected the defendants from the women testifying.

That's when he told me he had been working on a schedule that would form teams and put a team in a courtroom for a full month at a time, so that cases could be better prepared ahead of time. He told me I was to be one of the team leaders, and with three others assigned to me, I could avoid trying the abuse cases, that there would be one of the three who wouldn't mind them.

Administrative justice, or at least administrative fairness or administrative efficiency, often takes precedence to the rules of evidence and rules of law. The "criminal justice system" is billed as the systemic manner in which judge, prosecutor, defense, support staff, pre-sentence investigators, probation officers, jailers, wardens, parole officers, scheduling and secretarial assistants all work together to attain justice for all. Well, it doesn't work that way.

66

As a prosecutor, often the aim was to win and the belief was that a conviction would bring justice. As a defense attorney, I never had a client who came to me and said, "Fred, I want you to get me justice." Rather, the client did not want to go to jail, or if jail was guaranteed, he or she didn't want to go for any longer than necessary. In all most every case, at least one of the participants has a bias for the victim or defendant going into the trial and the bias remains throughout the trial. It is a pure myth that every defendant is dealt with even handedly, regardless of means. A well- connected, or rich, defendant most often gets a favor from at least one of the participants that the poor, un-connected defendant does not get.

In some cases, regardless of the standing of the defendant, it takes a GOOD, unbiased prosecutor to see to fairness, if not justice, when the defense attorney is so bad that he or she is a detriment rather than an advantage. In some cases, it takes a good defense attorney to overcome the incredible bias of the "system" for the prosecution, regardless of quality of prosecutor. Sometimes, a good judge has to see to fairness in the face of incompetence on the part of prosecutors and defense attorneys.

When a party steps in to make sure the competence of the system is preserved, is that an example of administrative justice? Maybe or maybe not, it's just an example of administrative balance. Do the examples defy the Constitution? That is an interesting question for the serious scholar. But to those of us in the pits, it didn't seem to matter. We did what we had to do to try to strike a balance.

I was really put to the test when I was assigned a guy Charley hired because he wanted to help out a friend. The guy had worked in the clerk's office while going to night law school and was not really very quick. He was a good guy. When the day came that he was to be assigned during staff meeting, all team leaders were holding our breath. Howard Cardin was absent because he was still in court. He told me to make sure he didn't get the new guy. I said, I would do all that I could to see that he did get him. Self preservation came before friendship.

Charley started off by announcing that the new guy had been admitted to the bar. We had already heard that from old Jim Coles, the permanent clerk in the Part I courtroom where the presiding judge of the criminal bench always sat. Jim was the best of the clerks, had the best memory for cases and defendants, but was also the most outspoken and biased of the clerks. Just a day or two before, he passed Howard, Pete Ward and I in the hall and said, "Well, the idiot passed the bar and got admitted. One of you guys will be stuck with him. Just keep him out of my court."

Jim always chewed on the stub of a cigar between court sessions. He carefully placed the stub on the ledge of the marble counter in front of his work area, right at the base of the bench. He was what H.L. Mencken would call a "curmudgeon," always able to frown and find fault with inept attorneys. He could do the same with good attorneys who just didn't do things the way he would have done them.

Jim was the number one information man in the courthouse. He knew all, heard all and told all that suited his purposes to tell. He barely crept along most of the times. But if you saw him streaking down the hall, you knew he was scurrying to be the first to spread a new rumor or fact. When he was in scurry mode, there was no evidence of the arthritic pain of which he constantly complained.

His cigar stub was not in his mouth, we thought probably he was so intent on delivering news that he was afraid he would bite through it.

Charley asked us for suggestions as to where to assign the new guy. Damned if one of my good friend's didn't speak up and say he should get the opportunity to work with and learn from the best. He ought to go to Howard or me because we had the best teams who could train him. Charley smiled and looked at me, waiting for me to comment. I said, "Well, charley I would love to have the chance to work with him and train him but I think it would be better for his advancement if he were with Howard because we are stuck with the narcotics cases which involve so many technical motions and rules that he won't get access to the full application of the evidence rules." I was proud of my quick thinking. Charley smiled and said, "Oh, Fred, I think you can guide him through the evidentiary snags in narcotics and when he wins there he will have a lot more confidence. Besides, Judge Sodaro is patient and will go easy with him while he is learning."

By the time I walked into Part I the next morning, Jim Coles had already heard. He said, "My God, you're one of the pets over there and you couldn't pawn that bird off on somebody else?" I said, "Well, Jim, I think the reason Charley assigned him to me is because you're the best clerk and you can teach him so much about courtroom procedures." He looked at me, scowled, pulled out the stub, lit it, and turned on me and walked out of the courtroom.

At the end of that day's assignment, Jim told me that Judge Sodaro wanted to see me in chambers. When I walked in, The Judge said, "Well, Fred, I hear you got the new man who used to be in the clerk's office. I can be patient, but you must be careful which cases to give him. And someone must be in the courtroom at all times with him, because as you know he is not quite sharp." My duties were clear: babysit the new guy. When I walked out of chambers, Jim was standing just outside the secretary's office chewing on his cigar, and around the cigar he said, You had it coming, big shot." I wondered if Jim just programmed the judge, or had a listening device in chambers.

The first week after the new guy joined my team, the Maryland

Prosecutor's Association convention was scheduled for Ocean city. Charley wanted all of us there, or as many as possible with the need of keeping at least four courts operating. Several of us had written articles for the Prosecutor's Manual for the National Association of Prosecutors, and we were scheduled to speak.

I knew we couldn't leave the new guy alone with Judge Sodaro, so I volunteered to miss the convention and stay behind. Charley said no, we should leave the new man alone. So I went in to Judge Sodaro to warn him. The judge said he could understand why Charley wanted me to speak, and wanted to reward the others on my team because they had worked hard. He said if he noticed a case that he or Jim could remember was a serious defendant, he could postpone it. Jim was standing with us in chambers, and he scowled and said, "Judge, it's going to be a damned long day, a Black Friday." Judge Sodaro laughed and said, "Oh, Jim, it won't be so bad, we'll make it through all right." Jim chewed on his cigar, and said, "Well, I'm going to stock up on bourbon in my water cup."

My number two chair, Jim Dudley (who was a terrific trial lawyer) and I looked at all the files and assured ourselves that they were all users and not pushers. So off to Ocean City we went.

On Monday morning, I walked into Courtroom one and encountered a grinning Jim Coles. The grin was because "he told me so." He said, "Well, we had a banner day, a record day and almost perfect. We had eighteen cases on the docket, and sixteen acquittals. *You sure as hell trained him well.* You owe me a bottle of the best damned bourbon bottled." I looked at the docket sheet he had held out to flaunt me with. Sure enough, sixteen "NGs" for not guilty and only two guilty. I went in to apologize to Judge Sodaro. He said, "Oh don't worry about it. We'll see those sixteen again. I just decided to let the chips fall where they might and he didn't get the evidence in. But I did recognize a couple of serious defendants and I helped him get the evidence in on them." It took the judge to reach some kind of balance in the "justice system."

67

There were times when we put administrative justice into play on the streets too. I have talked about "The Block" on Baltimore Street, just about two blocks from the courthouse. In the four blocks of "The Block," were strip bars, porno book stores, gypsy fortune telling stands, a pinball machine palace known as "Pollock Johnnie's," which also had the best chili dogs this side of South Carolina and entire wall of various and sundry condoms, a hamburger shop with delicious grilled burgers and about twenty pay telephone booths in the back to serve the bookies who frequented the grill and the Gayety Burlesque House where prominent strippers, including Blaze Starr, came to entertain. Anything illegal, including a hit on someone's life, could be purchased on the Block.

At one end of the Block, the Baltimore court house and federal courthouse was a block away; at the other end was, the Central Police Station.

Captain Tony Glover was head of homicide-robbery for the city, and his squad was stationed at Central. He was one of my very favorite officers. There wasn't an officer in his command who I didn't trust and like to work with. Some were finesse oriented, others were street strong but all were very competent and were very cooperative in working up a case so it could be successfully prosecuted. Some officers resented any request or suggestion by a prosecutor as to what extras were required for successful prosecution but not in Captain Tony's command.

Glover and his men also enjoyed having a good time. I remember the first day he called and told me they had just gotten a bulletin about a homicide fugitive from North Carolina who might be in Baltimore or Atlantic City. He asked if I wanted to go with his group to "turn out" the Block. I asked him, "What do you have that says he might be on the Block?" He said, "What do I have that says he is not on the Block?" Getting the point quickly, I took Bob Stewart and Joe Kiel, two of my assistants and we met the homicide guys about a half block from The Block.

We walked around the corner that ends the Block and went quickly into the first strip bar on the Block. As we walked in, every customer put his hands on the bar, the bartenders put their hands on the bar, one officer unplugged the juke box, another officer headed straight back toward the office, while another told the bartender not to hit the silent alarm button.

The stripper, not a bad- looking blonde, was "dressed" in a tight pair of silky panties and just pasties on her breasts. She was totally bored when we walked in. When the music was cut off, she hardly missed a step. She kept right on dancing, without music, and looked even more bored. As she went through her dance routine, she watched what we did and listened to the conversations going on out in front of her. As the officers searched the seven or eight men still at the bar, she kicked her legs, did the split movement, and bent over the bar with her breasts swinging down right in front of the officer searching the guy in that area. As she moved closer and hit his head with one of her breasts, I thought he was going to come out of his skin. I have never seen an adult react so vividly to physical contact. The little lady simply stood up and started dancing again.

Glover and I walked into the office to talk to the manager. We showed him the picture of the fugitive and asked whether he had seen the guy. He said he hadn't seen him but would call if he did.

Tony asked him how business was, and he said, "It was good until you jerks come in."

As we walked out of the office and back along the long bar, the dancer had stopped dancing finally and was leaning back against the pole. As we passed her she almost spit out, "Thanks for nothing you f--ks." Sterling Fletcher said over his shoulder, "That's not nice talk for a young lady." As we left the bar, we looked up the street and the sidewalk was filled with guys who had left the other bars as soon as they heard we were in the first one. They were lined up at the edge of the sidewalk, some leaning on parking meters. They were making small talk pretending not to pay attention to.

We walked the Block, showing the photograph and asking many, many very nervous guys whether they had seen the fugitive. When we came to a strip bar, we went in to see whether anyone had stayed inside. Nobody was inside but the girls, sitting around in fishnet stockings and skimpy outfits, waiting for the customers to come back in. As we went into the second club we came to, the dancer was standing right in front of the door in just her "g-string" and pasties. She glared at us and said, "What the f- - k are you jerks doing?" One of the detectives shot back, "We had word that your mother was dancing here, so we came to check it out." Being yet untrained as to the Block, I said, more seriously, "We're looking for a homicide fugitive. Have you seen this guy?" She said, "I ain't seen nobody unless they shove cash in this chastity belt. So why don't you take a hike and let a working girl make a living." I said, "Okay" as we walked out.

As we walked both sides of the Block, the guys on the street just stood, talking, while they waited outside for us to talk to the management and dancers inside. None of the dancers came out, and we joked that the sun wouldn't be good for their make-up. While we walked the street, virtually every penny of profit for The Block was cut off. Finally, near the Central Station house, we decided to end the exercise, and one of Glover's funniest detectives announced, "Well, comrades, today we have done the Lord's work."

My assistants and I had such a good time watching a whole criminal enterprise stop for a few minutes in time, that we decided to go every once in awhile to have lunch at either the burger grill or

Pollock Johnnie's. When we decided to go, I always called Glover and when he could, he joined us with a detective or two. As soon as we passed the corner bar, the word spread that we were on the Block. People started emerging from bars, porn shops, and the gypsy fortune tellers up and down the Block. Many of the dirty book stores closed their doors and put the "closed" sign in the windows.

When we got to the burger grill, we walked in, gave our order to the chef at the grill and sat at two of the four tables. Along a very long counter with twenty or thirty stools, the bookies sat, drinking their coffee. About the time we got our burgers and fries served, the telephones in the pay booths in the back of the shop started ringing. It was time for the bets to start coming in for the Pimlico races that day. The telephones rang and rang. And none of the bookies got up to go answer them. They just sipped their coffee, visibly nervous, looking around at us and grinning when they found us looking back. At one point, one of Glover's men asked, "Isn't anybody going to answer those phones in case it's an emergency?" Not a word in answer. The bookies just looked around at us, then at each other, kind of shrugged off "No, I guess not," and let the phones ring. We finished our lunch, and then sat and talked while we enjoyed our Cokes. Finally the phones quit ringing. Pimlico's first run had ended. For nearly an hour, we stopped track business for the bookies that day.

68

We also would walk to Pollock Johnnie's and have a chili dog. It was about in the middle of the Block, and our visit pretty well stopped everything in the book stores and the gypsy fortune telling shops that were near Johnnie's. It was always fun to watch the customers rushing out of the gypsy shops, trying to tuck in their shirts as they moved. The strip bars all emptied too. When we went into Pollock Johnnie's, people even quit playing the in-line pinball machines. Johnnie had fifteen of the machines sitting at the rear of his store. Even though the pinballs didn't pay out money from a chute like a slot machine, there was a payoff. The player had to get his payoff from the store keeper or bar keeper, and no one could collect their machine winnings while we were there. As we ate our dogs and drank our drinks, some people would stand awkwardly at the machines, leaning against them so no one else would play them and mess up the number of games that indicated how much was owed the players. It was really hard for them to look disinterested when they knew their winnings were dependent on their being able to save those games shown on the machines.

One day, the "card" of Glover's squad, Sterling Fletcher,

"tripped" over a power cord from one of the pinballs, groused about how unsafe the cords were and went along unplugging them all. A general groan went up and those had been protecting their games disappointedly slinked away, I'm sure cursing cops. Others, who hadn't won anything, went outside and stood leaning against parking meters until we were finished and left.

One of the porn shop keepers pimped out two girls from the back of the store. One day, while we were having our chili dogs, they came in, dressed in short, short shorts and halter tops. They ordered lunch and came over to a table to sit down. We started talking to them and asked if there was any action with women on the Block. They said, "Yeah we're all the action you'll need." I said to them, "No, I think we need some older dancers for a bachelor's party." One of the girls said, "You'll be making a big mistake if you don't take us, we're better than anybody else you'll get down here. We're better than those battered up old strippers." I asked about the price and they said, "Two hundred an hour." "Each?" I asked. When they said, "Yes," I said, "That's a little steep." Then the bargaining began, and we finally got them down to one hundred twenty-five dollars an hour apiece.

We agreed to pick them up at the other end of the Block in fifteen minutes so we could "audition" them. They left, and after we used the pay phone to call the vice squad, we walked down to the point to meet. When the girls arrived, I asked them what they were going to do for us for the one hundred twenty-five dollars and they listed off every sex act I had ever heard of and some I hadn't. I pulled out some bills and handed them to the girl, and the vice officers made their arrest. We gave the girls the chance to become informants for the vice squad and avoid the arrest and charges. They instantly agreed, and left with the officers to be debriefed as to where they worked and how they worked.

A few minutes later, I realized that I hadn't gotten back my money. I called the vice squad, and an officer said they would search the girls for the money. In a few minutes, I got a call back that said the police woman's search of the bodies had not come up with any money but they would do some invasive searches. In another few minutes, the call came that the one hundred twenty-five dollars had been found. I did not ask where, or what invasive search turned it up.

We learned that when we went to Pollock Johnnie's, the boys at the bookie station in the burger grill went on with their business as usually. So we started splitting up when we went down for lunch, two or three going to Pollock Johnnie's and two or three to the burger shop. We didn't want to discriminate against one or the other. Those of us who picked Pollock Johnnie's opted for great chili dogs, eaten in a classic pin ball salon-must have been the loudest chili dog establishment in the world. Behind the cash register, covering an entire wall from floor to ceiling was a mass display of condoms. Every color, every theme topic, every surface texture, but we never witnessed anyone buying. May have been that we put a damper on the business.

We also tried to stop in at least one book shop on each trip down to the Block. These shops had racks containing nothing but pornographic magazines and pocket books. Had it not been for my experiences with the pornographic import business in the U.S. Attorney's office, I would have been as surprised as the rest of our group at the huge number of such magazines. Previously, *Hustler* was a shocking example of *Playboy* gone wild. But walking into one of the Block book shops took one to a new plateau in the world of graphic sex. These magazines contained no "redeeming social value" in the form of articles or features. The "redeeming social value" is the old standard of obscenity established by the Supreme Court of the United States. Even given the standard, there is more truth than fiction to Justice Potter Stewart's personal test for obscenity: "I know it when I see it." We saw it in the book stores on the Block.

As we picked up copies of magazines and turned pages, the clerks got more and more nervous, trying to make small talk. We made it worse by just answering their questions with answers like "Oh we're just making a last minute check", or "Well, we're trying to check out what we've been told." Always there was at least one hushed talk on the telephone, which rang not long after we entered the store. As I later would find out, when I actually represented some distributors who owned these stores, this was the distributor who owned the store trying to find out whether we were going to seize magazines, and wanting to know what we bought, if anything.

We often joked about the fact that we probably cost crime more on our jaunts for lunch, or on a homicide sweep, than we did in a year of cases in court. Whether we were right, or jut dreaming, it was fun to watch crime slow down. In retrospect, looking back on our trips to the Block, in the light of what I found out after I entered defense work, we did deprive them of a lot of money-but not in the way we thought. We did disrupt their cash flow while we were there and strip club customers were on the sidewalk outside but the greater damage was what we caused in the changes owners made as a result of our trips. Many changes in operations took place for several days after a trip. The strippers were toned down on sexual acts performed in the booths and that activity was a real cash cow. Bookies changed their routine for a few days, and any change of routine caused confusion and disconnect with regular gambling customers. Movement of stolen goods through the book stores was curtailed for quite awhile after our trips. All owners were worried that any one of our trips was a precursor to a raid, or to a focus on undercover officers setting up arrests.

69

One final example comes from a sideline to conducting serious raids on drug houses. Probably the finest of the detectives-most honest, most ethical and most prepared-was Sergeant Steve Tabeling of the Northern District. He was a workaholic who left no stone unturned when he was preparing a raid, or preparing a case for arrest and then later for court. He was not a favorite of the Central Administration of Police Commissioner Pomerleau, because he didn't suffer politics well and didn't suffer administrative shenanigans that covered up problems at all. When he worked a case, it did not matter who the defendant was, or what his or her connections were. If the defendant violated the law, he or she had to worry about Tabeling and about the fact that he wasn't for sale.

When we worked up a warrant with Tabeling and his squad, we began going with his men to learn why cases were later not successful in court. When a raid was conducted by plain clothes detectives like Tabeling's, it was policy to call for uniform officers in marked police cruisers to accompany us to the site of the raid. This was necessary so people in the community where the raid was executed knew it was police, and not a raid by drug competitors. A group of men busting open a door in the dead of night, with shouts of instructions to the people being raided and to other officers, created quite a scene. It was important for anyone in the neighborhood responding to the noise to see the police presence.

Why raid, instead of just knocking on the door and making an arrest? These houses that we were raiding were regularly heavily armed and the occupants always prepared to fight off drug competitors. The doors were fortified by two- by- four blocks, and some with iron plates shoring up the door. These precautions were taken not to keep the police out but to provide protection against warring factions in the drug trade. If one competitor knew that a huge delivery had been made to a house that served as a "drop," it became a prime target for a crime raid.

The people who were armed were often high on cough syrup, and there was hardly any substance that could cause a person to fight more than the syrup. The houses were stocked with plentiful drugs of all kinds, because no house owner wanted to turn away customers. Many of these houses also served as "shooting galleries," places where a heroin user could go to make a buy and have someone heat the heroin to solution state and inject it into a vein. The user then went into his stupor and could rest or sleep in the "gallery" until he could function again. If these people got startled by someone moving around and searching, they could come out of their stupor with violence.

It was safer and more effective to hit the doors, front and back, break them down quickly and get to the people inside before they could prepare to fight and before they could destroy the drug supply. The raiding officers then could also locate the shot- up users and get them neutralized.

But Tabeling never arranged for back up until we were ready to conduct the raid under the search warrant. He would drive to a location a good distance from the actual search site and call for "back up for a turn out." He told me that he did this so no one in the department could warn any operations near the site that there might be a raid coming. He was convinced from his experiences in the department that there were payoffs even in the communications area. For a long time, I thought perhaps Steve was just paranoid because of his many run-ins with the Department brass and who played the political game. Steve had most of his run-ins trying to enforce gambling laws. Protection of the gambling trade and the "bigs" in that trade went high up into the administration. So he would put in his call in for back up from a site distant from the actual raid location. When the uniforms showed up, he then gave them the actual address and they led us there.

One night Steve said, "You think I'm paranoid, tonight I'm going to show you." We drove to a spot by the lake at the fringe of Druid Hill Park. He pulled over in a dark location and pointed out a building up the block. He said, "That's Jackie's whore house. Just watch what happens when I put in the call." He then radioed for "uniform support for a 'turn-out'" at the specified location. Then we sat in the quiet of the late evening. He explained that Jackie had once run a "house" in his Northern District but got tired of his hassling raids and positioning cars outside her place every once in awhile. So she moved into the Central District where there was no Tabeling. Steve had told me that operators like Jackie paid money for early warnings from communications.

Just a couple of minutes after his radio call, out from Jackie's place rushed three girls and three men, one carrying his shoes in his hands. They all scurried to cars and sped off. Then out came this very short, very hefty woman, who kind of waddled as she tried to run. Under a street light over what proved to be her car, I could see a head of short red hair that looked like a brillo pad. As she neared her car, Tabeling yelled out, "Hey, Jackie, we ain't after you tonight." She stopped, turned toward us about a block away and screamed out in a squawky voice, "Tabeling, you son of a bitch, you'll get yours." She slowly waddled back to her door, stopping again to shake her fist in our direction and call Tabeling some other names that I couldn't decipher-she had calmed her voice after the first surprised outburst. After all, she had to keep up the standards of quiet in the neighborhood. Steve said, "Well, that takes care of her for the rest of the night."

(Years later, after I left the States Attorney's office and was defending criminal cases, Jackie was my client and I reminded her of that night and told her I was with Tabeling. She remembered the night, called me a "son of a bitch," then took the edge off her voice and said, "But, you saw the light, honey." She told me that Tabeling's "stunt," as she put it, cost her five thousand dollars in lost profits that night alone. And, she lamented, the three guys who had to be hustled out, never came back. But even though she acknowledged it appeared that she had paid off someone for early warning, she never told me who it was, or what she paid.)

INFORMANTS

70

Police crime clearances would be much lower if it were not for informants- a class of people probably less popular than even lawyers and politicians. Criminals live and operate in a dark, underground subculture where police and honest citizens are unwelcome. The residents of this subculture don't volunteer information to the law, don't freely answer questions, they don't admit to seeing what is right before them and always "look the other way" to assure survival.

Without informants, most contract "hits" (murders) would not be solved and punished, most organized armed robberies and professional burglaries would not be solved and punished and most drug dealers would evade the law even more than they now do. Without informants, even the placement of undercover officers within the criminal structure would be much more difficult and dangerous. Informants provide the information about the hierarchy of the organizations that allow undercover officers to be eased into the operations.

Undercover agents like Joseph D. Pistone (of "Donnie Brasco" fame) are necessary elements to the prosecution of organized crime "families." His penetration of the infamous Bonanno family resulted in two hundred indictments and one hundred convictions of mafia members. Most criminal clearances from "undercover secret" information come from "informants" rather than law officers working under cover. Criminals and friends of criminals who want to avoid prison themselves turn on their friends, and provide information to law officers even as they continue to break the law.

Some informants provide information in exchange for money and police departments maintain funds from which they can take money to pay for that information. But the vast majority of informants provide information in exchange for immunity for themselves, to evade prison terms for their own violations of the law.

When the organized crime division was first established in the Baltimore State's Attorney's Office, we started operations without any informants providing information directly to us. We helped police officers with preparation of affidavits for their search warrants, with seizure operations and with arrest process, on the basis of information from informants unknown to us. That's how we wanted it. We had no process for protecting the security of informant information,

Long before the organized crime unit was initiated many of us noticed on our routine rotation into the narcotics court there were no defendants who appeared to be big drug dealers. We tried lots of drug users and users who dealt with other users. But where were the "big" dealers, where were the dealers who distributed to street -corner dealers, where were the distributors who brought drugs into the state? To tell the truth, I asked the question only in passing and paid little attention to the lack of enforcement against the "big" dealers. Only when I was plodding through the cases I handled during a day's assignment to the court handling drug cases was I even concerned.

When I first went into the State's Attorney's office, narcotics cases were tried only in one of the criminal courtrooms, usually no drug cases were tried in any other court. As a usual thing, two days before court an assistant got a docket sheet attached to those files identified on the docket that could be found. The docket sheet was an oversized yellow sheet that contained courtroom number, name of judge, case numbers of the cases scheduled, names of defendants, charges involved in the cases and the pleas entered at arraignment.

In each court, one assistant was in charge of making sure the docket was ready and the cases were ready to go. It was up to him to assign case files to himself and to the second assistant for preparation and presentation. Drug cases were handled in this manner, just as all non-drug cases.

As a usual thing, the files for drug cases contained nothing more than an indictment, a police report (if one existed) and a transcript of the grand jury proceeding (which was usually a page or less of summary of the case). Preparation for trial of the drug cases consisted of making a telephone call to make sure the narcotics officer would be present in court. The officer brought with him the evidence and the lab report verifying that the seized substance was a prohibited drug, or that the paraphernalia (syringes, glassine baggies) contained traces of a prohibited drug. Each of the narcotics officers could be qualified as an expert to testify that paraphernalia was used in the drug trade. Most of the cases were either in for pleas of guilty, or were tried by the court on an agreed statement of facts. Most were handled in perfunctory fashion.

These regular dockets were prepared by the assignment clerk in our office. Unlike civil cases, which were assigned and scheduled by the clerks of the courts, criminal cases were scheduled by the State's Attorney's office. As you have already read, a homicide case was specially assigned to an assistant when the case came into the office. Certain other "big" cases, such as white-collar fraud, corruption, big gambling cases, major robbery cases, and any case of special interest to Charley or George because of sensitive interest by the public and were specially assigned to assistants. Such specially assigned cases were only scheduled when the assistant asked the assignment clerk to set them.

The great bulk of cases, were just regularly assigned to courtrooms and were handled by assistants assigned to those court rooms on the days the cases were on the docket.

71

When I drew assignment to the narcotics court for a day, the docket was filled with charges of possession of drugs or paraphernalia for use of drugs. In a city where drug use was beginning to overwhelm neighborhoods to the west, north, east and south, we weren't trying any "big" dealers or sellers. The sales cases we saw involved sales on a small scale by a user mainly to pay for his own habit.

The rotation of assistants from court to court caused interruption in the processing of cases. If, on a given day, the defense requested a postponement in the court where I had the docket and the officer had no objection, I made no objection. That case did not stay with me. It got assigned for a future date by the assignment office, without regard to which assistant was assigned to the court. When the postponed case was again in court, it was handled by a different assistant who knew nothing about the prior request for postponement and would usually pose no objection to another postponement. A good defense attorney could use the rotation system to postpone indefinitely the day of reckoning for his client. That's what the defendant wanted -to stay on the street and continue dealing for his own use. A defense attorney could charge a higher fee if he could keep the defendant free and continuing to earn money on the street.

The rotation also prevented an assistant from even gaining an instinct that a particular defendant was important in the drug trade. No one knew the "nicknames" or "street names" of the big dealers and even if such a dealer happened to be charged, the assistant would not know the importance of the defendant. The case would be treated just as a normal user case.

There was no way for the assistant ever to assess any kind of pattern of use of informants, because once the case got to court, there was no need to review the probable cause of the arrest or search unless the defense raised a motion to suppress, and those motions were rare. If there was a motion to suppress, it normally involved the existence of probable cause for a street arrest and seizure, rather than challenge to a warrant. The issue of credibility of an informant was rarely encountered. And assistant's involvement in the credibility issue was limited to the information he was provided by the officer.

If a case actually did involve a jury trial, the case was rarely finished on the same day it commenced and carried over to the next day in the same court. The carryover caused at least two problems the regular docket for the next day in that court had to be handled and cases either postponed or moved to other courts and if the assistant had been scheduled in a different courtroom for the next day, his or her assignment had to be handled by some another assistant. Consistency in the handling of cases was impossible. This aided the defense immensely.

Witnesses whether police officers or citizens were rarely considered in the postponement decisions. As a result, witnesses often faced serial postponements and were required to return to court on several occasions. It wasn't uncommon for witnesses to despair and quit responding to subpoenas. Prior to asking for a postponement, skilful defense counsel perused the courtroom to see whether witnesses were present. If they were, a postponement request was made. If they weren't present, the defense let the case be called for trial and the state had no case. If the state asked for a postponement, the defense would ask for speedy trial and dismissal.

The "system" worked against the prosecution and the people of the state.

Charley Moylan solved most of these problems with one move when he established the trial team process. During our month's tour in narcotics court, we started asking detectives from the districts why there were never any big drug sellers in our court. Each district station house had a detective unit that answered to the captain of the district, not to central investigative services. The district detectives were at first very reluctant to talk to us about it.

Finally, Jim Dudley, an assistant with a lot more experience than I had, sat down with Sargeant Steve Tabeling of the Northern District and told him we needed some information, needed some help in order to find out why we never saw the major dealers and distributors. He said he would tell us because he couldn't be in any more trouble with the city "brass" if he tried. Jim, Steve and I then discussed some issues that raised major concerns.

He told us about rumors, both within and without the department, said many of the big dealers had arrangements with the narcotics unit in central investigative services, and with officers throughout the city. They informed the officers about users and petty dealers so that drug, gambling and other arrests could be made, and the officers left the big timers alone. Steve told us that there were also rumors, within and without the department that big dealers paid off certain officers for "protection" against arrest. He said that even dealers privately told of such payoffs, and that some such protection arrangements were subject of open discussion on the "Avenue," which was Pennsylvania Avenue, heart of the Western District -at that time the heart of the drug trade.

Tabeling also told us it was pretty strict policy that drug arrests should be made only by the narcotics unit of central investigations. Detectives in the districts, and patrol officers in the districts, were not to focus on drug operations and were to avoid drug arrests. Unless drugs happened to be on a person arrested for another crime, drug charges were to come only from the narcotics unit.

When we asked officers of the narcotics unit the same questions, we were told that major dealers were just too well protected by their own organizational structure for the officers to be able to get to them.

They told us their informants were afraid to provide information needed to get to the majors.

What was true of narcotics cases was true of gambling cases too. Rarely, if ever, did we see anyone even resembling a major gambling figure in our court and we seldom saw any defendant who had a status higher than a numbers runner on the street or a bookie on the street or in a local barbershop. The numbers racket was a lottery type of game. The purchaser bet two dollars or more on a number or series of numbers, placing his or her wager with a person known to the bettor as part of the numbers operation. Each day the winning number and series of numbers were announced and the winning numbers were applicable to the whole city. If the bettor won, he or she picked up the winnings from the same runner who had taken the bet. The bettors never dealt with anyone higher than the runners on the street or in the barber shop, the liquor store, the newsstand or the corner bar or lounge.

Off- track betting on horses was also illegal in the city and bettors placed their bets on horses, at the Baltimore and Maryland tracks or elsewhere, with bookies who took bets in person or by telephone. Your regular bookie might be a bartender, a barber, a shoe shine man, a newspaper stand operator anyone trusted enough by the gambling organization to process the bets.

In the narcotics-gambling court, we saw no major dealers or distributors of drugs and no one higher than a numbers runner or bookie. The information shared with us by Tabeling and gradually by other officers in the districts, finally explained why. But once Charley established the organized crime unit, the situation changed drastically. As the first director of the unit, I had seven assistants to handle drug and gambling cases and other forms of organized crime, or professional criminal, cases. We now had the time to start asking the tough questions and follow up on the answers.

72

The more our teams talked to detectives throughout the city's districts, the worse the picture looked. We found that drug users, dealers and big distributors had no fear of uniformed police and openly dealt on the streets in each of the districts. We heard that when captains and lieutenants went to Commissioner Pomerleau to complain about the overriding problem being caused by the growing heroin trade, he passed them off with the answer that "the narcotics unit will handle it." The "narcotics unit" consisted of a dozen officers at most. A dozen officers trying to handle a problem that filled the narcotics criminal courtroom every day, Monday through Friday, with drug possession cases. A dozen officers trying to handle a problem that filled all the criminal courtrooms Monday through Friday, with burglars, thieves, robbers, killers- perverts high on drugs or looking for drug money when they committed their crimes.

We also found that gambling cases were handled almost exclusively by the gambling unit in the city's vice squad working out of central investigative services. The districts did little about gambling except when a bookie or runner got so blatantly obvious that the district officers had to act.

We heard that management officers of all the districts had asked the commissioner for assistance, and to all he answered, "The problems will be handled from downtown." I found that virtually impossible to believe until I heard it from officer after officer. They not only said the commissioner turned his back on them and on the problem but that they heard rumors daily that members of the "narcotics unit" were on the take, thus protecting dealers. Rumors and rumors only. Lee Tomlin was one of the narcotics unit officers in whom I had trust and faith. I considered him a good officer, and that was confirmed by every officer I talked to. I never discussed with Lee the rumors about the other officers in his unit. I didn't know that he also went to the commissioner about the problem. I learned that just awhile back when reading Michael Olesker's, *Journeys to the Heart of Baltimore and Baltimore, If you Lived Here You Would Be Home*

I don't doubt for a second that Lee did ask for help. I believed him to be a dedicated officer who, as a sergeant, worked his team efficiently and honestly. I still do. As a matter of fact, as loyal an officer as Lee was, he had to be extremely concerned to have gone outside the chain of command and directly to the commissioner.

Even though no one complained to me about Lee during my talks, neither did I find anyone who trusted the narcotics unit as a whole or who wanted to share information with them and work with them. As one lieutenant in the same vice squad, which housed gambling and narcotics units told me, "There's some good guys in drugs, but you never know when they will say something to the bad guys and then it's on the streets."

At the time I felt that Lee Tomlin had to be very frustrated to be an honest officer trying to fight an ever growing problem without adequate help and with the knowledge that others in the force and on the streets didn't trust his unit.

We quickly realized that if we wanted to get dealers, we would have to start building our own probable cause information by talking to the users we arrested, by making deals with the users in exchange for information. As we discussed it as a group, we formed the theory that if we arrested enough users, and listened to them, and cross- checked their information and put it all together, we would get the dealers.

One distinct advantage we had was that we could work well with Tabeling and his detective squad from the Northern. I have never worked with anyone who knew more about the art of investigation, the art of crime-fighting, than Steve Tabeling. I have never met any officer, or person, more honest. If he told me that if I stepped out the window on the fifth floor I would not drop to the street, I might well try it.

In writing my stories, I read the *Baltimore Sun* articles discussing how Tabeling had been asked to study the current dreadful homicide clearance and conviction rates in Baltimore. I thought to myself, "Tabeling is still the man they have to go to, to right the wrongs in the criminal justice process". Why? Because any professional in law enforcement with a brain knows that Steve will objectively study the problem and will make his report honestly, and straightforwardly, regardless of who his report offends. That's Tabeling. That was him in 1968, when I first knew him, and from press accounts that continues to be him.

I asked Tabeling if he would be in trouble if he executed a warrant obtained by the States Attorney's office for a location in a district other than his home district, the Northern? He said he would hear about it from the brass downtown, but wouldn't be in any more trouble than he always was. He just insisted that, at least at the last minute before any raid, we notify the district and get uniform support from district. His insistence on that procedure was not motivated by him protecting himself, but by his loyalty to the department and his knowledge that it helped morale if officers believed they were trusted enough to be brought into the raids, even if at the last minute. He was right in that too, as proven over and over in my experience.

I told Charley about my conversation with Tabeling and he decided that we should start gathering information so we could shake up things in drug crime enforcement. Meanwhile, he took me to a meeting with Pomerleau, where we asked about the limited authority to make drug arrests. Pomerleau did his song and dance about the narcotics unit being charged with drug arrests because they understood the nuances of the drug trade and knew how to handle informants. I spoke up when I shouldn't have-one of the lesser- degree problems that Charley had with me. I said it was my understanding that a uniform officer couldn't make an arrest even if he saw a drug sale openly take place right in front of him on the street.

Pomerleau did his standard hem and haw about it not being an official policy, but he and his administrators believed that the complexity of probable cause and of the drug culture was better handled by the specially trained officers in the narcotics unit. Before Charley could take over the conversation again, I said something to the effect that, "So an officer can make a probable cause arrest for a larceny, which is one of the trickiest parts of the criminal law, but he isn't smart enough to figure out that a drug deal is being made when a packet of white powder is sold right in front of him?" Very likely I threw in some comment about the uniform officers knowing more about what was going on in the district's streets than central services could ever know.

As always, Charley saved the day by effectively shutting me up and we departed. But in spite of my indelicate comments, Charley had made it clear that his office was going to pursue drug dealers and distributors while not directly challenging the commissioner.

Starting with the Northern District, we began collecting information provided by informants brought to us by Tabeling and his district detective unit. We prepared enough information to prepare affidavits for, and secure search warrants for several "shooting galleries" in the district. (The "galleries" were apartments or houses where drugs were sold to individual users and the users could "shoot up" right there with needles provided by the operator. The users could then stay in the gallery and sleep it off if they had nowhere else to go. The man or woman in charge of a gallery did not keep on hand large amounts of drugs, just enough to handle the individual trade. If the gallery ran low, then a runner would bring more drugs from the dealer who supplied the gallery. Normally a gallery did not get supplied by more than one dealer. So when a gallery got raided and closed down for the night, the dealer who supplied it got hurt economically.)

The affidavits were signed by the Northern District detective and the warrants were then served by Northern District officers. At first, we might secure warrants for one, two or three galleries to be served on the same night. All would be executed at the same time, so that word of one raid could not be spread in time for the other galleries serving the same dealer to close.

73

Raiding the galleries was dangerous. They were located in areas of high crime rates where police presence was resented. The galleries were protected by heavily fortified doors, some with iron plates on the inside. The fortifications were used long before there was any danger of regular and continued police raids. They were used to help defend against raids by competitor dealers who would break in, steal what drugs were there, and disrupt the competition for that day or night. The unlawful raiders then would spread the word that the raiding dealer's galleries were safer for users.

When the officers conducted raids on the warrants we helped with, they called for uniform back up- uniform officers to help keep the peace in the streets where the raid took place and sometimes to help control the users inside the galleries. The uniforms were not requested until just a few minutes before the raid so there was no risk of even random talk about the raid. The lead detective, often by radio, called for uniform support for a "turn out," and would ask the officers to meet his squad several blocks away from the actual raid site. Then, after briefing the uniforms, the raiding party moved fast to the site and crashed the door.

All persons in the gallery at the time of the raid were told they would be arrested and charged at least with continually frequenting of a nuisance house, for example, a house where drug paraphernalia or drugs were present. If they wanted to talk to us, we took their statements and let them go. If they didn't, they were taken to the district lock-up and the next morning, after initial appearances were transported to the City Jail. By the time they arrived at the jail, they had been without drugs for at least twelve to eighteen hours and were beginning to hurt. As they got ready to talk, we made officers and lawyers available to take their statements and add their information to our now- growing mass of information about sellers and suppliers.

Bob Stewart kept our information files, carefully detailing our informants and the information they provided, cross- referencing the information, and steadily building toward probable cause for more difficult -to -reach galleries, for sites where large supplies of drugs were kept, and for the homes of dealers. Bob kept careful records of raids where drugs were found, to show the reliability of the "anonymous informants," who provided the information leading to the successful seizures.

We were unrelenting, and the raids began to increase in frequency weekly. It became normal to have seven or eight raids conducted on one night. We even reached the point at which several raids in adjoining districts would occur simultaneously. We were told by officers, and by our own informants, that the drug dealers were nervous, not knowing when and where we would strike next. The word we got was that dealers were upset because they weren't getting advance information about the raids from their police contacts.

The captain of the vice squad came to meet with Charley and ask that we keep the narcotics unit advised of our activities and involve them in the raids so they could "work" the informants that came forward. In his usual diplomatic fashion, Charley gave him a "we'll try to do that" answer. But we never provided them with names of, identification clues to, or information provided by, our informants.

74

Meanwhile, detectives in the other districts were coming to us to get involved in what we were working with the Northern District. Using Steve Tabeling as our "north star," we asked him about the detectives who wanted to get involved, and when we had a good feeling for their honesty, we worked with them.

Captain Glover and his homicide and robbery investigators wanted in, and wanted to start using the drug raids to look for people and evidence they needed for their cases. The Northeastern and Eastern district detectives wanted in on the action. We were hitting shooting galleries all over the city.

Informants began giving us information directly when they discovered that information about our informants and warrants did not get leaked. Our informant bank grew fast. We soon had affidavits working for many of the big dealers and distributors, with information provided by informants who did not know each other and did not know anyone else was informing on the big names.

The raids on warrants, which we helped with, were normally conducted by the district detective squads, about four in number and at least one assistant State's Attorney and supporting uniforms.

We heard the catch phrase of the day on the street was "Grant and four, gone your door." The first I heard of this was when Mamie Oliver of the *Baltimore Afro American* told me that "figures on the Avenue" were nervous about where we would hit next. By "figures on the Avenue," she meant people in, or close to, the drug trade on Pennsylvania Avenue in the Western District.

As our case numbers climbed and the charges against dealers started to escalate, Charley petitioned for and got empanelment of a Special Grand Jury to hear organized crime cases and to facilitate investigations into all forms of organized crime, including gambling, extortion, bribery and other forms of corruption.

At one point we had some fascinating informant reports that there were papers, records and funds in possession of Colonels Maurice DuBois and James Watkins that would incriminate most members of the commissioner's internal staff and the central narcotics squad. DuBois had been a bland FBI agent assigned to stolen cars when I was in the U.S. Attorney's office, and had been hired into a high-level internal affairs spot by Pomerleau. That always intrigued me. Having worked with him on stolen car cases, I wasn't impressed with his astuteness. I always wondered what talent had earned him such a high place in the city police administration. I hoped to find out through our Grand Jury proceedings, but never did.

Rumors from many sources said that Watkins' association with various prominent "figures on the Avenue" resulted in protection for them. All we had were rumors and unverified informant information. Even though the information came from informants who had been reliable as to drug seizures and arrests, we did not act on it. This is because of the sensitive nature of taking on the Commissioner of Police and his chief assistants without substantial documentary evidence, or evidence that could be presented under oath to a trial jury in an open and public trial. We imposed a much higher standard on ourselves for such cases than we did for charging non-police defendants. I think we all knew, and when we might have doubted it Charley made it clear, that to take on a case against police officers without convincing evidence that could be presented under oath in a public trial would be disruptive to the entire system.

As to the particular documents, I requested production of any documents, records or funds that met the description we had from the informants. I made the request to both Colonels DuBois and Watkins, pointing out that the Special Grand Jury was interested in them and that we hoped subpoenas would not be necessary. I got only denials that any such records existed and both Colonels made formal requests for the names of any informants who had provided information to me or to the Special Grand Jury. Of course we didn't turn over any names or information to them.

As we continued to develop our cases, we had now turned several mid -level dealers into our informants. One such dealer gave us information sufficient to get a warrant to search the home of Big Lucille. The dealer who gave up Lucille was a federal informant who was allowed to continue dealing on a mid-level basis as long as he provided information to the Drug Enforcement Agency agents.

We had arrested the federal informant, not knowing that he was an informant. Once we had him in custody, he was allowed one call and instead of an attorney showing up, DEA agents showed up to demand that we release him. We refused and said we intended to charge him and try him for a long sentence.

I told the federal agents that we arrested their informant and found him in possession of heroin on the basis of information provided to Captain Glover's homicide detectives by a murder suspect. Working from that information, we secured probable cause and, working with Glover's and Tabeling's units, made our case. I told them that Glover would not give up this case unless something much bigger came out of it.

We did offer to work with them and with the informant if he gave us a major dealer. At first, he claimed that he knew none, and the DEA agents agreed; they believed he was outside the circles of major dealers. I told them he was conning them and now was trying to do the same with us. We had good, reliable information that this dealer's supplier was Lucille. I told the feds we knew enough about their informant to know that he did run and do business with the major players, and that he had to give them up to avoid prison.

We involved Glover and Tabeling in the talks with the feds and the informant. They made it clear to the informant that they had enough to give us a case that would put him away for at least a couple of twenty year sentences. It didn't take him long to decide that he wanted to work with us. Once he realized that we weren't going to accept anything less than a major dealer, he gave us Lucille.

When we prepared the affidavits and secured the warrants, we got additional warrants for various other locations throughout the city-locations that would have no connection with the informant. We hoped to use the other raids to try to cover the informant, to make it appear that even Lucille was given up by one of the other informants working throughout the city that night. We secured the warrants, but we were content to sit and wait until we got word from the informant that he was certain Lucille was "dirty" i.e., that there were drugs in her house.

75

Lucille was a huge lady, rumored to "keep" young boys as her boy toys, and to deal from her house only to very select people. Her drug dealership was carried on by a widely spread group who never came to her house. She lived in a flat on the third floor of an old, formerly luxurious residential building. We knew from various informants that the door leading to Lucille's flat opened to a long hallway that was part of the flat. She used that hallway as a run for her dogs, like an outdoor dog run. Her dogs used the hallway as their toilet area. She was so big physically that it was a real burden for her to get down to the street to care for her dogs. From that hallway there was a locked door to get through to get into the main living quarters.

Finally we got a call that said that Lucille had at least two ounces of heroin in her house. Glover and Tabeling assigned themselves and their officers to execute the warrant on her house.

The federal agents had been a real pain during preparation of the affidavits, securing the warrants and planning the raids. As we rode to the site in Glover's car, I suggested that in all fairness we should let the federal agent lead the raiding party through the door from the main hall into the toilet hallway. We all decided that would be a good idea, and no one volunteered to warn the agent of the dog run he would leap into.

When we arrived, the federal agent was asked if he would lead the raiding party in right behind the officer with the maul who would break down the door. He was eager. We went to the third floor, one of Tabeling's detectives wielded the maul, the door crashed in and the federal agent went through the shattered door on a dead run. He hit the dog mess, slipped and slid several feet down the hall through the entire toilet area.

We moved past the toilet hall, and, following the maul- wielding officer, entered the main living quarters. Lucille was in bed with a young- looking man in a silky dressing gown. She started yelling "Who are y'all? What are you doin in my house? Who are y'all?" Tabeling said, "Lucille, you know who we are, we're the police." She just continued, "I don't know y'all. Who are y'all?" Meanwhile, our hopes began to dim as each room was searched and no drugs found.

A detective named Augie was in this search party. I can't remember his last name but he was known for his terrier-like searching, never quitting until he figured out where the drugs were and found them. Little Augie had just about exhausted his ideas in this case.

He sat down on the side of the bed and asked Lucille where her drugs were. She went into the "who are y'all? Ain't no drugs in here. I don't use line drugs." But, Augie told me later, for just a brief moment he thought her eyes darted toward a portable radio sitting by the bed. All I knew at the time was that Augie started taking the back off the radio. As he did, before he found the drugs there, Lucille all of a sudden said, "Mr. Grant, I don't know why y'all are here, I don't have no heron." (The word heroin was almost universally shortened to heron.) Glover said something to the effect that "Lucille, I thought you didn't know who we were. How do you know Mr. Grant" As she said something like "I seen him on the television," Augie got the back off the radio. Before any of us could see inside the radio, Lucille said, "What is that? Who put that in my radio? That's not my heron. Who put that heron in my radio?" Augie reached in and pulled out a solid pack of white powder that later turned out to be two ounces of heroin, or in the language of the street, "heron." What a relief!

When we got outside, and Lucille was approaching the back steps to the patrol wagon, the uniformed driver took her arm and helped her up into the wagon. She said, "Thank you, sir. At least there's one gent' man here," and gave Tabeling and me dirty looks intended to wilt.

Then Glover and his detectives told the federal agent that he was going to have to get a federal car to take him back to the offices, that they couldn't let him in their car with dog mess all over him. It was a good night.

76

As we presented the case against Big Lucille to the Grand Jury the next morning, we also presented the testimony of an informant who had been reliable on several warrants under which drugs were found in significant quantities. He said Big Lucille was a long -time friend of Colonel Watkins, who had bragged that he would never let her get caught with drugs and go to jail. The Grand Jurors were upset that they had not been given the records we had requested.

I told them Charley and I had an appointment that morning with the commissioner to see whether we could get the information the jurors wanted. As I finished and started to leave the room, the foreman called out, "Well, are we going to indict them today?" I wasn't really focused on indictments other than those of Lucille, which had already been voted, so I very quizzically asked, "Indict who?" The response was, "the Commissioner, DuBois and Watkins." I laughed and said "No, not yet." His reply was "Well, let us know when you're bringing in the charges. We've been talking about it and none of us want to be gone when we take that vote."

I told Charley about the foreman's remarks on the way down to the central administrative building and he made me promise to be quiet and behave myself. He didn't even laugh when I asked, "Don't

I always." He looked at me and said, "Quiet and behave." As I have and will say over and over, Charley had a way of looking very sternly into your eyes when he was dead serious, and as he talked to you he emphasized his points by nodding his head affirmatively. He stopped me, did the stern look and nodded repeatedly.

So, we entered the meeting. Across the table was Pomerleau with DuBois and Watkins as bookends beside him. Charley started out by asking for the information that we had requested. He said he didn't want this to deteriorate into a situation where subpoenas had to be issued. DuBois and Watkins took up the old falderol that the information requested didn't have any relevance and didn't prove any wrong-doing. Charley's response was that if that were so, then our inspection would take just a short time, we could return the information and documents, and the matter could be closed. DuBois said the problem was that if the information became public, people could be hurt unnecessarily. Charley at that point told them nothing would be made public, that the Grand Jury review would be private.

All of a sudden Pomerleau opened his mouth for the first time and said he was tired of being threatened with a Grand Jury, and tired of rumors of a Grand Jury, and that if the Grand Jury was going to act let them get on with it, I couldn't resist at this point, so I said, "Well, as a matter of fact, commissioner, the Grand Jury wanted to indict you just this morning, and I talked them out of it until we could see what would come of this meeting. They wanted to indict you and Colonels DuBois and Watkins."

Pomerleau usually talked with his head kind of cocked to one side. But all of a sudden that head went up straight on his neck, and he looked like a deer in the headlights. Charley said, "Well, we'll be going, please let us know before the day is out."

Out we went and Charley was silent as we walked back to the courthouse. I guess he wasn't happy with my version of keeping quiet and I behaving myself. At 4:30 p.m. a box full of documents and records arrived at the office.

As I recall, the contents revealed nothing to confirm the rumors. But the whole inquiry stirred some interest at the police administration.

Much later, after several more indictments of major dealers were returned-the type dealers or "figures" who could identify directly bribery if it existed-Lee Tomlin, who had been promoted and re-assigned to DuBois, came to my office and demanded that I turn over to him the manes of our informants and the information they had provided. I laughed and told him he had to be kidding me, and asked what he really came for.

He was not kidding. He said DuBois had sent him to get the names and if I didn't turn them over they were going to make it public that I was having an affair with a judge's secretary. I just picked up the intercom phone and asked my assistant, Diane, to find the reporters from the *News American and Baltimore Sun,* who probably would still be in the courthouse. I asked her to tell them to get "here and right now." I said, "Lee, I always live as though I may see whatever I do in the next building and day's papers."

Lee just looked at me, kind of smirked, said something like "I knew this wouldn't work," and walked out. Fortunately the reporters had left the building already, so I didn't have to make up some reason why I asked for them.

77

Information from informants provided the base for the whole narcotics breakthrough that brought some mid-level and high- level dealers to the courtroom for the first time. Court became not just a stopping point on the way to destruction of addicts.

The narcotics trade is so harmful and vile, that it doesn't surprise me that officers and prosecutors sometimes go beyond the pale in trying to get dealers off the street. Anyone who has seen the human pathos that comes with and follows drug use can imagine a time when he or she might bend the rules to get to a dealer.

I remember one night, sitting in a police car waiting for an informant to come back from an ultra- high- level dealers' apartment in a luxury high-rise. We had enough probable cause to search his home and had a warrant in our possession. But we didn't want to waste that warrant, one unsuccessful raid and the guy might guess who the informant was. Two officers, another assistant and I were waiting in the car. Waiting, and waiting. This would be the highest level distributor we had caught. I had told Charley earlier about the warrant and our plan before he left the court house for the day. This dealer was so big that as soon as we found drugs in his house,

I would call Charley so he could make a news release immediately that night.

We waited an hour, then half an hour more. Finally, down the street came the informant, strolling casually, being very careful. He got in the car, and told us he did not see a drug supply in the usual place the dealer placed it. The dealer did not keep a huge amount on hand at any given time, but when deliveries had just come into the city, two or three ounces of heroin would be on hand there. The informant could not tell us that there were drugs in the house.

I started questioning him, probing to try to get a feel as to whether we should execute the warrant. I asked what the chances were that the drugs would be somewhere other than their normal place. He said the chances were good, that he never understood that there was only one place where the dealer placed the drugs when they were in his house. I asked where else in the house the drugs might be. He didn't know for sure. I asked him how sure he was that a big shipment had come into the city. He was very sure because a steady stream of the distributor's street dealers had been entering and then quickly leaving the house all afternoon. That happened only when a delivery had just been made.

Those dealers did not come to the house except for big distribution. He was sure because earlier in the morning the distributor had been nervous and a tense. Tonight he was relaxed, in a good mood, as he always was when a big delivery had been made successfully and distributed.

I asked him to use his experience and instincts and tell us whether he believed the drugs were in the house. He thought about it for a few seconds, and said, "I think he's holding." I asked him how sure he was. What a silly question but we were all desperately hoping that we could make a successful seizure that night. He gave it a lot more thought than the question deserved and finally said he couldn't be sure, he just "thought" the distributor was holding. Not wanting to let any chance slip by us, I continued to question him. His answers didn't get any better.

Finally, he said, "Ya know, I could go back up there to watch movies with them (the distributor and his three women that he kept) and slip an ounce of the stuff down behind the cushion on the sofa. After awhile when I left, y'all could bust in on him." I hate to say it, but we sat there in silence for what seemed like an eternity, thinking. Finally, we all said, at about the same time, "No, we can't do it wrong." In retrospect, I couldn't believe we actually considered doing that. I like to think that even if we had agreed to the plan, we would have stopped it before it was carried out. At any rate, we didn't, the warrant was returned unexecuted, and we had to wait for another day.

While I was with the office, that day never came. This particular dealer was well protected. Whether he suspected anything that night we never knew, but the opportunities for our informant to be close to him grew less and less frequent.

Big Lucille could have given us this dealer too. After her arrest and indictment, she was held in jail, on very high bail. After a few days in jail, I asked one of our State's Attorney's police officers to go visit her and see whether she wanted to deal. After awhile, he called and said she would come over to the courthouse to talk, but I had to agree to her terms. He put her on the phone and she said she would come and talk to me, but it had to be as part of a trip that looked like a court appearance, that it couldn't appear that she was talking to me. I agreed to arrange for that. Then she said, "Mr. Grant, if I give you who you want, he'll tear my arm out at the socket and beat me over the head with it." I tried to assure her that we could use her information without naming her. Then there came a big condition: she wanted eight juicy cheeseburgers and French fries and "Coka-cola." She said after she ate those, she would talk to me. I told her I could arrange it and asked where she wanted us to pick up the burgers.

We set up an appearance called for by the prosecutor's office to determine whether she had counsel, so trial could be set. After the appearance, she was brought right from the courtroom to the Grand Jury room. The jury session had ended and the room was empty and was secluded enough from general view from the hallways in the courthouse that we ran little risk of being her seen.

We let her start her meal in peace and didn't come in until she was on the seventh. It hadn't taken her long. A guard told us later she "Scarfed 'em down like she was starvin'." I told her to go ahead and finish and then we would talk. Through several mouthful bites of burger and fries she told me that if she gave up the "man," she wouldn't live long enough to plan her own funeral. She said, he had told her that if she ever gave him up he would tear her arm off from the socket and beat her over the head with it. I laughed and asked whether he had ever done that to anyone. She said she didn't know, but she believed he meant it.

When she had finished the last of the burgers and fries, she said she was ready. She then started telling us about small time dealers lower on the totem pole than she was. As she tried to tell us about each of these low –level- guys, I would stop her and say she needed to help us with people bigger than her, people who delivered to her for her sales, not lower-level dealers. I kept coming back to the "man." Finally, she looked at me and with big tears rolling up, said, "He would tear my arm out of the socket and beat me over the head with the stump," and she just said she could not do it. We sent her back to the jail to do her own thing.

78

I never ceased to be amazed at how the dealers continued to trust informants even when it must have been obvious who was providing information. One of the characteristics that we were told was uniform with dealers was that they were extremely paranoid, always afraid and accusing friends and close acquaintances of "ratting them out."

Several years later, when I was in the alcohol and drug rehab center in Idaho trying to get on with grappling with alcoholism, one of the friends I made in the center was a dealer in cocaine. She told me that she and her husband slept with their clothes on some nights because they just "knew" that a friend had, in her words, "copped them out." She said one night after their best had been there for dinner and gone home, she and her husband were so sure the couple were informants, they left their car engine running so they could make a quick getaway. I asked whether they got rid of the coke, got it out of our house when they were paranoid that way. "Oh no," couldn't do that in case a good customer needed a supple. An interesting paranoia.

I saw the paranoia in dealers, yet they continued to trust the informants they accused. Captain Glover and his crew came up with one of the most colorful informants we worked with. He was a dapper dude, dressed "swell" and always had spit polished shoes and a fancy fedora on his head. I have no idea whether he is still alive, so I won't use his name but we knew him as "Peanuts."

Glover introduced him to me and asked that we help them put together a series of warrants that would help focus attention away from the informant and the main case he was ready to give them. My first question was what they had on the informant. I never trusted informants if they just walked in and volunteered something without some charge hanging over their head.

I always thought that was an interesting angle. As a prosecutor I didn't trust them unless there was some charge and they needed to make a deal to spare themselves. When a defense counsel attacked the informant's information or challenged the testimony of a co-conspirator, it was always on the basis that you couldn't trust anything said by a person trying to get out of a criminal charge.

Glover told me this informant thought he was about to be arrested on a series of fraudulent transactions growing out of the theft of credit cards and forgery of stolen money orders. He had a record and would face some serious prison time if convicted. He came forward with information about a drug- related murder. He had given Glover's troops some information that they checked out and it proved accurate. They had information from another informant could get them probable cause to get into the house, but they needed Peanuts to tell them when their suspect was present and in possession of drugs.

We went to work and figured out with Tabeling and his squad places that could be hit through a combination of the information being given to Glover and information from other informants. Several hours were put into getting affidavits ready for nine or ten sites to be raided that night. They were in various districts of the city, so other district personnel had to be alerted to provide backup uniform support.

Glover and Tabeling rounded up the raiding parties and took care of giving very flimsy advance information that there might be some vice raids coming that night. No mention of drugs and no mention of sites or even general areas of sites. We got warrants signed at Judge Carter's home that evening and by ten p.m. were ready to go. The raids came off successfully, with drugs and paraphernalia found in all sites searched. Glover and his men got their suspect, in possession of heroin when he was arrested.

We took the murder case to the Grand Jury the next morning and got a presentment on the charge. (The Grand Jury issued what was known at that time as a "presentment," which was a paper directed to the State's Attorney from the Grand Jury saying the Jury presented to the State's Attorney a charge of whatever crime for an indictment to be issued against defendant "X." The actual indictment, the formal charging document, was prepared by the State's Attorney's staff. Sometimes in these stories I had skipped over the presentment, because often when we took cases in after a night of raids, we went in with presentments and the indictments were already typed and ready to be issued as soon as the Grand Jury voted.)

Later that morning, as I was walking down the main hall of the Courthouse, Peanuts came strolling down the hall pleased as he could be. He asked something to the effect of "Your main man did his job, didn't he?" No caution, no whispering, just outright. I said that the whole project came off well, and he asked when his cases were going to be taken care of. I told him I would wait for Captain Glover to contact me about the cases so I would know what district to deal with. He said, "Ain't no district, it's out of DuBois and Watkins territory." What a shot in the mid-section. I said, "All the more reason I have to wait for Tony."

When I got to my office I called Glover and he said "Not to worry," that the murder case was not of interest to them. He could tell them the informant helped with locating the suspect and everything would be all right. I asked about Peanuts' usefulness in the future, and Glover was skeptical that he would get past the paranoia to be of much more help.

I thought nothing more about Peanuts. Bob Stewart entered his information and identified him by code in his warrant data base for future reference and perhaps future use.

79

Then a few weeks later, Steve Tabeling called and said Peanuts had information he needed to trade to get out of a possession charge against him. He told me Peanuts claimed that he could give us the probable cause for two men who were to enter into a buy and delivery of a substantial amount of heroin that night. Fortunately the possession charge was in the Northern District, so that wouldn't be a problem. Steve brought Peanuts to our office where we questioned him and got the probable cause information necessary to go into the affidavit. My secretary typed up the affidavit and warrant, and Bob got it signed by a judge still on the premises.

Even though we used the "Reliable anonymous informant" source, I didn't see how the defendants could miss the fact that Peanuts was the source of the information, including the knowledge of the time and place of the delivery. But he wasn't concerned.

This was one of those nights when Bob Stewart and I joined Tabeling and his squad of detectives in their tight little quarters, removed by an entire alley's length from the northern station house itself. They joked about being the stepchildren of the house. There was a little grocery store up the street that served chili dogs, and that night as well as many other nights we dined on two or three of those dogs followed closely by Tums. The chili dogs were so tasty good, but we all needed Tums right away. An hour or so after chili dogs were eaten, we got the call from Peanuts and we headed for the exchange site.

Bob and I sat in a car a block or so up the street from the exchange site. Tabeling had two guys positioned on the street, one just sitting on a stoop seemingly visiting with the owner of the house (Favorite thing to do in Baltimore in spring or summer: sit on the stoop and hope for a breath of breeze), and the other going door to door selling books. The exchange was to take place when the buyer arrived and got into the seller's car. Acting on the faith Peanuts was right, the police were going to rush the car and use the warrant to search the car and the buyer and seller. If Peanuts was wrong, his identity would be blown for nothing; if he was right, we had ourselves two pretty fair- sized dealers and from the seller, a possible tie to a D.C. drug organizations.

At just about the time we expected, the two cars pulled into the block and stopped across the street from each other. One man got out and crossed and got into the other car. Tabeling's two officers ran toward the car and Tabeling raced his car to the spot, as a uniform marked car came in from the other end of the street to box in the suspect's car. Sure enough, there were drugs in the front seat with the men, and the search revealed a trunk load of heroin. It was a very big bust.

A couple of days later, Tabeling told me the word on the street was that Peanut's was in hot water, that the buyer and seller were telling everybody that he was the informant, that he was the only person who knew when and where they would meet. Tabeling said Peanut's had called and told him that he had to get out of town for a while until things cooled down. I doubted we would ever hear from him again.

WRONG. Was that the first time I was ever wrong in my life? To quote Jim Rome, "Errrrrrrrrrrrrr, no."

80

This time the contact was through Tony Glover. Peanuts had gotten into some kind of entanglement with interstate drug dealers who had some ties with or at least information on, an informant murder in New Jersey. Not knowing anyone there, and facing more possession of paraphernalia and larceny charges, he turned to his old Baltimore friends. The larceny charges related to theft from two of his female companions, each of whom believed that she was "The only one" and handed him money to buy things for "Their living together." In each instance, Peanut's disappeared with the money, and the ladies filed larceny charges. When he was arrested on the larceny warrants, he was in possession of a syringe with which he injected himself with his "Energy source."

The charges were in Delaware, so first we had to approach Frank Mazone of the state police, with whom I had worked on several other cases. He was a great officer, an effective supervisor of an outstanding unit. He was a successful undercover officer known as the "man of a thousand faces" because he was phenomenal at changing his undercover appearances. We knew he did a lot in cooperation with Delaware because of the close proximity of Wilmington and its crime problems.

Frank was interested when I told him about our history with Peanuts, and arranged to meet him. It was an interesting encounter from which Frank took some very valuable information about statewide gambling, and the full details of the Delaware charges. He was optimistic, so we agreed that Glover would contact Newark and tell them we might have some information for them.

Everything came together and Peanut's met with and helped Newark get sufficient information to get a warrant for a suspect who turned out to be a "hit." He was charged and later convicted. Delaware had agreed to dismiss the charges against Peanut's based on the homicide help to Newark PLUS futures to be named, as they say in baseball and football trades. Peanuts had come up with help for Newark help for Maryland, and some information that was to lead to our cooperation with Frank for a series of warrants and raids.

Frank had been working on some cases in Baltimore and Harford counties, and with what Peanuts offered he was able to put those together with some links through drug operations to Baltimore City. Pulling out his immensely valuable informant index, Bob Stewart started linking and interlinking— all without computer help —the old fashioned manual way. I have a very live memory of Bob's glow of anticipation when he put together a linkage that was going to lead to success — carrying that well- sharpened pencil with which he was connecting the dots.

Affidavits were prepared based on information from such a multi-linking of informants that no one would be able to point to an informant and "know" that he or she was the source of information. We got the warrants signed, and with Frank as the chief of operations, the raiding parties were put together, notifications for uniform support were made, and we were on the way.

The raids were successful, admissible evidence was found at all sites searched, and several successful prosecutions resulted. As always, the success led to more informants, as the information about organizations in gambling and narcotics expanded.

81

Just a few weeks later, Peanut's was back again, this time involved in a real messy case, less than homicide but far more than petty larceny from a girlfriend. To help him, I was going to have to make a special plea to a very tough judge, and Tony Glover was going to have to explain to a group of outraged officers, why Peanut's got off the hook. His explanation would be risky because we had no idea whether any of the officers would then talk about Peanut's involvement as an informant. But the risk was worth it because Peanuts was offering something very big.

He was! He was offering enough, coupled with our informant information bank, to supply the probable cause for hitting a string of fifteen major shooting galleries. Hitting that many galleries on a given night would put a real economic hurt on the dealer served by those galleries, and on his distributor who was big in the District of Columbia. But to get the top man or a lieutenant we would have to name the informant. At this point, Glover, Bob Stewart and I believed it was worth it. We knew it would end Peanuts' usefulness, but what was going to end anyway. His involvements that we have to help clean up were getting more and more serious.

This one could prove to be embarrassing if we failed. Before talking to the judge, I told Charley what we would get if successful and what relief we would be seeking to get Peanut's out of his mess. I also told him t we would have to give up Peanut's identity to make the probable cause for the top man.

Everyone thought the final effort, would be worth it if successful, and we wouldn't know whether success would come unless we took the step. I went, hat in hand, to plead with judge, armed with all the specific results that had come from Peanut's information through the past many months (including successful prosecutions and gaining of new, valuable informants), to plead with the judge. It was not an easy sell. I also revealed what we thought we could do with his current information if we got him past his problem with the judge.

The judge agreed to go so far as to postpone the case but keep it pending on his docket, pending, until our current efforts were ended. Then he would review the results and make a determination as to whether the public had been served sufficiently to justify either dismissing the charges or imposing a non-custodial sentence.

With that, Glover went to work with the officers. Given the elements of command and police cooperation, he had an even tougher job than I had. Finally, he got their sign off, and we proceeded.

This time, we involved Steve Tabeling, the detectives of the eastern district, Glover, Frank Mazone, and, reluctantly, the federal DEA agents and Treasury agents (because of some counterfeit possibilities). In the affidavit, we named Peanuts as the source of information, and identified him as a witness to be produced at trial. We got warrants signed, and I showed them to the Judge who was holding the charges against Peanuts.

The raids were successful. In some sites no big discoveries were made but enough to justify "nuisance house" and possession charges against an operator of each of the galleries raided. In at least one site, we seized guns, proven later to be stolen. We seized some counterfeit bills but no production equipment. We also seized some revenue ledgers and were shot at in one raid.

Bob Stewart and I had gone with a Glover group to the site at which we thought we might find the lieutenant we were hoping for. Lieutenant Sterling Fletcher performed the mandatory "knock and announce" notification at the front door. It was a door that led directly to a staircase that went right up to the second floor apartment. As Fletcher banged on the door and shouted "Police," an officer with a maul crashed the door. Just at that moment a shot rang out, Fletcher went backward off the stoop, and I thought he might have been shot. There was a metal dumpster sitting in the area near the door, and Stewart and I ducked down behind it. We could hear bullets clanging off the other side of the dumpster. I remember looking at Bob and saying, "What the hell are we doing here?" It occurred to me that I had wasted a lot of hard work in law school to end up shot in a narcotics raid. But I admit most of those thoughts came after the fact, not while we were crouched behind that dumpster.

Finally, after a lot of shouting, and the sounds of scrambling feet going up that stairway, things were calmed down. It turned out that Fletcher had not been shot, thank God, but when the first shot came as he was standing in the open doorway, he stepped back instinctively and fell off the low stoop. With nothing to grasp for support, he fell backward off the stoop and wrenched his back pretty badly. He participated fully in our search and arrests made on the second floor, but suffered mightily through the next few weeks.

We got drugs, ammunition, stolen guns, and the lieutenant we were after. That junior lieutenant was charged with assaulting an officer and assault with intent to murder. He almost immediately became an informant, but we had to process him through the criminal charge because of the shooting and for appearances in order to shield him. Our deal with him was to help reduce his sentence.

As it turned out, we didn't have to work on his sentence. His charge was tried before Judge William O'Donnell (who I have previously described as being known as "Wild Bill"). We had no evidence that the defendant was the actual shooter, we were relying on the fact it was his apartment, the gun was at his feet, the gun was the gun that fired the shots and we had evidence that he operated the drug dealings from the apartment. Defense counsel had waived the jury, so the good judge was trying the case himself, thus he had vast territory of abuse of the prosecutor in which to range. I had taken the case myself and thought it was a slam dunk, so I didn't take preparation seriously.

The judge's question was, "What did the tests show as to gunpowder on his hands?" Well, wouldn't you know with the excitement and with the fact that the defendant had turned "talker" so quickly, right there in the apartment, we didn't do any tests. I didn't request any tests and the officers didn't pursue any. I had to acknowledge that the state had no tests. I pointed out that we were relying on his obvious activity in the organizational structure of the crime, so he would be an accessory, and under Maryland law that made him guilty as a principal.

The judge was ready for that one, it was a softball floating up to him like the Katie Couric questions of Sarah Palin, and I missed the return as badly, almost, as Palin did when she failed to even remember what newspaper she read.

He posed the sarcastic question, somewhat like this: "He may have been involved in the organizational structure of the nuisance house and drug operation but the gunshots were not necessary elements of those crimes. When the decision was made to shoot, it was made without consultation with the others in the organization, so how do you make him an accomplice without linking specifically to the shot or the gun?"

The prosecutor did his best in a losing cause, arguing that in the middle of a robbery if a shot is fired the robbers are all responsible. The Judge was ready, "But a robbery contemplates use of a gun, and the robbers are armed. The operation of a gallery does not contemplate, necessarily the use of a gun." He looked to the back of the court room where I was standing and addressed his next question to me, "Mr. Grant, how many other gallery raids has your office participated in this year where gunfire was involved?" I acknowledged, "None."

He was just getting started. "I remember asking you several weeks ago during a trial why the State's Attorney's office thought it necessary to send trial lawyers out on the street to be involved with police doing their job and you said that it was a learning experience so that attorneys would understand the evidentiary problems facing the officers in a gallery and could offer assistance to the officers to help increase success of prosecutions. Isn't that right?" Of course, it was.

Then, the finale, "Well, since you yourself, the chief, the head guy right under Messrs, Moylan and Helinski, were there to help secure a successful prosecution, why didn't you insist on the nitrate test?" Temporarily I thought back to Bobby Fertitta's remark to me about the good Judge's question as to a photo, and I almost said, "For a very good reason sir." It wouldn't have worked: there was no jury, and he would have bulldozed on to the answer anyway. I just said, "Because, your honor, I didn't think of it."

He looked a little dismayed at first, as though he hadn't expected honesty with such little effort. "So, the success of all these officers' efforts depends on your failure to remember to request critical evidence?" "Yes sir." All he could do was move on, with a "Well that's not the way things ran when I was in that office."

He, of course found the shooter not guilty of the assault charges, but guilty of nuisance house and drug charges, which would be much easier to get around if and when the defendant gave us valuable information.

As the prosecutor finished the presentation of the case and rested, and the defense rested, and judge issued his verdict. After he left the bench, he still continued to look at me in dismay, as though there was something else I was going to offer in my defense. I couldn't. I didn't have anything else. Truth is, I didn't even think about ordering a test of the defendant's hands.

But the process that the officers used in gathering the evidence in the apartment was perfectly in accord with the process that we had all set up after observing the chaos faced when officers entered a gallery. One of the most important elements of the process was the designation of an "evidence officer" before every raid. That officer's duties were to remain in one place, others were to bring evidence to him, so he could note who found what and where. When the raid was over he had the evidence and his notes to support introduction of the evidence at trial. After we put that process in place after the first few raids we accompanied, convictions in nuisance house charges increased dramatically. The "evidence officer" idea came from Bob Stewart.

When the case ended, I went over to Charley's office and told Charley and George what had happened. Charley just gave me that serious look, nodding his head affirmatively as if to impress on me his disappointment, but with a bit of a sardonic grin moving his lips. George was not as subtle. He laughed out loud and thanked me for making it possible for "Wild Bill" to take a shot at him and Charley.

82

Our world now moved on without Peanuts, we had named him in affidavits as the informant. We knew from word on the street that the affidavits had been copied and passed around so people would know the identity of the informant.

One night at home, a week or so later, I got a call from Steve Tabeling. "Counselor, when I tell you what I've got to say, you're gonna shout, "It ain't so!" "What's up Steve? I asked" (who hardly ever called at home). "Our %$##%^&& Peanut's is back and claims that he is on a deal where he can witness the sale of big product with us waiting on the street to make the hit." I asked how in the world that could be. He said, Peanut's said he had been through some pretty hot grilling but had convinced everybody that he was set up by the cops and prosecutors, that he hadn't been the informant and that they used his name just to throw everybody off track. He said he convinced them that he refused to cooperate with us so we got revenge by naming him.

I told Steve I had trouble believing that and asked what Peanut's wanted. He said Peanut's wasn't in trouble right now but he wanted to leave town and needed some "points he could use wherever he went in case he got "jammed up."

I asked Steve if he wanted to mess with the guy, and he said at least he would like to talk to him to see how believable his story was and would like me to meet with them. I said, "Okay."

Two nights later, in the former Hooper's restaurant, which had been ruined by being sold to a downtown delicatessen, just a couple of blocks from my house in north Baltimore, within a long stone's throw from Belvedere and York Roads, we met. Peanut's seemed to be fairly flush, bought us both coffee, and proceeded to tell his story. Steve had brought a member of his squad with him, a guy who had the most amazing ability to spot "BS" before almost anyone else in the world. I won't swear to it but I think his name was Weaver, a big, heavy set Afro American cop who detested the chili dogs we thrived on at Tabeling's office.

Peanut's laid out the deal that he was in on. He offered to go into the deal wired for sound, with us waiting within quick striking distance so we could make the arrest when the deal went down and he had taken possession. Weaver nodded "yes" to Steve and me when he finished. It was one more time around the merry- go-round. I did ask Peanut's, "How did you convince these guys of your cover story?" He said he had some help from the "Big Guy's" girlfriend who vouched for him. I asked him how he pulled it off and he launched into a pretty sordid and detailed story of how he pleasured her on the side so she didn't want anything to happen to him. I asked him what would happen to him if his sexual activities were found out, and he said that if the "Big Guy" found that out he would tear his arm out from the socket and beat him to death with the stump.

I looked at Steve and started laughing. I couldn't figure out the fixation on having an arm torn from the socket and used as a weapon to whomp on the victim's head.

The Next day, we set up a meeting—Glover and his lieutenant, Tabeling, his squad, the federal agents from the DEA and the officers set up how they would like to see the project go down. It seemed okay with me so we brought in Peanut's and started with information for the affidavit. We got a search warrant for the site where the exchange was supposed to be made. Early in the evening on the night of the exchange, the officers very carefully wired Peanut's, strapping the wires as far away from easily observed parts of the body as possible. To discover the wires, the crooks would have to make Peanut's strip himself of even his undershorts.

Before the critical time, unmarked cars were parked within a couple of blocks of the site in several directions. I was in a car with Tabeling and Glover, and I think Bob Stewart was with us. We were on a direct line of sight so we observed Peanut's when he arrived at the house and went in. We heard him greeted at the door by a woman who we could not see clearly with binoculars. She was very friendly to the informant and they went to some other room in the house. Sound quality was very good. They talked about everything but a delivery of drugs. It soon appeared pretty clear to us that this was the girl friend that Peanut's had been playing around with. She offered him a drink, and after awhile, their conversation started getting personal and detailed as to their attraction to each other. Time went by, and went by, and it got later and later and we realized that the deal was probably not going to be made. As the time had gone by, it became apparent that the two had switched from alcohol to something stronger. Speech became more and more slurred. Noisy interference now made it difficult to understand them. Their words and sounds made it appear however that they were physically mixing it up. We heard something like "Just get rid of it" and the sound went dead. After a few minutes, we realized that here we sat, like fools, watching a house where inside a wired informant was now having sex with the big crooks' girlfriend. I really do think it was Bob Stewart who finally said, "You know what they're doing don't you, while we sit here like idiots." Joking about the fact that we should leave because if the big crook got there now, there would be a homicide by use of an arm pulled from the socket and we would be witnesses, we left the scene.

Next morning, early, Glover called and said that Peanut's had appeared at Central District about 4 a.m. and had waited there until Glover arrived a little after eight. Peanut's had been told by a desk sergeant he would just have to sit on the steps, there was no place to sit on the steps. He had the wire equipment with him and a story that he had to rip out the wire because the girlfriend had gotten suspicious. Glover assured him that we knew what had gone down, and Peanut's admitted that he just couldn't resist her. He told Glover that the Big Guy had called about 3 a.m. and said the deal would have to be put off for a couple of days. Peanut's said he would be in touch with us.

Two days later, he called Glover and said the deal was set and it would also involve a big distributor from the District of Columbia and another from Atlanta. This was to be a major exchange. Peanut's told Glover, everybody was really up tight.   The details of the exchange weren't going to be spelled out until a few minutes before hand. All he knew was the deal was to be made at the Holiday Inn close to downtown.

There was going to be a problem in arranging an arrest right at the time of the exchange because of lack of prior knowledge. Peanut's, also was afraid that he might be carefully searched for wire because people were on such tinder hooks. He said he had received several calls from the Big Guy asking what he thought about the feds and the State's Attorney's office. Peanut's had managed to make the guy think he was on the "in" with us after our earlier "revenge" on him by using his name in the affidavit. It is amazing how gullible some of these people were including me and many others within the law enforcement family.

After a lot of beating around the bush, Peanut's got to the point of suggesting that we put him in a rental car and then put the car under surveillance. He said when he parked at the Holiday Inn and went in, the officers could close in. He would leave the room number on the dash of the car.

As you can imagine, this one called for some real soul searching. The feds couldn't rent a car without going through paper work that couldn't be completed in time for this move. We couldn't furnish a car that could be linked in any way to the city, county, state or federal government, because we had no idea who might be watching and checking on any car Peanut's used. It all boiled down to one question: whether the State's Attorney's office was going out on the limb for a rental car.   You've already read some of the costly projects I had gotten us into and wasn't sure Charley would go for this one. I took Glover, Tabeling and a Fed with me for my meeting with Charley. In fact, I let the Fed do the talking about how big this case might be maybe even bigger than just the exchange, with information as to the identity of the people who showed up at the hotel.

At the end of the officers' presentation, Charley asked me if I was willing to go out on the limb for Peanut's. I didn't question him as to what "going out on the limb" meant, because I wasn't sure I wanted to know. I said yes, and the project was put into place.

Our office had no active part in this one. All police activity would be by surveillance cars and then by staked out officers moving quickly on the hotel. I went home to wait for word.

As I got calls from Glover, the updates were not encouraging, Peanut's drove around town, making stop after stop at phone booths. He called Glover after each call and reported in. It seemed everybody was so scared they couldn't decide whether to go through with the deal or not. The Only thing was holding it together was the huge amount of money involved and the opportunity to link up with the Atlanta contact.

The word was the deal was going forward. By now it was dark and surveillance by car in the traffic along Lombard Street was going to be tough. The surveillance cars lost Peanut's after he made some strange, weird, twists and turns on one -way streets. One of the police cars just went to the Holiday Inn parking lot for the officers to wait. After awhile, Peanut's called Glover and told him he had to take evasive actions because he didn't recognize the cars that were behind him.

He said he was now approaching the Inn and would drive into the parking lot. He said that on the last call he had been told plans had changed a little bit. The exchange would not take place until he left the room. The "why" of this was his role, as we had always known, was to be the test as to whether the law was onto the exchange. He was to watch for officers, most of whom he knew by sight and when he arrived and told the main party of "figures" the scene was clear and then the exchange would take place. Now he said the exchange would not take place until he left. The Atlanta contact did not want him to witness it. We were to wait to make a hit until he came out of the hotel and drove away.

Much later, I got the report. When Peanut's came out of the hotel, he tipped his fedora in direction of the surveillance cars, got in the rental and drove away. Federal and city officers made their hit. They found a well- known Lieutenant of the big dealer we were expecting having sex with a prostitute and no one else present. But there was a bag, a shopping bag from Giant food stores, filled to the hilt with hundred dollar bills. According to the drug lieutenant once he got over the shock of a score of officers with bullet -proof vests and weapons drawn breaking down the door of his love nest he had been assigned to wait there with the money until the drugs arrived. The officers asked him whether Peanut's had been there and he said that he had. Peanut's had told him that the drugs wouldn't arrive for another two hours.

83

There we were once again. A load of money to become government funds through seizure, information going through the roof from the Lieutenant who would never be good as an informant in the future. And enough information for the feds to get court permission to check a dozen or so phone records, through which new names were identified. But no big drug exchange. One arrest had to be made to protect the value of the information received from the lieutenant. The players would know about the big strike on the room, so would know the whistle had been blown. If he hadn't been arrested, the information he had would have become useless immediately.

The whole case became one for the Feds. I told Glover I really wanted to hear the story Peanut's would dream up when he checked in with the car. But that didn't happen. The next day, no car, next night, no car.

We reported the car as stolen, gave the name of the suspect our informant and had the insurance on the car begin dealing with the rental company. The only good thing that any of us could see was that we were finally finished with our friend.

He had provided information that had resulted in many arrests, convictions and seizures of drugs, money, stolen guns, stolen goods, counterfeit bills, and names that we never had connected with the Baltimore drug business, information links with D.C., Delaware and New Jersey that might be very helpful through the years, and a strong working cooperation between Glover's and Tabeling's troops and the State Police and Federal agents. Peanut's furnished us with laughs for many months.

Much later, early one morning, about 2 a.m. our time, the phone at home rang. It was the Arizona State police, calling with regard to an undercover employee of the State's Attorney's office. The sergeant apologized for the lateness of the call, but my name was given as the supervisor of the employee and it was important that Arizona clear up the matter quickly. He gave me a name of the "employee," and I didn't recognize the name. I told him I knew no one of that name. Then he told me that the man had been stopped by a highway patrol unit because he was driving a car that was on the interstate stolen list. The "employee" had explained that the stolen report was simply to "cover" his activities. In the car was quite a supply of drugs that the "employee" said he was taking to an exchange being monitored by my office and the federal agency.

I told the sergeant that I had no such employees, knew of no such project and did not recognize the name at all. I told him that I couldn't understand where he had gotten my name. The sergeant had me hold on for a few minutes. When he came back on the line he said that the man said to mention the name "Peanuts" to me. Suddenly the lightning struck me and I realized that this was Peanuts, captured in the stolen rental car.

I told the sergeant that Peanuts was an informant who had broken his agreement with us and had run off with the car, leading to the stolen car report. The sergeant was quite incensed that we had put a car in the possession of an informant, and then inconvenienced the interstate system with the stolen process. In fairness, I listened to his complaint for some time, and just took it. I really did have it coming. Finally, after he felt better about getting it off his chest, he asked if I wanted to talk to the informant to work everything out.

I told him, "No," that I would ask Captain Glover to contact him the next day. Tony did call, told Arizona that he was theirs to do with as they wanted, that the drugs had nothing to do with us, had no part of any case in Baltimore, and that he wasn't doing any work for us.

Other than hearing that the car was pretty well run into the ground, having amassed thousands of miles of travel, and was returned to the insurance company at a value they set as zero dollars, I never heard of or from Peanuts again. Several weeks later, Glover said he had heard a rumor that Peanuts had set up some deals for the DEA in the Southwest. I was not surprised.

LADIES OF THE NIGHT

84

The **"ladies of the night"** that I encountered, both as a prosecutor and defense attorney really deserve their own section of the book. Prostitutes operating in some organized business structure, not street workers that I knew were some of the most honest, direct people I met.

Several times, we tried cases in the organized crime section based on prostitution arrests. Often, we tried to make a deal with the prostitutes to get them to testify against their pimps or madams so we could make a "pandering" case. Prostitution or operating a house where prostitution took place where fairly "soft" offenses and didn't usually bring jail time. In fact, we didn't often ask for jail time.

But, "pandering" was a serious felony. It is the crime of using prostitutes for income, as a way of making a living. Any pimp or madame is a panderer. But without testimony of one of the prostitutes working for them, we wouldn't have been able to get to, much less past, a motion to dismiss.

My job brought me into contact with all kinds of prostitutes. There were street walkers who worked for pimps who mistreated them, kept them dependent on drugs and took most of their money so they were dependent on the pimp for even the most elementary basics of life. The work on the streets, trying to pick up men driving around looking for a prostitute, men who are frequenting the bars and strip joints in a "red light" type area, any kind of man in any kind of area. Mostly they frequent "dangerous" areas of the city, and areas along main routes of travel.

Although, where street walkers operate in mass, the streets will become main routes of travel for the "johns" looking for a short time of "bliss". I know that there were some sections of the city like this in Baltimore, but I don't remember that any spots were as bad as 14th street northwest in D.C. Even in my days in Baltimore, police traffic controls were necessary at some intersections such as 14th and U streets N.W. on Friday and Saturday nights. Police placed traffic cones in the streets in order to funnel through traffic that was trying to move on 14th Street. Without the traffic funnels, there would be no movement of cars because of all the "johns" cruising slowly along the curb, looking at and through the assortment of women showing their wares. Round and round the block guys would go until they finally settled on their girl for hire. The lucky men got their sex right in the car, the less fortunate went to some dumpy hotel room, or alley, where they were more vulnerable to muggings by the "lady's" pimp.

The last time I saw this 14th street display was in the 80s when I was in D.C. with two attorneys to take depositions of FBI agents who had screwed up their testimony in a criminal case. The night after the depositions, they wanted to see this phenomenon of the nation's capital. I guided them to the spot where the orange cones and few traffic flares, marked the lanes to try to move traffic and restrict the area in which the "johns" could linger.

One of my western associates pulled up to the curb and stopped. I asked, "What are you doing?" He said, "I'm curious, I want to see what you would say to them." By this time a half dozen and half dressed ladies had approached the car, and started to "close" a deal by beginning to remove parts of their clothes to show more than was already shown. I said "get the hell out of here", and the urgency of my voice caused him to start the car and move away. He wanted to know why we had to rush out of there. I said "we're in a Virginia car, if the police are going to get anyone here its going to be Virginians. And you wouldn't want to go to the DC jail." He said something like, "we wouldn't be there long. We could get a bondsman." I said, "even if it were a half hour, it would be the longest, worst half hour you ever spent in your life."

Over the years various efforts have been made to straighten up the 14th street carnival atmosphere, and I have no idea how well they have worked. The most interesting effort that I can remember was in 1989 when the police, apparently under orders from the Mayor, gathered up a dozen or so prostitutes and marched them toward and over the 14th street bridge into Virginia. The Washington Post reported that interviews with Virginia authorities pointed out that they often sent prostitutes, homeless and mentally disturbed folks back toward DC.

In Baltimore, the only place that I can remember an abundance of street walkers, outside the girls who worked from the open doors of bars on and around the Block, was on St. Paul and Calvert Streets up around North Avenue.

No matter where they are encountered, these street walkers are the most dangerous to those picking them, from a violence or theft standpoint.

85

Red Merritt worked many different areas of Los Angeles where street walkers created major problems. He told of police activities, by individual cops, not by department policy, in Watts to try to drive the streetwalkers and their pimps into another district. The main means of control of prostitution, according to Red, was to force the workers and pimps to move into another district and thus outside the cops' jurisdiction.

Officers resorted to raiding "cribs", apartments or rooms from which the pimps worked their girls, removing all the workers and pimp. While the bookings and posting of bonds were taking place, officers would conduct harassing activities in the crib such as replacing Vaseline with HEET, placing long dead rats in the back of drawers in dressers, and sabotaging cooling fans or window air conditioners—things designed to reduce profit for the pimp and designed to move him on to another district with his girls. Red had a thousand of stories about how the officers in one district would set out to cause problems for officers in the higher rent districts where street problems were not as great. They loved to move problems from Hollywood to Beverly Hills, for example. He told one gross story that illustrates the venom that officers felt for the "uppity" districts. There was a Mexican food restaurant in the Hollywood district that he was working. The tacos were explained as "out of this world". One lunch hour, Red and his partner had a break in cases and decided to pick up a quick lunch of tacos. They pulled up in the alley behind the restaurant because there was no open parking in front. As they went into the back door into the kitchen, they found one of the owners mixing taco meat and relieving himself into the mixture. They didn't take any health type action, they just went to one of the printing shops and had "free taco" signs made up, advertising the restaurant, and then distributed them to the Beverly Hills station house and to all the places they knew Beverly Hills cops hung out for coffee. Over the next few weeks, they and their Hollywood associates heard many times over from Beverly Hills cops how good the tacos were.

He said that there were officers who would take almost any steps to avoid making an arrest which meant endless reports, paper work, and lost time waiting in courts for hearings. One officer, who he said was close to Joseph Wambaugh who wrote books about LA police, would go to the extreme of taking the felon and the evidence into another district and then call the district station house and report the crime.

It always reminded me of a Northern District officer that I met once. He had been assigned to guard my wife and son during a period of time when there was a contract on my life and on Sergeant Tabeling's. I introduced myself to him and said that I didn't remember meeting him at the courthouse. Most of the Northern officers I had met at some time. He said "no, you don't see me at the courthouse, I don't make arrests." He went on to tell me that he hadn't made an arrest in over ten years. When he was first on the force, he was an eager cop. He made an arrest, rushing to the scene so that he would be there first. He spent hours and hours and hours and hours in doing and re-doing reports in the case which turned out to be a receiving stolen property involving loads and loads of property all of which had to be inventoried. Then he lost off-duty hours while attending court for five different postponements. He decided then and there, that he would never be first officer on scene again, he would be second or third so that there would be no arrests to be made.

Well, once again I divert. Back to "types" of prostitutes.

86

There were girls who worked for a Madame in an established "house" where men came to them by appointment. The Madame took care of the girls much better than a pimp. It was fairly normal for the girls to live at the "house" for a full shift, whether that was two days, four days, or a week. Then they took an equivalent shift off. During their shift at work, they slept, ate and lived at the "house". Sometimes the Madame lived in the house, and sometimes she left at night, to return in the morning and start "working" the girls. The Madame did not take most of the girls' income they "shared", when the girl collected from the "john", she took the money out to the Madame who kept track of earnings for each shift. That way, the customer never saw money reach the hands of the Madame. Thus, the Madame couldn't be charged with pandering without testimony of the prostitute. Rarely did the police find a prostitute who wanted to testify and put her working status in danger.

There were "call girls" who worked from their own apartment or house, taking calls personally, or taking referrals through an "agency". These were normally older, more mature women, more experienced, and much, much higher priced. Rarely were they ever arrested. You hear about arrests of call girls only when there is a big "sting" put together by the FBI or some organized vice task force. These girls carry a load of protection because of the social and political status of their clients. Their web of protection exists among the line police officers, supervisors, and more often than not among the prosecutors and political officials within the city. They openly discussed their protection techniques—involving payment of money, payment with sexual services, and pressure through threatening to reveal the relationship. What they were not open with me about was the source of their protection. They hinted, but never identified.

Some call girls work a regular round of convention hotels too, often sharing their fees with hotel employees who either look the other way while the girls work the bar, or steer customers to the girls. Some call girls actually do work for Madames who manage their schedules and appointments. Some do work for pimps who make their appointments for them; these pimps are no more worthy than those who mistreat the street walkers, they just make more money and work with a higher social scale of customers.

Street walkers are normally arrested by vice cops on their routine shifts, just to clear off the streets every once in awhile. Some citizens "clean up the streets" organization may make complaints, and then there will a concentrated effort to make wholesale arrests. But, normally, arrests are just routine street arrests.

As I said, street walkers are the most dangerous of the ladies. Men they pick up and take to some dirty, run down apartment or third rate hotel, or to an alley-way, are vulnerable to shake downs. If an out of town business man gets lured to one of these places, the pimp has a ready made extortion victim. Or, the guy just becomes victim to getting rolled and having his cash and credit cards stolen. He can't really afford to make a complaint with the police because that would force him to reveal his relationship with a street walker.

If the street walkers are more presentable, the pimps may work them in a convention hotel trying to pick up visiting out of town business men. But, the likelihood of their being involved in a successful hotel business is not great, because they are usually easily picked out by hotel security officers or bell men and concierge.

Most in-house Madames do not send their girls out on calls.

Some do for special customers who they know they can trust completely. If the customer calls for "guests" for out of town visitors and/or friends, the Madame may work with him. But, normally the Madame works only from her house, where she can control the setting. They are far less vulnerable to stings and arrests if they operate only from their houses. They are also less vulnerable to being involved with girls who have boyfriends that engage in muggings. The profit of these in-house Madames depends on trouble-free production, on a mass assembly line basis which isn't interrupted by police raids or arrests or investigations.

Arrests and raids at these in-house operations mostly occur as a result of complaints from neighbors who are irritated with the volume of traffic coming and going from the house. When complaints come in, either a local police station house or the central vice squad will put the house under surveillance and gather information about the traffic, and then decide that there is prostitution going on and send in an undercover officer. The officer signals the officers outside the house when money changes hands with the girl.

87

One of the more successful Madames in Baltimore was Jackie, a gnome of a woman with hair like a brillo pad and a vocabulary like a sailor. When her house was raided, it was usually based on a warrant, because she was very careful about identifying her customers. When a lot of complaints began to back up about the traffic to and from her house, the officers would put it under surveillance and come up with statistics of traffic and her known record for prostitution, and get a warrant. They went in and arrested the girls and let the male customers go. If the vice squad got enough complaints, or the district in which she was operating got enough complaints, she would move to a different location and live free of police trouble for several months.

The first time I ever heard of Jackie was in a telephone call from Lt. Andrew of the central vice squad. He called me at home one night, calling me from Jackie's house. He had led a raid on her house. The front door led right to a steep staircase that led to the second floor of the building. At the top was a steel enforced door, with a bar on the inside which helped support it from being broken down. He told me that the officers broke down the front door that lead to the staircase, but were having trouble breaking through the steel enforced door. He was talking to Jackie through the door and she was insisting that nothing illegal was going on and she wouldn't open the door. He was calling me from a telephone at the corner store. I told him to try to get her to call me, or to give me a number where I could call her. I might be able to "negotiate" them into the place.

I was quite surprised when the phone rang and it was Jackie. Just as sweet as pie, asking what she could do to get out of the mess she was in. She said that Lt. Andrew told her I was an honest man so she would listen to me. I explained that Lt. Andrew was a stubborn and determined man who was going to get into her house one way or the other. I told her that through surveillance we knew that she had three customers in the house, and we were going to station men outside her front door and marked cars outside on the street and stay there until the customers had to come out. I told her that I was going to authorize Lt. Andrew to arrest anyone who came out for obstruction of justice and book each and every one. She asked me what I was prepared to "offer" and I said the customers would be allowed to go without identifying themselves and without arrest, she wouldn't be charged, but the girls would. She agreed, and the standoff ended. The next day in court she told the assistant prosecutor that I was evil, but Lt. Andrew was a real gentleman.

I didn't hear of Jackie again until I got another call from Lt. Andrew. This time, they managed to get the upper door opened through a ruse. They arrested one of the girls, but couldn't get to the other two. They had holed up with Jackie in the kitchen/office where four "yapping dogs" as he called them were holding off the officers. One more time she called me and I told her that if she let the officers in the girls would be arrested, but we wouldn't charge her with pandering and wouldn't charge the customers. I told her that I understood she called me evil the last time we talked. She was just so sweet, saying that Lt. Andrew must have misunderstood her and that she thought I was a perfect gentleman. Once she was off the phone, and the officers entered the kitchen/office she let loose with sailor like four letter words to describe me.

When I left the prosecutor's office, she came to me to represent her. She wanted to put me on a retainer to just come when called. I explained that an attorney can't take a retainer to represent someone on criminal cases, that the IRS looks at that as evidence that the lawyer is part of the criminal activity. I also explained that if she called me to represent one of her girls, I represented the girl, not Jackie.

The first time she called me, she wanted me to represent a girl named Brenda. She was scheduled the next morning in the Central District court at 9am. When I got to court, I introduced myself to Jackie and she introduced me to Brenda. Jackie told me she wanted me to enter a plea of guilty, get the fine imposed quickly so Brenda could get back to the house. I told Jackie I couldn't plead any one charged with prostitution guilty in front of the judge who was presiding. This judge often proclaimed that prostitution, stripping, pornographic book stores, and dirty movies were the elements that were destroying society. He was known for putting prostitutes in jail. At his regular dinner spot, Valeggia's in Little Italy, he loved to expound on how he served the moral values of the city by being hard on prostitutes. I explained that I couldn't plead Brenda guilty and have her go to jail. I told her that it wouldn't do my reputation with clients any good at all if one of my clients went to the City Jail for prostitution. I told them that I would ask for a jury trial, get the case sent up town, and then plead her guilty later in the higher court.

Jackie asked me how long that would take. I told her about an hour, that the judge would take guilty pleas first and then move on to the other cases. Jackie told me she couldn't afford to tie Brenda up that long in court, that she had over the road truck drivers out of Pittsburgh who had already made appointments for Brenda and they would be to the house in less than an hour. I just refused to do it.

Finally, Jackie told me that the judge was one of Brenda's best clients, that when he called she would send Brenda out to meet him. I didn't believe her, and said so. I thought she was trying to con me into pleading guilty. Brenda assured me, though, that the judge was a regular client. Very reluctantly, I agreed. Her case was the second one on the docket. He called the case, and never looked up as I walked up to the trial table. Looking down at his docket book all the time, he asked "are you represented by counsel?" I said "yes, your honor, Fred Grant for the defendant." He said nothing, but "what is the plea?" I said "guilty", he said "100 dollars plus costs." He never looked up. We took the slip from the clerk, he kind of shrugged at me, and we took the slip out to the cashier's window and paid the fine.

I can't say that the judge was a regular client, or a client of any kind. What I can say is that the next day when I was in that court, he put two prostitutes in jail for ten days each. I never doubted Jackie again when she told me someone was a client.

One late afternoon Jackie called and told me that one of the "girls" had been arrested, too late to get before the judge at the Central district for setting of bail. I called and found the judge was still at the station house and he said he would stay and set bail. I went to the station house, appeared with her, got the bail set had the bondsman post the bail and I left with the girl to return her to Jackie's "house". I parked about three or four parking spaces from the entrance to the "house" and as the girl and I walked to the house and waited to get through the locked door, a group of teenagers across the street were chanting "gonna see the hos", "gonna see the hos" and other more descriptive phrases. I wanted to just shout out, "I'm their lawyer" but decided that wouldn't solve anything or even answer anything so just stood with my head down while Jackie got around to unlocking the automatic lock.

I went into Jackie's "kitchen or office," the scene of the "yapping" dogs holding off Lt. Andrew, to collect my fee. She served up a glass of bourbon (good quality Jack Daniels Black Label) and as I sat there, Brenda came in naked and handed Jackie some money for her current client. She looked at me, spoke to me and laughed at my obvious embarrassment. She said, "I never did get to thank you enough for getting me out of there. If you want to wait, I'm sure Jackie will let me thank you." Jackie just cackled and told her not to waste her time, that I was a lawyer and only interested in hard cash. She then threw in another insult to the effect that the only screwing that a lawyer got into was when he screwed his clients. They both had a great laugh at my embarrassment and deliberately carried on the conversation longer than necessary.

Finally, the naked Brenda turned and left, saying as she left, "If you change your mind, just wait for me." I finished my drink, told Jackie about her "cheering section" outside and hurried out and back to my car. When I got home, I told Lodice about what had happened, and her remark was the one I was to hear so many times in the future, "I'm so proud."

The next time I saw Brenda was when her husband got arrested in Anne Arundel County for receiving stolen goods. He had a record for the same offense, so was afraid he was headed for jail time. She brought him to me for representation. I didn't recognize the name because she and her husband were using their "real" names. So, when she walked in with him, I was pretty shocked. I kept my mouth shut about knowing her because I had no idea whether her husband knew what she did for a living or at least for spending money now that I knew she was married.

No need to worry. Brenda said right away, "I've told Benny how good you are at getting Jackie's girls out." I heard about the case, decided that I could probably win on a motion to suppress, collected my fee and made arrangements to see them at arraignment where I would ask for a jury trial. I assured them that the case would move on a pre-trial motion. Brenda counted out the fee to me, looked at Benny and said, "No use offering him me for part of this, he already turned me down in favor of money at Jackie's." Benny just laughed, they left and I wondered how a husband handles that. Obviously, well, if the wife makes more money, or all the "honest" money coming in.

88

Jackie never called me at my home. But, Pamela did. Pamela was a beautiful former "girl" in a house like Jackie's. She had been a very loyal worker, with an eye for business. So, she was allowed to "move up", and currently had her own call girl group operated out of a massage parlor. She had made enormous amounts of money and had a log home on a large site in the Dulaney Valley, the area north of Baltimore where many thoroughbred farms were located. In fact, the beautiful grey champion Native Dancer was at stud near her property.

I represented Pamela and any of her girls when they were arrested. When Pamela called, she called me at home. She had a very seductive voice, and when I would get home Lodice would say "your friend Paaaaamelaaaa called", mimicking the aristocratic tone that Pamela liked to assume.

She wanted to know what Pamela looked like and I told her she was like a gnome, with red hair that looked like a Brillo pad. She said that it didn't sound like that from her voice. I said voices can be deceiving and hers certainly is. Pamela was tall, had Raven black hair, and did move like an aristocrat. When she dated some visiting businessman in Baltimore or DC, he could take her anywhere and she was not out of place in the highest levels of society.

One night Pamela called me and told me that one of her girls was scheduled to be in the western district court the next morning. I told her I would be there. Lodice and I had planned to go to the Amish country in western Maryland the next morning, so I told her we would just stop at the station house on the way out of town. She stayed in the car while I went in to make a quick appearance and get bail set. I was hoping that Pamela would not be there, and she wasn't. But, as I started back out into the parking lot, I heard that familiar voice, "Freeeed". I stopped and talked to her, said I had to hurry. She looked over and asked "is that your wife in the car?" I said yes and she offered to go over and be introduced. I said "no, we've got to hurry." She just laughed a throaty laugh and asked "what did you tell her I looked like?" I just left her laughing, and went on to the car hoping that Lodice had not seen her. I got in the car and was pleased because there was no mention of Pamela. As we drove, about a half hour later, suddenly she said "Well, that's the best looking brillo pad that I ever saw." During our conversation over the next two hours of driving there was no "I'm so proud."

Pamela once was charged with pandering, a felony, on the basis of a statement given by one of her "girls" that she fired for using drugs. She was in my office one afternoon, working with Earl Arvin the investigator who helped me with cases. Earl was an absolute gem. He could get into ghettos, into organizations, into communities where no one else could safely be, and come out with statements and witnesses that saved the day for me many times.

Pamela was briefing him on the key witness so he could make inquiries and get all the current violations of the law she was being excused for in order to get her testimony. Pamela had been dropped off by her male friend who shared her home with her so I drove her to her massage parlor when we were finished. I went in with her while she closed and locked her office and then was to drive her home into the Dulaney Valley. She opened what appeared to be a closet in her office and I saw whips and chaps, and other elements of dominating sexual activity. I of course couldn't keep my mouth shut so I asked about it. She told me that sado-masochism brought in such profit that it paid her complete overhead for the massage parlor.

Her stories over the next hour while I drove her to her house revealed practices that I only had come in contact with in sado-masochistic literature which formed part of a research project I had done on the First Amendment and how it gets perverted by obscenity. She told me of one old man in his seventies who lived in what had been an elite apartment in the early days of Baltimore, in the Eutah Place area of the city which now has been rejuvenated again. She went to his apartment once a month, undressed to black lingerie, seamed black hose and high heels. She fixed him mashed potatoes, wrapped a stage prop chain around him, danced for him and taking off the lingerie until she was naked. Then she fed him the mashed potatoes, got dressed, got paid and left. She asked how I would like to do that for a living. I allowed as how I would rather be representing the lady that did that rather than be a participant.

89

The real life of prostitutes, call girls, and madams is filled with stories beyond the comprehension of ordinary citizens.

One category of hired sex that was outside the realm of these ladies of the night was that of the regular housewife who engaged in action to supplement her budget. One such lady came to our attention in the Northern District. There was an undercover policeman who looked exactly like the undercover officers in some of the police shows like the old Hill Street Blues—they just looked like street people who had just landed on earth. This guy was even called "animal". He was dressed in clothes that looked like they had come out of dump. He even could rotate his eyes so that one of them tilted away from you as you looked him right in the face. He worked one undercover action after another and no one ever toppled to him being an officer.

The Northern detectives had received a call about a lot of foot traffic going into a private residence on Lothian Road in the Belvedere-York Road area of Baltimore. The report was that even utility trucks would park, and the drivers go into this residence on a regular basis.

So, "animal" was dispatched to put the place under surveillance. It had snowed, so he went armed with a snow shovel. He went to the door of the residence and asked the lady if he could hire out to shovel her walk for her. She agreed, paid him and he started shoveling. As one motorist after another arrived, went in and came out, he would talk to them while he shoveled. He had secured jobs with the neighbors to do their walks too, so he shoveled away and heard from the various guys "what a treat" the lady was. Finally a telephone company driver came out and "animal" asked him, "how it was", and the guy gave him the details of all he had gotten for ten dollars. "Animal" finished his shoveling, came back to the station house and they called us to help them with a warrant.

Service of the warrant lead to seizure of evidence, sexual activities and the brief detention of two guys who were waiting when the officers entered the house. The lady was married to a regularly employed insurance salesman who was apparently pretty cheap with her. So, she set out to make her own "spending money", and advertised word of mouth. The two guys detained didn't waste much time telling their stories in order to avoid being charged. The lady then agreed to plead guilty quickly to get the case over with. She admitted to having as many as twenty clients in a given day--- working only Monday through Friday. I agreed that she didn't have to be arrested, that she could come to the station house the next morning. I knew there was nowhere for her to run.

She showed up, with her husband. Apparently it had been a long night for both of them. At any rate, I filed the charge, she pleaded guilty, promised the judge she would quit using her residence for prostitution, got fined and released. We, or at least I, never heard another complaint about traffic at the house.

"Animal" said that he would have liked to have been there to hear the conversation between husband and wife. I told him that I had no doubt that if he had shown up at the door with one of his incredible costumes and stories they would have let him in during the conversation.

90

The **"Block" in Baltimore was** a strip of about four blocks on East Baltimore Street which contained strip clubs, the Gayety Burlesque House, pornographic book stores, gypsy fortune telling booths, bars with daytime "bikini dancers", some bars which didn't have day time dancers, Pollock Johnnies---which had the best chili dogs in town, great Polish sausages, twenty or more pinball machines, and an entire wall of condoms behind the cash register---and the hamburger grill where the bookies operated from the many pay telephones in the back.

Ironically, at the east end of the Block sat the Central District Police Station and Police Administration offices. It is from the homicide-robbery squad offices in that building that Captain Glover and his guys used to walk to meet me and other prosecutors to do our tour of the Block and trouble the bars, book stores and bookies.

I never was involved in a case in which one of the dancers was charged with prostitution, but prostitution went on in the bars and night clubs. When I was with the Court of Appeals as a law clerk in my first year in Baltimore, appeals came up from a series of convictions of owners and managers for sex acts committed in the bars for money. The press billed the convictions as a big "crack down" on the Block and on prostitution. But, by the time I was in the prosecutor's office, the action was back. Some of the police officers had informants among the girls who worked the bars and clubs. Some of them danced, others just worked the streets from the bar doors. Some were the actual strip dancers who worked the three "night clubs" on the Block.

As time went by, some of those informants also provided information to the State's Attorney's office, most of being the type of "deep background" information that just helped explain things we saw going on.

This was the most indistinguishable group of professional ladies in the whole city structure; it was very difficult to ever put together the hierarchy of pimps and organizers.

Some of the bars did form a haven for at least one prostitute each, working the afternoon hours. She would stand in the door making offers to guys walking the sidewalks or would work from the bar stool trying to lure guys to the booths where she would offer sex right there on the premises.

On one of the days that we made a tour down the Block to stop profits for awhile she was standing in the doorway of the bar where she worked. As we walked by, she lifted her skirt up showing that she was naked underneath and invited us in. One of the officers couldn't resist and showed her his badge. She just shrugged and said something to the effect of, "you'd like it too, unless you're queer." We had a good time with him about that for quite awhile.

Through a strange turn of events, that lady became one of our informants, and she was able to tell us how each of the bars used at least one prostitute on the floor, sometimes more when a big convention was in town. She said that the girls were free to "sex the guy" on the premises or take him to a hotel room she shared with other girls from the street. The only condition was that the fee be shared with the bar, and that she take the guy into at least three very expensive "drinks" (of seven up) before selling him what he wanted.

But, there were some operations on the Block where at least I knew of no prostitution or drug violations going on. The lady that owned the famous Two O'Clock Club, was Blaze Starr, the famous stripper who as a young girl had an open affair with Governor Earl Long of Louisiana. Her affair has been chronicled in her book and in the movie Blaze. Stories swirled around during the affair telling of her moving naked freely through the governor's mansion. The stories were made a prominent part of the State's First Lady's attempt to end the affair and the marriage, without losing the prestige. Long, who was brother of Hughey Long (the "Kingfish", prominent among corrupt Louisiana politicians), was committed to a mental hospital after his terms as governor ended. The commitment apparently was organized by his wife, using the affair as the base. Although, I always found it difficult to believe that having a relationship with Blaze Starr would be grounds for a judge to put a fellow man into a mental institution.

91

Blaze Starr was a voluptuous woman, whose stage presence was overpowering. One of her acts featured a couch which started smoking and broke into flames as she undressed on it. She assumed the role of a panther in one act, growling at her audience from a position on all fours. The act was initiated after the death of a live panther which she had trained to undress her on stage.

I can't say that Blaze was a paying client of mine, because I never charged her for any advice I gave her. But, several times I did advise her on civil matters, and on various issues regarding legality of what the police were doing on the Block. She was an articulate, very intelligent lady. If you had met her outside the Two O'Clock club, and didn't know that she was an exotic dancer, you would have thought she was a voluptuous, striking, intelligent business woman who dressed provocatively to take advantage of her build. She tolerated no drugs among the preliminary dancers who preceded her show, and she tolerated no drugs among her employees.

Her Two O'Clock Club was the only "legitimate" strip business on the Block, other than the decrepit old Gayety Burlesque House where Blaze had performed once on a tour when she was much younger. She laughed about how she wouldn't be "seen dead" in the place as it existed at the time I knew her. It had been the site for shows by famed strippers like Tempest Storm, Candy Barr (allegedly girl friend of an LA member of the mafia), and the infamously viable Busty Russell.

Blaze Starr was the only person even remotely connected with the Block that Lodice didn't find distasteful. She likened her to Gypsy Rose Lee, and to the legitimate world of burlesque.

I represented many of the strippers who worked the Block after I went into the private practice. The cases included drug possession, larceny, forgery, car theft, obscene dancing, divorce, and auto accidents. But, never a prostitution charge. The closest to that was one who was charged with larceny on the basis of a complaint filed by a salesman from Nashville. He claimed that during a "night on the town" with three friends attending the sales meeting, my client picked his pocket and stole two hundred dollars while whispering niceties in his ear at the bar.

His story differed from that told by most out of town businessmen who lost money on the Block. The information I had from clients on the Block was that most "victims" claimed that they were mugged, and that their wallets and money were taken. This guy claimed that my client picked his pocket, took the two hundred dollars in cash, and carefully returned his wallet, credit cards, a certified check for five hundred dollars and his identification. I never believed the story for several reasons one being that my client was smart enough to have known that the certified check was just like cash. Had she stolen the two hundred dollars, she certainly would not have left behind the five hundred dollars.

One of the most interesting clients I represented was the owner of the locally famous "Oasis" night club. During the Block investigations and prosecutions which I mentioned before, those which had reached the Court of Appeals during my year as law clerk at the Court, the "Oasis" was prominently involved. Several prostitution and pandering charges had focused on activities allegedly taking place in the club.

It was a basement night club, with a steep stairway descending to the front door right from Baltimore Street. She was also named

"Pamela" and her calls to my house weren't any more popular with my wife than those from the other Pamela.

Rumors and press reports were that this Pamela had been the mistress of the owner of the club, Julius Salsbury. Again rumors were that Salsbury was involved heavily in gambling operations throughout the city and county. Supposedly, he was one of the top people involved in gambling and related public corruption. None of that did I know. Gambling, other than the big pinball case, was never one of the elements of the city's vices that I was heavily involved with. Salsbury had been charged with a federal crime, and just prior to beginning a sure march to a federal prison, he disappeared. I never knew anything about where he went. Rumors at the time were that he had escaped to Israel and was being protected there from any extradition possibilities. Recently, I read in Michael Olesker's book "Journeys to the Heart of Baltimore" that he was secreted out of the city to Canada in the bottom of a horse van.

At any rate all I knew about Salsbury is what I heard from prosecutors, the newspapers and my favorite radio news man Eddie Fenton. When Pamela contacted me to represent her in some interests, she represented to me that she was the outright owner of the Oasis, and had legal documents on their face showing that she was the owner. I remember asking Eddie if he thought Salsbury was really gone, having transferred the business to Pamela. Over a series of drinks in my office on St. Paul Place across from the courthouse, Eddie assured me that Salsbury was gone, probably for good. I figured he knew more about the truth of the matter than anyone else in town who would talk to me.

He, of course, made me promise that if any good case came up involving the Oasis I would let him know.

Pamela had been the headline stripper at the club. When she performed again, she still led the card in class. The dancers performed on a squared off dance floor in the middle of the club. Tables surrounded the floor, and then second levels of tables were along the walls in darker areas of the club.

When most of the strippers danced, there was hardly a noticeable reduction in the din of patrons getting too drunk for their own good, buying "drinks" for the dancers between their performances.

But, when Pamela danced, she performed, and the customers and other girls paid attention. I once wondered whether it was the girls who felt compelled to quiet down and watch her perform, or the customers who were so taken with her that they focused on her and away from the other girls.

What- ever it was, when she danced everybody paid attention, including her lawyer. When she danced, she was always the main event, ending the first go round of rotation of dancers. When a girl finished her dance, she went to a dressing room to put back on some of her clothes, and then came back out table to table until she found someone who couldn't live without her joining him or them at the table for the cost of drinks. Pamela did not do the table mingling. When she finished her performance, and re-clothed herself, she went to her office or to a small bar in a corner of the front of the club. When I had to meet her at the club, we did business in the office and then I had drinks at the small bar. She would join me socially for a few minutes but then went about her business.

The police made several attempts to make some form of criminal or alcohol violation stick to her as owner of the club. The object was to gain the basis for seeking cancellation of her liquor license. That would have put her out of business. This was before the emergence of today's Gentlemen's Clubs where nudity and contact dancing, without alcohol, are the attraction. The time had not yet come for the idea of eliminating alcohol to avoid oversight by liquor licensing agencies. No one had yet come to the conclusion that naked dancing, naked mingling with the patrons, and "lap-dances" would make huge profits without alcohol. Who would have believed in those days that a twelve dollar coke could buy ones way into a mecca of naked females.

I believed that the real reason for the city's efforts to get her license was to pressure her into telling them where Salbury was. On a couple of occasions, a detective who had made an arrest at the club would "hint" to me that she could make all her problems go away if she told what she knew. I discussed that option with her, and told her what I suspected. But, she denied knowing anything about where Salsbury was.

Most of the charges were frivolous, considering all the actions that were going on openly in other bars on the Block and being ignored. I easily got them dismissed at the Municipal Court. Finally police filed a charge that worried me. It was a charge of allowing an obscene act in the club. Obscenity law was still in the formative stage, particularly as to live performances. Mr. Justice Potter Stewart had uttered his famous comment just a few years earlier, when he said that he wouldn't attempt to specifically define "hardcore pornography", i.e., obscenity, "But, I know it when I see it." For some time before this, and for many decades after, if an officer witnessed a naked dance as described by statute, he usually filed a complaint with the liquor licensing board rather than a criminal complaint. (It was and has been pointed out many times that the language defining an obscene dance or act was more pornographic than the challenged dance or act.)

92

In this case, two officers had gone into the club, stood watching three dancers and claimed that one of them displayed her entire naked body in the last segment of her dance. Of course, I doubted the veracity of the officers' statements. Both officers were known to Pamela's personnel. She always had two men standing at the front door watching and screening everyone who entered. They were alert enough, and big enough, that they served as "bouncers" as well as screeners.

When a police officer, or officers, entered, a signal was given to all personnel in the club that police were on the premises. On several occasions prior to my going into private practice, I would take out of town police or prosecutors to the Oasis because I considered it relatively safe and tame. When we entered, we did not know how the signal was given, but it was obvious that all personnel knew that we were "the law". No dancer approached us for drinks, and while we were present, table mingling ended. The bouncers knew these two detectives, and alerted Pamela and the personnel to the presence of the officers. I had just gained a dismissal of a bribery charge where the officer claimed that a dancer offered sex to him in exchange for not charging her with soliciting. The city charged Pamela as an accomplice.

The officer could not identify the dancer who supposedly made the bribe offer. He named her by first name only. But I was able to show that the woman charged as the principal was not at work on the date of the alleged bribe offer. I showed him photos of the dancers who were employed on the date of the incident charged. He, wisely, would not identify one of them because he didn't know who was working on that date and who wasn't.

Having just come through that case, Pamela called me at home as soon as she knew that two detectives had come into the club. I told her to make sure that no laws were violated, that the dancers performed very conservatively, and to make sure that the officers knew that recognized them. She called me in a few minutes and told me that she went to where they were standing, offered them free drinks "if they weren't on duty" and called over the dancer about to perform and introduced her to the officers.

Within an hour, she called to tell me that they had arrested her and a dancer, and had ordered her to close the club. This was a Friday night, and losing the last three hours of the night meant a big loss in money. This was not a stupid lady. She was every bit as smart and articulate as Blaze Starr. She would not have exposed her club and her business to known officers by allowing a nude dance to take place right in front of them.

I went to the police station that night because I wanted to talk to the officers quickly. But by the time I got there, they had already gone. Never did officers leave the station that quickly after an arrest like this one. It was pretty clear to me that they went in to the bar prepared to make an arrest. Cameras from one of the television stations had been waiting at Central District, just a block and a half from the club, to televise Pamela and her dancer arriving under arrest.

A friendly officer told me that the cameras were set up over a half hour before Pamela and the dancer arrived at the station so obviously they had been alerted that an arrest was going to be made. Unless the detectives went in knowing they were going to make an arrest, they couldn't have given such advance notice to the television people.

Pamela told me that the officer that seemed to be the lead told her as he arrested her in her office that she, "knew how to make the trouble go away." She said that she asked him what he meant, and he simply said, "you know what the brass wants." The dancer said that one of the officers said to her that since they had to arrest her anyway it was too bad they hadn't really seen her naked.

But I knew that all these statements wouldn't help in the trial. The officers would deny them, and the judge was not going to credit my witnesses over officers. I knew that I would get nowhere with my witnesses denying that the dancer was ever nude during her performance. I also knew that an obscene dancing conviction would no doubt lead to loss of the liquor license. So for one of the few times in my life I had to defend a criminal case on the specifics of the "law" instead of the facts.

I challenged the probable cause for making the arrest, on the ground that what the officers observed did not constitute "obscenity" as defined by the United States Supreme Court.

On the Monday following the arrest on Friday night, the liquor license was temporarily suspended and a notice of hearing on the license was placed on the door of the club and served on Pamela. The suspension was based on the charge.

I didn't know what the judge's position on the case might be. With both the Block and pressure from the brass both involved in the case, it would be impossible to determine prior to trial what the status of the judge might be. So I had to present my argument with the assumption that the judge had been primed and prepared by the police.

As soon as I got notice of the suspension of the license, I called Eddie Fenton and filled him in on the case and what I suspected about the case. I made sure that I needled him a little about the television station having been alerted by the police. That, he didn't like at all.

93

Two days prior to trial, I spoke to Milton Allen, the State's Attorney, in the hallway of the Courthouse. I asked him whether he had given any directions to the assistant State's Attorney who would handle the case, in other words was I wasting my time trying to deal the case. Milton told me that he had heard nothing about the case except what he read in the Sun and heard from Eddie Fenton. He asked me how I had gotten Eddie so fired up about the case. I told him that I had learned from watching him in action over the years. Uttering a laughing profanity he walked away. I believed what Milton said. He was totally honorable in my book. I never had any reason to doubt his word, even when he had no legal obligation to be truthful with me.

I spoke to the assistant State's Attorney the day before trial to see whether we could deal the case. We were good friends, and had been for many years. (As I have said elsewhere, the Municipal Courts were handled by assistant State's Attorneys who were part time. They had their own private practices, and handled only appearances in the Municipal Court.) He told me he would really jeopardize his standing with the department if he dealt the case. No more needed to be said.

Eddie Fenton showed up just prior to trial, and used a telephone in the desk sergeant's area to call in his story that trial of the city versus the Block was about to begin. His very presence made the judge, officers and prosecutor nervous.

The prosecutor called the lead detective as his first witness. I objected to his testimony as soon as he was sworn, and argued that he had no probable cause to even state the observations he made at the club because he did not know the elements of the crime prior to, or even after, the observations. The prosecutor said that my argument was not valid to keep out of evidence the physical observations made by the officers. The judge listened carefully, and said he was interested in hearing my theory.

I knew I had lucked out: either the judge was really interested in the argument, or more likely, he didn't want to have to rule against my client. Either way, it gave me a shot.

I asked the detective to define "obscenity", and he said simply that it was as nude dancing. I took him through all the elements. When I asked him to explain to the court the element related to "contemporary community standards", he was stymied. I went on to "prurient interest" and he was able to tell me that it meant something like sexual desire. But, he wasn't able to relate that to the "contemporary community standards". He wasn't able to tell me what, to him, "patently offensive" meant, and finally he blew the element related to whether the dance taken as a whole lacked "serious literary…or artistic..value". I quizzed him about the Gayety Burlesque House and nude dancing featured there. He admitted that he was aware that the dancers at the Gayety stripped to complete nudity almost immediately into their routine. I asked him how he could justify saying that nudity was part of such a small segment of my client's dance was obscene, when the community standards of Baltimore obviously accepted nudity at the Gayety.

The prosecutor objected that the link of nudity to liquor license regulations was different than the definition I was inquiring about. I argued that the only definition relevant in this case was the criminal, because this was a criminal trial, not a trial before the liquor board.

The judge agreed and overruled the objection. When I finished questioning the officer, it was clear that he could not define obscenity from a criminal standpoint. He could not define what the obscenity was that he would have been looking for, other than mere nude dancing.

I also had established through him that prior to the dance for which he made the arrests, my client came over to the detectives and introduced the dancer to them. I asked him how regular it was that someone would intentionally violate the law right in front of known officers of the law. The prosecutor objected, and I argued that as a vice expert he should be allowed to answer. The judge agreed, and the officer acknowledged that it didn't happen on a "regular" basis.

My argument to the judge was that when even the enforcing officers were not able to define the crime, the defendants were in an impossible position as being expected to comply with a law which didn't have specific guidelines. I argued that due process required that a defendant had to be able to know the parameters of a crime prior to being expected to comply. I argued that if the officers didn't know what the elements of the crime were, they could not possibly have formed probable cause in their minds for making observations they needed to make the arrests.

The judge's major question was how there could ever be an obscenity charge made under my argument. I answered that the officers could go to a judge, tell the judge what they observed, and let the judge determine whether under the law of obscenity there was probable cause for issuing an arrest warrant. I argued that because of the sensitivity of the First Amendment, it was necessary for an officer to seek the impartial review of the court familiar with the nuances of obscenity law, so that defendants were not subject totally to the subjective discretion of the officer.

The judge took a recess, and on his way into chambers, Eddie beat him to the door and asked whether he could use the judge's phone to call in his story. Eddie had left half way through the testimony, and had come back just in time for the argument, as though he knew exactly when it would begin. Of course, the judge was not going to deny the phone to Eddie, so WCBM listeners were given the up to date status of the case as seen by Eddie, as the judge stood and listened.

From outside the open door, the prosecutor and I heard Eddie emphasizing the First Amendment and free speech. The prosecutor laughed and said he doubted the judge could resist Eddie's approach. I told him that if I won, I probably owed Eddie a drink and he said, "more than one." The detectives were very nervous and hurried out of the court room to confer in the hallway. I told my clients to go out in the hallway and just stand there next to the officers. I told Pamela to ask the lead detective how she could get rid of the problem now. She never got a chance to ask. When they went out and walked over toward the officers, the officers hurried back into the courtroom.

By this time, I wasn't surprised when the judge ruled with me, limiting the application of the argument to the question of obscene dancing, and dismissed the charges. The prosecutor said that the city might want to appeal. I said that I welcomed the appeal so that we could expand the press coverage of the important free speech issue. There was never an appeal filed. I did treat Eddie to several drinks. Not that he would have done what he did just for me. He loved covering interesting news, and over the years he had covered many of my cases as prosecutor. This was the first defense case of mine in which I can remember him taking special interest.

Strangely, the license suspension was lifted within hours of the court's decision. I never had to file any formal documents with the board, and even though they could have looked beyond the criminal decision, there was no effort to push the suspension by the police or the regulators. I think the police justifiably were concerned as to what might come unraveled as the case meandered through the process.

All along I suspected that my clients from the Block, and from the prostitution business, paid police protection. But I never asked for and they never volunteered confirmation. So other than the one time when Sgt. Tabling showed me that Jackie deserted her house when he radioed in that he had a raid planned for her neighborhood, I never had any evidence of inside connections by these ladies.

CASES THAT MAKE YOU GO HMMMM!

94

One major case that came down from the Maryland Court of Appeals has always caused me to wonder what in the world our whole system of laws is supposed to be about. It caused a lot of turmoil in the criminal justice system throughout the state but mostly in Baltimore City where we were hard pressed to keep up with the regular day to day flow of criminal cases.

The Court of Appeals reversed a second degree murder conviction of a defendant who was a Buddhist. The judges reversed the case because, now get this, the Grand Jurors who heard his case and presented him to be indicted, had sworn an oath which ended "so help me God". Now, this was the Grand Jury, those people who only hear a portion of the evidence in order to determine whether the defendant is to be charged. They don't convict him or her. They don't have anything to do with the trial. They only decide whether there is "probable cause" to believe that a crime occurred and that the defendant did it.

The Court decided that a Buddhist was deprived of a Grand Jury of his peers if the jurors had to swear an oath before "God". How asinine. When you stop to think of all the young people who have fought and died for this country so that we can have the rights we enjoy—you have to wonder how many of them fought less, or tried less, because their oath was to "God". You have to wonder how many of them really thought they were fighting so that a Buddhist could escape the penalty of the criminal law if the Grand Jurors who charged him stated an oath to the "God" who was so important to every one of our Founders.

You have to wonder whether we get less justice when the last thing our Supreme Court hears before the case begins is "God Save This Honorable Court." Well, you get the idea of how stupid I think the decision was.

But what was really bad was that the decision didn't just affect the Buddhist murderer. The Court made the decision retroactive to apply to every case that had been decided, so that defendants who had been pleaded guilty or been found guilty and were serving their sentences had the opportunity to have their pleas set aside and their convictions set aside.

All of a sudden, over night, our case load nearly doubled. We had the current case load plus the old cases in which a defendant got to choose whether to accept the sentence he was serving, or have another go at "justice". Fortunately, for the most part, it was just an administrative nightmare. Anyone who had served most of his or her sentence, who had gotten a sentence less than the maximum, wouldn't risk another go. But sometimes a bad case slipped in on the docket. Our assignment clerk had no way of knowing how serious a case was so as the cases came up with the defendant's decision to have another go, the case got put on our regular, daily assignment.

95

One day on my regular docket assignment before Judge Meyer Cardin, there appeared the case of Melvin Junior Harris. When I opened the file, the day before the case was set it was bare except for the indictment. No police reports, no nothing. The defendant had been in prison for about 5 years already. He had been charged with rape, burglary, and had been sentenced to life plus ten years. With such consecutive sentences I knew it was a bad case. I asked Tom Coppinger, the lieutenant of the police squad that was assigned to the States Attorney's office, to see whether he could find the witness.

I requested a postponement on the day the case was scheduled, and Judge Cardin granted the request and set the case for a special trail date before him. The defense attorney waived jury trial, so the case was set for trial by Judge Cardin.

The next day Tom reported to me that he had gone to the address given for the witness and found no one home. So, he went back that evening and the witness's mother was there. In the meantime, we had dug up police reports, and the old grand jury transcript. It turns out that the victim was an honor student at a Catholic high school at the time of the crime. She got home from school, walked in with her arms full of books, and then turned to go back and close and lock the door. The defendant, Melvin Junior Harris, had walked into her apartment behind her, put a knife to her throat and raped her. He then took $10 from her purse and left.

I can't remember now what caused his arrest but he was chased and caught by a police officer within a few days of the crime. He waived a jury trial and was convicted of burglary for entering the apartment without permission and rape. As I said, his sentence was life plus ten years.

Now, the up to date news came from Tom. Our honor student was now a strip dancer at a "night club" in Atlantic City, and was girlfriend of the owner. Her mother said she would get the message to her to see how she felt about a re-trial. We knew she had to be in favor of a retrial, otherwise the only way I could get her into court would be by getting an order from a New Jersey court ordering her back to testify. That wouldn't do me any good if she wasn't favorable to coming back.

About a week later, Tom came in and said the victim had called him and was outraged that the defendant was getting new trial. She said she would come back to testify because the guy deserved to be in prison for life. Tom told her when the trial was scheduled, and she agreed that she would come down to Baltimore the week-end before the trial, visit with her mother, come in to go over the case with me and then be there for the trial.

The day before we had our meeting scheduled, she was supposed to call and let us know she was in town. No call came, and there was no answer at her Atlantic City number. The "club" said she had gone down to Baltimore on personal business. So, I asked Tom to go see whether she had gotten to the City. He came back from her mother's apartment and said the victim would be in right after lunch. He said he knocked on the door and there wasn't any answer. He tried the knob and the door opened to the length of the safety chain. He saw our witness lying on the couch in the living room naked. He quickly pulled the door back closed and knocked louder and said, who it was. When she opened the door, her robe was open and she was still naked underneath. As he just stood there, she grabbed the robe together and said something like "I must be embarrassing you."

He left and she promised she would have her mother drive her to the courthouse that afternoon.

Of course by the time our appointment arrived, every prosecutor had heard the story, so the hallway past my office was the busiest that day that it ever had been. She was stunning. She was wearing a slightly above the knee purple dress. She stood probably 5'8" or 9", had shoulder length black hair, and was just simply, stunning. Tom brought her and her mother to my office and introduced us. Trailing behind them was a line of prosecutors, all apparently with business just beyond where she was going.

She and her mother sat down, and I started talking to her about the events of that day of the rape. She crossed her legs, and her mother reached over and tried to tug down her dress. She brushed her mother's hand away and went on talking. Undaunted, her mother said something like "Sharon, pull your dress down, you'll embarrass Mr. Grant." She just smiled and said something to the effect "Oh, mom, I'm sure Mr. Grant has seen more than I'm showing him right now." I have no idea what I said, probably something like, "just feel comfortable" or some inane thing.

We went through the facts. Her voice was steady, slightly deep and very seductive. She had green eyes that just sparkled when she laughed or made some joke about her mom being too "prudish". We then went through her life at the present, and I prepared her for the fact that the defense might try to impeach her credibility with the type of life she was leading. She openly said she lived with the owner of the club and had nothing to hide.

I interviewed her longer than any witness I ever talked to before trial---in fact the only witness who ever came close in time would be Charles Clifford Cofeld in the bank robbery series.

Throughout the interview, prosecutors passed by the office, all slowing down as they passed. She remarked at how busy that section of the office was, and I told her I thought it probably had to do with her rather than business with me. She just laughed and enjoyed the attention. When finally she and her mother got up to leave, there was a group of prosecutors that were standing up the hall, kind of trapped in a hallway cul-de-sac. She turned and smiled and waved to them saying something like "bye for now."

96

The trial was in two days. The next day I went to the Grand Jury and had them issue a superseding charge, adding the charge of robbery because of the ten Harris had taken from her purse. By asking for a new trial, Harris had waived any right to be tried on the old Indictment, so I added the robbery charge. I had decided that in case of a conviction, he should pay a little extra for a charge that should have been made at the time.

The day of the trial, I left Sharon in the office with Tom until I was ready to call her. We took care of the pre-trial motions such as motion to dismiss the robbery charge which I resisted by arguing that I was just presenting the charges I would have presented had I been the prosecutor at the time. Just before I was ready to call her, Tom brought her into the courtroom. I think more than half of the prosecutor's office was in the courtroom. The jury box which was not being used was filled with prosecutors. The courtroom was full.

She was a magnificent witness—not overly emotional, but emotional enough to not appear disinterested. Her testimony took about an hour and a half and I took her through the details of her current life as a strip dancer, living with her boss. I wanted to get that in on direct.

On cross examination she did even better. At one point the defense counsel who was one of the very best challenged her statement that she had an almost photo memory. This came after she described the shoes that the defendant had on the day of the rape. Counsel asked her to describe the shoes he had on. Now, she couldn't have seen them for more than a few seconds when she walked in to take the witness chair, because she couldn't see his feet from the chair. She described his shoes to the "t", even as to his left heel being more worn than the right. He said "no other questions". I asked whether it was necessary to state for the record that she was correct, and he just shrugged and said no.

I had no redirect. She left the witness chair and was followed out of the courtroom by the whole entourage of prosecutors, like the High Priestess of the Nile with her following. Judge Cardin called counsel to the bench, and when we got there he grinned and said, "do you get the idea that the crowd wasn't here to see us?"

The defendant didn't take the stand. The judge found him guilty of all charges and then sentenced him to life plus the original ten plus a consecutive fifteen for the robbery, for a total of life plus 25 years. He made it clear for the record that he didn't impose the extra sentence as punishment for demanding a new trial, but as the sentence that he would have imposed had he been the original judge.

The result turned out all right. But just imagine what could have happened. Because some other defendant, a Buddhist, raised a religious issue, this rapist could have gone free after serving just a portion of the sentence that was justified.

How in the world a court of rational men could have ruled that a Buddhist was deprived of his rights because a Grand Jury had taken an oath to do their duty so help them "God", is beyond me. It was at the time, and is even more so today, absolutely ridiculous.

As a result, hours and hours were spent in getting ready for a new trial, transporting the defendant back and forth from prison to jail to the courthouse, inconveniencing the rape victim by taking her back through the entire event (although at times I think she was glad to have the chance to go after the guy again, this time as a mature woman). Just think of all the hours that were spent not just on this case, but on all the other cases that had to be re-tried because of the impact of an oath in the eyes of "God" administered to Grand Jurors who believed in "God", not in Buddha.

I heard later that several other serious felons withdrew their requests for new trials when they heard about Melvin Junior Harris getting more time the second time around. I never checked it out.

97

Maybe an even worse case is one that took place right here in Idaho. When I came back from Baltimore, and worked briefly in the Sheriff's office, I worked on a case with Red Merritt. The Nampa police had a whole series of larcenies reported where ladies panties had been stolen from clothes lines. There were also burglaries reported where the only property missing was ladies panties taken from dresser drawers. Canyon County also had a series of reports of panty thefts, with no suspect in any of the cases.

Then, one day a lady on the north side of Nampa got home from work and found her front door open. She went inside and was confronted by a man coming out of her bedroom with a handful of panties. He was also carrying a hand gun. In spite of the gun, she screamed and he ran past her and out the door. Several members of a family were eating in their front yard a few doors away, heard the scream, and ran toward her house. They saw the guy run out the door and around the corner. They followed him and were close enough to get the license number of a station wagon he jumped into and sped away. They said there was a child in the station wagon, either a girl or a boy with long blonde hair.

Red worked the case and got a license number check that linked the plate to a guy who lived in Meridian, a town half way between the site of the crimes and Boise. From all visible signs, he was a fine, upstanding citizen. He had been named as "man of the year" the previous year by one of the Lions Clubs in the Boise area, and was active in their Little League program. His last name was Larson. When Red started checking records, he came across a case from years before that had been worked by railroad police and a county sheriff in eastern Idaho. Red checked with the retired railroad detective and found that the name of the current suspect was the same as that of a kid who had been convicted of rape and murder. He said the case had been appealed so I found the case decision from the Idaho Supreme Court.

This same panty burglar had been convicted of raping a high school girl, beating her probably to death, and then throwing her from a very high bridge down on to railroad tracks far below in a steep ravine. Her body missed the tracks and was lying along- side the tracks. A railroad engineer spotted the body. The investigation led to Larson. The file in the case showed that he had attempted to kill a woman before he killed the high school girl. He entered her home, started to fondle her and then tried to strangle her when she resisted. He was caught and went through a series of examinations as a juvenile.

The psychiatric reports said that he had a serious mental disorder that caused anger toward women, and predicted that he would kill a woman. He was of course released and put under supervised juvenile probation which he was on when he killed the girl.

The trial judge who sentenced him imposed a life sentence "without the possibility of parole" and even though knowing that the last phrase didn't carry weight of law, he sent a sentencing report to the Department of Corrections in which he strongly recommended that Larson never be paroled.

Larson showed up again a few years later. A dentist's wife in Ontario, Oregon came home from shopping. As she walked up to her house, she noticed a station wagon parked in front with a young boy with long blonde hair sitting in the car. When she got to her front door she found it standing open. She entered the house and confronted Larson coming down the stairs from the upstairs bedrooms with a handful of her panties. She screamed, and he ran out the door. She followed him out and got the license number of the station wagon. The police traced the license plate to Larson who had been paroled from Idaho in spite of the judge's recommendation against any parole ever.

Larson's parole had been transferred to Portland, and within a few months the supervised portion of his parole was terminated, and he was left without supervision. The dentist's wife identified Larson's photo as the man who had confronted her in her home. His parole was violated, but evidently he had never been picked up before confronting the Nampa woman in her home.

Red got a warrant for his arrest and turned it over to the Sheriff's office to serve since Larson lived outside the county. We knew what station wagon he drove, and knew his license number. We knew where he lived in Meridian in a new, up scale subdivision. So, another deputy and I sat in a parking area up the road from the subdivision and waited for him to come from work. We spotted the station wagon, got in behind it and stopped him. We identified him as the Larson named in the warrant, both from photos and from his i.d. and from his license plate. We searched the station wagon, and under the floor of the back area, stuffed in and around the spare tire were dozens and dozens of pairs of women's panties and several pornographic magazines.

We took him into custody and took him to the Meridian police station to arrange for a tow truck to pick up his station wagon and to give him a chance to call an attorney. Instead he called the mayor of Meridian. The mayor arrived in just a few minutes, really fit to be tied. Boy, he was angry. He tied into me about making a false arrest and making unfounded charges in "my" town. I showed him the box of panties and the pornographic magazines, and I showed him a copy of the Idaho Supreme Court decision about the murder of the high school girl. I said something to the effect of "Mr. Mayor, you might want to check with your friend and see if he isn't the same man named in this murder decision." He looked at the case, took it with him and went in and talked to Larson for a few minutes.

When he came out, he handed me the decision, and without a word, slumped out the door of the police station. The officers on duty were delighted. Obviously, the mayor was a regular pain in the neck when they didn't treat his friend's right.

When I turned the panties over to Red to check with his burglary and theft victims, he had them checked for semen stains. The test was positive. Only two victims of the thefts could identify panties; there were two pair with unique enough patterns, and tears one dolphins, one kittens—that the women were sure they were theirs.

So, Red charged him with two petty thefts, and he was scheduled to go before the Magistrate to appear on those charges and the assault which had been charged in the case of the Nampa woman who had confronted him in her house armed with a handgun. The prosecutor told Red there was no need to appear because the cases would just be re-scheduled for preliminary hearing on the assault.

When I got to work that afternoon, I noticed on the court record that Larson was fined and released. I called Red, and he came to Caldwell. He checked the court records, and sure enough found that Larson had pleaded guilty to all charges, had been fined two hundred fifty dollars and costs and was released. Red tried to call the prosecutor from the sheriff's office and was told that he was in a meeting. Red told the pa's secretary that he was coming to the office.

The prosecutor's office was right outside, across the driveway from the sheriff's office in the jail. It was in a double wide mobile home with a front and back door. Red told me that he knew the pa would try to dodge him. So, he went out the side door of the sheriff's office and stood by the back corner of the pa's office. Out the back door hustled the prosecutor, and Red stepped right out in front of him. I swear I thought the pa was going to have a heart attack.

His explanation was that a friend of the Magistrate had called and told him that there was a big misunderstanding and that Larson was a real fine citizen and active in Lions Club work as was the Magistrate. The prosecutor said that he didn't have anything to dispute the judge, so he went along with a fine. Red handed him the police file, and told him that every paper in that file was in his pa's file. Red left him sputtering, and came back to the courthouse and went in to see the Magistrate. After reviewing the file, the judge called his friend and chewed him out, but there was nothing he could do because jeopardy had attached.

Red made efforts over the next few weeks to convince someone to pursue Larson on the Ontario charge, and to try to link him and his panty horde with some of the other larcenies and burglaries. I just dropped it. I had seen the paranoia of this prosecutor at work before as I've said in the defense attorney chapter, so I knew that "justice" had no place in his repertoire.

Now, this all happened right here in the land of "good living" where the evils of the city had not even reached, or so I was told.

98

Another case of grave injustice occurred through my own fault, mine and no one elses. One of the cases that I inherited when I became an assistant United States attorney in Baltimore was already old when I got it. It involved the subjection of a man's young, teen-age daughter to sexual encounters with his friends. The reason it was a federal case is that the guy lived in Maryland, and his daughter lived in Maryland, but he would take her to his friend's house in Philadelphia and while the men all played cards and partied, the girl would have intercourse with the men upstairs.

The girl had been fourteen at the time, but you would never have guessed that from the nude pictures of her that her dad sold. She looked every bit the part of a fully developed woman. When I got the case, she was 17 and was living in a state home for juveniles. I went with the FBI agent to interview her. She was pretty worldly as she described her actions with the dad's friends and with the dad. She said she really harbored resentment toward her dad because she had found out that he was charging the men for having sex with her. She said it hadn't bothered her until she found out he was charging and not sharing the money with her.

The FBI agent said that she would be ideal as an informant for the Bureau somewhere like New York City where she could blend in with the girls and women who were sought by members of organized crime groups. Otherwise, it was hard to tell what kind of a life she was going to lead.

She was the only witness who lived in Maryland. Her dad was in the city jail and had been there for about a year when I got the case. I was not experienced in trial law in fact at that point I had tried only one case, a simple property damage case. Trial of this case would involve a complicated series of court papers issued by the Maryland court, then sent to the Pennsylvania courts for issuance of papers there, and then arranging for getting the witnesses to Baltimore after the court paper work was completed. All this was necessary to get witnesses from outside the District.

I kept putting it off, putting off the necessity of convoluted paper work. I wasn't getting any pressure from the FBI to try the case because it was already so old. I wasn't getting any pressure from the defense attorney for obvious reasons. He was letting the case sit until he could seek dismissal for lack of speedy trial. In the federal courts at that time, the lack of a motion for speedy trial by the defense didn't matter; all that counted was the time that lapsed. I wasn't getting any pressure from the victim. She was better off in the home than she had ever been, and the only reason she wanted to testify was because she was mad that her dad hadn't shared money with her.

So I put it off, and put it off. Finally, the defense moved to dismiss for lack of a speedy trial. I put in a lot of hours on research, and was able to demonstrate I thought that the defendant's case had not been prejudiced by the time lag, and that he had never asked for a speedy trial. But I knew I was wrong, even though I thought my legal argument was correct. I knew I had blown it. The judge dismissed the case for lack of a speedy trial. My associates tried to comfort me by pointing out that he had served nearly four years in "hard time" in the City Jail without any outside exercise or other advantages because he was held as a federal pre-trial detainee. Probably they were right, that he had served harder time, and more of it, than he would have served under a federal sentence.

But, I never really got over it. I knew that I had failed the girl.

Whether she cared about the trial or not I had failed her as a victim. To this day it upsets me that I didn't have the nerve to just forge into that case and take on the monsters of paperwork with which I had no experience.

THE RIOTS

99

Palm Sunday—1968. I was up at first light, having a cup of coffee, standing on our back porch looking at the slightly lightening sky. My wife had gotten up to fix coffee, so we would have a few minutes together before I headed off to work. It was chilly, as it often was just before dawn on a humid day in Baltimore.

Normally, neither of us would have been up on Sunday morning at this time. But, this was not a normal Sunday or normal day. I was expecting to be picked up by a police radio car at 7am to be taken to the Eastern District police station where a rare and unusual court day was to begin.

The night before, a little before ten pm my boss, Charley Moylan, called and directed me to head for the Eastern District. A while before that call, we heard news broadcasts that fires, looting and rioting had started big time in the eastern City.

In Maryland, people arrested had to be taken before a magistrate for an initial appearance before they could be delivered to or held in the city jail. The District police stations had lockups where the people arrested were held until Municipal court sessions began. Each station house had a court room where the initial appearances took place. Normally, these court rooms and sessions were attended by part time assistant states' attorneys---private practice attorneys who contracted to handle just the Municipal proceedings at the station houses.

But this wasn't a normal time. Charley told me that the Eastern lock-up was already filling up, and we would have to handle initial appearances quickly in order to speed up the movement of prisoners to the city jail. He said that arrests for assaults, vandalism and looting were increasing by the minute, and we had to set up a rapid movement process. He said we also would be facing a curfew that would no doubt result in many arrests.

As the first signs of the sun began to dawn, we talked about Mass, and I told my wife that I would meet her and our son Andrew at St. Bernard's for the 11 am service. I was sure that by that time, we would have moved enough cases that we could proceed normally into the Monday regular court sessions.

It was obvious by this time that the day was going to be warm and humid. That "sticky" feeling that came after the chilly pre-dawn was already in the air.

Shortly after 7am, the radio car showed up. I had told Charley the night before that I could drive to the District but he said that the police would have to pick me up. The officers told me that the District was just like a war zone. They said that the walls of the station house were bulging with prisoners that arrests had continued all night---people being arrested for arson, fighting, resisting arrest, breaking and entering and looting. They said that no businesses were being spared and that the neighborhood business sections were being destroyed.

As we crossed the northern part of the city toward Harford Avenue, I looked down toward the eastern and southeastern part of the city and could see plumes of smoke rising from several different locations. From one site we could see flames shooting high into the sky midst the smoke. It was surreal---it looked like a scene from some foreign country engaged in an actual war.

The police radio continued messages with the code for "officer needs assistance", and reporting members of the National Guard needing help. The officers told me that in several places Guardsmen had been backed up into doorways and penned in by rioters who knew their guns were not loaded. According to the officers, it had been announced publicly by some quick thinking bureaucrat that the Guard had been dispatched to the city but were not carrying loaded weapons. Whether that was true or not, I have no idea, but I do know that during that Sunday I heard many stories of officers who had to rescue Guardsmen.

As we drove down toward the District station house and got closer to the riot area, I began to suspect that I was wrong in thinking the court process could be handled quickly. The sidewalks were strewn with broken glass, sirens were coming from every direction, fire engines were in the streets, some buildings were burning and smoking, and officers were arresting people as we passed. A radio call reported a fire just breaking out, and as we passed that intersection, flames were shooting out from a store. Officers were wearing riot helmets, and when we passed fire engines, officers were guarding the fire fighters. The radio continued to call out reports of sniper fire. It really was a war zone.

What lead to this war on the streets of Baltimore City?

100

Thursday, April 4, 1968—Memphis, Tennessee. Dr. Martin Luther King was assassinated shortly after 6 p.m. He was in Memphis to help organize the city's Black population in support of city sanitation workers who had been on strike for two months. On Wednesday, April 3, he had delivered an emotional speech in Memphis calling for a mass marching, peaceful demonstration the next day. Throughout the day on the fourth, he was in meetings with organizers, making sure that there was no repeat of the violence which had broken out the last time a walk was started in the city. He had rested for awhile in his room at the Lorraine Motel before leaving to deliver a major speech that was planned for that evening. As he ended his rest, he walked outside his motel room, and was shot down by a sniper lying in wait across the street.

Shortly after 7pm a hospital spokesman announced that he was dead, killed by a bullet wound to the neck. The bullet had severed his spinal cord, and brought a death that would disturb the nation.

The shock waves spread fast. Within hours, riots had broken out in Memphis and in Washington, D.C. We heard reports of shootings, arson and looting, and the officials of Baltimore were nervous and restless. Rumors developed immediately that a white man had been the sniper, and the rumors grew into reports that the police had a suspect who was a white man who had rented a room in a rooming house across from the Lorraine. Even without the official reports, we all assumed that a white racist had shot Dr. King.

And, the resulting riots in Memphis were not a surprise. There had been disturbances and problems in the major cities of the Midwest and East for two years.

Uprisings had occurred in the summer of 1966, but Baltimore was spared. During that summer, representatives of the Congress of Racial Equality visited the City and declared it to be the "target city" for social revolution. (CORE was a civil rights organization formed in Chicago and focused originally on desegregating public transportation and facilities in Chicago. That became prominent in the Freedom Rides throughout the South designed to desegregate public transportation facilities. Committed to non-violent tactics, CORE was not trusted by the White establishment, particularly law enforcement. J. Edgar Hoover had an absolute phobia about the CORE leaders and ordered regular surveillance of its leaders, especially James Farmer, its founder and first leader. I wish I had kept the blistering attack Hoover had issued on Floyd McKissock when he succeeded Farmer in 1966. McKissock was the leader who came to Baltimore to "target" the city. From 1066 on, CORE changed its emphasis to voter registration throughout the south. Even though committed to non-violence, CORE's activities hit at transportation and voting, both critical to segregationists, so its activities drew violent responses.)

In spite of being targeted, the City was spared outbreaks of violence. In Cleveland, San Francisco (Hunter's Point), Omaha, Rochester, Atlanta, Chicago and other major cities, violence resulted in injury, death and massive property destruction. But, Baltimore was spared. Probably for that reason alone we didn't expect real violence in April, 1968. Since we had escaped violence even when CORE chose the city as a target for breaking up segregation, why not expect to escape again in 1968.

One of the great ironies of Baltimore riot history is that police commissioner Pomerleau spoke to a police conference in Memphis, no less, during the summer of 1967 and announced that his police department was deficient in riot control training. He told the Police Executive Conference on Community Tensions in June, 1967, that 60% of his police officers had a less than high school level education and came from a natural environment which produced prejudice. But he said that his community relations programs were helping to draw his officers away from their prejudice. Fortunately, this speech escaped the attention of the Black community leaders of Baltimore City, and the officials of CORE.

He bragged about the fact that Baltimore had escaped riots during 1966, and said that the City was a "community of ethnic groups with strong religious training and interests, and with few exceptions, a desire to live in harmony".

He also told them that the deficiency of his men was "by design" intentionally planned because of his belief that control of riots should be the job of the citizen soldiers of the National Guard. He said, he preferred that the police handle regular police services while the Guard fought to control riot damage. He believed that if he committed his police officers to riot control, he would deprive "the majority of our residents" the police service and protection they deserved. On its very surface, this was a statement of the utmost prejudice. What he was saying was that the "majority" of city residents would not be affected by riots and should be entitled to the regular police services while riots were being fought. If this process were carried out, all non-rioting Black residents and White business owners in the riot areas would be deprived of police help, and be dependent on mostly young and inexperienced members of the National Guard.

He said, "At this point it would be well to say that my men are perfectly willing to get in there and do battle whenever the need arises, however, there is general agreement that if this unfortunate occasion should present itself, our community relations programs as we know them today might just was well be discontinued. We cannot in my judgement be friend, brother, or father and mother to all the people one day and a force prepared and expected to do battle for an extended period of time in coping with racial land other community disorders of any magnitude the next day."

He continued, "I do not feel the police should be used in quelling riots and anarchy. This seems to be a reasonable responsibility that can be assumed by our national guard. We are all aware that when these forces are committed in sufficient quantity, on a timely basis, control is readily regained. This citizens' army made up of mechanics, salesmen, lawyers, storekeepers, and other businesses, when transformed from their day to day pursuits to that of national guardsmen have a tremendous psychological impact on the community and the riotous forces. It seems to me that it is these citizen forces who have an obligation to subdue problem areas brought about by their fellow citizens."

He couldn't have been more wrong. The National Guard was neither prepared to, nor adequately equipped to, take control and end the riots. If in fact, he was right that his police force was deficient in riot training, he certainly did his men and women a disservice, because they were required to take the brunt of the riots until the regular army gained a foothold. On that first day in the Eastern District, the officers did carry the burden of trying to control the rioters as well as protecting the Guardsmen on the streets.

He told the Memphis conference that his plan, put together with General Gelston of the National Guard, was to never to have to commit more than 500 officers to riot service. In fact, he had to commit his entire department to the riots of 1968.

He also told the Conference that Baltimore was in need of refined planning for "custodial problems with respect to volumes" of detainees. He said planning for this issue was "of a continuing nature." Apparently the planning was too difficult to put together within the next 10 months because it obviously had not been completed prior to the April, 1968 outbreak.

1967 Race riots—The Watts riot of 1965 had served notice on the nation that Blacks, especially young Blacks, in the economically depressed urban centers, were distressed with the slow development of equal rights after passage of the Civil Rights Act in 1964. The destructive Watts riots were followed by the violence which broke out in the summer of 1966 in a score or more major cities. Then came the long hot summer of 1967. Fire bombings, looting, shootings, killings broke apart the fabric of more than 150 towns and cities from Hartford, Connecticut to Tampa, Florida—from Newark to San Francisco. The worst of the big city riots damaged Detroit and Newark.

In Newark, the riot started after a Black cab driver was pursued and arrested after he passed a double parked police car. He was severely beaten, and when civil rights leaders were allowed to see him, they urged that he be hospitalized at once. A crowd had gathered outside the police station protesting the police treatment of the cabby. When the rumor spread that he had died, they began hurling bricks and other objects at the police station. The crowd then began breaking windows and looting, and the violence spread to downtown Newark. The state police were mobilized, and National Guardsmen were dispatched to the city. The rioting continued for four days, and it resulted in twenty three deaths and over 700 injuries. 1500 arrests had been made. Racial unrest had grown steadily over the prior years as reports of police brutality increased in intensity—including three deaths of young Blacks who were in custody at the time.

In Detroit, the riots began after police raided an "after hours drinking club". For several years the infamous "Big Four" tactical squad of 4 men teams had roamed the streets, arresting prostitutes and raiding after hour clubs. Reports escalated that they treated Black youths with brutality on the streets. The raid which led to the riots resulted in the arrest of over 80 people who had gathered for a party for two returning Viet Nam veterans. After the arrests, violence broke out and spread through the city. Two days later, the National Guard entered the city, and on the fourth day the 82nd Airborne entered the city to try to quell the violence. After 5 days of rioting, there were 43 people dead, nearly 1200 injured, and 7000 arrested.

But, perhaps the most dramatic of the riots occurred in tiny Cambridge, on Maryland's eastern shore. Cambridge was a depressed town of about 13,000 which had a clearly divided and segregated society. Blacks were not allowed to use the city swimming pool, skating rink and other city facilities. Even though segregated schools had been ruled unlawful in 1954 by the United States Supreme Court, Cambridge had separate schools for Blacks and Whites.

Cambridge had gained national attention several years earlier when Freedom Riders came there to integrate interstate buses. Washington DC attention focused on Cambridge because of its nearness to the capital and because diplomats complained of discriminatory treatment as they traveled in the area. As early as 1963 Attorney General Robert Kennedy urged Black and White civic leaders to work together to end the racial intolerance. But, to no avail.

During the summer of 1967, H.Rap Brown, a militant Black Power activist came to Cambridge to urge violence as a means to gain equal rights. He told a crowd that "If Cambridge doesn't come around, Cambridge got to be burned down." (Brown started out with the Student Non Violent Coordinating Committee, but his bent was violence, and became famous for his remark that "violence is as American as cherry pie" and that "If America don't come around, we're gonna burn it down." In 1968 he left the SNCC and joined the openly militaristic Black Panther Organization. Later he was convicted of murder and sentenced to life.) Very soon, someone set fire to the school in the Black section of town. Volunteer White firemen refused to respond and fight the flames because they said they were afraid of being attacked. As a result, 20 buildings and 2 complete blocks were burned to the ground.

President Johnson appointed the Kerner Commission, named for its chair the Governor of Illinois, Otto Kerner, to study the causes of the 1967 riots. Specifically referring to Cambridge, the Commission report stated the cause of the riot to be years of discrimination and segregation in the town.

1968—"Burn baby Burn"—that was the slogan of the militaristic arms of Black groups which had grown impatient with progress in integration and equality as 1968 began. There was no doubt that the nation sat on a tinder keg. Any major incident would set off another year of destruction.

Early in the year, the incident occurred. In Orangeburg, South Carolina, Black students from South Carolina State College held a sit-in at a "whites only" popular bowling alley. Pushing and shoving spilled out into the parking lot, and responding police officers began fighting with the Black students. The students retreated to the campus, but their anger at the events, in the words of Tom Brokaw in his book, <u>Boom</u>, "festered for two days."

On February 8, 1968, the students built a large bonfire. State troopers responded, accompanying a fire engine. According to Brokaw, "the students began to taunt them...[and] began to throw things at the troopers." An officer pulled his gun and fired in the air, and, as is so often the case, the warning shots back-fired, and other officers pulled their guns and started shooting into the crowd of students. The resulting mayhem was known as the "Orangeburg Massacre".

101

At about the same time, the racially motivated strike of the city workers began in Memphis. The conflict began in January when 21 employees of the city's Public Works Department were sent home without a full day's pay because rain hampered work. They were all Black. White employees were allowed to stay on the job and get full day's salary. The Union of Municipal Employees objected.

On February 11, a Union employee meeting was held to discuss grievances with the city about disparate treatment of Black employees. Union officials reported that meetings with city officials had been futile, so 500 workers decided to strike. On February 12, 1000 of the 1100 sanitation workers did not report to work, and the strike was in full swing.

The next day, February 13, hundreds of workers marched on City Hall. The march ended in a meeting at a downtown auditorium, where they booed and jeered the mayor when he said the strike was illegal and that garbage would be picked up with or without them.

Angry exchanges between the mayor and union officials heightened tension in the city, and on February 16, concerned Black and White ministers urged the city and union to settle the strike. Instead, the city stepped up its anti-strike actions, with the mayor hiring replacement workers, and a state senator introducing legislation to make it a crime to assist striking city employees. The "replacement worker" action was unsuccessful, and as garbage stacked up in the city, tensions escalated.

Violence erupted on February 23 following a special meeting of the city council in a downtown auditorium. The council ignored the strikers' demands, and strikers began a march, accompanied by Black ministers from throughout the city. Reports disputed what started the violence, but police ended up spraying mace into the marchers' faces in the downtown business district of Memphis. The next day, the city obtained an injunction designed to stop the strike. Instead, the city's action led to a decision by over 100 Black ministers to support the strike and call for an economic boycott of downtown businesses. That decision resulted in the Black community joining strikers in daily marches and mass protest meetings.

On March 5, the city council again rejected strikers' demands by a 9-5 vote, but for the first time a White councilman supported the strikers. After the meeting, striking workers, ministers and community supporters staged a sit-in in the city council chambers, and over 100 were arrested.

On March 13, a police car was damaged by thrown rocks and bottles, and fifteen cars of police officers were required to disburse a crowd of hundreds of young Blacks near a junior high school.

On March 14, Roy Wilkins, director of the National Association for the Advancement of Colored People, spoke to a crowd of more than 9000 at a rally in support of the strikers. The news reported that ministers, both Black and White, asked Dr. King to come to Memphis to support the strikers in an attempt to push the city to settlement. His visits to other sites throughout the south had successfully brought about non-violent changes in city racial practices.

Dr. King was touring the South recruiting volunteers for a "Poor People's Campaign" which he planned for Washington, D.C. He interrupted his tour, and came to Memphis, where he spoke to a crowd of more than 13,000 on March 18. He supported the strikers and urged a complete work stoppage by all Black citizens of Memphis if the city did not settle the strike.

He pledged to return to Memphis and lead a mass march on March 22. That march was postponed because of a snowfall of 16 inches, the second largest in the city's history. The protest march was rescheduled for March 28.

On March 28, Dr. King, with other Black ministers, led a march of over 5,000 people who were described later as working-class, church-going citizens. But, about a half hour after the march began, a group of young Blacks started breaking windows and looting businesses in the downtown area. As marchers ran for shelter, police responded to the rioters with nightsticks and tear gas.

The first of the major Memphis riots was underway. 3500 National Guardsmen were sent to the city, and a city wide curfew was imposed. The violence resulted in a death and 62 reported injured persons. News photos of police officers beating Blacks with nightsticks, and of a small child with a bloody head, spread throughout the nation. Blacks in cities around the country decried the violence.

Dr. King told a news conference that it wasn't the marchers who started and participated in the violence. He said that people on the "sidelines" created the violence, and he vowed that peaceful protests would continue. In fact, he pledged to return to Memphis to lead a peaceful march in support of the strikers. The march was planned for April 8 and it was to be a national march, with marchers from throughout the country participating.

On April 3, Dr. King had scheduled meetings throughout the day with young people and community leaders to plan the march and future protests. He was served with a restraining order from a federal judge prohibiting another march without approval by the court. Of course no one including Dr. King planned to obey the obviously illegal restraining order.

After the full day of meetings, Dr. King gave his final speech on the night of April 3. During the speech, which has become known as the "I've Been to the Mountain Top" speech, he called for unity, economic boycotts and nonviolent protest in support of the strikers.

He had received many recent threats on his life, and during the final moments of the speech he seemed to contemplate his death:

"And, then I got to Memphis. And some began to say the threats, or talk about the threats that were out. What would happen to me from some of our sick white brothers? Well, I don't know what will happen now. We've got some difficult days ahead. But it doesn't matter with me now. Because I've been to the mountain-top. I don't mind. Like anybody, I would like to live a long life. Longevity has allowed me to go up to the mountain. And I've looked over. And I've seen the promised- land. I may not get there with you. But I want you to know tonight, that we, as a people will get to the promised has its place. But I'm not concerned about that now. I just want to do God's will. So, I'm happy tonight. I'm not worried about anything. I don't fear any man. Mine eyes have seen the glory of the coming of the Lord."

The next evening, Thursday, April 4, 1968, he was shot down from ambush.

102

In Washington, D.C. just down the highway from Baltimore, crowds began to gather in the streets and urged on by the inflaming words of Stokely Carmichael, they began to break windows and loot businesses. (Carmichael was leader of the Student Non Violent Coordination Committee, but was forced out in 1966 when H.Rap Brown took over. Carmichael was instrumental in starting the organization which grew into the Black Panther Party. He often tried to use Dr. King's non-violent marches and events to urge Black Power.) By 11pm, the city was in full riot status, as looting had begun in thirty other cities in the nation. In Chicago, rioting started in a black ghetto on the west side and looting and arson spread throughout a 28 block stretch of west Madison Street between Roosevelt Road on the south to Chicago Avenue on the north.

But, Baltimore was spared a general uprising during the night hours of April 4. I don't even remember being aware that around midnight a homemade Molotov cocktail was tossed through a window at Hoffman's Liquor Store on Park Heights Avenue. Police records show that there were several reports of incidents in the southwest part of the city, but I do not recall that the news carried any of those reports on Friday's early reports.

Friday, April 5—The city was nervous. News broadcasts carried interviews with ministers, Black leaders and city leaders, urging against violence, contending violence would dishonor the memory of Dr. King. News reports of the violence in cities all across America increased the uneasiness.

Assistant State's Attorneys like me went about our business on that day, unaware, I think, of the meetings going on throughout the city to prepare for the worst. At least I was unaware of them. I didn't even hear of disruptions at Coppin State College and one of the high schools until the end of the day. As a usual matter, we didn't keep up to date with news outside our work, unless an associate heard some news while at lunch.

Charley did tell several of us that plans were being made for the courts to be mobilized to handle arrests in case violence broke out over the week-end. He told us that the Chief Judge of the Supreme Bench said he would call in the judges of the Supreme Bench, if necessary, to serve as Magistrates for initial appearances of those arrested. Under Maryland law, any circuit judge could perform the functions of a Magistrate.

We finished our day in court, and several of us retired to Cy Bloom's Place In the Alley, the lounge we frequented just half a block from the courthouse. It was a popular after work spot but that evening three or four of us had the place to ourselves. We talked about the murder of Dr. King and the violence that was overcoming the nation and speculated as to whether we would make it through without riots. The bartender and hostess said that business had been off all day. Even the lunch hour crowd was sparse. They told us that their few customers had been nervous about riots.

Probably wishfully thinking, we talked about how the city had been spared so far while so many others had erupted in riots. We joked about Baltimore being "different", being "low key" or even "downright disinterested". We thought we would ease through without violence. We had no idea that trouble was already brewing in the streets. We even made jokes about what we would do in case of rioting, jokes that in retrospect were pretty feeble attempts to make light of what we feared. We even teased the hostess, who lived in Carroll County, that she should become our heroine and take us all in for the week-end. She was "up" for the joking and called our bluff by accepting our challenge. We joked about what might happen if we went awol for three days with the hostess from Cy Bloom's. The two of us who were married suggested that our worst punishment would come from our wives not being very understanding.

We all left much earlier than usual on a Friday night. On the way home, the streets seemed eerily quiet and deserted. That night, for some reason that I don't now remember, I rode the #8 bus that would take me up Greenmount Avenue, which would be alive with rioting within twenty four hours. The bus was almost empty and was deathly silent. Passengers were about equally divided, Black and White. As we moved north from downtown, the complexion of the passengers changed dramatically and by the time we reached Belvedere and York roads near the City's north boundary line, all passengers were White. A man sitting across the aisle, who had remained silent throughout the trip, looked at me when the last Black passenger left the bus and asked, "Do you think they're going to burn us out?" I said something inane like, "I hope not" and the conversation ended. When I got up to leave the bus, he said, "Good luck to all of us."

That night Lodice, Andrew and I ate our dinner on the back patio. Our neighbors on both sides also ate outside and we talked about what was going on in the country and how lucky we had been in Baltimore. We lived a good distance north, east and west from any Black neighborhoods and to the north of us was Towson, in Baltimore County with almost totally White neighborhoods. One of our neighbors talked about how the riots seemed to be limited to Black areas of the cities, and hoped that if trouble started in Baltimore, it would be limited to the Black neighborhoods.

We watched the late news and were relieved that as of that hour still no big disturbances had started in the city. The news focused on terrible scenes of violence in Washington, just over 50 miles away. There were national interviews with political leaders throughout the country, predicting high numbers of injuries and property damage. Locally, as I recall, interviews with city leaders, Black and White, focused on their urging calm and predicting that cool heads would prevail. Mayor Tommy D'Alesandro announced that Monday would be a day of mourning for Dr. King, and he asked that Sunday become a special day of prayer. I don't remember even being aware that Governor Agnew had put the National Guard on a state of readiness on Friday afternoon. As far as we knew that evening, we were still dodging a bullet.

On Saturday, when we did our weekly shopping, we avoided the inner city. We liked to go to the Lexington Market on the west side of downtown Baltimore on Saturdays. It is a huge marketplace of produce, seafood, meat, bakery and flower shops which was one of our favorite shopping spots. Earlier in the week, we had planned to go there to get a smoked ham for Easter dinner. I suggested we stay away from downtown, near the Black neighborhoods, just in case.

We spent our day in White northern Baltimore City and Baltimore County that day. There wasn't a particularly high state of nervousness among people as we shopped. We didn't discuss the possibility of riots and I didn't sense any extreme fear. I think probably the attitude was generally the same as I had, that any trouble would be restricted to Black neighborhoods and not affect the white population in the outer ring of the city! Amazing, in retrospect we were relying on the all White attitude that Spiro Agnew had helped formalize in Baltimore County—even as he was considered a moderate on civil rights.

Included in our shopping was the purchase of paint and supplies to be used that night in painting our Andrew's room. Lodice liked to buy paint at Sears but the Sears store was on the eastern side of the downtown area and in a predominately Black neighborhood so we bought elsewhere that day.

I didn't look forward to the scraping that came before the painting or the painting either for that matter. We had dinner on the back patio again and our conversation with the neighbors was much more relaxed than it had been the night before. I think the fact that we had gone through a Saturday without any outbursts made it apparent to us that Baltimore would escape the fate of the other big cities in the east, south and Midwest. We weren't aware that trouble had already started. We didn't know that late Friday night a firebomb had ignited a lumber yard in the Western District and that a member of the Congress of Racial Equality had been arrested. We didn't know that on Saturday the Maryland State Police had been put on short notice alert, that several fires had been reported and crowds were gathering and breaking windows in the Eastern District.

After our quiet dinner, we began the awful scraping job. As we worked later into the evening, we heard the news that violence had broken out very near the Sears store that we avoided that day. I told Lodice how glad I was that we had avoided that part of the City. Not long after, Charley called with the word that Palm Sunday would be a work day. He told me that a police car would pick me up early the next morning and take me to the Eastern District station house. He told me the lock-up was already filling up and we would have to establish a process for moving defendants quickly through the court and out of the station house to the city jail.

103

The **Eastern District Municipal Court**—There were police stations in the Southeastern, Eastern, Northeastern, Northern, Northwestern, Western, Southwestern and Central Districts of the city. In each police station house there was a court room used by the Municipal Court judges of Baltimore (called magistrates elsewhere in Maryland). Those judges presided over initial appearances where arrestees were advised of the charges against them and advised of their rights to be represented by counsel. They could also set bail and try and dispose of misdemeanor charges.

The initial appearances had to be conducted within twenty four hours of arrest. Each morning, the defendants arrested the night before were brought into court for their initial appearances. If the defendant was charged with a misdemeanor, the case could be disposed of right away if the defendant either waived counsel or proceeded to disposition or also had counsel who chose to try the case or enter a guilty plea. Many misdemeanors were disposed of quickly during the initial appearance. If the defendant was charged with a felony, he was advised of his rights, bail was set and an arraignment was scheduled. If the defendant was represented by counsel, he could, and most often did, either waive a preliminary hearing or schedule a hearing. If he waived the preliminary hearing, the charge was moved uptown to the State's Attorney's office for presentation to the Grand Jury. If a preliminary hearing was held, the Municipal Judge would simply decide whether there was sufficient evidence to hold the defendant for presentation to the Grand Jury. The Municipal Judge could not try or dispose of a felony charge.

Each of the police stations had a lock-up composed of just a few cells where defendants could be held until the next session of court. The Municipal Judges sat each morning and each afternoon, Monday through Friday and in the mornings on Saturday and Sunday at the police station houses.

When a defendant had been processed through his initial appearance and bail had been set, he either posted bail or as transported to the city jail where he was held until his next court appearance. The Warden of the city jail could not accept a prisoner without commitment papers signed by a judge.

There was nothing in the law to forgive non-compliance with the rule requiring initial appearance within twenty four hours of arrest. The rule was closely followed because one of the early United States Supreme Court decisions regarding appointment of defense counsel involved a reversal of the Maryland Court of Appeals as to the significance of the initial appearance.

No matter what the emergency, the law did not allow delay of the initial appearance. Thus, Charley gave us the warning on Friday before the riots broke out. I certainly didn't expect that we would ever really be pressed into twenty four-hour court service just to keep up with arrests.

I was quite surprised Charley had directed me to the Eastern District. I would have thought the worst trouble would immediately develop in the Western District. It was the center of the worst of the ghettos in the city, the center of the worst of the drug trafficking in the city and had the worst crime rate in the city.

The Eastern District included neighborhoods much safer than those in the Western. But the riots started in the Eastern and the District lock-up filled up fast. We had to set up a process that assured that any defendant who was committed to the city jail was accompanied by proper documents of commitment. The Warden could not accept a prisoner without the formal commitment.

104

CHAOS IN THE EASTERN—When we got to the station house, there was a large crowd outside the front door, not pushing and shoving, just standing as though waiting to get in the building. The officers pulled around into the back parking lot of the house and when I went in I could see the line extended backward from the sergeant's bench. These were relatives and friends trying to see defendants or get them released. The courtroom was already filled with a crowd that was quiet, not rowdy, faces anxious, not angry. The noise and confusion was in the overly crowded hallways and entry ways to the station house.

I went through the courtroom into the hall leading to the judge's chambers. There were two officers with shotguns just outside the chambers' door and they told me the judge was scared and wanted close protection. I walked in and found an ashen faced, subdued judge Broccolino who was normally robust, jovial and full of life. He said, "Grant, if we're not careful we're going to get taken out. We're the enemy down here right now."

I don't know why I wasn't scared—ego, stupid, excitement, don't know the reason, but it hadn't occurred to me that we were in danger.

I told the judge what we had to do was just set up a process for moving the prisoners through rapidly, either back on to the street or off to the city jail. I said something like, "Let's not dally around on any one, just move them through so fast their friends and relatives don't have a chance to set up anything."

On the way in, the officers in the radio car told me charging papers (stating the defendant's name, the charge, where the arrest was made, the arresting officer and any details he had time to write down) were being left with the desk sergeant so the officers could get back to the streets where they were critically needed. Even at this early point, Pomerleau's plan to not rely on his force was in the dumpster. These were the papers that, connected to the clerk's court document, governed the defendant's release or commitment to the city jail. If the prisoner was remanded to the jail, the court commitment would accompany the charging papers to the jail. We had to keep copies of the charging papers for future actions on the case in the courts. Without the right commitment papers, the defendant could not be committed or admitted into the city jail. Pomerleau's statements to the Memphis conference in 1966 cut backwards on him, less than two years later, the reports on national guardsmen and their failure to properly define the crime charged, to properly define the place and involvement of the offending Black citizen, showed their deficiency in riot preparation forced him to use his police officers to handle primary responsibility for the rioters, a responsibility which he believed should be taken over by the Guard. Every officer I came in contact with that first morning bemoaned the time they had to spend protecting guard members. The reverse of Pomerleau's game plan was being put into play and the city's residents needed the security of this turn-around process.

Oral histories from eye witnesses to the riots collected by the University of Baltimore, reported businesses destroyed by vandalism and looting police made no attempt to stop early on in the riots. I didn't witness such inaction on the streets, as did the witnesses who made the statements. My work was done at the station house and at the courthouse. When I read the stories, I found them hard to believe because of my experiences with the officers bringing defendants into the station houses.

The reports of inaction became completely believable when I found and read Pomerleau's speech in Memphis. He made it clear that Baltimore police were not trained to control mass riots and he didn't intend them to be primary controllers. He fully intended that response to violence and resulting property damage and personal injuries would be the job of the Guard. Obviously the Guard was not prepared to control the riots, thus there may have been inaction during the early hours of the riots before the control duties fell back on the police by default. My experiences evidenced the fact that within at most a few hours after the violence broke out the police took on the brunt of control efforts and did themselves proud in holding the fort until the regular army could take over.

When I entered the station house, I talked first to the sergeant who showed me the charging papers and I could see, scanning through several of them and most of the charges were going to be "curfew violation". Next was "looting". I wasn't aware of any "looting" statute on the books in the Maryland Code and I knew it had been used instead of the real offense of trespass, breaking and entering, theft, vandalism or any other form of illegal conduct related to a broken into business. I knew this was no time to quibble about the word used on the charging papers. The important thing was almost every defendant would be charged with curfew violation, the least of all charges or I could reduce charges to curfew violation in an effort to get rid of the case. I did a quick check and determined that I thought I could at least argue cogently to the Municipal judge that I could try a curfew case.

I told the judge likely we would not know the real facts of any of the cases we ran through that day there was a good chance he could try many of the cases such as curfew violations and get them disposed of but if the case couldn't be tried, I would take the heat by recommending personal recognizance release or remand to the jail. I told him if I could tell from the charging papers there was no violence involved, no burglary and no theft or if there was family or relatives in the courtroom, I would probably either reduce the charge to curfew violation so we could dispose of the case or recommend release so we could clear out faster the lesser charges. I told him also if I suspected the defendant might be a risk, I would recommend a high bail and remand to the jail. The ideal was going to take it on myself to be the fall guy if a mistake was made seemed to relieve the judge a bit. It was only fair. The burden was on the state to make a case for remand and we had no time for postponement to get the arresting officers off the street.

We started the clean out of the station house process. We first had to clean out the lock-up cells which had long since been stuffed full. Prisoners were now sitting on the floor of the sergeant's area, along the walls in the court room and someone of them were locked in police cars and wagons in the yard of the house. We were in the process of moving friends and families out of the courtroom so prisoners could move into their seats. Then, the noise got worse, as friends and relatives moved to the outside of the station house lost touch with what was happening to their relatives.

We moved the curfew cases pretty fast, with most of the defendants wanting to be tried on the basis of the charging paper or arrest report, without having to post bail or waiting in jail for a later trial. The courtroom was guarded by armed officers and the whole scene took on one of martial law. That factor, together with the difficulty of posting a bail or reaching family to help with bail, no doubt prompted many pleas and stipulated trials. On the "looting" charges, where there were no notes or information from the arresting officers and where there was a relative in the courtroom, I recommended release or, where appropriate, reduction to curfew violations. We moved those pretty fast. As we moved them out, the crowd seemed to get a little more relaxed too so there was little tension in the courtroom.

As other batches came in, the charges were mixed, some firebombing, some burglary, some assault, some resisting arrest, some "looting". On the more serious charges of resisting, assault, burglary and firebombing I recommended high bail and they were remanded to the city jail. As defendants were released or banned to the city jail, I expected the lockup population to thin out. But, officers were bringing in prisoners faster than we could move them out. The cells in the lock-up were crammed full, and we continued bringing handcuffed prisoners into the courtroom.

Strange it never occurred to me, as we met our objective of

moving prisoners quickly, getting the more serious charges off to the city jail, the warden of the jail had no idea how many people were coming to him and relatively little idea which ones were threats to order and which ones were not. I later heard the Warden had been pretty outspoken about his ability to hold all the prisoners we could send him. He said he could store the defendants on their heads to make more room.

As we moved through the day, criminal defense lawyers began to show up. Relatives had by now had time to call attorneys and they had been able to get through the traffic jams and emergency crews to the station house. Volunteer lawyers also started showing up from legal aid. With the experienced attorneys it made the processing easier for me. I trusted most of them enough after they talked to their client and heard the story and repeated it to me, unless there was something specific on the charging papers that disputed it, I accepted their story and made my recommendation based on their word. The relationship between prosecutor and defense attorney was so important that a good defense attorney would not deliberately mislead the prosecutor. They had a much better chance of making good "plea bargain deals" if they played it straight with the prosecutors.

The volunteer lawyers were a different story. Being inexperienced in the ways of the criminal courtroom, they seemed shocked by the speed with which we tried to move. When I suggested instructing ten or twelve defendants at a time as to their rights and as to what would happen if they agreed to plead guilty to a curfew violation or to go to trial on such a reduced charge on the basis of the arrest papers and without the arresting officers' presence, they questioned the legality. When faced with that argument, my response was to the effect, "You better talk to the defendants and see if they want to risk sitting in the city jail in the midst of a riot and wait for their trial." As they talked to each defendant, I continued to call individual cases. Before too many minutes went by, agreement was made and the "stipulated trials" began. I would offer the arrest or charging papers, the defense would stipulate the trial could be based on the papers as the state's case that would be presented if the officer were present, and then the defendant could say what he wanted in defense. The top penalty was a one hundred dollar fine, which in and of itself was a problem in a city where it might be impossible for a citizen to get to a bank or to a family member or friend with cash. But it beat sitting and waiting in a jail where they didn't know what to expect from a mass of rioters.

I suggested to the judge that when one of the good, reliable defense attorneys was there to represent a defendant, that the judge appoint him to represent several more defendants while they were in the courtroom. He did it and we moved many more prisoners through, faster, with the experienced attorneys who were willing to agree to stipulate trials on reduced charges. When the attorneys had a doubt or just didn't want to rely on the defendant's story, they would just say, "I can't help you with this one" or something like that. On those cases, fair or not, I recommended high bail and the defendants got remanded to the jail.

By mid-afternoon, we had moved enough prisoners that the arresting officers were able to bring their arrests right into the courtroom for processing. It made the process a lot easier because the officer could tell me what he saw the defendant do. My recommendations were based then on two things: whether a relative was there for the defendant and what the officer saw him do.

As we reached this point, the whole station house began to relax a little. The judge was getting tired, but he was over his angst and was moving right along. I began to think this wasn't going to be as bad as I thought.

105

Then, Charley called and said he was sending a replacement and I was to head for the Western District. The Western station house was in even a worse condition than the Eastern had been that morning and getting worse. Just my luck, get the Eastern cleared a little and then head for the Western, a district that no prosecutor liked to work at any time, even under normal circumstances.

The Western was in the midst of the worst Black ghettos in the city, it had the worst crime rate in the city, had the most intense drug usage and delivery in the city, also had our lowest conviction rate was in cases from the Western District. The officers assigned to the Western did not have the same attitude toward seeing their cases through to completion as officers in the other districts. I got upset with them, but I had real empathy for them too. It was a tough place to work and keep a good attitude.

Let me give you an example. In my regular assignment one day I had a burglary case from the Western District. The case had been in for trial twice before and each time postponed because the civilian witness was not present. We got our files for regular assignments usually two days before trial. Unless it was a very serious case, or one was specially assigned to me, I didn't try to contact witnesses until the night before the trial. Often it wasn't possible to reach them, especially in the Western District because they didn't have telephones or they had moved from the address and phone number they had when the arrest was made. When that was the case, I called the District and either asked the officer to contact the witness during his shift or leave a message with the sergeant asking the officer to contact the witness.

We simply could not rely on the sheriff's service of subpoena on the witnesses. We didn't usually get his return until the morning of trial. And, we couldn't rely on the return either. It might say the witness was served when in fact the witness had died while trial was pending. It might say the witness was served at an address where there was only a vacant lot because of urban renewal or where the witness had been kicked out of an apartment or simply moved on.

On this particular burglary case, I could not reach the witness because the number had been disconnected. I left a message for the officer with his sergeant. From the nature of the sergeant's response to me, I had no doubt the message would never be delivered. Just before court started, I called for the witness and no one responded. The officer came up to the table and I asked if he had contacted the witness. He said he had not, also he said the witness had moved and he had no idea where she was. I told him I couldn't call the case until she was there or the judge would force me to dismiss because of the number of times the case had been postponed. The defendant was on bail, so no demand for speedy trial had been made but defense counsel was waiting to move to dismiss because of prior postponements. This defendant had a lengthy record of larcenies and burglaries.

Twice more during the morning the officer came to the trial table between cases and asked when I was going to call his case. Each time I asked if the witness had shown up and each time he said, no. He told me he had looked at the sheriff's return of service and it showed he had served the witness at an address and was now a vacant lot.

Just before I called the last case before lunch, he came up again. I said, "No witness?" and he said, "No." I asked him why he didn't make some calls and see if he couldn't find the witness. He looked at me with tired eyes and said something to the effect, "It's not my job to find the witness. I made the arrest, you should make the case." I told him I wouldn't call the case until after lunch to see whether the witness didn't show up. He told me he wouldn't come back after lunch. He had to get home to get some sleep because he was on the midnight shift. I said, "You don't seem to care whether this case gets dismissed," and he said, "I don't care this guy will do it again and get arrested again." I told him I didn't like his attitude and maybe I'd better call his captain and report him. He looked at me and said, "Call whoever the hell you want to. There's nothing more they can do to me. I'm already permanent midnight to eight in the Western District. What more can they do to me?"

I thought to myself that this poor guy had hit the bottom of the job opportunities and I felt sorry for him. I told him to go ahead home and get some rest and I would dismiss the case that afternoon. Without a word, he turned and walked out. When I told one of my co-workers about it the night during a after work drink, he just muttered, "Poor bastard."

A year after this incident, I ran into the officer again. He had been transferred to the Northwestern District and the difference in his attitude was amazing. He had contacted the witness and had him present in court, he had his reports organized in chronological order for my review, had photos, and had the evidence in hand from the evidence room at the district.

A Black ranking officer from the Western had made the politically incorrect statement to a colleague and the one time I had the sure cure for the crime rate in the District, fence off several blocks of Pennsylvania Avenue, line the fenced off street with tables, stock the tables with cases of wine and knives, put the top three hundred criminals from the District inside the fences and at the end of the melee just send the survivors to the pen. Needless to say he never made that statement publicly. But that was the District I was headed into.

The officers in the radio car taking me to the Western warned me there was chaos at the house. Crowds straining to get inside, the lock-up jammed to overflow, some defendants being held right in the courtroom and many defendants without any charging paper at all. I asked how that happened and they said that officers were so busy on the street if there was a paddy wagon nearby, they would call for it to come pick up their prisoner. In the handoff of the prisoner to the wagon, the papers either didn't get exchanged or they got misplaced. There were many defendants in there without evidence of their names, their charges, or the arresting officers.

The last three blocks to the station house were jammed bumper to bumper and it took at least a half hour to make it through the mess. As we came within sight of the house, I could see a huge crowd pushing, shoving and shouting at the front door to the house. The crowd's unruliness was evident and was different from any of the crowds at the Eastern from the beginning of the morning.

As the car pulled into the back parking area, and I got out, the strong smell of gas hit the officers and I. Just before we got there, a prisoner being put into the wagon for transport to the city jail had made a run at the officer and tear gas was released. It still hung in the air, and my eyes starting tearing and running and burning, and my nose and mouth started burning. We made it into the house and tried to get in the men's room and it was jam packed with people. We went through the courtroom where the court was in recess, went back into the judge's chambers we used his bathroom to douse, wash and rinse our eyes. It was my first and last experience with tear gas. I can understand why some people want to surrender when hit by it and why some just get mean when hit by it. I was so mad about it I might be one of the mean ones under the right circumstances.

During the recess and after my eyes were at least bearable, I talked to the part time prosecutor who had been working prisoners at the Western.

It was clear that no real smooth process had been set up for moving prisoners. The judge who had been sitting was ending his tour of duty and the recess had been called so that the new judge could get ready to go to work. I told the part time guy he and I could divide up the prisoners, him taking one batch while I tried to prepare the second. I would then try my batch while he prepared the next batch. He seemed to agree, although I later realized that he never said, "Okay" or anything affirmative. I started working on the first batch that the lock-up officer brought in and I went out to the hall to talk to the part time guy. I couldn't find him. I asked the sergeant if he had seen him and he said, "Yeah he left right after you got here." It didn't upset me. I remember laughing and saying to the sergeant, "I guess that's his idea of dividing the work load." I didn't blame him.

Charley did send help right away. It amazed me that no matter what problem I faced or what time it was, I could reach Charley who seemed to be tireless throughout the whole process. Many times I have tried to imagine how we would have functioned under his predecessors. It isn't a pretty sight in my mind. He had a sharp legal mind to the point of being a scholar but he also had a keen organizational mind which is often lacking with scholars.

The crowd in the courtroom here was angry, noisy and boisterous. When the first batch of prisoners was brought in and seated in the front row, they turned and were talking to friends and family. The hubbub was loud and overbearing. The judge came in and used his gavel, demanding quiet in the court. It didn't help much.

I have read the accounts of lawyers' experiences as they remember the riots, in interviews collected by the University of Baltimore for its 40th anniversary of the riots and many of them tell of the armed atmosphere of the courtrooms, with rings of helmeted officers and guardsmen standing around the courtroom. They didn't spend the hours and hours that we prosecutors spent in those rooms—during times when there was no protection other than perhaps one officer. Often, during the late night and early morning hours, the only officers in the house were the lock-up officers who brought prisoners in and out of the courtroom and the desk sergeant who was up to his neck in trying to get prisoners booked in. Had the judges, clerks and prosecutors given in to what should have been natural fear, the process would have totally disintegrated. We were the enemy of prisoners, their families, friends and the entire community that came into those station houses.

I have also read some of the interviews, particularly one of a Bolton Hill lawyer, who said there wasn't wide spread fear in the city and the riots were more limited disorders than riots. That lawyer did not venture to the Eastern District station house on Palm Sunday morning or to the Western District station house that night and on Monday. The lawyer must have spent volunteer time deep within the recesses of the main court room or in some administrative office, because he or she couldn't have been on the streets in the riot areas or in the crowded, loud, unruly station houses. He or she couldn't have seen the fear present on the faces of officers, defendants and victims in those station houses.

I had explained to the judge how we had worked the process at the Eastern and he said he wanted to handle the cases that way, with me recommending and he relying on my recommendation. I did tell him it was going to be a bit more difficult because on some of these defendants we didn't know what the charge was. He said, "Use your instinct and make a recommendation, if I sense something different I will just ignore your recommendation." So, off we went.

The first defendant was without papers of any kind. I had found out his name from his mother who was in the courtroom. I called the case and advised the court his charging papers had not caught up with him yet. The judge asked him what he was charged with and he snapped out, "You white son of a bitch, you tell me the charge or kick my ass out of here." The crowd let out with that chilling, low rumbling, "Ummmm" that was ominous. Without a second's hesitation, the judge set a ten thousand dollar bail and remanded the defendant to city jail on a charge of contempt of court. The "ummmmm" got louder and more ominous. The rest of the first ten defendants were also remanded to the jail even though their charges were curfew and looting. Same with the second batch and I had by that time quit making recommendations. He took a recess after he had remanded about thirty more defendants to the jail. It occurred to me that in about an hour, we had sent more prisoners to the warden from the Western than we had in half a day at the Eastern.

During the recess, the judge said he guess he had made his point and would now get back to the process we had discussed. He thought what he had done had quelled the emotion of the crowd but the clerk, the lock-up officer and I saw it differently. The crowd worried us. Now, for the first time in the day, I was scared. Whatever had prevented fear before wasn't working in the Western. Keep in mind this was before metal detectors were placed in police stations and in courtrooms. We knew the chances were good and crowd members were armed with weapons of some kind.

To this day, I don't know why we weren't victimized in the station house. The officers were so busy on the street about the only officers in the house were the one lock-up officer and the desk sergeant. The judge, clerk , lock-up officer, sergeant and I were just sitting ducks but fortunately no one decided to duck hunt.

Each time I walked out of the courtroom into the jammed outer hallway leading to the desk sergeant's bench, I was in the middle of yelling, shouting and pushing. Two officers brought in a defendant and told me they wanted to stay with him so they could testify that they had seen him throw a firebomb inside a pawn shop. They said as they drove into the station house, a woman in the crowd threw a liquor bottle at the windshield and that led to rocks and bottles being thrown at them. They told me if the National Guard heavy trucks hadn't moved in behind them, the crowd would have pursued them right into the parking area. That's the first I had heard the Guard had brought in heavy equipment to help set up a perimeter around the house.

I took the officers and their defendant right into the courtroom. When the recess was over, I called this case first. I identified the defendant, told the judge the charge was arson and the arresting officers were present to verify the charge. He looked at the defendant, called his name and asked if he had heard the charge. When the defendant said he had, the judge advised him he had the right to hire an attorney and if he couldn't hire one, there would be one appointed at the arraignment. He set the bail at fifty thousand dollars and remanded the defendant to the city jail. I heard a woman at the back of the courtroom yell out, "Jesus, Mercy" and the "Ummmmm" swept through the whole crowd. I told the officers to get the defendant out quick. In fact they took him right out to their car, I took them out the commitment and they drove the guy to the jail themselves.

We just never got caught up with the incoming defendants at the Western. We were moving the prisoners faster than we had at the Eastern because of the way the judge was handling the cases.

But every officer in the District was on the streets and the arrestees just poured in.

106

Along about dark, Charley sent two prosecutors to the District to relieve me and a radio car took me down to the main courthouse at Calvert and St. Paul. Charley met with several of us and filled us in on what he had learned through the day at briefings with the mayor, the chief judge of the Supreme Bench, the police commissioner and General Gelston of the National Guard. He said the Supreme Bench judges were going to begin hearing the initial appearances at the main courthouse. There were four large courtrooms and one smaller courtroom on the second floor of the courthouse which could hold bigger crowds than the station houses. If the prisoners were brought to the courthouse from the street where they were arrested, it would ease the pressure on the station house lock-ups and speed along the process of moving defendants back on to the streets or to the jail. He also told us that soon the city jail would reach absolute maximum, since it was already beyond normal capacity. He said officials were discussing holding some prisoners at the civic center, a downtown auditorium which was home for concerts, hockey and basketball. We also learned that we should try to get rid of looting cases on a reduction to curfew and should try the curfew charges on the basis of the stipulated arrest report.   I didn't want to cause him further stress by pointing out I had been reducing charges to curfew and trying by stipulation all day. He sent two of us to the city jail to meet with the warden and discuss any problems with the way prisoners were arriving. After our meeting, I returned to the courthouse and my colleague stayed at the jail to help with problems.

Before I left, I had to help with a major problem there was a busload of prisoners with no papers of any kind. The school bus had brought them from the Courthouse, without the papers. That meant we had no idea what charges were filed against the defendants, what district they came from or who the arresting officers were. I addressed the prisoners and advised them that we were going to find out where there papers had been misplaced and they would have to wait on the bus until we found the papers. About a half hour later, after finishing up a meeting with the Warden, I checked and still no papers and not a clue where they might be. I went to the bus and made that announcement. I told them that I would be in the jail building for about ten minutes those who wanted to stay and wait for their papers so they could clear their names should stay right where they were.   I didn't mention what those that didn't want to wait to prove their innocence should do. In ten minutes when I came back out, the whole bus load of inmates was gone. Problem solved—at what cost?

As we drove through the streets of downtown Baltimore, the streets were empty and still—eerily still.   Only police, Guardsmen and regular army were visible. I was aware that the regular army had been called in. We were not able to keep up with the news from outside but Charley told us that the army was on the job and an occasional newsman would come into the court rooms in the main courthouse. That's how we kept up with what was going on. Inside we were told that street activity was slowing down considerably since the army had come in with real strength. We just hadn't seen the slow-down in prisoners yet.

Coming back from the jail, no cars moved except police or jeeps or trucks. The wail of sirens came from all directions. The police radio still carried constant calls, and repeated "officer needs assistance" codes. The officers had heard a rumor that several people had been killed in a fire in the Eastern.

Back at the courthouse, I did get to call home for the first time all day. Lodice was fine but worried about me. She and the neighbors had eaten dinner outside. She said the sirens just came from all directions but way off in the distance. So far, violence had been limited to the Black neighborhoods. That would remain the case. I marveled at the fact that the violence was aimed at destroying the businesses that supported their neighborhoods. Little corner grocery stores where a person could buy six eggs or two eggs if they couldn't afford a dozen, were getting the daylights beat out of them. The pent up hostility toward whites was obviously more important than considerations of neighborhood convenience.

I felt some comfort from the fact that the rioters and looters were mostly on foot, moving quickly through the neighborhoods they were ravaging. On foot, they would not move too far out of their home areas—thus the mostly White neighborhoods to the far north where we lived might escape the violence. Even though at one point about the third day, it appeared that some trouble was moving north on York Road, it never got closer to our home than about twenty blocks.

I don't remember exactly when I took up assignment in the main courtroom in the courthouse, whether it was the first night or the second day and night. I do know my first work with Judge Sodaro came during a night session because at the end of his tour, the police drove him home and they let me tag alone and get some time at home for a short night's rest and a bath and meal.

Judge Sodaro was one of my favorites. A former States Attorney of Baltimore City, he was a no-nonsense judge. He cut right through the issues to the bottom line and trial before him, whether court or jury was a real pleasure. When he arrived to take over for the prior judge assigned to the courtroom, he sent for me to come to his chambers. He told me to keep my eyes open for danger to any of the court personnel and he didn't want to risk the safety of his court reporter, clerk or bailiff.

The courtroom was packed when he took the bench. Because these courtrooms were much bigger than the station house courtrooms, several loads of prisoners could be brought into the courtroom to wait for their appearances. The prisoners now were being brought to the courthouse in school bus loads. The buses were lined up around the square city block courthouse. As one load was processed through court, those going to the jail would be brought out and put back on their bus which took them to the jail. At that point, another bus would be emptied and the prisoners taken into court.

I remember at some point during the week, Charley said to me he just knew that someday in the future, someone would discover a school bus loaded with prisoners driving around and around the city in circles, not unlike the Flying Dutchman. I laughed and said, "I wouldn't doubt it at all."

Judge Sodaro processed the prisoners through in good, speedy fashion. He was not a time waster, yet he never seemed to be hurried. As the night wore on, the crowd in the courtroom got more restless. The crowd did not thin, because busloads of prisoners replaced everyone processed. At one point, the judge called me to the bench and asked me to see whether I could get us some protection in the room. The Judge, his clerk, the reporter, the bailiff, one police officer sitting in the back of the room and I were the only whites in the room. He was worried about the restlessness of the crowd. He didn't like that ominous, "Ummm?" anymore than I did.

I knew it was futile to seek more protection because there just weren't any extra police officers in the building. As I started out of the courtroom, I stopped to talk to the officer at the back of the room armed with a shotgun. I told him to stay alert because the crowd was restless, the judge was worried and I was on the way to see if I could get him some help. He just quickly said something like "sure thing", and I walked out.

As I walked down the main hall, suddenly I heard the loud blast of a shotgun. In that courthouse with its marble walls, the sound reverberated back and forth across that hallway. I ran back to the courtroom. The officer was smiling, the crowd was deadly silent and the judge had left the bench. The officer looked at me, winked and said, "I must have dozed off and the gun went off accidentally." I thanked him and went back into chambers and explained to the judge the officer had done what he could to get the attention of the crowd. He went back out on the bench and the crowd remained meekly quiet.

In the main courthouse, we heard more rumors and information about what was going on throughout the city. Some meals were brought in from time to time from at least one of the Italian restaurants in Little Italy which stayed open for police and emergency workers and the military. Officers told us armed men surrounded Little Italy, with some staked out on rooftops. Apparently the rioters didn't want to tangle with the Italians and left the area relatively untouched.

We were also told that the Lumbee Indians, who lived in a section of the city along east Baltimore Street not far from Little Italy, were armed and had advised the rioters to stay out or be killed. These were members of a tribe that originally came from North Carolina. Apparently the rioters didn't want to mess with the Indians either and their neighborhood remained unscathed.

Days and nights just blend into each other as I remember the experiences of round the clock court appearances. When I rode with the officers taking Judge Sodaro home, we experienced that eerie silence of the streets in the early morning hours after midnight. We headed north on Charles Street and saw no vehicles except military jeeps and police cars. No civilians were on the street. As we passed the Basilica and residence of the Cardinal Archbishop, we saw National Guardsmen and equipment completely surrounding the block. We were in an unmarked car and had to stop at a military check point and be cleared. As we went further north out toward the Catholic Cathedral, even the military and police presence thinned out and our car seemed to be the only vehicle moving.

As the week wore on, a homicide officer called and wanted me to go with him to see a prisoner at the Western District who told the lock-up officer that he had information on a murder that he would trade for release. As we moved west, they heard a radio call that a pawn shop which had a big supply of guns had been broken into. The site was near us, so the driver changed course and raced to the site. As the car screeched to a stop, two men took off running from the front door of the pawn shop. Both officers jumped out and gave chase. I got out of the car and, again, was afraid, thinking, "What the hell am I doing here in the middle of this war zone?"

As I stood there alone on the sidewalk, one officer came back with one of the men and handcuffed him to the door post, one hand through the front window, the other through the back. The officer then went back out of sight around the corner.   All of a sudden the second officer came running to the car, jumped into the driver's seat and shouted, "I'm going to cut him off." He took off, with the handcuffed prisoner high stepping as fast as he could to keep up with the car and not get dragged. I swear his feet and knees were coming up almost to his head. He started yelling and I did too. The driver stopped and then took off on foot again.

When both officers were back, we talked about what had happened. The handcuffed guy still had eyes as big as saucers. I told the officers I had better get a release from the guy. I asked what he stole from the pawn shop and they said it wasn't a gun and by the time they caught him he had dropped whatever it was. They didn't consider him a big arrest.

I went over to him with a notebook that was in the glove compartment. I told him that he might well have a civil case against the city. I told him he had a choice. He could be charged with burglary and taken in to be processed and then remanded to the city jail or he could sign a release excusing the city from any liability and then he could be released and on his way. He wanted to sign and get out of there. I wrote up a release, had him sign it, I witnessed it and gave it to the officers who took off the handcuffs. The guy looked at me and I told him he could go. He took off on a dead run and when he rounded the corner he never looked back.

As the regular army under General York moved on to the streets, the violence began to subside. We continued trying cases in the main courthouse but the number of arrests decreased as the firm discipline of the army set in.

I was only in the presence of the "power players," once —that was in the armory when General York first arrived. He met with the Police Commission Pomerleau, General Gelston of the guard, city officials and Charley Moylan. I do not remember why Charley dragged me along to that meeting, but I was there.

General Gelston and the other police and city officials welcomed General York and city officials welcomed General York as though he was there simply to support their efforts. He quickly, but civilly advised them he was taking charge and they would support him when and how requested. Even though he was gentlemanly about it, feathers were ruffled and things got a bit tense but only for a moment. He showed a document to a representative of the Attorney General's office it was a document with more ribbons on it, than ink. I did not read it, but when the Attorney General's man finished reading it, he told Gelston and Pomerleau (both of whom were appointed by the State) that General York was in sole command.

General York then advised that the command center was being moved from the relatively safe armory to the street at the site in the Western District where the action was taking place.

From that moment on, as the boots of the army hit the streets, the violence waved.

By Thursday afternoon, most of the city was operating again. Whole neighborhoods had been decimated, some probably never to be restored. Captain Glover and his driver took me out to the Eastern District to interview a witness to a homicide that occurred two weeks prior to the outbreak of the riots. The homicide squad had been looking for the witness who appeared in one of the last batches of riot arrests on Wednesday night. An Eastern District desk sergeant noticed the name which had appeared on a look out list and notified homicide. We drove through neighborhoods where the smell of smoke was still strong and the haze still irritating to the eyes and nose. Broken plate glass windows and doors were being covered over with plywood boards. Small riots of residents stood talking softly. Store keepers were sweeping out, broken glass and debris and hosing down sidewalls. Several buildings had been gutted by fire and at some sites fire engines and crews still stood by in case of flare ups.

We saw many Black residents carrying their clothes and belongings, moving from apartments destroyed by fire and water damage, which resulted from ground floor stores and businesses.

An automatic burglar alarm was blaring and nobody seemed to be paying attention to it. There was at that site nothing of value left to burglarize.

At a stop light, Glover's driver called to a short, fat man hurrying through the cross walk—"Hey Artie, how's business?" "Not worth a damned," Artie yelled back without breaking stride. Glover told me he was a neighborhood bookie. The barber shop where he did business was ransacked, the door hanging off its hinges.

Stalls at the market had not yet reopened because there were no people on the street shopping. A big furniture store was completely cleaned out, walls and supports buckled from the heat of the flames. (When I reviewed eyewitness statements prepared for the University of Baltimore's — 40 year remembrance event I reach the poignant story of a witness to the destruction of this family owned furniture store which had been in business for decades telling how repeated calls for police help went unheeded before the store was finally firebombed.)

When we entered the station house, a maintenance man was mopping the floor with what smelled and looked like pure disinfectant. The strong odor was startling. The desk sergeant kind of flip saluted the captain and said "Nothing will live through that Captain." Glover said "Where is everybody?" The sergeant pointed to the maintenance man and said "Harry drove them all out with that pine goop." There was no lock-up officer to help us, so Glover took the key, opened the cell and took the witness into the courtroom. The witness was willing to help us if we made sure he got to his cousins house in Ellicott City. He was afraid to be released in the City because he did not know where the killers might have relocated. He didn't want to go to City jail for fear they might have been locked up during the riots. I called a Municipal Court Judge, we took the witness with us uptown and got release papers signed. The sergeant shouldn't have let us take him without the release, but he was in no mood to stand on ceremony. We then stopped at homicide, took the statement, the witness signed it and two officers set off to deliver him to Ellicott City and then to take the release back to the Eastern. It seemed good to be back at regular work.

On Good Friday morning, very little was going on in the Courthouse, other than getting ready to get back to regular court schedules on Monday. Downtown was not busy, even though offices and businesses were reopened. The day was not normally busy downtown on Good Friday, but this day was even less buy than normal.

With little to no case preparation to do, a friend and I left early so he could give me a ride home. As we headed for his car, we passed Burke's, our spot at Light and Redwood. A sign in front advertised special on mint juleps. After all it was spring, Kentucky Derby time and thus mint julep time. My friend said he had never tired one, so we had to go in for one.

He liked it so much he ordered a second. I warned him that the julep slips up on you and strikes you down. I told him he might get away with a second, but no more. I switched to bourbon on the rocks, much less deadly than a second julep.

He slipped down the second and said he needed one more. He gushed at how they were as good and easy as homemade lemonade. I told him about having witnessed men a lot bigger and heavier than him go to their knees with three juleps. He would not listen.

After his third and my third bourbon, we left for the car. I thought he seemed in control of himself so I decided he was the exception to the julep rule of no more than two. We started up Charles Street, moving north through almost deserted streets. As we reached the portion of the Street widened into a divided boulevard, suddenly his car lurched and seemed to be moving along lopsided. I said, "We must have had a blowout." Then I realized that his left tires were on the median strip and we were in fact moving along in a lopsided car.

We laughed about it and he was able to swerve the steering wheel enough to right the car. About the time a police car came up behind us with lights on. The driver hit the siren just a "bleep" and we stopped.

The two officers walked up to the car, recognized us and the driver said, "It's been a tough week for your guys too." He asked how we were and I told him that we had about three mint juleps. At once he said, "Okay, here is what are going to do, Mike will drive our car, I will drive your car and you two will ride with me and that way we will all get home safely."

Throughout this exchange my friend had just looked at the officers with a blank look and a kind of silly grin on his face. I imagine I was not much better. We took off, the officer driving my friend's car and the other following in the radio car. All the way to my house my friend sat with a grin, not saying a word. I got out, thanked the officer, told my friend I would see him Monday and he just looked at me with the grin and glazed over eyes. What a way to end the week. I sat in the backyard with Lodice and Andy that night. We ate dinner and hardly talked at all. It was so refreshing to be outdoors, free of the noisy turmoil of station houses and a 24/7 courthouse operation. Andy wanted to play police and crooks, so I was the crook, he was the police and Lodice was the judge. The whole tumult of the riots seemed so far removed. The city would be back to normal. It was never again as it had been.

As the courthouse began to return to normalcy, the school buses disappeared and the judges started thinking about getting back to the regular work of the courthouse, many of us just sat drained. We knew what we had been through, side by side with officers toward whom my attitudes would be changed forever. Some officers for whom I had never had much respect, jumped way ahead in my eyes because of the way they handled themselves in such a dangerous time. I can honestly say, from having been right at the place where arrestees were first brought, I was impressed with the little and if any, evidence of brutality or physical abuse inflicted on rioters.

As we settled down, trying to get our minds back to regular court work, the whole experience became like a dream and round me were reminders, officers on the street still were helmeted and the streets still were mostly deserted even though the city had been returned to normal hours, without curfews.

107

The appeals from riot condition convictions—After the riots ended and after a brief week of relaxing with the regular routine of "normal" criminal cases, it was time to plan for handling the nearly one hundred appeals that had been filed from those cases disposed of at the Municipal Court level. Any defendant tried and sentenced by a Municipal Court judge had the right to appeal to the Supreme Bench. Those cases were put on the docket as trials, "de novo." In other words, the Supreme Bench judge did not sit as an appellate judge he sat as though he was trying the case for the first time. He was not bound by the verdict or the sentence imposed by the Municipal Judge. Most of us hated appeals because often we had nothing but the appeal papers and the judgment of the case below—no arrest reports, no transcript of witness testimony and no list of witnesses. We had to seek out the officer in advance to see whether any special preparation had to be made.

Charley held a staff meeting and advised that all the appeals already filed would all be set in Judge Sodaro's court and all would be scheduled on one week's docket. My team of prosecutors was assigned to Judge Sodaro's court, and Charley said it was up to us and the Judge to figure out how to dispose of them without unnecessary postponements. The docket sheets were going to show as many as twenty cases set for "de novo" trial.

I talked to Jim Dudley who was my number two prosecutor on the team and a good practical lawyer. I suggested that we each pick the top four cases on each day's docket, cases where the charges were serious enough we thought Judge Sodaro would impose at least the sentence was imposed below or a more serious sentence. We needed to avoid cases where the judge might think the Municipal Judge acted too heavy handed, we couldn't afford reduced sentences or every appellant in the courtroom would be inspired to pursue his case. Our hope was if in one or two cases the Judge either imposed the same sentence or even better, a higher sentence and many appellants might withdraw their appeals.

I went in and told Judge Sodaro what we planned. He had called me in with concern when he saw his docket for the week. His first question to me was, "How in the world do you expect us to get through all these cases?" After I explained, he thought it was worth a try.

On the Monday morning the appeal trials began, I had selected a fire bombing case where the defendant had agreed to be tried at the Municipal Court level, was convicted and sentenced to only one year which was the maximum sentence that the Municipal Judge could impose. The defendant was an unlikely fire bomber. He was attending Yale University and had no criminal record. He had been active in civil rights demonstrations by his own admission but never anything violent. I put the officers on the stand and they swore that they saw the defendant throw a Molotov cocktail into a dry cleaning shop ("Molotov cocktail" is a bottle of liquor (often Vodka for what reason I don't know) with a burning torch in it, the "cocktail" is thrown and when the bottle bursts, the flame spreads out with the alcohol.) The defendant denied his guilt and said he came around the corner just as the officers responded and they assumed he had thrown the bomb. On rebuttal, I put on one of the officers who testified the defendant had not just come around the corner, they officers saw him standing in front of the store talking to another man who took off and ran just as the defendant threw the bomb.

In closing argument, I urged the court to convict the defendant on the officers' testimony and I urged the court to impose a sentence far higher than that given at the Municipal level. I made sure that my statement was making clear the crowded courtroom that the defendant got only one year at trial and I was asking for the maximum of five years from Judge Sodaro.

In his summation, the Judge found the defendant guilty, basing his decision on the credibility of the officers then he went to lengths to clearly point out that on the basis of the facts he heard, he would not be bound by the Municipal Judge's sentence of one year. As the trying judge, on the basis of the facts heard, he would have imposed a five year sentence had he been sitting in the Municipal Court and was the sentence he was imposing, emphasizing he was raising the prior sentence by five times.

The crowd started the expected "ummmm" and whispered comments were heard, some rising to conversation level sounds.

Jim Dudley immediately called his case. I don't remember the facts but it was another case which was disposed of by a one year sentence because that was the maximum the Municipal Judge could impose. When the case was ended, Jim made the same argument I had made and Judge Sodaro imposed an increased sentence. The Judge immediately announced a recess. As Jim and I left the room the crowd was in an uproar, attorneys surrounded by their defendants. Within a few minutes, one of the best of the criminal lawyers sought us out, sitting in Jim's office. "Can we make a deal?" Jim responded "only by withdrawing your appeal. We've been instructed to try these." We waited fifteen minutes and walked back into the courthouse and started marking as "withdrawn" all the appeals that attorneys were caving on. Many defendants, not represented, came up to us and asked about withdrawing. All of these defendants had been free on appeal so we didn't even have to worry about jail releases. I went in and told the Judge we were ready. He only asked, "How did it go?" and I said, "We're going to have a short day." All, but one of the appeals were withdrawn that day.

On Tuesday, we repeated the process, with the same results. From there on out that week, the word had gotten out and we probably wouldn't have had to schedule our "prime" cases first and second but we did. Most of them we didn't even have to try.

108

When the week was over, I thought a lot about what I had been through. How many innocent people were remanded to the city jail on my recommendation? How many dangerous people were released back to the streets on my recommendation? How many of those charged with looting, theft or burglary had been innocent but just agreed to plead to curfew charges or be tried on curfew charges because of the pressure of being separated from any means of posting a bond? I had absolutely no clue as to either answer.

I had helped set up a process that gave those arrested one right, the right to initial appearance. But was the process adequate to satisfy the purpose for such an appearance? Shouldn't there have been more information for fixing of bail than a hunch or some hearsay rumors given to me from an arresting officer through the lock up officer? Was the demand on physical space for holding prisoners sufficient reason to try to pry pleas out of defendants on reduced charges, when they may have been innocent or on the other hand guilty of far more serious offenses. The defendants received process but was it the process that was "due?" Did the community get "due" process?

The soon to be felon Sprio Agnew didn't think so and was later critical of the reductions of charges and thought the entire system treated violators too softly. I thought about all these questions but I decided I had done what I had to do and safety of all of us involved in the process justified what had been done. I still think so today, after forty years. When the city was at war, as it was, the process given to people arrested could not be the same as it would be absent the street war conditions. That is the rub, the criminal justice system cannot function normally or legally when mass civil disorder occurs.

When I think of the mass processing of arrestees, I think of the Denzel Washington movie, "The Siege" and how the innocent can get swept up by mass public reaction to civil disorder. Given the right circumstances or rather the wrong circumstances, any of my family could be victimized just as I'm sure many of those I processed were victimized. There ought to be a better way but I don't know what it is. The system just doesn't work in mass disorders. Sometimes I think maybe it works better in such cases than it does in specific cases where innocent victims are victimized further.

One commendable element of the riot experience was the performance of Charley Moylan. I can't imagine how anyone could have done a better job of mobilizing and organizing the office to help move cases in order to reduce stress on all elements of the system.

As I started testing my memory as to the riot experiences, I looked to the University of Baltimore site which featured a good deal of research for preparation of an April, 2008 the 40th anniversary conference on the riots. I found a Committee report on the court and prosecutor response to the disorder, prepared by the Committee on the Administration of Justice under Emergency Circumstances. The report pretty fairly pointed out the problems we faced and created by reducing charges in a militaristic court setting but also pointed out the positives of our performance. I never remembered reading the report but found it was issued very shortly after the Riots in May, 1968. I thought "That's pretty good for government work" and looked to see who had been on the Committee's staff. I found I was not only on the staff but was a coordinator of subcommittees. I obviously did not point out all the flaws in the system. I began to reduce the charges down to curfew violations early on the first day if there was nothing that indicated that there had been actual stealing or violence connected with the arrest. I would reduce the charges if the defendant would plead guilty or let the judge try the case on the arrest paper plus whatever the defendant wanted to say. I would explain this process to a whole new batch of defendants as they were brought into the courtroom from the lock-up. I can't remember whether Charley had even sanctioned this during one of our many telephone calls. I know sometime during the day or the next day we got instructions to do as I was doing. But I saw no alternative—we were making any significant progress in loosening the logjam in the station house and crowds got more and more nervous the later in the morning it got. In fact when Agnew issued his criticism, I remember thinking and I wished he had been there instead of in his Annapolis Ivory town.

I remember to this day the look on the faces of some those defendants. When I would explain what I was going to do to the ten or twelve defendants en masse, some would just shake their heads, some would actually lower their heads as if in despair that there was nothing else they could do. I almost believed that the ones who seemed anxious to do this probably had a lot to hide and wanted out before we learned it. The others, I really wondered if innocent people had been caught up in the net. Years later, thinking about it, where would an innocent person have gone, what would he have done with violence and fires sweeping his neighborhood. The stores that were looted and destroyed were often first floors of apartment buildings. In fact, all the single family stores were. If I lived in an apartment above a store that was being broken into and looted, and out the window I saw fires breaking out, would I just hunker down and hide there. Or would I have gone out on to the street to see better what was going on and see whether there was a way for me to get clear and free from the violence. I know what I would have done, I would have gotten out. Once on the street, as far as the law in Baltimore went that day, I would have been a law violator. I had either violated the curfew as we understood it at the time or I would get swept up with anyone else the police arrested at that point for looting the store where I stood.

Another problem that had plagued us was that if the National

Guard took people into custody, they did not bring them to the stationhouse. They turned them over to the nearest police officer and in the drama the officer often didn't get the guardsman's name or the charge. We either had the wrong charge or the wrong arresting officer or we had a charging paper blank except for the name of the defendant and sometimes "detained by Guard". These defendants too were "given the option" of pleading or stipulated trial as to curfew or go to the city jail. What "real choice" did they have? If you had been there you would know the answer to that is "none." The old "voluntary waiver" of the right to plead not guilty and go to trial, the old "voluntary confession of guilt" went by the boards in that war-like courtroom.

The Committee on Administration of Justice under Emergency Conditions was not just a "sweep under the rug" group of civic pixies. George Russell, a great judge and a very smart and skilful City Solicitor. Charley was on the Committee along with the United State's Attorney. Many of my colleagues who had seen all round the clock duty during the riots were there as members of staff. I have no memory of that work on that Committee but as I read the report I can see the contributions of Charley's staff. Pretty much the scenes I have described were set forth there but in nice legal report language. I saw, in particular, the mention that some sentences from the Municipal Court were increased on appeal and as a result many appeals were withdrawn.

The Committee report made some great recommendations for post arrest processing of cases. But from a practical standpoint, I wonder how many of those recommendations are part of an actively practiced and trained policy today. I wonder if the States Attorneys' staff today is prepared for a gigantic riot tomorrow or the next day. I don't really "wonder." I doubt it sincerely. What's more, even if trained in a better process, will they focus on it well enough to let the process run them when the fires break out and the station houses are overrun? And, if they do let the process "run them", will they be able to adjust, as we did, in order to meet the always changing demands of a city gone mad?

It is my belief that the criminal justice system, the manner which our civilian government has set up a court system, will not work effectively AND DELIVER JUSTICE in the time of mass disorder. Keep in mind that I believe that the communities deserve justice from the system too. The citizens who were family and friends and dependents of those that got swept up on the streets of Baltimore got no justice. They got what the system was willing to give them.

One can argue that the system kept the great bulk of citizens in the city safe from harm. No, it didn't. Arresting and detaining over five thousand people in those few days did not protect the rest of the city. The natural barriers of the city's racial geographic PLUS the heroic work of police, guardsmen and the regular army, not to mention the armed Italians and Lumbee Indians, protected the rest of the city.

109

Another interesting footnote to the riots was the emergence of Spiro Agnew. He had first run for Baltimore County Executive when he was stripped of position on the county planning board of appeals. He was bitter about losing the position. A real ugly split developed in the democratic -party, and Agnew became the first republican county executive in many moons.

After a term in that office, he ran for governor. The Democrats had to choose between three candidates. Carlton Sickles had been a congressman but lost his district through re-districting. Thomas Finan was attorney general and he was the heir apparent for the party nomination. Sickles wouldn't accept the party preference so both men entered the primary. A third candidate was from the eastern shore of Maryland and was probably a white supremacist. He was at least anti-civil rights. His campaign slogan was, "Your home is your castle, protect it," meaning defend it against Black violence and crime. Finan and Sickles split the responsible democrat vote and the supremacist won the democratic nomination. Agnew won the governor ship easily. He was heavily supported by the Black voters.

Agnew turned on his supporters. When the rioting had

subsided, Agnew called Black religious and civic leaders to a meeting to discuss the riots and civil rights in general. One hundred Black community leaders showed up. He almost immediately started attacking Black militants and called them "Circuit riding, Hanoi visiting, caterwauling, riot inciting, burn America down leaders." At least eighty of the leaders walked out on the meeting and Agnew got news coverage about his placing blame for the riots on Black leaders.

When Richard Nixon started looking for a candidate that would appeal to the South, Pat Buchanan started touting Agnew because of his notoriety for lambasting the Black leaders. The rest is history. What didn't get widely reported and must have escaped Buchanan's notice was the fact that Agnew later apologized to the Baltimore Black leaders for his remarks.

Tom Brokaw points out in his book *Boom* that after Buchanan convinced Nixon to choose Agnew, the former Maryland governor became the "attack dog" for the ticket, "taking on the anti-war protestors and civil rights agitators." Later in the campaign, Buchanan had to come to Agnew's aid after he had gotten in trouble by referring to a reporter as a "fat Jap," and had referred to another group as "Polacks." Buchanan explained to Brokaw he got Agnew out of trouble by writing him "some serious speeches on social security and so on."

GUYS AND DOLLS

110

I am a fan, in the fullest fanatic way, of the Damon Runyon yarns about the characters thriving among the teeming masses of "THE city", New York City. "Guys and Dolls", one of my favorite musicals, is based on several Runyon short stories.

He wrote about gamblers, bookies, numbers runners, prostitutes, call girls, burglars, thieves, crooked athletes, police officers, dancers, musicians, painters, pimps, lowlife lawyers and judges, all the people who breathe life into the city.

Through the years since leaving Baltimore, I have often thought in Runyon terms of the characters with whom I worked. As in "Guys and Dolls" drama, comedy and pathos filled our lives on a daily basis. I can imagine my friends and foes filling out a cast created by Runyon. They would put on a show I would love to see.

111

Earl Arvin— **was a good,** close friend. He was my investigator. His main income was from insurance company adjusters. But he liked me, he liked my practice and he enjoyed the "toughness" of the criminal practice. I got him in his "spare time," which often was full time when I needed him during a trial.

He was a unique character with a fluorescent imagination perfect for developing defense strategies. His contacts provided full access even to the center of the ghettos. He found witnesses who would have never come to light through "regular" investigative techniques. Even if I could have found them those witnesses wouldn't have given me the time of day without Arvin's influence. When he brought them forth, they were ready to testify. In most cases, it wasn't fear that had held them back. They just didn't want to get involved in other peoples' business. Arvin focused them on the importance of helping a "brother", and they followed him like he was the pied piper.

Earl was a sharp dresser, sporting flashy clothes on the cutting edge of fashion. He was articulate, funny, ready to laugh at himself and the world around him, always eager and ready to help no matter what the issue. I can still see him and hear his voice—laughing out loud, joking, and then all of a sudden, very seriously, "What you need boss?"

Sometimes, in court appointed cases, I just turned over to him the whole fee which the city paid me. In those days, before public defender offices had been established, the courts appointed attorneys to represent indigent defendants. The fees were not good, and the appointed attorney did not get paid by the hour. He got a flat fee for the case, depending on the charge. I think the fee for a murder case was seven hundred fifty dollars I know the fee was way too low for the amount of time it took to prepare and try the case.

In many of the murder cases, I paid Arvin even more than I received from the city—because I didn't like to lose, especially when a defendant's life was on the line.

One such case involved an old man who dispatched two young thieves with a baseball bat on the front stoop of his home.

When I first interviewed him in the City Jail, he told me that the two had beaten up on him and stole his disability check the month before, leaving him without food for two weeks. He begged on the street, waiting for his next check. On the day he usually got his check in the mail, they showed up before the mail was delivered. They told him they would be back and they would hurt him if he didn't give them his check.

He said, he went inside and armed himself with his old baseball bat. When the robbers returned and blustered up to him, he simply ended the threat with two swings of the bat.

I believed the old man's story and frankly, the police officers did too. They knew the young thugs had records of violence in the neighborhood had no witnesses to confirm the old man's story.

While the young criminals may not have deserved to be killed as they were, they both had long records of juvenile robberies, thefts, assaults and vandalism.

After talking over the options with my client, I offered the state a plea of manslaughter which meant a killing without premeditation and without malice. I had explained to the client that self defense would be difficult to prove because he armed himself and then attacked before the thugs actually assaulted him. I told him we might convince a jury that, as an old disabled guy he had no real alternative to avoid being beaten and robbed. I explained the risk of a much longer sentence if we tried the self defense issue and lost. He agreed to the manslaughter plea.

The young prosecutor on the case turned down my offer. This was his first homicide case and he was hung up on the old man arming himself with a bat and waiting for the robbers, instead of hiding out and trying to avoid them. He was analyzing his case from a technical legal standpoint as he had been taught in law school.

I understood how he felt. It hadn't been that many years since I prosecuted my first murder case. I considered murder to be of the greatest importance and had never really considered that there were "lesser" murder cases in which "justice" might accept, even demand, greater leniency. Law school doesn't prepare one for the case of an old, crippled man being beaten and robbed right on his front stoop by strong, young thugs.

In my first case, I turned down a manslaughter plea offered by a veteran criminal attorney. His client shot and killed a lifelong friend in a foolish argument. The two friends had gone to a Yankee-Oriole doubleheader and consumed a lot of cold beer during a hot day and night "header." On the way home on the bus, they started arguing about the Oriole strategy in the second game.

With all that alcohol at work, they became enraged. One threatened to shoot the other and the second man said something to the effect, "Come and get it." The first man got off the bus near his home which was four blocks from the home of the second man. He stood around and waited to see whether the second man was going to push the fight. The second man got off the bus, went into his house, got a gun, came outside and started walking back toward his friend's house.

As the two men approached each other, the armed man thought he saw his friend move his hand toward his waistband so he pointed his gun and fired. His aim was fatal, and his friend was unarmed and dead.

The case was set before Judge George Russell, one of my favorite people of all time. He was a brilliant trial lawyer, and would later serve the city well as city solicitor. I watched him defend criminal cases before I came across Calvert Street from the federal courthouse to the state's attorney's office. He was very, very good. As a judge, he had not forgotten the "empathy" that today's hard core republican senators, Jeffrey Beuregard Sessions II of Alabama and Lindsay Graham of South Carolina, abhor. During confirmation hearings in the Spring of 2009, they castigated Judge Sonya Sotomayor for having "empathy" for parties appearing before her in court. Their spiteful attacks failed and she was confirmed as the first Hispanic woman to sit as a United States Supreme Court Justice.

I have never appeared before any judge who was worth his or her salt who didn't have empathy. The word is defined as "the ability to identify with and understand somebody else's feelings or difficulties." Judge Russell had that ability.

Weeks before the scheduled trial, defense counsel, Joe Rosenthal, offered a manslaughter plea and I turned it down. Like the young man who now had my case, I was hung up on the premeditation shown by getting the weapon and deciding to use it and on the fact that the shooter had a whole host of alternatives to avoid the act. On the day of trial, I again turned down the offer.

Joe waived the jury and asked for a court trial on statement of facts. In a "statement of facts" trial, the prosecutor stated the facts that would be presented if his witnesses took the stand and testified. Defense counsel then agreed that the facts represented what the testimony would be and made a statement as to what defense witnesses would say if they took the stand. The case then was presented to the judge, sitting without a jury, would then enter a verdict of guilty or not guilty and if guilty? The degree of the offense.

Joe's action stunned me. I just couldn't imagine a defense attorney submitting a murder case with evidence of premeditation to the judge on a statement of facts. I wasn't yet prepared for the concept that "there were murders" and then "there were OTHER murder cases."

I presented the facts Joe presented what witnesses would say as to the long-time friendship between the two men and how many beers they had consumed at the game. Joe then asked for a manslaughter verdict, trying to back the shooting up to the heat of the argument which took place on the bus.

Judge Russell listened to my argument that premeditation was presumed from the fact that the defendant went into his home, picked up the gun and then re-entered the street and confronted his friend.

After listening carefully and asking questions to clarify the facts, he entered a verdict of guilty of manslaughter, based on his findings that while the alcohol did not excuse the crime, it did modify the mental attitude of the killer, to the point at which the shooting was done in a heat of argument. What he saw was the tragedy of a lifelong friendship ending this way, of the great loss suffered by both families and of the tremendous guilt that the shooter would feel the rest of his life.

I asked for a date for sentencing and Judge Russell said that he didn't need a pre sentence report. He said the pre-sentence investigators couldn't tell him anymore than he already knew about the two friends and the facts that lead to the shooting. His statement was to the effect that, "There is no use backing up the caseload by heaping one more chore on the pre-sentence people, when I already know pretty much what is right here." He asked me if there was any criminal record and I said, "No," any juvenile record and I said, "No." He turned to the homicide detective, George Christian, who he knew from years in defense of murder cases, and asked, "George is there anything that you know of that makes probation an inappropriate sentence?" Christian said, "No, your honor." Judge Russell asked me if I would stipulate that the detective would testify that he saw no reason to oppose probation and I did so.

In one ninety minute segment of court time, George Russell taught me more about understanding the difference between cases and understanding that cases turned on their own peculiar facts, than I had ever learned.

The sentence of supervised probation was imposed on a man who the judge believed would never be violent again a man who the judge believed would condemn and punish himself every day of his life. From that moment, I understood that every homicide case had to be viewed in accordance with the specific facts of the case.

When I first met Arvin, he told me that he worked that case up for Joe Rosenthal.

As we faced trial, I fully understood why this young prosecutor didn't want to accept my plea offer. He had to learn as I had learned.

When he first refused the plea, knowing that I would need a jury to have any shot at self defense, I hired Arvin. A couple of days prior to trial, he came in late one afternoon and said, "You owe me a drink, I've got the witnesses and they WILL TESTIFY." I agreed, and we retired to Cy Bloom's Place In the Alley, just half a block down St. Paul and up the alley halfway between Lexington and Fayette. It was a stylish lounge which served as an after-work hangout for young professionals, i.e. "yuppies", although we resented the tag. At lunch time, the bartenders save seats at the bar for lawyers who were in trial and needed to grab a quick lunch.

As Arvin and I drank our bourbons, his as a straight shot and mine on the rocks, he described our two witnesses. One was an elderly woman who overheard the two teenagers talking about stealing the old man's check and how they were going to do it again. The second was a young cousin of one of the teenagers who was invited to go with them to steal the check. He said he wanted nothing to do with robbery because he was an adult, not a juvenile. If caught, he would do adult prison time.

Earl said both would testify but he had to pick them up and get them to the courthouse and buy their lunch downtown. I told him that if they showed up, he should take them to the Chesapeake, at the time one of the finest restaurants in Baltimore. He said no, they had heard about Burke's, a lounge-grill located at Light and Redwood streets and that's where they wanted to go. They wanted crab cakes. Burke's was a fun place, good drinks, good crab cakes, and especially good breakfasts when one had time to slip in there before work.

I choose to divert from the trial momentarily to give you another look at Arvin. There was a regular morning customer at Burke's who mesmerized young lawyers who stopped in for coffee. Every morning, just before regular office hours began, at about 8:50 a.m., a fine looking lady stepped up the bar and ordered a boilermaker. The bartender poured her two, and she downed them one right after the other. She always dressed in expensive styles, from shoes to leather coat—full length or jacket. She or someone spent a lot of money on outerwear. When she finished the boilermakers, she laid down her money, turned and with a throaty voice called out, "Mornin' everybody" and was gone. No one knew her or where she worked. Some of us decided that we needed to know. One Friday evening we had a drinking contest to see who "won" the task of approaching her and finding out who she was and what her story was.

I "won" the tournament, drinking more shots of Jack Daniel's Black Label and still being able to walk. The following Monday morning, I walked up to the bar and asked if she minded if I joined her. "Not at all," she said, then proceeded to ignore every inane, nervous comment I made, drank her boilermakers, said a spirited "good morning, everyone," looked at me and said, "And you too, hon'." I was forever labeled "Burke's flop. To escape my humiliating failure, I asked Arvin to find out who she was. He joined us the next morning, and when she came in, he ambled up to the bar and engaged her in conversation. She agreed to meet him there after work. He met with her they sat for two hours or more, and then left. Do you think he would tell us a thing about her? He said it would be unethical because she asked him not to share. I won the drinking tournament, but Arvin won the lady.

Back to the trial—the presiding judge was Solomon Liss, a whale of a man both physically and personally. He had been People's Counsel as well as a very successful civil lawyer, and understood the system from all standpoints. We picked the jury pretty quickly and I was surprised that the prosecutor left on the jury a self-admitted "bag lady" that lived off the streets. I thought that was a vote in my pocket.

The state's case went fast and I established, through cross examination of the police officers, that the defendant had reported the robbery of his prior month's check and had identified the two teenagers as the robbers.

I started the defense by calling the western district detective who had investigated the robbery complaint. He testified that he interviewed the two teenagers but they denied guilt and had an alibi from two other youths. He knew he didn't have enough evidence to overcome the alibi but he knew the boys were the robbers. He labeled the case file "open, unsolved."

I then called the woman and young man found by Arvin. Their testimony established the basis for my being able to argue self defense to the jury—hoping to get at worst a "compromise" verdict of manslaughter.

We argued the case and it was in the hands of the jury by 4 p.m. By the time we argued, Arvin had taken the witnesses to Burke's for a late lunch.

I expected a quick acquittal. But two hours later, Arvin returned to find us still sitting and waiting. Finally, at about 7 p.m., the jury told the judge that they were hung and couldn't make a decision. Judge Liss called them in and asked whether more time would help. The foreman said, "No, we have one juror who absolutely has said that she will not change her mind even if we stay here all night." So the judge declared a mistrial.

As the jurors left, Arvin cornered the foreman and asked him what happened. He said the "bag woman" was holding out for first degree murder while the other eleven were for "not guilty." When I reported that to Judge Liss, he was as amazed as was I. One "sure thing" juror who should understand what it is to be without food as a result of street violence and she wanted "first degree" murder.

Judge Liss suggested that, in view of the way the jury was focused on "not guilty," the prosecutor should accept a plea and get rid of the case. The prosecutor agreed to take a manslaughter plea but I said I couldn't do that in view of the eleven votes for not guilty. I said, "I can do better the next time, and will argue hard for self defense." I did say that I would urge my client to plead to involuntary manslaughter or assault with intent to kill but nothing more severe. The prosecutor bristled at that but the judge reminded him of the eleven not guilty votes.

The prosecutor caved in, I entered the plea. Judge Liss sentenced him to three years with "credit for time served awaiting trial," suspended the sentence and placed the defendant on probation. The probation office was closed for the day so the judge ordered the defendant to report to the probation office the next morning and let him go to his home, such as it was, that night. He had no way home, so Arvin took him home and then picked him up and returned him to the probation office the next morning.

Earl was a great dancer, and often charmed the nightly crowd at the Place in the Alley with his dancing to Proud Mary, a favorite at the time. He knew everybody in town. He could, and did, take me places that no white could go in safely, such as the Apollo club. He took me to visit and talk with people who never would have talked to me without him. I heard things that I never would have heard had I not been with him. I also mingled with some high fashion members of society featured weekly in the *Afro American*. Some were far from being lawful members of society, and they viewed me with skepticism as I did them. Ms. Mamie Oliver always heard about my forays into Western District society clubs and wanted to interview Arvin and me for her social column but we resisted.

Earl's wife sent him off every day dressed to "the nines" even though she knew his work that day and night might well involve some "high stepping ladies," as he called them. He had access to a world of helpful trivia and junk information, as well as to important news of "happenings on the Avenue" (Pennsylvania) and throughout Baltimore. He kept track of street noises as to witnesses for the state, keeping an ear out for things that might be helpful in challenging their testimony, their memories and their credibility. He knew far more about what was going on in the police districts than he or I should have known.

I invited Earl to go to two games of the World Series in which the Birds destroyed the "Big Red Machine" Cincinnati Reds with Johnny Bench and Pete Rose. After the first game, we went to his favorite place on the "Avenue," had a couple of drinks with a group of his friends who I didn't know, and then he drove me home. The next morning, he showed up early at the office. I was surprised to see him because I didn't have anything going on—the second game started in the early afternoon.

He told me that one of the ladies at the table the day before wanted to meet me. He said she was a girlfriend of one of the guys I had tried for years to convict. I said, "Arvin, I don't need informants anymore, and really don't want that kind of information."

He told me she wasn't looking to be an informant, she was looking to be my "girlfriend," He said she offered to get me all the legal work for her "main man" and all his lieutenants in the drug and theft trades. I said, "Arvin, I'm married, and even if I weren't it would be unethical, not to mention very dangerous." He said he told her all those things. She told him she knew I was married, she wasn't interested in marriage, she just thought it would be exciting to be my girl friend and share in the excitement of criminal law. She told him she didn't care about ethics and she could handle the danger from her main man. I said, "No, no, no."

Arvin said I was right but he had promised to discuss it with me and arrange for us to meet so I could give her my answer. He said he would tell her "no" because it wouldn't do for me to meet her. I asked why and he said, "Cause if you see her, you might not say no, and then I'll have a hell of a time keeping you out of trouble."

Arvin was always full of surprises always with a big money—making or news—making idea, always with some romantic angle going on, always delivered the goods when a witness was needed.

I have thought of him every day since I left Baltimore. I have missed his always interesting presence in my life. He was indeed a Runyan character and could have handled any song—and— dance role on Broadway.

In fact, in my production, Arvin would be the catalyst. It would be Arvin to whom the plot would always return, Arvin who carried the story line in each direction. He would have been the polestar in my *Guys and Dolls* performance.

112

Tony Glover— **captain of homicide** was a giant of a man who could easily fill the role of Lt. Brannigan in Guys and Dolls. Runyan would have a field day following this guy around, focusing a story on him. In my production, I would have him disrupting the gamblers on the Block on a daily basis.

He was a great leader of the homicide and robbery divisions, insisting that his detectives and the prosecutors worked closely together to get convictions. Often he called for prosecutor assistance with the strategy for interviewing suspects or witnesses. When a prosecutor needed help preparing a case, a call to the captain took care of it. All his officers were professional and talented in investigations. They knew how to investigate, how to gather evidence and preserve it. They knew how NOT TO LOSE.

Tony had a great sense of humor and really enjoyed our walks along the Block at lunch time or in mid-afternoon, disrupting the routine economics of the Block as we walked. I still laugh out loud when I remember our stops for lunch in the hamburger joint was a main bookie spot. As race post times neared, the phones in the back of the joint rang and rang and the bookies just sat nervously at the bar, trying to avoid eye contact with us, thinking of all the bets they were losing. Glover would frown at the bookies and ask, "Isn't somebody going to answer those phones?" They could only grin nervously, trying desperately to look calm as their money went down the drain.

Working with the districts, with Sgt. Steve Tabeling, the federal agents and with the state police as he did while working with our organized crime unit, Tony showed how police work was more important to him than credit. Oh sure, he enjoyed the praise when he and his troops got it but the enjoyment was in successful operations, not just credit.

As I now read the *Balimore Sun* reports of current or recent problems with handling homicide cases in Baltimore, I am amazed. I guess I never foresaw a time when the professionalism of Glover and his men would be lost in the Department. I know if Glover had been around, he wouldn't have tolerated what I read about state's attorney's office practices as to homicide cases and witnesses. He might not have been able to change thing but the state's attorney would have known what "heated battle" was before Glover finished a day's work. And he would never have given up until big changes were made.

What Glover knew about the upper brass of the department I never asked. But I do know that they pretty much left him and his men alone and didn't attempt to intrude into his business.

As close as Glover and I were when I was prosecutor, the relationship ended when I went into private practice. I can't remember even visiting with him after that point. He came to my "going away" party when I left the office but from then on greetings came only through prosecutors and officers in court telling me that "the Captain sends you his best."

Tall and imposing, he looked the role of a homicide chief. Although not Black, he always reminded me of the captain of homicide in the acclaimed TV series *Homicide, Life on the Streets*— tough on his men, but Katy bar the door if someone else criticized his officers. He was a strict believer in "keeping it inside the house."

113

Judge Anselm Sodaro— **was an** Italian judge who spent most of his assignments in the criminal court. A former state's attorney, he was practical moved cases along with no entangling, frivolous or red herring issues. He was fair and objective on the application of the rules, and on sentencing. A violent criminal could count on a maximum sentence as set by the Legislature. A non-violent defendant who could evoke empathy would get a break on sentence.

He was a very short man, and one of the only short men I have ever met who did NOT have the SHORT MAN'S EGO. He was completely unpretentious in his courtroom yet ran it with dignity and a very quiet voice. I never heard him raise his voice to a defendant, but rather could silence a shouter with a quiet, soft, reasoned and disciplined tone.

He took copious notes of testimony he thought relevant. And when he had heard enough of a witness's testimony, he placed his pen back into the pen stand on the bench. That was a pretty good sign that he wasn't going to pay much attention the rest of the way in. It always amazed me that counsel didn't read that sign. Often, he would carefully put his pen in the stand (and did it so deliberately that you couldn't miss it if you watched him) and say, "Anything else, counsel?" That was the cue to say, "Nothing else your honor." But when a non—observant attorney said, "Yes, just a few more questions your honor," with a little sigh of exasperation Sodaro would say, "Oh ALL RIGHT" and snatch the pen back out of the stand. If you, as opposing counsel, were watching closely you would catch a look in your direction as if to say, "I gave him a chance."

I will never forget how frightened Sodaro was during the first night session of riot hearings he held, when he asked if I could get more National Guardsmen or army in the courtroom. Unable to do that, I talked to the police officer who "misunderstood" my concern and his shotgun accidentally went off—quieting the crowd in that courtroom for the rest of the night. That night, Judge Sodaro rode home crouched way down in the front seat of the radio car between tall Dick Nevin of our state's attorney's police squad and me. He asked several questions about which seat was the most dangerous target of snipers, and then fell into silence. But in that courtroom the next day, no one would have had any idea of any fear at all. He always commanded his courtroom with a quiet voice and hand.

The law clerks and bailiffs to the criminal judges were quite a friendly bunch, and they used to joke about the judges. They gave Judge Anseelm Sodaro the private nickname of "Ants." You can be sure they never said it in public. One afternoon, the lunch hour had run long for some reason and it was a laid back docket assignment for that day, so nobody was pushing very hard. As the clerk came into the court room he announced, "The Criminal Court Number One of Baltimore city is now in session, the Honorable ANTS Sodaro presiding." The judge took about two more steps, realized what had been said, and turned to look at the clerk. The young man's face was twenty five shades of red. Sodaro just said very quietly, "That's Anselm and it means 'protected by God'." The clerk was so rattled, he slipped out, "yes, God." Judge Sodaro laughed out loud and took the bench. The young man never again referred to the judge as Ants.

Judge Sodaro would have been an ideal Runyon study as a judge. He would be the lead in my musical numbers for the courts.

114

Joseph Rosenthal —Joe Rosenthal had long since passed his prime as a trial lawyer when I met him. I heard stories about his earlier years and his prominence in the trial room, and read some of the old newspaper clippings related to some cutting—edge civil rights cases that he tried. Joe was still the "man" to hundreds, if not thousands, of people who knew what it was to be the underdogs in the process.

He was a long—time friend of Dr. Lillie May Jackson, the Grand Lady of civil rights in the city and a legend in her own time. She had started the NAACP in Baltimore and was president of the state NAACP for twenty years. In the early 1930s she led a movement to end job discrimination in the city, and continued working against segregation and discrimination throughout her life.

When I first studied the case that forced the University of Maryland Law School to desegregate, I was studying history and political science at the College of Idaho. I had no idea that Dr. Jackson even existed, and certainly was unaware of her importance to the case. From the study of that case I developed my interest in Thurgood Marshall, who served as counsel for the plaintiff Donald Gaines Murray. The case was the first stepping stone to the history changing school desegregation case Brown v. Board of Education won at the Supreme Court by Marshall in 1954.

The importance of *Murray* was not only that it resulted in the desegregation of a state university law school, but the manner in which Marshall argued the case. The law school had rejected Murray's application with one sentence based simply on the fact that he was a "Negro." Marshall did not merely argue that segregation of the school was unconstitutional he argued that what the school offered in the way of out-of-state law training did not even meet the "separate but equal" standard that was then the "law of the land." He pointed out that Murray wanted to practice in his home town, in his home state. To do so, he would need to study the laws of the state of Maryland. Those laws would be featured at law schools within the state, but not at a law school outside the state. In other words, he argued, if one wanted to practice in Maryland, he needed to study at the University of Maryland where Maryland laws would be paramount. To study in Pennsylvania or another state he would be deprived of the special focus on Maryland laws that he would have at Maryland. Thus, Marshall argued, training at an out-of-state law school would not be equal to training in the state. With no equality, there could be no "separate but equal." Marshall won the case, and the long trek to *Brown* had begun.

What I didn't know was that Dr. Jackson pursued and encouraged filing the case and secured the services of a New York attorney who brought Marshall in to assist him. During my time in Baltimore, it became clear to me that Dr. Jackson was indeed a hero of the civil rights movement. I met her only once, and that was through Joe Rosenthal.

Joe entered his appearance for the appeal of a case I was handling in the United States Attorney's office. I had argued and won the case at trial and at the Fourth Circuit Court of Appeals. But it was clear to me that the U.S. Supreme Court would reverse, and that the Solicitor General would confess error rather than file a brief and argue the case. The General at the time was Thurgood Marshall, having agreed to leave the Court of Appeals to become President Johnson's Solicitor General—the first Black to hold that office. He had accepted the Solicitor's job with the promise that he would be appointed to the Supreme Court as the first Black justice when the next vacancy occurred.

I told Joe that the U.S. Attorney had already told me if the Solicitor General confessed error rather than argue the case I would have to file a new case against Joe's client.

The cases were obscenity cases in which the Customs Director of the Port of Baltimore convinced my boss to seize thousands of magazines showing naked men and women, rarely together, not involved in sexual relations, but posed in a provocative manner.

My boss took the position that we could not simply ignore our wins for the government at trial and appellate levels—particularly since the chief judge of the district had ruled with us at trial, and arguably the best panel of arguably the best of the circuit courts ruled with us on appeal. He felt, most understandably, that we couldn't let those victories go to waste unless there was an actual contested decision by the Supreme Court. When the Director of Customs first asked for cases to be filed, the U.S. Attorney assigned the cases to me. After reviewing the magazines involved, I felt that from the beginning that even under existing U.S. Supreme Court decisions, I would have no chance of winning. The magazines were nudist magazines published in Sweden and imported through the Port of Baltimore to distributors who then sent them throughout the nation.

One of the magazines, *Exclusive*, contained photographs of nude females in very seductive, sexual poses—but there was no photo of any sexual activity, no posing of naked women with men, just straight nudity. These were not the old nudist colony magazines that many of us secretly looked at whenever we could get our hands on them. Those magazines contained photos of men, women and children who frequented nudist colonies, and the sexual organs were always shadowed out. They also contained articles about the advantages of nudism.

Exclusive had no "shadow outs." It had no articles. It consisted of photos graphically showing every part of the female body with focus on the sex-related parts of the body, heavy emphasis on seduction. I had no doubt that the magazines met the "prurient interest" element of the Supreme Court's test for obscenity. The photos were obviously designed to, and did, appeal to the prurient, lurid interest of the reader. But it would be difficult to get past the "beyond contemporary community standards" and "without any redeeming social value" elements of the test.

I tried the case against Harold Price Fahringer of Buffalo, New York, the premier obscenity lawyer in the nation at that time. Chief Judge Roszell Thompson tried the case, and completely unexpectedly, I won. Fahringer filed an appeal, and I argued the case to a panel of the Fourth Circuit which included Chief Judge Haynsworth of South Carolina and Simon Sobeloff, another legend of the law in Baltimore. Sobeloff had been Solicitor General under President Eisenhower, and was appointed to the Fourth Circuit to wait for Felix Frankfurter's retirement from the Supreme Court. Sobeloff was to be the "Jewish" replacement for Frankfurter. Haynsworth and Sobeloff were both real students of the law, and for the most part they were a step ahead of the Supreme Court in constitutional interpretations. I fully expected that Judge Thompson's decision would be reversed. But it wasn't. I also won the appellate argument.

In the meantime, another shipment of nudist magazines, these containing nude male photographs, had been seized in the Port. Curiously, the law that we used to seize the magazines was the law of admiralty, and the hearings on the seizures were governed by admiralty rules. This case was going to be harder to win because of the difficulty in arguing that the nude male photos appealed to the "prurient interest" of the "average reasonable man." I didn't have much problem arguing the "prurience" of the enticing photos in *Exclusive*.

To that point, the Supreme Court had not specifically, or even closely, come to a position that held that male nude photos met the "prurient interest" element of the test. All the Court had said was that it was not within the knowledge of jurists as to whether there was any prurient appeal of a male photo to males. For the government to make a case with male nudes, it would have to rely on expert testimony because of the Court's underlying position that a homosexual was not part of the makeup of the "reasonable man," which set the standard for community interests.

I sought out the great and well—respected Manfred Guttmacher, the psychologist consultant and adviser to the Supreme Bench of Baltimore. He testified, as an expert witness, that the photos would appeal to the prurient interest of male homosexuals. He testified that the magazines were deliberately designed for homosexual males as shown by certain symbolic placement of the nude figures alongside natural symbols of the penis, and by the high price placed on the magazines. (I think the price was ten dollars, high in the early 60s.) He said the high price indicated the market was the homosexual market, because the price would make the magazines special to them, quite apart from a publication for the general public which wouldn't pay that price. Guttmacher testified that a likely homosexual purchaser would be very possessive of the magazine, cherishing it and jealously guarding possession of it.

Right at that moment of this testimony, I had been standing near the witness chair, by the empty jury box, while asking the questions. When I got the doctor's last answer, As I started back for my chair at the trial table, I reached out to get the magazine he was holding as I went by him. Guttmacher pulled the magazine back and said, "No. This is mine." Then, realizing how that came across right after his "possessiveness" testimony, he laughed and held it out to me, "But you may have it if you wish." It brought laughs from the judge as well as counsel for the distributor. Fahringer did not represent this distributor, which was Potomac News of D.C., run by a publicly avowed homosexual. Stanley Getz was counsel, and he was top notch.

Amazingly, Judge Thompson ruled with the government, and ordered the magazines seized and destroyed. On appeal, the Fourth Circuit again amazed me with an opinion affirming Judge Thompson.

At this point, the distributors, or at least one of them, hired Joe to substitute in as counsel. The U.S. Attorney and the Director of Customs were adamant that unless the Supreme Court actually reversed the decisions, we had to stand on those decisions and continue to seize shipments. Mr. Kenney and I both knew that chances were that the Solicitor General would "confess error," which would mean that the government accepted the fact that the lower court decisions were wrong and would not be followed by the government.

Thus, Joe said he would get us an appointment with General Marshall so I could try to convince him to argue the case and let the court issue its decision, rather than confessing error. I laughed and told him I would go with him if he could get an appointment. I really thought Joe was just blowing smoke.

Joe made an appointment for us to meet with Dr. Jackson at her home. He said she could convince Marshall to see him. I felt that I was in the presence of greatness, but a humble and gracious greatness, when I met with her. We talked for quite a long time, and she told me about some of the cases that Joe handled at great personal sacrifice. She told me about some of the cases involving charges of police brutality that Joe took on, often without fee, which brought down on him the derision of the white communities, the city, and the police department. She told me about criminal cases Joe took on at her request when no other lawyer in the city would touch the defenses. I heard stories about a young Joe Rosenthal that I never had pictured.

Joe requested that she call Marshall and ask him to meet with us. She wanted to know what the case was about, and she certainly didn't approve of him representing shippers and sellers of obscenity. He talked for several minutes about the importance of freedom of speech, and how important it had been to the civil rights movement. After letting him carry on for a while she waved her arm in one wide imperial sweep and said, "Nonsense," but what is it you want? He told her he just needed an appointment with "Thurgood," and she said, "Okay, I owe you a few favors."

I was stunned when she went to her telephone and directly called and talked to the Solicitor General. She must have had the direct number to his secretary, because she called the person who answered the phone by her first name and asked if "Thurgood is free to talk with me." She didn't have to tell the person on the other end of the line who she was. In just a minute or so, she said hello and chatted for just a few moments, then said she had a favor to ask, that she would like for him to meet with Joe Rosenthal to discuss a case. He must have asked about the case, because she said that she would let Joe tell him and handed the telephone to Joe saying, "This is the Solicitor General."

Joe called him "Thurgood" and told him about the cases and that he and the assistant U.S. Attorney who won the cases below would like to discuss them with him. After a few more moments of conversation, Joe handed the phone back to Dr. Jackson. We heard her say, "Yes, I really would like for you to meet with them." When she finished in a minute or two and hung up, she looked at Joe and said that the General would meet with us at four the next afternoon. To say I was impressed is a major understatement.

The next day we were there early, and Marshall took us in early. Joe and Marshall talked about "old times" and "old cases" and had a few minutes of personal conversation before we got to the issue at hand. Joe had me explain the cases. I did and then told the General that I never had thought that the government would win, but we had and so were now at his mercy.

Why were we there? Why didn't I just handle filing the brief myself? The U.S. Attorney's office handles appeals at the Circuit Court level, but at the Supreme Court level the Solicitor General handles all cases and makes all decisions about the handling of them on appeal. I told him that if he simply confessed error, I would have to go through the whole process again with another shipment.

He looked at me for a seemingly endless period of time, silently, and then in that great voice asked, "So, you mean that you are asking me to present these cases to the Supreme Court for decision, when I know the decisions will be reversed, just so you won't have to go through the whole process again?" I thought about the question when asked that way, and just said simply, "Yes, sir, that's what I'm asking." He was leaning way back in his chair, the way he would sit during his later years on the Supreme Court. He thought for a minute, then leaned his head even further back and laughed a loud, long laugh. "All right, son, I'll do it because you must have done one good job of arguing to get good judges to rule the way they did. But we will only file a brief, I'm not going to have anyone from this office go up and argue these things and make the Court think that it should give serious thought to these cases."

I thanked him profusely, Joe said his personal goodbyes as I waited just outside his office, and we headed back to Baltimore. Traveling back, I could hardly believe that within 24 hours Dr.

Jackson had secured us an appointment with Thurgood Marshall and I had actually met and talked with him.

True to his word, the Solicitor's office filed briefs, but waived oral argument. A few weeks later the Supreme Court issued *per curiam* decisions reversing the trial and appellate decisions, thus causing release of the magazines to the distributors. (A *per curiam* decision is one in which the Court is unanimous, and for which the Court believes there is need to state the base of the decision in the form of an opinion, or even assign a Justice's name to it.) A percuriam opinion is a clear sign to the losing side that it "shoulda stayed home." But it was a decision, and I was off the hook. We didn't have to seize any more of the nude photo magazines. I always wondered if the market was so good after it became known that the federal prosecutors were not going after the magazines as obscene.

The Joe that I saw and heard about during those two days with Dr. Jackson and General Marshall was 360 degrees from the Joe I saw every day in the criminal courts. He never went to trial, all his cases were solved by plea bargains, or by court trials (judge sitting without a jury) or trial by agreed statement of facts. He was so consistent, and his clients were usually so little threat to the community safety, that most all of us worked with him cooperatively on virtually all his cases.

At the time, I thought, "Lord, the man can drink." When he arrived at court in the morning, he would walk back into the hallway that connected the courtroom to the judge's secretary's office and the judge's chambers. There he would pose someone, like the prosecutor, as a shield for him as he downed a miniature of whiskey. He drank all day, and then for an hour or two at the end of the day. Little did I know that one day I would get to the point where I could challenge him in the drinking game.

Rarely did he ever call about a plea the day before the case was set. But, when we saw Joe's name as counsel, we knew it would not be trial, and could plan around it. When he came to court on the morning of trial, he came up close to you, turned to you so his back was to the courtroom, then looked up at you and asked questions that would get you to respond, often with head shakes. Because Joe was very short he was always looking up at your face when he talked.

Whatever we worked out that morning was the plea that he entered. Sometimes he would come in and ask for a postponement, usually saying that his client had not paid him in full yet. Since we would have called off the witnesses, knowing the defendant would not go to trial, we usually agreed.

Later, when I became a defense attorney, I had clients ask me how much cash they would need to bring to court to pay the prosecutor and judge. I told them there would not be payment made to anyone, and the first few who asked this. I asked why they asked. The answer was universal. At some time either this client or a friend or relative had been represented by Joe, who had told them that when he was talking to the prosecutor in the courtroom he was working out how much cash he would have to pay for the deal.

Suddenly, a light came on and I remembered how Joe would manipulate you into talking to him with his back to his client. Those were the times when his clients believed he was working out bribes. When he told them how much he needed for the case, they gave him that much in cash, which was in addition to his fee.

One client told me that I had been the prosecutor on a case in which she was the defendant, represented by Joe. I did not remember the case, but I asked, " How much did Joe tell you he had to pay me for the deal we made?" "Four hundred dollars," she said. I told her that I never got any of that money. But, she didn't seem indignant that Joe had made an extra fee. She said that she asked him whether she could pay it in sex, and Joe said, "No, Grant wants the cash." So, Joe was not the Southwest Airlines of the criminal bar. Instead of putting the whole cost in one straight- across- the -board fee, he hid the costs like the other airlines do—so much cash for bribing the state's attorney, so much cash for bribing the judge, so much cash to file paper work after the verdict or judgement of the court was entered. From the standpoint of a low starting fee, he had the advantage over other lawyers.

Not only was Joe was very short, he was jovial, always laughing. He would have made a great pixie or leprechaun in an Irish movie. He would be a perfect cast member in *Guys and Dolls*, a great foil for Damon Runyan's straight officer of the law. And that's the role he would fill in my pretend musical.

Joe jealously guarded his clients and, unlike other criminal lawyers who got overloaded from time to time, he would not send a client to another lawer. But Joe was ready and willing to introduce his friends, even lawyers, to all the known figures of the Black social community and to all the known figures who operated the Block—and if business came from those folks, that was fine with Joe.

115

Arthur Murphy, George Russell, Milton B. Allen— These unique men were the Black lawyers with whom I had the most contact. All were fine lawyers—ethical, dignified, imaginative.

Arthur was flamboyant, colorful, outgoing, and wanted to be noticed and semeetings were just awfully hard to sit through.

If there was any truth to the rumor that members of the staff enjoyed a world series game in the office during the first series the O's played after Frank Robinson joined them, and that they watched the game on a color television set wheeled around from the FBI evidence room where it was being held as evidence in a high jacking case, and that they enjoyed the game while sipping southern Maryland moonshine mixed with coke, then you can count on the fact that Arthur, Roger and I would have been involved. But, remember that I said "If there was any truth to the rumor". It was too good a game to miss by being caged up in an office.

If there was any truth to the rumor that certain members of the staff were raucously reviewing and admiring the photographic "Exclusive" magazines seized in the obscenity cases, in my office, and that the U.S. Attorney returned from D.C. sooner than expected and walked into the office just as one of the staff was holding up a photo, regaling the others with anatomical comments, and that the staff members were summoned individually for "counseling" sessions with the U.S. Attorney himself, you can bet that Roger, Arthur and I would have been involved, and that Arthur was the one making the funny-at-the-time comments. But, remember I said "*If* there was any truth to the rumor." I wasn't very impressed with the session I had.

I can remember Arthur taking up position in the hallway outside his office each day just before 5pm. It was the time of the march of the FBI steno pool ladies to the restrooms before leaving the courthouse for the day. We often commented that the guy who screened applicants for the steno pool had one of the best jobs in the world. We also wondered who in the Bureau had good enough taste to set the obvious physical qualifications for hiring. It couldn't have been just a coincidence that they all fit such a perfect mold.

Arthur was always there to greet them and let them know how much we appreciated them. And, the more we kidded him about it, the louder he laughed and the more he enjoyed himself. On one unforgettable day, Roger walked down the hall to talk to the "Chief" at FBI parade time. He found Arthur standing proudly talking to some of the ladies, and noticed that his fly was open. Roger sauntered up to Arthur quietly and said "Chief, your fly is open." Arthur laughed and said, "Sure it is", then realized that it was, zipped up and laughed even louder. You simply couldn't get him down.

In court he was a tiger, leaving all levity behind him. What an example he set for charging hard in court at every minute of a trial----"never let up, and when you get them down, finish them off" was his motto which he drilled at us constantly. When he went to the Grand Jury, if he had a "sure thing" charge, and a "not quite so sure a thing" charge, he had the guts to charge both, and make the defense worry about the more serious charge. I learned a lot from him, which shaped my attitudes toward developing strategies---"If the law doesn't say you can't do it, try it." It works for prosecutors, defense attorneys and those attacking government bureaucracy and arrogance.

I have already talked about George and Milton, and how much

respect I had for them, how great they were as performers in the process and as role models.

These three were such fine examples of professionals and were so omnipresent that I think they masked for a lot of us the absence of more Blacks in the high ranks of the process.

Their presence assured that quality Black professionals existed, and with the color blindness of so many other whites, I went through life and my work without giving much thought to the exclusion of Blacks from the profession and from substantive governmental roles.

It was one of those things you do your work without taking time to "think" about racial and social issues or causes. You just do your work with the people filling the roles needed to make your work successful. Then, you go home and watch the news coverage of racial, social problems in other parts of the nation and world, and think "it's too bad that people can't get along like we do here." We had one Black and no women assistant U.S. attorneys. At the time there were no Black federal district judges in the District of Maryland and no Black FBI, Secret Service, Postal Inspectors, Alcohol-Tobacco-Tax, or Drug Enforcement agents.

When I went to the State's Attorney's office, there was one Black assistant, Joe Howard, only one Black judge on the Supreme Bench, and only one Black judge on the Municipal Court. There were only a handful of black defense attorneys.

Yet, I went about business, admiring these Blacks not as Blacks moving ahead of their peers but simply as professionals.

116

Juanita Jackson Mitchell— **She was** a great lady and a lawyer with compassion. No one in the City could ever overlook or forget her wide array of colorful, eye-catching hats. She was never in court without the hat, and the classic photographs of her catch the style.

But, she was far more than just a stylish lawyer. She was a lawyer of substance, dedicated to the civil rights of every one of her clients. When she appeared in criminal court, she did not plead just for a lesser sentence, she pleaded for acquittals, for her clients to avoid a criminal record. She knew how critical a criminal record was to a young Black man. She was not focused just on the outcome of each criminal case, she was focused on avoiding that criminal record which could later in life block the client from getting a job, getting into the military service or getting into a school of advanced learning. Many lawyers try for the short term success through a plea bargain; their attitude is get the best deal today and let tomorrow take care of itself. Ms. Mitchell did not take that short cut. She was interested in the future of her clients, their full life experience.

When I was prosecuting, most of her clients were very young, first time burglary offenders. Her cases were those that other lawyers were trying to "plead out" for probation. She fought for innocent verdicts, or probation without verdict, to avoid that criminal record.

I remember one day in Judge O'Donnell's court she was representing a young Black man charged with burglary. He had been arrested in an alley leading away from building in which there was a broken window. The breaking of that window set off an alarm and a police officer in the immediate vicinity arrested Ms. Mitchell's young client. She urged that the young man had just stopped off in the alley to urinate.

Judge O'Donnell said to the effect, "Ms. Mitchell, if I were to believe every story that I hear about someone stopping in an alley to urinate the gutters of Baltimore would run yellow." Undaunted, Ms. Mitchell persisted. Finally she wore down even Judge O'Donnell who turned to me and asked whether I opposed probation without verdict. I said I did not, and he put the young man on probation with a stern reminder to urinate at home or in a public toilet. Always a lady, even when advocating for her client, Ms. Mitchell very cordially thanked "Your honor" and then me on the way away from the trial table.

She had saved one more young man from a record, at least for that day. She did what she had to do to protect her client, both in the case and for his future. She could have entered a plea of guilty in exchange for probation and saved herself at least an hour in court time. But she was interested in her client's future and did not take a short cut that endangered his future. I am sure she hoped, more than many of us in the criminal practice did, that the young man would see the error of his ways.

She never misled me. She actually believed her clients, and wanted desperately to prevent the beginning of that criminal record. She was always humble in her approach to the courts, and respectful to the prosecutors. With her position in the community, she could have been demanding—as to both her time and her position. She could have parlayed her name and reputation into special treatment just as many prominent civil rights leaders do today. She was not. When her client's case was last on the docket, she settled in to wait his or her turn. Some in her position would have blustered and blown, trying to move up the docket because of "My busy schedule" or "My appointment with the Mayor." Not Ms. Mitchell. She came to court to do a job for her client and knew that "Getting on her bandstand" would not win the sympathy of the Court.

That said, whenever I could, I moved her case up because I knew that criminal cases did not constitute the bulk of her work. I knew that her time in criminal court would simply take away from community work that was needed. And I did it because she was so cooperative.

I think I would cast Ms. Mitchell as the choral director, leading rousing songs of celebration of victory for some underdog.

117

Charles D. Harris— **He was** one of m favorite judges, except at sentencing time when I was on the defense side. He was a distinguished looking and acting judge, very strict in application of the rules of evidence and in sentencing. But I never shied away from trying a case before him. The one thing I made sure of is if I had a slam-dunk case against me on defense, I pursued the case through a "not guilty statement of facts trial." As already explained, this meant the prosecutor would summarize the evidence his witnesses would provide. I would agree that such would be the testimony and I would make a statement as to what the proof, if any, would be from the defense. Judge Harris preferred a statement of facts trial to a plea of guilty because it took so much time to make a record showing that the defendant voluntarily, knowingly, and all the rest, waived or gave up every right he or she had. In the statement of facts trial, the only waivers to work through were waivers of the jury trial and the right to have the witnesses take the stand and actually testify to what the prosecutor summarized.

Judge Harris did not suffer well wasters of his time. If the client had no real defense, you did not want to take up time with a jury or even a court trial if you were caught in his court.

As a prosecutor, I immensely enjoyed his courtroom. He presided over the biggest gambling case I ever prosecuted. Not long after I joined the State's Attorney's staff, Charley Moylan took on the in-line pinball machine industry that placed gambling devices in stores all over town. The machines were in bars, lounges, Mom and Pop grocery stores, sandwich shops, strip clubs, truck stops, Polock Johnny's shop on The Block (featured which in-line pinball machines, cigarettes, beer, condoms in hundreds of shapes, colors and textures, and the best chili dogs and Polish sausages anywhere), and at least one house of prostitution. The machines were not rigged for direct payoffs as were the old slot machines. But the machines collected games won in a cumulative total, and when ready to cash in the player got paid by the bartender or person in charge. The payoff was based on a set amount per game won. Everyone knew the machines facilitated gambling, and juveniles were not allowed to play them.

In the United States Attorney's office, Tom Kenney had taken them on with instructions from D.C. He served as lead counsel at the trial, with me sitting second chair. I had interviewed and prepared the FBI expert on gambling machines, and I conducted the examination of the witness at trial. The expert carefully explained how the machines were designed for gambling, how the payoff was worked through, and why the machine was not a satisfying experience for the non-gambling pinball player.

In the federal system, in a gambling case such as that, a jury first decided whether the machine was used for gambling, then the court had to decide whether the machine fit the definition of a "gambling device" under state law. The jury found that the machines were used for gambling, but Judge Edward Northrup, an old legislator from southern Maryland where gambling was highly popular (and still existed legally when I first went to Maryland) held that the machines were not "gambling devices" under Maryland statutes. It was an ironic, but not unexpected, decision, given the legislative background of the judge. He was from a heavily pro-gambling part of the state and was prepared to bet on anything positive.

The Department of Justice decided it would be futile to appeal his decision, so the pinball industry dodged a bullet.

When I got to Charley's office, he wanted to take them on under state law, not as devices but on the basis of actual gambling activity. So we put together quite a team of undercover officers to go throughout the city playing the in-line pinballs, getting paid off and recording winnings, who paid them and where and at what time of day on what date.

Frank Mazone played an important role in this undercover operation. It was on one of his successful pay off days that the bartender told him he had to be careful in making payoffs because he always had to worry about that "damned" Mazone of the State Police. Frank asked who that was, and the bartender said it was a state cop who went undercover and fooled people into breaking the law. Frank asked the guy if he had ever seen Mazone, and the bartender said, "I've never met him, but I've got a picture of him and will know him if he ever comes in to use my machines." Frank wished him luck, pocketed his winnings and went outside and recorded name, time and place.

On several occasions I prosecuted drug dealers who had bragged to an undercover Mazone that the "undercover fink Mazone" would never get to them. But he did.

I spent two full days interviewing the FBI expert on the machines and how they operate, and how they differed from regular pinball machines. The first time I was scheduled to go to D.C. to interview him, I put on a bright blue shirt and red tie. It was a good feeling to get away, even for a day, from the same old white dress shirt and conservative tie. Just as I was walking out the door, I got a call summoning me to Judge J. Gilber Prendergast's courtroom. When I got there I found that he was inquiring about a sentencing case that mistakenly appeared on the court docket. I apologized for taking so long to get to court, and told him that I was just on the way to the District of Columbia to have FBI training on the in-line machines that plagued Baltimore. He smiled and said, "Ahhhhah, *that* explains the pinball machine costume."

When trial time arrived, I put the FBI expert on the stand and had him testify as to how the machines were wired so they would accumulate the number of games to be paid off. He testified that during his early training, he worked undercover and observed bartenders or managers pay off the player in cash when his run was completed or he was ready to cash out. The number of accumulated "payoff" games was treated just like chips being turned in at a casino.

I followed up with testimony from officers who, as undercover players, had been paid off for winnings in establishments throughout the city. We had evidence from each of the police districts in Baltimore. The officers also testified as to statements made by bartenders and managers as to how the owners of the establishments wanted the payoffs to be made. The defendants were the owners/operators of the establishments. In those rare cases where we had no specific evidence to tie in the operator owner, the individual who made the payoff was the defendant.

Judge Harris found the defendants guilty of violating the gambling laws. Sentencing was delayed for several days to give the defendants the opportunity to file motions for a new trial. After the motions were filed and denied, sentencing was set for a Monday morning. Charley and I believed there was better than an even chance that Judge Harris would deal out some jail time. This was his chance to sentence the upper level of gambling, not just the numbers runners and street bookies who were the usual defendants. Jail time for these defendants would hurt the industry, and might even lead to some informants against the very top dogs in the industry.

The Baltimore Sun, which was strongly anti-gambling, wrote that the industry was worried, that the successful prosecution had shaken them, but jail time would make the mountain quiver.

On the Friday afternoon before the scheduled sentencing, I went through the courtroom to get to Judge Harris' chambers to talk about the next week's schedule. As I went through, out came Theodore R. McKeldin, former mayor and governor of Maryland. McKeldin had delivered the "I like Ike," "Here comes Ike" rousing nomination speech for Dwight Eisenhower at the 1952 Republican National Convention years before. Simon Sobeloff had written the speech, so two Baltimoreans had an important role in the "Ike" movement that swept the country.

As governor, McKeldin had appointed Judge Harris to the bench. He had played no role in the defense of the gambling interests, but his law partner was lead counsel. As we passed in the empty courtroom, McKeldin said, "Nice trial, young man. Come see me when you've had enough." I said "Thanks," with a sinking feeling. I did not mention to Judge Harris that I had just seen McKeldin coming out of his chamber area. When his secretary let me in his office, he was standing behind his desk with his hands in his pockets, looking downcast. He said to me, "Fred, one day when this is all over, we will have to have a drink and I will tell you a story about how old favors are never completely paid off." I didn't even let on that I knew he was talking about sentencing in the gambling cases.

I went to Charley's office and told him what I had seen and what the judge had said. We pretty well knew at that point, there would be no jail sentences. So Charley did the only thing he could do, began to prepare what he would say to the press on Monday *before* sentencing, so that it would not look like we were disappointed when no jail time was imposed.

Monday morning the press was there in force. *The morning Sun* always was on an anti-gambling campaign, so George Hiltner was there early. Eddie Fenton had smelled the blood of a real story so he was there to scoop the newspapers with dispatches right from the courthouse to WCBM. He already had a phone staked out and reserved in the State's Attorney's front office, just a few feet from the courtroom. Hollace Weiner from the *News American* was there. Charley gave them a joint statement that we had done our job, we had pointed out how the gambling industry had invaded popular, neighborhood spots all over town with gambling machines. He gave them the opening to ask him about what sentences he expected, and then told them that the prosecutor's job was to seek justice, to get convictions where the evidence merited, and sentencing was properly in the hands of an objective bench. He said that whatever the sentence, the impact on the gambling industry would be the same—because they knew now that we could get convictions any time we invested the time to go after them.

It was as good a press statement as I ever heard him give. When he was finished, and we went to the trial table to await the formal proceedings, Eddie Fenton slipped up to me and said, "So, they got to the judge, huh?" What a guy was Eddie! He didn't even wait for me to say anything, he hustled off to his telephone to call in a dispatch that said that the State's Attorney did not expect jail sentences to be imposed. Of course, he was right, and Judge Harris surprised everyone except the defendants, Charley Moylan, Eddie Fenton and me by imposing fines, instead of jail sentences, on the defendants. I know it was a hard dose for such an honorable man to swallow.

He had a great sense of humor. Given to suffer from a slight stutter at times, he did not seem too defensive about it. In one case, I had a defendant charged with delivery of drugs, possession of drugs, and conspiracy to violate the drug laws. He worked as a shoe clerk in an east Baltimore department store. An informant had turned him in, and an undercover officer went in to make a buy. Apparently smelling a rat, my client pretended not to even know what the officer was talking about when he proposed making a buy.

Having failed to get a direct delivery, the officers executed their search warrant without the "buy." They found a stash of heroin in an empty shoe box in the stacks.

Because they had not been able to make a direct buy, the state produced the informant as a witness at trial. I attacked credibility by proving that the officers and prosecutor had promised to dismiss eleven drug charges against the witness, and that they had delivered by dismissing the charges prior to the trial of my client. I asked the witness whether he would have testified if the state had not dismissed his charges. He said "No." I asked if there was any other reason he testified and he said that he had a grudge against my client because he had refused to to go into business with him. My client had told me this, but I took a real chance in asking the question because I could not prove it without putting my client on the stand, which I could not do. This is one time when the "forbidden" question was worth it, and worked. I followed up by asking him why the defendant would not go into business with him. The Witness said it was because he sold drugs at school grounds and to school kids, and the defendant did not believe in that. It could not have been a better series of discrediting questions and answers.

Those credibility answers gave me a lot to argue as to the "justice" of the justice system, with police officers making deals with school yard drug predators.

The jury found my client not guilty of all delivery and possession charges, even though the amount of drugs found in the empty shoe box in his shoe department was large enough to make a delivery charge stick. But the jury found him guilty of what they thought was the lesser of the offenses, the conspiracy. Actually, under Maryland law, the conspiracy charge carried the same maximum sentence as the offense itself. Had I been allowed to argue penalties, I think I would have gotten a complete acquittal.

As it was, the verdict was not valid. The only basis for a conspiracy was the specific offense on which the jury found my client not guilty. Under those facts, the conspiracy verdict could not stand. So Judge Harris set aside the verdict, and we agreed to submit the conspiracy to him for a statement of facts trial based on the evidence produced at trial. He found my client guilty, but put him on probation because of the jury verdicts.

That night at a bar association dinner, I was getting a drink when the judge walked up to the bar. He mentioned that I tried a good case, and I said, "You know judge, for a moment there I thought you were actually going to put a "not" in front of that "guilty," but "you just couldn't get the "not" said." I was referring to the fact that as he announced his verdict he had stuttered and had to compose himself before continuing. He just laughed and said, "Not in your lifetime, Grant".

On another occasion, I tried and won a jury trial before Judge Harris on a court appointed case. When I got the check from the city, it was for a measly two hundred fifty dollars, when I had expected seven hundred and fifty. I didn't make a special trip over to the courthouse, but I had a case scheduled with Judge Harris that afternoon. After we finished chambers meeting, I remarked to him that I was surprised at the amount I got paid in the case and wondered if the city had made a mistake. Harris had complimented me at the end of the trial.

He told me "no," that neither he nor the city had made a mistake. He said, "Fred, you tried too hard to get an acquittal in that case where you knew the defendant was guilty." I said, "Judge, you mean

I would have been paid more if the jury had convicted my client?" He replied, without hesitation or remorse, "Yes, and even more if you had pleaded him guilty."

In one case, I was called to defend the assignment clerk in the State's Attorney's office on a drug conspiracy charge. Her husband was caught in a drug sting and she was charged because of drugs found in the house. They arrested her at work at about 3:30 p.m. She called me and I went right to the lockup in the courthouse. She was right then most concerned about her kids who she needed to pick up at 5. Also, this was a Friday evening and if we didn't get bail set quickly, she would sit in jail all weekend. First I assured her that her kids would be picked up, and I called Arvin to have him start making telephone calls to members of her family. I went to Judge Harris who had received the indictments from the Grand Jury that day, and fortunately he was still in the building late on a Friday afternoon. He set an immediate bail hearing. I went over and notified the prosecutor assigned to the case, who wailed about me getting "special treatment from the judges" but came along to the hearing.

I requested release on her own recognizance. The charge grew out of an undercover operation that had gone on for three months. I argued that if she was not a danger to run during all that time, she was not a risk now. I told the court that her kids would be expecting her and that she was not about to run because of her kids and her home. She had no place to run. I also got a chance to take a shot at the prosecutor by saying, "I don't think, either, judge, that it is 'special treatment' for me that you agreed to hear this motion immediately as the prosecutor alleged to me. It's the kind of justice that any judge ought to give to any defendant regardless of what the prosecutor charges."

I could tell that Judge Harris was getting ready to do something he thought was funny because his eyes started twinkling. He said that I had made such an eloquent plea that he was moved. But, he said, he could not just place her on her own recognizance because of the message it would send as to favoritism to an employee of the prosecutor's office. He then asked, "Counsel, are you willing to assume responsibility for your client, and if so, I will release her to your personal custody." Now, his eyes were positively dancing. I had to say "yes," so I did. Because of her position of employment, and Eddie Fenton had shown up for WCBM, George Hiltner of the *Sun* and *Hollace Weiner of the News American* were all there. So in their presence and with great fanfare for the press, Judge Harris released her to my "personal custody and care", for me to take personal responsibility for her," for me to "keep her in my presence at all times and care for all her needs" until a subsequent bail hearing could be conducted. He left the bench, smiling openly, and remarked, "Have a good weekend, Mr. Grant."

The release was made, and she was free to go home, after I assured her that she and her kids did not actually have to come live with me for the weekend. On the way home, I heard Eddie with the lead news story, which would be repeated hourly throughout the night and the following slow news Saturday, that the drug defendant had been put into my personal care and custody. Of course the TV stations picked up the story from Eddie and the Associated Press, and the *Sun* and *News American* saved the story for their widely read Sunday editions. Both papers had pictures of the defendant, who was really a good looking, seductive looking woman, and me—with captions like "counsel keeps client close. One of the papers it may have been the *Afro American*, had a line under a photo, "Judge orders client to be up close and personal with lawyer.

My wife, Lodice, found no humor in the whole thing, but the rest of the city, or at least all my friends, did.

I would definitely make Judge Harris the producer of my "Guys and Dolls" show.

118

Meyer Cardin—I have mentioned Judge Cardin several times in the book, but feel a need to single him out further. He was a member of a very successful family. His son, Howard, one of my closest friends in Baltimore, was, as I have said, one of the best trial lawyers I ever saw. His son, Benjamin, a successful lawyer in his own right is a United States Senator from Maryland——-a highly regarded Senator with great seniority. Other members of the family were successful in business, the law, and in political positions important to the people of Baltimore and Maryland.

But, he didn't play the role of a wealthy judge indifferent to the plight of the victims and defendants who came before him. He treated witnesses, victims, court personnel, and practicing lawyers with kindness, with an attitude of caring about their concerns and interests. He didn't have to wield an iron fist in order to discipline his courtroom. Many times I watched him straighten out an offending lawyer with a simple disapproving look. When he walked into the courtroom, he was smiling obviously content to perform the duties he took on with the oath. If the smile disappeared, whatever was going wrong was soon righted.

He never gave less than his best in the courtroom. He never shirked from assignment loads, and never complained when we overloaded his docket in order to move cases. We did that often because he was a no-nonsense, bottom line judge who didn't like postponements and didn't like delays.

Neither did he shirk helping out other judges and court personnel when they were overloaded. When a judge saw that his docket had bogged down or would bog down, his suggestion was usually "see if Judge Cardin can help out." Almost always the answer was "yes." The clerks and bailiffs who worked his courtroom were used to accepting the extra workload. They didn't complain about it because they knew their judge would just smile at their complaints and take on the extra work.

Within a few days of coming to the state's attorney's office, I encountered a reason for a requested postponement that I had never heard in the federal courts. An attorney requested a postponement because "rule one has not been complied with." I was mystified, and leaned over to the lead attorney that day and asked "what is rule one?" He laughed and said "that means that the client hasn't paid the fee. Rule one is that the client has to pay the fee before the lawyer goes to court." Of course, there is no such "rule one" in the procedural rules. But, on that day the judge granted two or three postponements for that reason. And, I was given to understand that there was no reason to oppose the request because the judges wouldn't force the lawyers to go to trial if they hadn't been paid.

So, the first time I heard the request made in Judge Cardin's court, I didn't respond with objection. I figured that the Judge was practical enough that he would just grant the request. Instead, he asked the lawyer how many times the case had been postponed because of "rule one". The lawyer answered that this was the third request. Judge Cardin replied to the effect that "I would give you a break the first time, but you should have collected the fee by now or dropped the client. I'll put the case off until after lunch so you can send him out to get the money to pay you. But, we're going to dispose of this case today, one way or the other." All the time, he was smiling, speaking directly but not harshly. That afternoon, apparently there had been compliance with "rule one" because we disposed of the case without further request for postponement.

Many times a defense attorney would ask for a bench conference and suggest to the judge that the client intended to plead guilty, but needed time to get his affairs in order, including getting enough to pay the fee. So, the attorney would ask for a postponement with the assurance that the client would plead guilty when the case was re-scheduled. Judge Cardin would get that little smile on his face and say "let's take his plea today, and I'll give you plenty of time before sentencing." He knew that postponements led to further postponements, and that the quicker the plea was entered, the better the chance that the case would get resolved in a shorter period of time. Rarely did the plea not get entered on that day.

When I hear trial judges complain about their work load, and go out of their way to avoid over-scheduling. I think of Judge Cardin. Several times in Idaho, I have been in the courtroom of federal district judge B. Lynn Winmill and heard him complain about the case load and the back-log, and wonder how he could handle the extra work that might be required in a case in order to give every party a full voice in the proceedings.

I was first in Winmill's courtroom watching a case in which an anti-rancher, anti-livestock grazing architect requested that the court prohibit grazing by the ranchers in Owyhee County, Idaho. Family ranchers sat in court, with their livelihoods—their lives— on the line, and Winmill complained about his case load and the extra work that would be required if he speeded up the case as the ranchers requested. As taxpayers, the ranchers were paying for the courtroom, the law clerks, the secretaries, the Marshalls, the court building, all the utilities, the law books in the court library, the judge's salary, the salaries of the government bureaucrats involved in the case and the federal attorneys representing them. And, directly from their own pockets, they were paying their own attorney. Yet, sitting there working on their dime, Winmill begrudged them the time to consider their case.

I thought of Judge Cardin. I compared his "let's do it" attitude to that of Winmill's which more resembles that of a whining bureaucrat. I wondered why someone would want to be a judge and then bemoan the time it takes to perform the duties that go with the oath. Could it be that the concept of "anointment" rather than "appointment" is the motivation?

Judge Cardin would be my producer of "Guys and Dolls," watching the casting, the rehearsals and the final production from out front, with a smile on his face.

119

William J. O'Donnell— He was a brilliant judge. He was very bright and he had as thorough a grasp on the law and rules of procedure as anyone I ever encountered. But I hated to go before him. Even when prepared, I could count on him raising some question that neither I nor my officers had thought about. When he caught me in one of those situations he was then brutal.

He was the Baltimore City State's Attorney just prior to my boss, Charles Moylan, taking office. Charley worked for "Wild Bill" as we called him. O'Donnell reveled when he could tell us "that is not the way things were done in my office" or "you would know the answer to that question if you worked for me." He went easier on police officers who were on the witness stand. When he found something that the officer had neglected, he put the blame on the prosecutor: "Well, officer if the state's attorney's office had done the job right you would not be in this fix" or "a good efficient prosecutor would have prepared you for my question."

I have told the story of the night Bob Stewart and I were hiding behind the dumpster, hearing bullets clang off the other side—the night Sterling Fletcher avoided being shot but fell backward off the stoop and injured his back. What started out as a well organized search expedition turned into a nightmare with the firing of the first shot from the upstairs apartment I do believe that the shooter did not know that we were the law. I accept the fact that he thought we might be drug trade competitors out to rob him. The reason is that as soon as the uniformed officers went through the door and started up the stairs the shooting stopped.

Once the search party of detectives got into the apartment they found several women in various stages of hysteria as a result of the raid and the shots fired. Our evidence officer took up position in the center of the apartment and other searchers brought evidence to him, identifying where the evidence was located in the apartment and who was nearest to it when found. The gun was found and taken to the evidence officer and the man who rented the apartment was the closest to where the gun was picked up from the floor.

All those in the apartment were charged with frequenting a nuisance house because of the quantity of drugs found throughout the apartment. The tenant was charged with possession with intent to deliver drugs, with operating a nuisance house and with assault on a police officer. Our theory was that since he was the person with legal right to resist a person breaking into the home he had more reason to have shot the gun than any of the women who were present. After he was charged we received the report that verified that his finger prints were on the gun. There were other prints on the gun as well.

The charges were scheduled for trial before O'Donnell. When the evidence officer was on the stand testifying as to the taking of the gun into evidence O'Donnell asked whether a paraffin test had been made on the defendant to determine whether he had recently fired a gun. Of course there had not been such a test performed. In the chaos surrounding the search scene after the shots were fired and the search party ran into several hysterical women in the apartment, no one thought about performing a paraffin test. In fact no one from the crime lab qualified to make such test was even present right after the entry into the apartment. In those days officers would be lucky if the crime lab personnel arrived on a scene two to three hours after detectives arrived. There were times detectives had to wait hours before the crime lab arrived on the scene of a homicide.

Judge O'Donnell took up the assault on witnesses and the state's attorney's office for the failure to perform a test that would have shown whether the defendant fired the gun. He regaled the crowded court room with his comments that there were two prosecutors present including the chief of the organized crime division who should have had the presence of mind to order the test be made. He questioned why prosecutors would even go along on a search if they were not competent enough to step up and fill an evidentiary void. Then in a crowning moment of sarcasm he dismissed the assault charge on the grounds that the state deprived the defendant of test results which could have cleared him. Comfortable and satisfied with himself he then sat back in his chair, looked at me in the back of the courtroom, nodded smilingly, and let the trial proceed on the other charges.

Before Charley instituted the trial team process for assignment of a trial team to a specific judge and courtroom for a month, handling a continued trial before O'Donnell was a nightmare. Two attorneys were assigned to a courtroom to handle the daily docket of cases scheduled for the day in that courtoom. If one of them started a jury trial that did not finish by the end of the day, the trial had to carry over to the next day. That meant that the docket for the next day had to be moved to make way for the continued jury trial. If that move was not accomplished prior to the beginning of court O'Donnell was fit to be tied. That would launch him into a tirade about how "this would not have happened in my office."

The carried over trial not only fouled up the next day's schedule for the attorney trying it, but the next day's schedule for the courtroom and a different pair of prosecutors. If I had a jury trial carried over I had to arrange for someone to handle my work for the next day and the attorneys who had the courtroom assignment for the next day had to find a way to dispose of their cases. Prior to the start of the day the prosecutors had to have arranged for the scheduled trials to be moved to another courtroom and judge in order to escape O'Donnell's wrath.

The first time I had a continued jury trial I arranged with Judge Cardin early in the morning to take on the extra cases. A jury trial scheduled for his courtroom had been settled at the last minute, so he could take on the whole O'Donnell regular assignment. When I went into chambers and explained to the judge that the docket had been moved without hitch he seemed to be very disappointed. His response was "good" but he just looked disappointed because he could not blame me for delay.

He told the defense attorney and I that he would use the time saved to take care of a "couple of things" before resuming the jury trial. We waited in the courtroom for nearly two hours while the jury sat enclosed in the tiny, cramped jury room that served the courtroom. When the judge finally came out and called for the jury we were at least two and a half hours into the day and it was lunch time. When the jury was seated in the box apologized for holding them up. He said that the assistant state's attorney had to move the day's regular docket because he had not been efficient enough to complete the state's case the day before. He did not precisely say that I caused the delay, but he gave the jury that impression and all of them at one point or other looked at me during his remarks. He released them for lunch, expressing his hope that I would be prepared to proceed after lunch so that the jurors would not be further inconvenienced. They all gave me an aggravated look on the way out of the courtroom.

After lunch he welcomed the jurors back and made the comment that perhaps I had enough time to get my house in order and complete my presentation in a more efficient manner. What could I do? Nothing but grin and bear it and try my case.

He did not single me out for this kind of treatment. We all got it. But a major problem was averted once we went to the trial team process. When a jury trial did not end and had to be carried over, the other member of the team simply went to work to move the next day's docket.

With a one month assignment to a courtroom the process for dealing with postponed cases and carry over cases was vastly improved. But it meant that when we got assigned to a tough judge we had to deal with it for a solid month.

The month we spent with Judge O'Donnell was monstrous. He was a good judge, but we could not do anything right. No matter how hard we worked-no matter how carefully we prepared he would find something overlooked in every case-whether it was relevant to the outcome or not.

Of course, we wouldn't be lucky enough to avoid arraignments in his court. Each criminal court took arraignments on a rotating basis. With five courts sitting at that time, could we get a break and have arraignments hit his court a week before we went there or a week after? Of course not.

Arraignments were a nightmare in his court. Our arraignments sheet had 25-50 cases assigned for handling before our trials for the day started. In Judge Sodaro's court, arraignments took less than an hour. Each defendant was called; if he or she had an attorney a plea was taken; if there was no attorney yet, the court either appointed counsel or postponed for the defendant to get counsel. We had no information on the case other than what was on the arraignment docket sheet; defendant's name, case number and, charge. We had no files on any of the cases because they were there for arraignment only. Odds were that the prosecutor handling arraignment would not even try the case. The jail guard who transported in-custody defendants knew nothing about the cases.

So, most judges didn't ask questions of anyone but the defendant. Not so with Judge O'Donnell. He asked questions about the charges, the amount of bail, about the defendant's family, about why the defendant was not charged differently. He had the indictments in front of him. We did not. So of course, we had no answers. He liked to keep track of the number of "I don't know your honor" he got each day. So the four members of our team took turns in the barrel and the unlucky on who had Monday got a second shot on Friday. At the end of arraignment week, Judge O'Donnell announced the number of "I do not know your honor" answers and all variations thereof.

Once arraignments were over, the fun of trials began. Nothing he hated worse than a case that ran smoothly for anyone of us. He would lean way back in his chair, looking at the ceiling, for the world to see, as though he was bored stiff. All of a sudden, He would roll his head sideways and rip the prosecutor with a question out of the blue. He did it even in court trials, but, loved doing it, during jury trials. Often, I just stood there, wondering how I was going to stay cool and not be held in contempt, and how I was going to avoid a mistrial. In court trials, more than jury trials, he launched into how things were done in "My days as State Attorney," how "My people knew they had to do things," how there was better preparation "In my office where your boss was slow learner," how things would be done differently by "Real trial lawyers like me and my assistants," and how "I never would have tolerated such sloppy work in my office." The latter came only on arraignment days because we were not "Sloppy" lawyers. I have told about how Bobby Fertitta finessed him on my first day in the State's Attorney's Office. When one of us could back him into a spot where he did not dare go farther for fear of mistrial, we were very satisfied with ourselves. The court trials were murderous. He could challenge us endlessly with no fear of mistrial.

That first arson case I tried before him on my first day was probably the best experience I ever had with him. I think maybe he was just sizing me up to see whether I could try a case. At the end of the court trial, he found the defendant guilty. Then I set about to make my life easy with my co-workers. He said, looking at the two other assistants in the room, "Give your boss my regards. He has finally hired a trial lawyer." I thought, "oh great," but soon realized that they knew what he was up to.

Remembering that Charley had doubled our assignment in Judge Prendergast's court, after the third week I got Charley's promise that he would not extent our time in O'Donnell's courtroom.

As we moved into the last week, we made sure there was no case scheduled on Friday that could hold over. Then we began to plan our "Getting away" party for that Friday evening. On Friday, we had only two court trials scheduled. The first one concluded just prior to noon. I had the last case and knew I could finish by five p.m. We picked up after lunch at 1:30 and by 3:15 I rested. Judge took a recess for completing some "Personal business," we waited and waited, and soon I walked around to his secretary's office to see when we might resume. The bailiff from another courtroom asked me how we were doing. I said, "Waiting for the judge." He said "Yeah, I saw him leave about half an hour ago." I said, "Leave?" and he said "Yeah, had his hat on and walked out." I thought maybe he was through for the day. I went in and his secretary said he had some errands to run.

We were patient. All our team was in the courtroom to witness the end of the week.

We waited and waited for his return. We had been very careful not to let him find out that we planned a "getting away" party because we knew he would try to spoil it by holding us over for another day.

Finally he came back about half past four. The trial resumed and the defense called its first witness. I had no cross examination. The defense had told us he had three witnesses. Half way through the testimony of the second the judge interrupted to say that he had an important engagement that evening and would have to continue the remainder of the case until Monday morning. Defense counsel asked to be allowed to proceed quickly through the rest of the testimony of at least the second witness and the judge said no.

He recessed the court after he continued the remainder of the trial to Monday. I walked back to where my team was sitting, kind of despondent about not having completely finished our month there. We still intended to party because only I would have to come back on Monday. Leaving the bench, as he opened the door to his chambers, Judge O'Donnell looked around and called to me. When I responded, he smiled and said "Hope this doesn't upset your party plans too much. Maybe you can party again on Monday if we finish in time." With all our efforts at keeping the party a secret he had found out about it and took his long break that afternoon just to thwart our happy ending to the month.

He did not plague me as a defense attorney nearly as much as he did when I was a prosecutor. He was very careful about not stepping on a defense counsel to the point that an appellate court might say he had interfered with a defense.

About two years after I left Baltimore I returned for a conference in Washington, D.C. I stayed with our good friends, the Doellers, who lived just two houses away from us on Rosebank Avenue. One evening we went to O'Brecky's Crab House in East Baltimore. There was always a line at O'Brecky's, and sometimes two lines. On this particular evening I saw Judge O'Donnell and his wife standing in the other line. I thought "Oh good, I get to be harangued while

I stand in line to eat." I thought perhaps he would not see me or would not remember me. I turned away and kept my back to him. All of a sudden I felt a hand on my shoulder and his voice said "Grant, where the hell have you been? I've missed you." I explained my return to Idaho and we had a most enjoyable conversation while we waited for tables. When we finally were called to a table, he said "Come by and see me if you get a chance. You were always one of my favorites." I would never have known it!!

Judge "Wild Bill" O'Donnell would have to be the executive producer of the show; nothing else would fit his need to run the whole project.

120

The Idaho Ensemble— A group of my good friends in Idaho would have fit in well with the Baltimore cast; they could have held their own in the courthouse mingle. They helped me survive depression aggravated by my abuse of alcohol- periods during which I blamed my condition on my having left my talent back in Baltimore. They are both such special friends that some might say that I am biased as to their abilities and talents. I do not believe that I am.

We three share the ideals of family home and God; we share a belief in personal commitment to those we love. We share a major dislike: not one of us suffers fools well. Bur, we also differ dramatically in peripheral concepts that round out life. Our political views range from the ultra liberal through the moderate conservative to the ultra conservative. Our entertainment interests range from German opera to Blues, from the highest brow theater to Greater Tuna, from the Wizard of Oz to Raising Arizona to the Greatest Little Whorehouse in Texas. Our sports interests range from willingness to watch ant play stick ball to watching games only because friends are watching. Our social commitments range from favoring more executions to outlawing the death penalty, from outlawing all welfare programs to taking full care of those who cannot care for themselves.

121

David Johnson—David is a family friend who entered my life in Idaho, long after I left the trenches in Baltimore. He was the Canyon County public defender's Earl Arvin. He seemed tireless, his best work continuing when others had completed their days. At night and early morning he found the witnesses to provide the facts---to tell what really happened. Like Earl, he also spent hours and hours in the jail, talking to defendants, listening to their tales of woe, hoping to hear and detect something that would help their cases.

David wanted to believe that the clients were innocent, even when the facts so clearly showed the opposite. He gave of his time far and beyond that for which he got paid. But, in the end, when guilt was too apparent to ignore, he worked hard to gather facts that would help at sentencing. Like Earl, he did the work without which the lawyers would have been as useful to the client as a third thumb on the left hand. On any case worked by David, the lawyer knew that all stones had been turned before he or she walked into court. If there was useful evidence, it had been found.

I remember how difficult it was for David to accept the reality that in a death penalty case, the need was for development of the worst possible features of a defendant and his life. It does no good to present redeeming factors to a judge considering imposition of the death penalty. Rather, one must present the sordid, sub-human manner in which the defendant was raised---in order to show that he or she did not even grasp the importance, the sanctity, of the life which had been taken. As a person who tries to find the best in all people, David was at first hard pressed to believe that he had to portray the worst from the life of a capital defendant. But once he accepted his fate, he did outstanding work in dredging up the worst. One particular case led him to uncover a defendant's family background of such inhuman degradation as to shock and dismay a sentencing judge. The result was a life sentence rather than death which almost assuredly would have been imposed but for David's discoveries.

During the years when I worked with that office, I looked forward each morning to David's first appearance in my office carrying a cup of strong coffee. Like my friend Earl, he faced each day optimistically---an attitude needed to balance out my pessimism.

Like Earl, he added the dimension of life to my day---both had interests other than the cases they worked. They shared those interests as valuable breaks in the monotony of case stress. They both knew all the latest gossip and secrets of the courthouse, the jail, the police officers and the prosecutors. I never wanted to discuss any item of news, society, literature, religion, politics or history, that they did not freely join in and add gems of thought and insight.

David and I debated thoughts far removed from the stark reality of the criminal world in which we worked. Which of the Gospels---Matthew, Luke or John---provided the richest base for the evangelist? Which of the political philosophies---liberal or conservative---best portrayed the American revolutionary spirit? David always stood on the Daniel Moynihan base, while I stood with William Buckley. (Mind you, I did not advance or support the so-called "conservative" views of rabid, extremist right wing republicans; rather, the conservative views of William Buckley, Everett McKinley Dirksen Barry Goldwater and, I believe, most of our Founders. I often laughed, and still do, at the fact that during a democrat sweep in Idaho in 1972---when governor Cecil Andrus won re-election with over 70 percent of the vote---a school teacher in Canyon County won election to the state senate as a democrat, then switched to the republican ticket and was re-elected for several more terms. I do not think she voted as a republican more than a handful of times during all the years in the senate, but she was re-elected over and over in a County in which Hitler might stand a chance if his name appeared on the republican ticket.)

Many times Earl and David helped preserve my sanity.

Like Earl, David has healthy southern-based superstition. He is from Texas, and he is a Texan I credit with being southern, not southwestern. Once, a man came into the office seeking representation in an estate dispute in California. My good friend, Van Bishop, maintained his license in California, and called David and I into the interview. We both quickly lost interest when the man described an experience in the California house which involved levitation and a mysterious knife suddenly plunged into a bed without evidence of a human wielder.

David and I retired to my office where he expressed the old southern attitude of, "Not letting the thought even get into my mind." The concept is that once a thought is settled in your mind, the damage to your psyche has been done; so the person must turn his or her mind away from the thought immediately. I agreed--- the southern approach to the unexplained always made sense to me. "Keep it out of your mind, do not let it creep in and settle."

Once, in Baltimore, a gypsy fortune teller wanted to retain my services. She wanted me to file suit to stop her sister in New Orleans from "hexing" her through mind control and a voodoo doll. She believed her sister to be a "voodoo priestess". She had loads of cash to pay a healthy fee. But, as she told of the "hex" activities, Earl's eyes got wider and wider. He got up, stood behind her, looked me right in the eyes and shook his head "no", mouthing silently the word "no" over and over. I turned down the case, but tried not to insult the lady because I did not want her to go out and "hex" me. I referred her to another lawyer who I knew would take the case. I did not want her to go to another lawyer and be turned down again. That might irritate her.

After she left, I said to Arvin, "we just messed up on a big fee."

He would not even discuss that aspect of the case, just muttered "no, no, no" and walked out.

One day after Van, David and I spent a couple of hours in the jail interviewing a murder defendant, I said "David, I need a surrogate drinker, are you up for it?" He said his usual "sure", and, as I had my club soda, he downed a shot of Wild Turkey for me. It helped.

David, like Earl, took care of all the outside logistics needed to get the job done in court. No detail was too slight or minute to gain their attention, and action.

David would be the director of my "Guys and Dolls". He would do everything to make the performance "go" on stage. I would ask his wife, Allison, to be our public relations agent, working closely with the director. Allison was one of my favorite reporters when she wrote for the *Idaho Press Tribune*. She was an honest reporter who understood her role as a journalist, and performed that role with equity and ethics. Plus, she was a good writer.

David and Allison are Godparents to two of my grandchildren. They and their daughter, Grace, are family to me, and to my family.

122

Ralph Nichols —**Ralph, my good** friend, is the epitome of a devoted father. When he and his wife decided that divorce was desirable, the critical issue for Ralph was custody of their son. Ralph wanted joint custody in a state in which that status was just plain not in the cards. Idaho judges blindly applied the presumption that the mother was the proper full custody parent, whether or not it was justified by truth.

Undaunted by legal precedents, Ralph hired a lawyer willing to challenge the presumption. Ralph undertook the bulk of the necessary research. After lengthy legal arguments, the judge agreed to designate, joint custody in Ralph and his wife. It was a major victory, and created a turning point in the law.

At the time, Ralph was an exceptionally talented political reporter for the *Idaho Press Tribune*, the primary local daily newspaper for a rural population of probably eighty to ninety thousand.

His wife's new husband acquired a job in Seattle and had to move. Rather than go through a court proceeding to determine how to handle the shared custody in view of the move, Ralph gave up his job and moved to Seattle. He became a news reporter and writer for the *Seattle Times*.

When his wife moved to Anchorage, Alaska, Ralph followed so that his son would have both parents around him. Ralph then reported for, and wrote for, the *Anchorage Daily News* until his son graduated from high school. After graduation Ralph's son enrolled in the University of Washington and Ralph returned to Seattle where he lives today.

Ralph shares one of my vices apparent from this book: the inability to keep my mouth shut at critical times. He exercised that vice when leaving the *Seattle Times*, so the option of returning there for work had been removed. He reported for and wrote for a well-read weekly newspaper. His columns covering the city council almost always stirred controversy. Today, he is a free lance writer.

While reporting for the *Idaho Press Tribune*, Ralph developed a healthy suspicion that one of the Third Judicial District judge might not be as ethical as one would hope. He began closely covering the judge's cases during an election season when the judge was up for election. In Idaho at the time, the Governor appointed district judges who then had to stand for election at the next regular election.

One afternoon while the trial was in progress, Ralph was in the newsroom working on his stories for the following day when a tipster called. The judge, said the caller, had told this party in open court, "If that sign were to come down it could affect the outcome of this case." A couple of other reporters who worked with Ralph would have shrugged off that rumor and continued putting out journalistic brushfires – but not Ralph. He believed that if judicial ethics were set aside for political gain in a small case, then this judge would think nothing of sidestepping justice to suit his own ends in a major case.

Immediately after conferring with his editor, Rick Coffman, Ralph requested a transcript of the court proceeding and talked to attorneys for both parties. His articles, accompanied by a photo of the campaign sign, led to the judge's loss at the polls a month later. Ralph had given all parties [especially the judge [the opportunity to comment on and explain the facts surrounding the placement of the sign. Ralph's interview of the judge was not confrontational, which helped get the judge to open up and say more than hoped for and more than he should have said. The articles were objective and fact based. Ralph's words told the story of a highly unethical incident that led to action by the readers at the polls.

Much earlier in his career, before I knew him, he reported for and wrote for the *Idaho Statesman*, the daily newspaper published in Boise, the state capital. He discovered and reported a political blow-up between a mayor of Boise and the police chief. Only days after he reported the dispute, the chief was fired. Whether Ralph's articles directly led to the firing, they certainly hurried the action.

During his career Ralph covered such political powerhouses as Senator Frank Church who was the only Idahoan ever to chair the Senate Foreign Relations Committee. He remembers well the Senator's foray into the presidential primary race to challenge Jimmy Carter, and the Senator's last campaign when he was defeated by a young Steve Symms. As Ralph says, Senator Church suffered the fate of many chairs of the Committee—those duties are so all consuming that the Senator loses close contact with the folks at home.

In Alaska he covered another colorful Senator, the always interesting and newsworthy Ted Stevens. His recounts of covering the varied political characters should be put into a book. But Ralph procrastinates as do I.

His success as a reporter was due to his skill at generating information from sources who knew that he would protect their identities, topped off by his ability to write clearly and forcefully. His skill, ability, and expectation that public figures should perform their duties ethically combined to make an excellent investigative reporter.

But, my friendship with Ralph is based on his personality and life interests, not his reporter skills. We had social faults which we unabashedly shared—never kidding ourselves that we were justified. I say "had" because we have reformed—old age does that to one. Ralph visited me in the hospital shortly after a five by-pass heart surgery several years ago. He walked into my room eager to regale me with shared memories of past unacceptable conduct that St. Paul condemns in his epistles. Instead, he found a priest preparing to give me Holy Communion. The priest looked at Ralph, who is not a

Catholic, and asked if he wanted to participate. Without hesitation, he said, "Yes." (By that time, Ralph, once a devout Episcopalian, felt abandoned as many do by that church, and was searching for an Anglican parish with an orthodox bent, which he later discovered.)

After Communion, the priest said, "We need all the help we can get." I repeated his words with, "Yes, we need all the help we can get." Both Ralph, who suddenly looked very serious, and I knew that I meant help for more than just physical needs! When the priest left, Ralph said, "Fred, that was a sign. We must change our ways." I said, "I know," and today we do pretty well in walking the straight and narrow. Occasionally we lapse into memories, laugh a lot about incidents in which Ralph often came off as Woody Allen and I as a reprobate, then return to our new lives at an older age. To this day, when I need to laugh as the cardiologist directs, I can call Ralph and be sure that laughter will result.

Like David, Ralph brings full life into my days. He loves the opera and fine arts. But, he also appreciates the lower levels of entertainment. At times in our earlier lives we made research forays into the venues of such lower levels of entertainment. Perhaps someday we will put our research findings on paper for publication—and perhaps we will not.

A Means to an end

123

As I wrote these stories, and reminisced by reading Michael Olesker's books as well as the chronicles of the 1968 riots, I marvel at how much I overlooked and missed in the sea of life around me in Baltimore. I led a colorful life. Rarely did I think about what it might be doing to my wife and sons, and to my family in Idaho.

Even more rarely did I think about what my actions might cause and cost others. For example, I have already referred to the Irving Lee Wilson death sentence that was set aside because of my over-reaching.

The reversal of the judgment of a jury and distinguished trial judge resulted not from innocence of the defendant, but from my over-reaching conduct. Wilson killed Walter "Kid" Henderson, a kingpin of gambling and drugs in Baltimore. We had specific evidence of Henderson's prominence in both criminal activities. We knew about his propensity to violence, and we knew that his lieutenants, like Wilson, were also violent.

We knew that the "Kid" always faced the threat of one or more of his lieutenants trying to overthrow him for top dog position. We knew that if someone attacked the "Kid", there were loyal lieutenants ready to wreak revenge. We also knew that if the Kid died, there would be a wild scramble for succession.

When we heard that Henderson had been shot and killed in his bar, we immediately started combining our information to get search warrants for his bars, houses and cars. A few minutes later we heard that Irving Lee Wilson walked in to the Western district station house, turned himself in and said that he killed Henderson. We turned our attention to finding out all we could about Wilson. We presumed that the Kid was assassinated for revenge or take-over of power.

With that thought in mind, we began our investigation. We began with the premise that this was murder in the first degree.

We prepared a series of affidavits setting out the Kid's operations in both gambling and narcotics, and describing the probable cause for searching his premises and cars. We hoped to find specific evidence of his criminal operations, as well as evidence of motivation for his murder. Warrants were issued and a group of search parties began their work.

The Special Grand Jury in session had been informed of the Kid's operations, and we had prepared them for an eventual presentment of the Kid on gambling and narcotics charges. We had taken no presentments to them because we had no one who dared to testify against Henderson.

During his life, we had been unable to develop probable cause to search the houses and autos. Our informants absolutely refused to give us specific information about Henderson-all of them using that favorite threat that "he would tear my arm out of the socket and beat me to death with the stump." In fact, informants who were closest to him told us that he rarely had drugs in his possession. His lieutenants and their dealers handled the drugs.

None of the informants I have described would even talk to us about the "Kid". He ran a tight ship and demanded absolute loyalty. We knew that with so much profit coming to the guy on top of the heap, there would always be people looking for an opportunity to topple the king.

Once the word was out that our search parties were scrambling to the "Kid's" holdings, the *Afro American* was after a story as to why police were crawling over his belongings like locusts. Ms. Oliver was not a reporter and writer to be lightly put off. Many underestimated her, but I was not one of those. I talked to several people about strategy, but the decision to make the statements to her that lead to pre-trial publicity problems was solely mine. Once made, I carried out the strategy without ever thinking twice about it. I told her we believed that Henderson had been killed either in a takeover attempt or for revenge. I told her that we were searching for any evidence that might lead us to the motive, and to whether there were others involved in the crime. What I told her was true, except that I did not emphasize the purpose of tying Henderson himself to racketeering activities. I did not tell her that we hoped we would find evidence that linked him to the real top people in the trade--- people who walked the streets as highly regarded political and social leaders, who "made" or "broke" politicians every day.

Frankly, we hoped that we would find something to link him to Willie Adams, who had immense power in the city. Not too long before Henderson's death, two of us had ridden with state police detectives in a helicopter viewing the enormous, well-protected estate owned by Adams on a huge bluff overlooking the river. The troopers wanted to show us that it would be impossible to stage a raid at the premises.

When I made the statements to Ms. Oliver, I knew the story would be a huge feature in the newspaper, and would be widely read in the Black communities of Baltimore. I also knew it would get no, or little, play in the *Sun* or *News American,* so would have little or no impact on the White population of Baltimore. When I made the statements, I also knew about the United States Supreme Court decisions regarding pre-trial publicity.

One of those cases that I had studied carefully through the years was the Shepard case involving the publicity that no doubt denied Dr. Sam Shepard a fair trial. (Shepard was the inspiration for *The Fugitive* television series and, more recently, the movie.) Frankly, I don't know that I ever consciously considered the impact of those cases when I spoke with Ms. Oliver. Had I done so, I would have believed, as I still do to this day, that an impartial jury could have been selected in Baltimore City.

Today, even more than then, I believe that. Through the years, I have seen trials allowed where anyone who had not read or heard about the specific facts of the case would have had to be a recluse. I have seen trials allowed where jurors who said they had not been influenced one way or another by the publicity lied or misled the court, either because they wanted desperately to be on the jury or because they didn't even recognize influence. In fact, the only times I have ever seen a juror say that he or she had formed an opinion because of pre-trial publicity involved jurors who wanted off the case and wanted to avoid jury service at all costs.

Once, when I was summoned for jury duty, as I sat in the main jury room in Canyon County, Idaho, the guy sitting next to me was a commission salesman. He told me how he could not afford to miss time for jury duty. I said something to the effect that it was going to cost me too. He said something like "well, do what I'm going to do. I'm going to claim that I am prejudiced in some way. I'll listen to the statement of the case and find a way to say I can't be fair. If it's a Mexican defendant I'll claim I am prejudiced against all Mexicans. I'll even say I hate all police officers. I've gotten off many times. I just can't afford the time."

When we were called into court, I was excused by the judge (who was a close friend of mine) right away, with assent by counsel. The judge said, "In reviewing the jury names, I see Fred Grant's name here. This is a case involving interpretation of an insurance policy and he knows more about how to interpret legal questions than I do or either of you two do, so I suggest we excuse him." Both counsel were friends and they laughed and agreed. I thanked the judge and got up to leave. The salesman was sitting right behind me and he gave me the thumbs up sign as I went out. As I checked out with the jury commissioner, out came the salesman. He said, "Lucky for me, I knew one of the lawyers and said I couldn't be fair."

So, today, probably more than then, I don't put much stock in the pre-trial publicity issue. Sometimes defense counsel has to assume that the jurors are pre-disposed and challenge them to set aside the pre-disposition and do their duty, as I often did.

As to Wilson, I never dreamed that his counsel would remove the case, knowing that he couldn't get as favorable a venue ANYWHERE

IN THE STATE as in Baltimore City. He didn't have a chance in hell to get a majority Black jury in any other venue. He didn't even stand a chance of getting more than a token number of Blacks on a jury anywhere but in Baltimore City. That includes Baltimore County, where in those days the County was holding itself out as an outpost for Whites to escape the Black population.

124

As a defense attorney, I would have relished the defense of Wilson before a Baltimore City jury. Of course, I can say the same from the standpoint of having prosecuted him in the City. But I really believed then, and still do, that I would have been hard pressed to get a verdict above second degree in the City. So, I let myself use the case to further the objective of the organized crime unit that I was responsible for. Frankly, nothing could have surprised me more than when Wilson's defense attorney asked for a change of venue. Big mistake, Before a Black jury in Baltimore, he might well have faced no more than manslaughter, and might even have had a chance at self defense. Before a White jury in any other part of Maryland, Wilson had no chance. Before a Black jury in Baltimore, he had a whale of a chance. Such a city jury would have known something about Walter "Kid" Henderson, even if they didn't admit it. During the trial, a good defense attorney would have made the case of Henderson's involvement in crime, of Wilson's knowledge of his violence and of his propensity to fire first, and would then have heard how Wilson thought, when Henderson reached his hand down toward his waistband, that he was going for a gun as he had in the past. All this would have "sold" with a city jury familiar with the ways of the street. In fact, the pre-trial publicity in the *Afro American* which reached virtually no White citizens would have been read by most Black city residents and they would have been prepped for the type of case Wilson could have put on.

Perhaps the worst thing I did was take the stand for the defense in the case in Caroline County. I was stunned when defense counsel called me, and I sent Alan Horowitz, sitting second chair, to call Charley and George Helinski. I think I objected, I know I made the point of awkwardness of being called to testify for the opposition during my prosecution of a case. Then, when I had to take the stand, I should have just flat out refused, and if I had been up to date on the Standards brought to my attention by Mr. Keating in the post conviction process, I would have known that the trial judge could not make me testify.

When I did take the stand, the defense attorney asked such open ended questions that I could have taken more advantage of the defense than I did. When asked what I thought when I heard of the shooting, I used the terrible word "assassination" which in and of itself implies premeditation and deliberation. I should not have been on the stand, but I should have better guarded my truthfulness on the stand. I seriously did believe, and still believe, that Wilson was sent there to kill, to assassinate, Henderson. But, never should I have been put into the position of saying so as a witness. It violated at least two rules as to prosecutors set by case law with which I was familiar: no prosecutor should ever vouch for the truth of his position or the credibility of a witness, no prosecutor should ever tell the jury what he or she believes is truth. Opinion, argument, based on someone else's testimony is permissible, but not vouching for the truth. Here I was put in the position of what I *believed* and my response created error, even though never picked up on appeal.

But, I should not have made the statement even when in the position to do so.

To this day, I do not and cannot understand what possessed the attorney to move for change of venue. The change of venue was automatic in a capital case, so once requested he was at the mercy of whatever county the case went to. Caroline County was no worse for him than Baltimore County would have been. In fact, because of the unique talents of Judge DeWeese Carter in Caroline County, he was better off there than he would have been in Baltimore County. But, no where would the defendant have been better off than in Baltimore City.

The blame has been put on the attorney for making that venue decision, but where was the defendant during all this time. He wasn't a mute, and he didn't lack street smarts. How and why did he simply sit back and let his attorney make a decision that he must have known didn't make sense. Then, and now, I believe there was some reason why Wilson didn't speak up and stop the change of venue. There was also some reason why Wilson didn't hire an experienced criminal lawyer. The officers, others in my organized crime unit and I were all surprised when Wilson's attorney entered his appearance---only because of his lack of experience in criminal cases. We fully expected that he would be joined by one of the Murphys, or Milton Allen, or Allen Murrell, Joe Rosenthal (with Norman Yankellow handling the trial work), Nelson Kandel or one of the many other highly experienced and competent criminal defense attorneys in the City.

The fact that Wilson went to trial, with so much at stake for people in the drug and gambling trades that he had to know about, with inexperienced counsel amazes me to this day. There is an untold story there.

But, when Anton Keating was assigned the post conviction defense of Wilson, he waged a strong attack based on the American Law Institute Standards by which prosecutors should guide themselves. Those Standards, as they relate to pre-trial publicity, urge avoidance of any discussion of fact or prosecutorial views or conclusions prior to trial. Truthfully, as I testified in the Wilson hearing, I was unaware that they even existed.

When Keating asked me whether I was aware of their existence at the time I gave the publicity statements to Ms. Oliver, I honestly had to say "no".

Why wasn't I aware of them? I didn't spend time in the library reading ALI materials, or even new materials regarding any type of oversight by the ALI. My reading was limited to new case decisions that might effect my trial of cases. I wasn't even aware of the ALI Standards when I was defending criminal cases. I didn't learn of them until I was appointed court coordinator and compliance officer for the Idaho Law Enforcement Planning Commission, a job I held when summoned back to Maryland for the Wilson hearing. We used the Standards extensively in determining planning and development funding for courts, prosecutors and public defenders throughout Idaho.

The amazing thing is that later in my career, I relied on those standards continually in arguing for pre-trial restraint, and then arguing that violation of the standards called for reversals. In fact, when I returned from Maryland where I was pretty well taken over the coals by Keating, I set out to find out what the standards were really all about. I got so involved with them in my work at the Law Enforcement Planning Commission that I served on national committees regarding implementation of the Standards, and chief federal district judge of Idaho appointed me to serve on a Federal Speedy Trial Committee to make recommendations as to new federal standards and rules.

I found a remarkable new horizon of legal thinking in the ALI standards as to all forms of trial process, and even used the standards in several seminars I gave on strategy. In each of them, I told the story of my humiliation on the stand in Wilson. In my entire career, I never felt more like I had wasted all my talent, all my education, all my training, and all the faith that my bosses had placed in me, than I did when I left that courtroom.

And you know the real irony of that trip? At the end of the day of my time on the stand, the decision was made that they might need me back the next day. It was just a few days before Christmas, and I had reservations for the next morning early on a flight to get me back in time for my sons' Christmas plays at school. I told the judge that, but rather than stay later and complete the examination, he ordered me back. When I got there the next day, there were no further questions. I missed my boys' plays, the only ones I ever missed. I couldn't get a plane out until Christmas Eve and finally got an American Airlines flight to Salt Lake City where I knew I could get a bus on to Idaho and be home in time for Christmas. I knew then, as I know now, that the anointed one did what he did to punish me for the way I had handled the Wilson prosecution years before.

That fact alone made me realize that too often every player in the so called system puts himself/herself above the interests of witnesses or victims. And from that day on I pledged to myself that as a hearing officer, or participant in any way in adjudication, I would never subvert knowingly the interests of a witness and/or victim. I have served as hearing officer in personnel cases, zoning cases, road validation cases, and discrimination complaints. Always, at the request of a witness or counsel to go past the hour for the convenience of a witness, I have agreed to do so. In fact, often I have made the offer.

125

During an evening zoning hearing that was important to the county, the attorney for the challenging land owner was scheduled to leave on vacation the next day. I committed to him that we would try to finish that evening, even though the testimony would be long and tedious. At about 11 pm the Commissioners were ready to stop for the night, and so was I. But, to continue the hearing would interrupt the plans of the attorney to start his family vacation. I thought about that pre-Christmas episode in Caroline County, Maryland, I thought about the judge who really didn't give a damn about my interests or those of my sons and wife.

I told the Commissioners and the audience about my experience with that learned judge in Maryland, and advised that we were going on into the night. The hearing ended at 2am. No one was harmed by spending a few hours of overtime, and a family was spared needless disappointment.

The system is designed around the convenience of the main players, beginning, and unfortunately often ending, with the convenience of "His or Her Honor". Witnesses and victims are not players, thus are left out of the convenience planning. It doesn't have to be like that. Any judge who doesn't take into account the interests of the families of the witnesses and victims who are caught up in the process is not really worthy of sitting the bench. Judges tend to think of themselves as being "anointed", not "appointed." The judge who heard the Wilson case was upset with me because of my attitudes and performance at the time of the trial. He knew he had me at his disposal and at his mercy, and by God he was going to wield his power.

So many times I have seen the same type of attitude, and so many times I have realized that there is a reason why the public holds judges and lawyers in such low esteem.

I realize that I brought on myself the problems because of performance that didn't take into account the cutting edge of legal thinking at the time, that didn't even take into account good common sense. But, the players in the process should not let another's lack of common sense or poor performance- control their decisions.

I turned off my mind as to anything as subjective as a set of national standards that did not have force of law. Just as I, and so many other Baltimore citizens turned off our minds as to the racial disparity that existed prior to and following the riots of 1968.

How often I cheered Lenny Moore as he ran into the hall of fame as a Colt. How often I admired big Jim Parker and the protection he gave Johnny U. How often I cheered Frank Robinson and Paul Blair, and especially the day that Frank cleared the left field wall of Memorial Stadium, knocking the ball clear out of the park and out into the parking lot where a flag was installed to mark the spot.

Did it ever occur to me that they lived as secondary citizens from the standpoint of being accepted into white communities? Olesker's discussions with Lenny Moore should make every Colt fan ashamed. John Steadman's story of how the unprincipled owner of the Redskins, who we knew was a racist, slurred the name of Lenny, one of the most exciting runners I ever saw, even when Gayle Sayers came along. We all knew, or should have known, that our stars were deprived of equal housing and other elements of society just as were most of all Black citizens in the city.

It never occurred to me after one of those exciting afternoons at the Stadium that Lenny, Jim Parker, and Lenny Lyles would not be going home to an integrated neighborhood in a social setting that was justified by their position and their income.

It never occurred to me that Frank, Paul Blair, Wes Unseld, Earl "the Pearl" Monroe and others were not accepted into white society on a par equal to all whites who shared their uniqueness and incomes.

From my own professional standpoint, it never occurred to me that Blacks were deprived of equal opportunity in the government of Baltimore City, in the prosecutor's offices, in the law firms of Baltimore City. Didn't I think it strange and discriminatory when Arthur Murphy was the only Black assistant in the U.S. Attorneys office, when there were no Black FBI agents, when Joe Howard was the only Black assistant state's attorney when I joined that staff, when there were no Black command officers in the police department with which I worked closely, when there were so few Black detectives among the waves of white detectives who worked with our office and division, and when there were no Black federal judges---district or 4th Circuit---and when there was only one Supreme Bench judge and only one Municipal Court judge? No. Why? Because I didn't think about it. I lived my prosecutor's and defense attorney's life during the day and most of some nights. I went home to a completely White neighborhood near the north City boundary with nearly all White Baltimore County, and didn't spend time thinking about what was happening in the city.

Neither I, nor my friends, did anything about it. I guess we thought Baltimore was different. Because it was easier not to see, we didn't see the segregation and abuses that were evident in other cities because of television and newspaper coverage.

That's why we sat on the Friday evening before the riots began and weren't really all that worried about riots in Baltimore, because "Baltimore is different". It was all around us to see.

I had seen it during one very memorable surveillance assignment. I was sitting in a police car in a ghetto neighborhood, one in which I would have done anything in my power to keep my wife and son out of. A man dressed in work clothes came out of a row house with a very cleanly dressed little boy. The two of them walked, hand in hand, toward the corner. It could have been any white dad and son in the city. They got to the corner and waited. Soon, the mother got off a bus, dressed in a white uniform, greeted and hugged the man and little boy, and she and the little boy walked back to the house, hand in hand, while the man got on a bus to go to his night shift job. It occurred to me what a tragedy that this working family had to live in a neighborhood rife with drugs and violence. I told Lodice about it that night, and the thought of it has never left my mind. I have often wondered how that little boy fared. But, what did I do about it? I put it out of my mind and carried on.

I wasn't brought up in South Carolina to be a bigot. My people were not, but they and I lived and accepted the fact of segregation. It was a way of life that too many of us accepted throughout our lives wherever we lived. I remember an incident when I was only about seven years old, when the Black delivery boy who worked for my grandfather Bogan Cash Kelly wanted to take me to the "picture show" (as we called them then) with him on a Saturday night. My grandfather approved, gave him the money for our tickets and loaned him the store's delivery bicycle to carry us to the show. We had to go to the alley door of the movie house because Blacks were not allowed to buy tickets at the front box office. They could not enter the front door of the theater, and had to sit in the balcony. The only entrance to the balcony was by way of the alley door. From that door, the stairway to the balcony was enclosed so that no Black person could, even by accident, mingle with the Whites. Nobody wanted to risk a Black getting on to the hallowed main floor of the theater (interesting isn't it how today many whites consider the balcony to be the elite watching spot).

When we got to the ticket window that night, the ticker seller would not sell him a ticket for me to go with him into the balcony. No whites could go into the Black balcony.

So, we went home and I was very disappointed. When we told my "Big Daddy" what happened, he loaded us into his big Hudson and off we went to the theater. The three of us went to the alley ticket window and my grandfather said he wanted to buy three tickets. A very nervous ticket seller said she couldn't sell tickets to whites. He told her to get the manager. When the manager came, he knew who my grandfather was---everyone in Hartsville, South Carolina knew

Bogan Cash Kelly. The manager very patiently explained that he just couldn't sell tickets for whites to go into the "colored" balcony. I can still hear my grandfather's booming voice, "well, I don't give a damn about 'whites', you'll either sell me three tickets so we can go into this picture show or I'll buy this damn place and you'll be the first one fired." We went into the balcony and the three of us watched a double feature, viewing those picture shows until long past my grandfather's usual bedtime. Very likely it was the only time during segregation when two whites sat with a Black friend in the balcony and watched a movie.

But did that change the "way of the south" in Hartsville? No. It didn't even change the way in which I grew up within the "system" of segregation and accepted it. Why didn't we question it or challenge it? Probably because we didn't see anything we could do about it, and stayed focused on our own lives.

126

My wife and I lived in south Chicago for four years, in one of the most segregated parts of any major city. For the first year, we were the only two whites on the entire block on University Avenue just north of 63rd street. 63rd was the longest, uninterrupted business street in the world—all of it lay through heavily segregated south and southwest Chicago.

When we went somewhere on the bus, we were the only whites until we got toward the northern half of south Chicago. But we survived without incident. Then, when we moved into University housing, near 55th street on Ellis Avenue, we lived in one of the most advanced sites of integration in any American City, along Hyde Park Boulevard, in the neighborhood of the University of Chicago.

My moot court partner was Waverly Clanton, a very bright law student, married to a wonderful lady, Carrie, with a bright little son "Chip". I spent hours every day with Wav, and we dined and visited often with the family. It just happened that they were Black. The fact was really inconsequential. Wav and my close friend was Robert Newhouse, a Black law student who had an interest in politics and a personality to be very successful in law or politics. On Lodice and my first trip back to Chicago from Baltimore, we had dinner with the Clantons and spent a lovely evening with them. None of us ever discussed race and the great divide in this nation.

In Baltimore, we settled into the all white residential area near Belvedere and York Roads, just a few blocks south of the Baltimore County line and the city of Towson. We didn't consider our neighborhood to be segregated just because it was all White. And, that's the way we lived our lives.

We all should have seen the riots coming. God knows I have said many times that if I had been born Black I would probably have been angry and demonstrating long before 1968. We had seen Watts, Chicago, Detroit, Cambridge, Newark, and we should have seen it coming in Baltimore.

But, Baltimore was different.

A presidential study following the Cambridge, Maryland uprising in 1967, warned of the seething resentment caused by our divided societies. It warned that America was divided into White and Black societies, and that deep resentments would erupt into violence.

But, Baltimore was different.

Dr. King knew the night before his murder that he did not have long to live. I am convinced that his speech that night was not just theoretical; he knew, he felt, that he had to be killed by some white who could not stand to see change. His words were prophetic, and not by accident:

"Well, I don't know what will happen now. We've got some difficult days ahead. But it really doesn't matter with me now because I've been to the Mountain Top. And, I don't mind. Like anybody, I would like to live a long life---longevity has its place. But I'm not concerned about that now. I just want to do God's will. And, he's allowed me to go up to the Mountain. And, I've looked over and I've seen the Promised Land. I may not get there with you. But I want you to know tonight, that we, as a people, will get to the Promised Land. So, I'm happy tonight. I'm not worried about anything. I'm not in fear of any man. Mine eyes have seen the glory of the coming of the Lord."

As he spoke those words, no doubt I was drinking with friends at Cy Bloom's or Hartley's on Baltimore Street—paying no attention to Memphis or the simmering resentment throughout the nation. If someone had said to us that night, Dr. King just about predicted his own death and looks for trouble in Memphis, we would have said "but, Baltimore is different."

According to Olesker's book, Mayor Tommy probably thought the same that night. After all, he had made longer strides than any of his predecessors in bringing Blacks into government, in recognizing that much more needed to be done. And, after all, Baltimore is different.

Since starting to put this book together, and remembering the nights and days of the riots, remembering the hopeless, despairing look on so many Black faces of people simply caught up in a curfew—I know that for my own sake I need to review more of what went on both before and after the riots.

The University of Baltimore documentation on the 40th anniversary of the riots shows that the events of those days between Palm Sunday and Easter, 1968, had a profound effect on the city.

Now that I've started this writing business, I don't want to stop. The post-riot violence in Baltimore intrigues me, perhaps because I lived through it without even developing a real interest in it. I was doing my own thing, defending clients, socializing more than I should, working long hours and drinking even longer hours. Since I didn't defend any of the involved defendants, and had no personal or case stake in the issues, I just didn't pay attention. I only vaguely remember the so-called "Panther"cases. Until my reading during preparation of these stories, I didn't even recall the tragic shooting of the officers.

I'm going back now to review those cases and their effects on the City and the system.

127

I will start with the policies of Colonel DuBois to serve the interests of Commissioner Donald Pomerleau and Attorney General George Mitchell. I never had much use for DuBois as pointed out elsewhere in this book. He was at best a mediocre FBI agent whose ascent to such heights with Pomerleau mystifies me. I wouldn't put it past him, for a second, to plant informants with instructions to deliver charges whether truthful or not. Well do I remember when he sent Leon Tomlin to get our informants and their information. Why? None of the other officers with whom we worked ever demanded, or even wanted, the names of our informants. The "why" is that our information was getting us closer and closer to DuBois and his squad.

I never sympathized with the Black Panther party in its early days in Oakland. I never paid attention to its activities in Baltimore, but had no reason to sympathize with them any more than I had earlier. I knew Arthur Turco who it turns out had a critical role in the post-riot year violence in the City. I met him, and even had drinks one night with him, but never cared for his beliefs and his endless discussion of them. He briefly dated a fine lady who worked in the court system and was a friend of mine. That's how I came to spend an evening with Turco, and I chose not to spend any more time with him. His diatribes just didn't interest me.

Vaguely, I remember when an informant was found dead, having been tortured before being murdered. And, vaguely I remember hearing that he was suspected of being involved. My friend in fact was questioned about Turco's attitude and appearance on the night of the murder. I remember having the thought that if the suspicions were true, it wouldn't surprise me.

William Kunstler was instrumental in bringing Turco into Baltimore. I never cared for Kunstler and his tactics. I didn't know him, never was introduced to him and never wanted to be. His arrogance, his condescending attitude toward Baltimore, didn't bode well. I remember thinking that anyone who studied at the knee of Kunstler might well believe that violence was justified "for the cause".

I never accepted the argument that it took such arrogance to make a dent in White society. I knew better. I knew and respected Thurgood Marshall, Juanita Jackson Mitchell, Dr. Lillie May Jackson, and the Mitchell lawyers. They did far more toward changing societal patterns all the Kunstlers and Turcos in the world. I knew Arthur Murphy, and I knew George Russell and Harry Cole and Milton B. Allen---I knew them, I worked with them, and I know that they did more for societal changes, and for gaining acceptance of Blacks into White structures than all the Kunstlers and Turcos in the world.

128

Now, for my own sake, it is time to re-visit the times and my thoughts. The case that most intrigues me is the case of Marshall Eddie Conway, who is still in the Maryland prison system after three decades. As I understand it, he was convicted primarily on the word of jailhouse snitches who may or may not have worked for DuBois. My limited research to this point and my gut instinct as to DuBois tells me they did work for him.

A personal advantage to my taking a long, good look at the Conway case is the opportunity to delve into DuBois and his activities the way I should have when I had the chance.

Perhaps the temperament of the city led to an effort to calm the temper of the overall city at the expense of some few individual Blacks. I have always believed that we rushed to judgment in the assassinations of Dr. King and John Fitzgerald Kennedy because the powers that be thought that the American people couldn't withstand the impact of knowing the deep facts behind the murders. It will be interesting to see if I come to the same conclusion as to the conviction of Conway.

Sometimes, the system puts the interest of calming a tempest ahead of what is right and/or just.

It is dangerous for the truth, when a prosecutor goes to any length to win, or uses a case to win some other battle that is going on as I probably did in Wilson. Even though I still doubt that Wilson was simply acting in self defense, even though I still think there is more to the story than anyone other than Wilson knows, I do know that I wasn't smart in my handling of the case.

I never used a jail house snitch, i.e., a cell mate who claims that a defendant admitted the crime to him. The defendants that I dealt with as a prosecutor, in cases significant enough to have merited a jail house snitch, were not stupid enough to confess to a cell mate. If they were going to confess, they would have been making some kind of a deal with the state.

The defense attorneys that I knew, for the most part, were smart enough to warn their clients about keeping their mouth shut in jail. I know that I certainly warned the officer-kidnapping defendant to say nothing to any inmate, and he obviously did not.

My inclination about defendants was borne out as I defended the type of defendants who would be subject to cell mate confessions. They were too smart to confess to some inmate who could use the information to further his own cause. After all, defendants know the informant system as well as, or better than, law enforcement does. They have too many of their own go down because of informants, to openly admit a crime to an inmate.

Today, there is growing evidence of the lack of reliability of jail house snitches. Exposes in several cities have brought the fact home. A serious scandal was discovered in Los Angeles several years ago, where it was discovered that the same jail house snitches were making case after case, being moved from place to place by the state to gather information. It was shown at that time that the testimony was false, and that the use of the snitch continued even after the entire population of Los Angeles knew the snitch by name and picture. Yet, he continued to testify that defendants opened up to him and confessed their crimes. Not hardly.

129

In Idaho, one of the worst cases of injustice coming from testimony of jail house snitches kept an innocent man on death row for nearly a decade. Finally, the use of dna cleared him of any possibility of being the rapist and murderer of a young school girl.

Charles Fain was charged with the rape and murder of a young school girl in Nampa, Idaho, a rural town in the middle of a rural agricultural community. Fain denied his guilt from the beginning. His statement to a police investigator, who did a job about as bad as any in history, did not admit guilt. He was given a polygraph test which he passed, but of course the test was not allowed in court by the trial judge.

Seminal swabs were made at the autopsy, but no one knew where they ended up, or what happened to them. At least during post conviction, the defense was able to show that the autopsy was run a lot like a carnival side show. Scores of people were present because this case had dominated the press and the fears of a community for weeks. The Nampa police chief brought his secretary (later turned out that she was his girl friend at the time) as though the autopsy was a social event. Testimony of participants showed the conduct of the autopsy was scandalous. Evidence was dropped as it was handed from hand to hand. Evidence was handled by people other than the coroner and chief evidence officer.

And, what happened to the crucial dna and rape kit swabs? The medical examiner testified that he gave them to the evidence officer. The officer testified that he never got them. Everyone testified that they were made. But, the FBI said that when they got the sex kit, there were no swabs. So, in that carnival atmosphere, somewhere, the swabs were lost or deliberately destroyed.

A state medical lab technician testified that had the swabs been saved, she might have been able to determine the exclusion of the defendant as the killer. The trial judge and the Supreme Court leaped on that "might have been able to" as evidence that the absence of the swabs was not sufficient to affect the due process of the defendant.

So, the case came down to two jail house snitches. The first was a step son of a deputy sheriff. He was specially assigned to Fain's cell, even though for his offense normally he would not be placed with a defendant facing death. He testified that Fain, in great and vivid detail, told him how he sexually satisfied himself with the victim and then killed her.

The snitch, Bobby Roberson, contended that within an hour and a half after being put into the cell, Fain came up to him and confessed to the crime. The jury believed that Fain, who had repeatedly denied his guilt (and who remember had passed a polygraph, but the jury was denied that information) came up to a guy he didn't know and confessed in detail.

Roberson then asked to be taken to see a detective. He told the detective, who was no more than an inadequate patrol officer who had been promoted because of longevity and a good old boy system, about what Fain had said. The detective said that he would get Roberson moved, but for the time being he should go back in the cell. Knowing that Fain was represented by counsel, the detective did not notify him of what Roberson had said, but he did in fact notify the prosecutor.

Roberson later said that when he went back into the cell, Fain then went into vivid detail about his actions with the victim, and even allegedly drew maps of where he picked up the victim and where he dumped her body. Imagine that! Roberson asks to be removed from the cell. Everyone in the cell block in that small jail knew that Roberson had been removed from the cell and talked with a detective. There are no secrets in the Canyon County jail. Everyone on the cell block, including Fain, knew that Roberson had talked at some length with a detective while he was out of the cell. How in the name of sanity, can we believe that Fain then openly told him about the crime and drew maps?

But, in one of the most remarkably absurd portions of Roberson's testimony, he claimed that Fain crumpled up the maps after showing them to him and threw them in the toilet. This was a lidless, toilet located right in the cell, within 8 to 10 feet of each inmate in the cell. Roberson said that he went and sat on the toilet, and when Fain wasn't watching, picked the maps out of the toilet and put them in his pants for safekeeping. How do you suppose Fain didn't notice Roberson, in clear view, reach into the toilet, pull out wet maps and stick them into his pants? No one ever proved, or even inquired into whether, the maps were in Fain's handwriting.

Roberson said that he then asked the jailer for pencil and paper and he began making his journal notes of Fain's confession. How it stretches credulity to believe that an inmate, who had left the cell once to confer with detectives, could openly ask for supplies and then keep a journal without causing Fain to be suspicious of what was being written. The whole alleged incidents prove incredible to anyone knowing anything about jail inmates and the subculture that rules within a jail.

The defense offered mental records as to Roberson which showed that he was a "manipulative person who seeks in a 'rather dramatic way of placing himself on center stage' and who has 'faked' situations in which to achieve personal satisfaction." This evaluation report was made by the New Mexico state psychiatrist just a little more than a year before Fain supposedly confessed to Roberson. It is very doubtful that the "manipulative person....who...'faked' situations" had changed in that year's time.

The problem is that the trial judge refused to admit the evidence to refute Roberson's credibility.

130

The second supposed confession was made to an inmate named Ricky Chilton, a cell mate with an atrocious record of escape and perjury. Chilton told his attorney about Fain's statements that he overheard in the cell. The attorney gave the information to the prosecutor. Yet, Chilton claimed that he wasn't promised any consideration, and didn't expect any benefit, for testifying. And, the trial court bought the story. This trial judge was a worldly guy, who had been an excellent civil trial attorney, who couldn't possibly have really believed that Chilton didn't expect any benefit in exchange for testifying.

According to Chilton, Fain admitted the crime to him, and also discussed his guilt with another child abuser and murderer who had conveniently been moved into his cell just after Chilton was placed there.

On the basis of the Chilton and Roberson testimony, as pointed out by the dissent from the one member of the Idaho Supreme Court who was intellectually honest, the jury had no choice but to convict. The dissenting judge was Justice Bistline who became known as the one member of the court who actually listened to counsel and paid attention to the facts.

I had prior experience with his listening ability. Canyon County and Blaine County, in Idaho joined in a contest of the state's constitutional ability to demand that county assessors raise tax appraisals. The case was filed in the Supreme Court because it involved every county in the state. One of the arguments advanced in the joint briefs filed, was abandoned by counsel prior to the hearing of arguments. The prosecuting attorney for Blaine County, Keith Roark, a crafty and intellectually sound attorney, and Bill Brauner for Canyon County, one of the best "old country lawyers" that I ever saw, had decided that the issue simply raised too many collateral problems. So, when Keith began his oral argument, the first point he made was that the counties were abandoning the argument. He spent several minutes explaining the reason for the abandonment.

When the Supreme Court, Bistline dissenting, ruled against the counties, a good part of the decision was spent in discussing the abandoned issue and deciding it against the counties without any mention of it being abandoned. How could that happen? Because the decision had been written before the argument, and the drafting law clerk didn't hear the abandonment which came during the court hearings.

At a Christmas party not long after the decision was issued, Mr. Justice Bistline told one of the county's attorneys that the decision had been written before the arguments, and that he had already started on the dissent prior to the arguments. So much for the appellate process in Idaho, and so much for judicial honesty of the Court which allowed the conviction of Fain to stand on the cell mate testimony.

Many years later, after more than a decade on death row for Fain, dna processing improved to the point at which some of the specimens taken at the autopsy could be tested. Fain was cleared of the crime, to the point at which he was absolutely EXCLUDED as even a possible offender.

131

One other interesting element of the evidence allowed in the trial against Fain was the admission of testimony from an FBI agent that a cast of a footprint found at the site where the body was found "could" match the footprint of the defendant. Much, much later an independent evidence lab in Oakland, California determined that the agent had mistaken the toe of the shoeprint for the heel.

When the miscreant agent was subjected to post conviction depositions, he had no explanation for how he had made such a mistake. Ironically, while counsel waited for the deposition to begin, in a conversation with another agent, the discussion turned to the old FBI technique under J. Edgar Hoover to send malcontents and inept agents to Butte, Montana. The agent said the only thing that had changed was that Mobile, Alabama had taken the place of Butte. When the negligent agent's deposition began he was asked where he was assigned, and the answer was "Mobile, Alabama".

The books are replete with cases in which defendants have been freed after dna results proved that jail house snitches lied. Those cases make it clear that alleged jail house confessions are the most untrustworthy and unbelievable evidence known to man.

Just think about it. In most cases in which jail house confessions would be sought, the defendant has been accused of a significant crime. In most cases in which such confessions have been used, the jailhouse snitches are necessary because the defendants have maintained their innocence and have not confessed in spite of expert inquiry by the police. So, why would these defendants, wise to the ways of the street, confess openly to a cellmate? These defendants are abundantly aware of the fact that their cellmates will do or say whatever is necessary to escape punishment for their own crimes.

With my long standing objection to using cell mate confession testimony, I have been intrigued by reading about Conway's conviction and the manner in which it took place. Why did Turco, who was a cellmate of Conway, want so desperately to defend Conway? Why did Turco work so hard to convince Conway to insist on him as a defense attorney when he had to know that the courts would not allow it. Stranger twists have taken place than a scenario in which Turco wanted Conway to take a big fall.

The specifics of the claims regarding the jailhouse confession testimony that sank Conway are confounding and convincing. Reading about the cases has done two things: brought back to me the memories of how I dodged, along with many others, any recognition of responsibility for racial unrest and dissention, and an abiding interest in studying Conway's case and the involvement of DuBois. God willing that will be next.

I know Red would approve. Red never believed that Fain was guilty, and never believed the cellates Roberson and Chilton. He would have a field day exploring the Conway case and DuBois with me.

LaVergne, TN USA
09 March 2010

175343LV00002B/2/P